Thinking Through Cultures

THINKING THROUGH CULTURES

Expeditions in Cultural Psychology

Richard A. Shweder

Harvard University Press
Cambridge, Massachusetts, and London, England

Library of Congress Cataloging-in-Publication Data

Shweder, Richard A.
    Thinking through cultures : expeditions in cultural psychology /
Richard A. Shweder.
        p.   cm.
    Includes bibliographical references.
    Includes index.
    ISBN 0-674-88415-9 (cloth : alk. paper).
    ISBN 0-674-88416-7 (paper : alk. paper)
    1. Ethnopsychology. 2. Personality and culture. 3. Cognition and culture.
    4. Ethnology. I. Title.
    [DNLM: 1. Cross-Cultural Comparison. 2. Ethnopsychology.
    3. Cognition. 4. Personality.
HM 251 S562t]
GN270.S48 1991
155.8—dc20
DNLM/DLC   90-4796
for Library of Congress   CIP

To those who doubt that there are such things as concepts, propositions, and gods subsisting outside of time and beyond our world, and to those who doubt not, I dedicate these essays.

I offer them to my fathers, Louis Miller, Nilamani Senapati, Jerome Shweder, Evon Z. Vogt, William L. Walter, and John W. M. Whiting, who in their ways taught me about science and romance in anthropology, and in life.

Contents

Thinking Through Cultures

Introduction

The Astonishment of Anthropology

If there is a piety in cultural anthropology it is the conviction that astonishment deserves to be a universal emotion. Astonishment and the assortment of feelings that it brings with it—surprise, curiosity, excitement, enthusiasm, sympathy—are probably the affects most distinctive of the anthropological response to the difference and strangeness of "others." Anthropologists encounter witchcraft trials, suttee, ancestral spirit attack, fire walking, body mutilation, the dream time, and how do they react? With astonishment. While others respond with horror, outrage, condescension, or lack of interest, the anthropologists flip into their world-revising mood.

Undoubtedly, there is some irony in this pious devotion to the virtues of astonishment. In the postmodern world that cultural anthropology has helped to construct (see, for example, Clifford and Marcus 1986; Clifford 1988; Geertz 1988), everything from science to literal description to one's own subjectivity is self-consciously redefined and revalued as artifice or art. In that world, piety is figured as a form of either innocence or insincerity, both of which stand, quite naturally, in need of defense. The following essays try to provide one part of that defense of astonishment, by "thinking through cultures" in search of our psychological nature.

The expression "thinking through cultures" is polysemous; one may "think through" other cultures in each of several senses: by means of the other (viewing the other as an expert in some realm of human experience), by getting the other straight (rational reconstruction of the beliefs and practices of the other), by deconstructing and going right through and beyond the other (revealing what the other has suppressed and kept out of sight), witnessing in the context of engagement with the other (revealing one's own perspective on things by dint of a self-reflexive turn of mind). Because these essays are exercises in thinking through cultures in search of the human psyche it seems appropriate to refer to them as expeditions in cultural psychology. They are expeditions in cultural psychology that, it is to be hoped, exhibit some of the astonishment of anthropology.

The idea of a cultural psychology is the idea that individuals and traditions, psyches and cultures, make each other up. Because the idea of a cultural psychology implies that the processes of consciousness (self-maintenance processes, learning processes, reasoning processes, emotional feeling processes) may not be uniform across the cultural regions of the world, any serious or astonishing treatment of the topic must address the problem of rationality (or psychic unity), as well as several closely related issues, including relativism, romanticism, realism, and the trilogy of modernisms (pre-, post-, and pure).

One of the central myths of the modern period in the West is the idea that the opposition between religion-superstition-revelation and logic-science-rationality divides the world into then and now, them and us. According to this myth the world woke up and became good about three centuries ago when Enlightenment thinkers began to draw some distinctions between things that premodern thinkers had managed to overlook.

Many modernist authors (for example, Ernest Gellner in anthropology, Jean Piaget in psychology) construct an image of the premodern period as a dark age of intellectual confusions: the confusion of language with reality, of physical suffering with moral transgression, of subjectivity with objectivity, of custom with nature. That image of the premodern mind is built out of presupposed separations or distinctions—of language versus reality, subject versus object, custom versus nature—that over the past several decades have been challenged by postmodern scholarship. Today, deep into the postmodern age, there are other stories about rationality and religion waiting to be told.

The problem of rationality (or psychic unity) is one of the central themes of *Thinking Through Cultures*. The problem presents itself to anthropologists and other students of cultural psychology in the following form: What inferences about human nature are we to draw from the apparent diversity of human conceptions of reality, and what justification is there for our own conceptions of reality in the light of that apparent diversity?

Nicolas Rescher (1988, p. 140), in his recent writings on rationality, formulates nicely what is at stake in debates about conceptual diversity. The logic of his formulation goes like this, although I have taken considerable liberties with his wording and added the examples.

Consider the following four propositions. Each will seem plausible to some readers, yet taken together they are incompatible. One or more of them must be rejected, but which?

1. We, the members of our ethnic group, are rationally justified in our conception of things; for example, that when you are dead you are dead, that virtuous people can die young, that souls do not transmigrate, and that authors have a natural inalienable right to publish works critical of revealed truth.
2. They, the members of some other ethnic group, have a different conception of things; for example, that the spirits of your dead ancestors can enter your body and wreak havoc on your life, that widows are unlucky and should be shunned, that a neighbor's envy can make you sick, that souls transmigrate, that nature is a scene of retributive causation and you get the death you deserve, that a parody of scriptural revelation is blasphemous and blasphemers should be punished.
3. They, the members of that other ethnic group, are rationally justified in their conception of things.
4. If others are rationally justified in their conception of things and that conception is different from ours, then we cannot be rationally justified in our conception of things, and vice versa.

The four propositions are mutually incompatible. Accepting any three entails rejection of the fourth. Here one is presented with a fateful choice, for rejecting first one and then another of the four can resolve the inconsistency in a variety of ways.

Rejection of the first proposition is entailed by acceptance of the other three. Those who go searching in other cultural traditions for a lost paradise or age of truth often adopt this stance, which might be described as reverse ethnocentrism or inverse developmentalism. If you are an inverse developmentalist you view your own culture as retrograde, or as oppressive, or as a form of false consciousness, or as a source of illusions. Carlos Castaneda's Don Juan beckons. Colonized peoples sometimes adopt this stance, if they identify strongly with the worldview and practices of the colonizer.

Rejection of the second proposition is entailed by acceptance of the other three. Those who adopt this stance think that all differences are merely apparent, or superficial, or idiomatic. This is the stance associated with the humanistic ecumenical spirit of universalism and the Platonic quest for pure form. From an ecumenical perspective, for example, ancestral spirit attack might be viewed as just a way of speaking about repressed childhood memories or fantasies about malevolent aspects of parents. Or it might be argued, in the name of universalism, that although a queasiness about widows is not part of our public discourse, we, too, manage to isolate them socially and keep them out of sight. In other words, deep down, or viewed in a unitarian light, that faraway place that seemed so different is not so different after all.

Rejection of the third proposition is entailed by acceptance of the other three. This is the stance that underwrites the monotheistic proselytizing spirit of the nineteenth century and the familiar developmental contrasts drawn by Sir Edward Tylor (1958 [1871]) and Sir James Frazer (1890) between magic and science, primitive and modern, superstition and objectivity. Ernest Gellner is a witty contemporary exponent of proselytizing developmentalism. Describing his view of the practice of anthropology, he states:

> What in fact [anthropologists] do is give an account of a given society, or some of its practices, against the backcloth of *our* world, and not of *its* world. An anthropologist who would explain witchcraft beliefs and practices of a given society by saying, "Well, as a matter of fact, in their country, witchcraft works, like what they say," would simply not pass muster. If relativism genuinely were the practice of anthropology, such an explanation would be not merely possible, but mandatory. In fact, what the anthropologist does do is explain how witchcraft beliefs can function notwithstanding their falsity. (1988, p. 26)

One logical possibility remains: rejection of the fourth proposition. Any defensible anthropological relativism requires the rejection of that proposition and acceptance of the other three. Many of the following essays explore that possibility.

Yet is it coherent to claim simultaneously that we are rationally justified in our conception of things (for example, that nature is indifferent to virtuous conduct; that Salmon Rushdie should be free to publish unharmed) *and* that others are rationally justified in their conception of things (for example, that nature is just; that Salmon Rushdie should be punished), and that this is so even though our conception of things and their conception of things are truly different, and inconsistently so?

The rub, as Rescher and many philosophers are fond of pointing out, is that we could not possibly know that others are rationally justified in their conception of things (proposition 3) if we could not make rational sense of their conception of things "by our lights" or, as Gellner puts it, "against the backcloth of our world."

In other words, if we can make rational sense of their conception of things, then their conception of things is not *that* different from ours, for it must make sense in terms that are understandable to us. It is *our* rationality that we explore when we confront *their* conception of things, for how else could we understand them, unless their meanings, beliefs, and modes of justification were in some sense available to us?

Does that mean that claims of genuine difference (proposition 2) must be denied? That would seem to depend on what we mean when we claim that the conceptions others have of things are different from our own.

One thing we just cannot mean is that the other is fundamentally alien to us (see Spiro 1990). Others are not fundamentally alien to us, just inconsistently and importantly different in their conception of things (as expressed in their texts, in their discourse, in their institutions, in their personalities) from our conception of things, at the moment.

Yet the conceptions held by others are available to us, in the sense that when we truly understand their conception of things we come to recognize possibilities latent within our own rationality, or existent in the history of our own reason, and those ways of conceiving of things become salient for us for the first time, or once again.

In other words, there is no *homogeneous* "backcloth" to our world. We are multiple from the start. Our indigenous conceptions are diverse, whether they are centered in our official texts or our underground newspapers, in our public discourse or our psychoanalytic soliloquies, in our customary practices or our idiosyncratic routines, in our daytime task analyses or our nighttime fantasies.

There is, of course, in that formulation a sense of universal latency, in which everyone has got everything. There is also a sense of manifest particularity, in which it matters a lot precisely how someone has got it—"it" referring to some conception of things (such as the idea that misfortune is punishment for moral transgressions, or that the opposite sex is a dangerous species).

Typically, the cross-cultural differences that interest us are differences in the way in which some conception of things has become manifest—the degree of its salience, centrality, generalization, legitimacy (local rationality), and institutionalization as a customary practice or personal motive in this or that ethnic tradition. In some parts of the world whether or not men and women sleep together and make love during the woman's menstrual period is discretionary, perhaps even a matter of taste; in other parts of the world it is mandated that women stay secluded for several days.

"Maintenance-loss" models of the capacity for cross-language speech perception, as described by Janet Werker (1989), provide a suggestive metaphor for the idea that an original latent multiplicity of highly differentiated forms (everyone has got everything) coexists with specialized institutionalizations of incompatible and diverging manifestations.

While I would not want to suggest that babies are the bearers of the universal subjectivity of humankind, it appears to be the case that the newly born come into the world with a very complex, detailed, and elaborated capacity to detect categorical distinctions in sound. The research on speech perception has been done with infants of English-speaking parents listening to language-specific phonemic contrasts in Hindu and in the appropriately difficult-to-pronounce American Indian language Nthlakapmx. The dramatic finding is that four-month-olds seem able to discriminate the phonemic distinctions peculiar to those disparate languages, a capacity that adult English speakers no longer possess. If this early capacity to detect a sound contrast in foreign tongues is kept alive through even a small amount of initial second-language learning during the first two years of life, it is maintained into adulthood. Typically, however, it disappears by the end of the first year of life, with the onset of exclusive single-language learning, and can be recovered later in life only with difficulty. It is recoverable. For example, [ra] versus [la] is not a phonemic contrast in Japanese, and monolingual Japanese adults are unable to discriminate [ra] versus [la] when listening to English. It takes several years of English-language training for Japanese speakers to detect the sound contrast reliably. On the other hand, if the recent research with American infants can be generalized, four-month-old Japanese infants who have had no previous exposure to English will have no difficulty discriminating between [ra] and [la] or between sound contrasts in other languages that play no part in the child's native speech community.

It would seem that in the case of speech perception, knowledge is prior to experience or, alternatively put (speaking for a moment as might a Darwinian or a Hindu), knowledge has its origins in experiences that are prior to the experience of this individual in this life. Yet it is this-worldly experience, this time around, that sets the threshold for the accessibility or availability of that which is known. One wonders about the relevance of maintenance-loss models to other domains, such as the emotions (see Chapter 6). Human infants come into the world possessing a complex emotional keyboard; yet as they become Eskimo, Balinese, or Oriya only some keys get played. Do the other keys get stuck because they are hardly played at all?

———

The problem of rationality (or psychic unity) continues to be an issue in the interpretation of conceptual diversity. It has a distinguished religious and philosophical ancestry. The "problem" is really a gloss for an oft-diagnosed form of intellectual and spiritual uneasiness, which, judging from textual history, East and West, has been a vexation for our kind for a very long time. It is the tension between the claims of tradition for our allegiance versus the claims of our ego to autonomy from the limitations of our customary practice and belief. The philosophical source of the uneasiness is the demand of individual consciousness to be free from the influence of established things. The theological source is the idea that this-worldly existence is some kind of negation of pure being.

The idea that existence is a negation of pure being can be traced in the West from Plato through Descartes to various contemporary "structuralisms," which aim to recover the abstract forms, universal grammar or pure being hidden beneath the "superficialities" of any particular person's mental functioning or any particular people's social life.

In the structural traditions the search for an autonomous being or pure consciousness typically proceeds in one of two ways. Descartes made famous a method of erasure (through radical doubt) whereby everything sensuous, subjective, embodied, temporary, local, or tradition-bound is viewed as prejudice, dogma, or illusion, and pure being is reserved for only those things in which an autonomous reason could have absolute confidence, namely, its self and deductive logic.

Others have made famous a method of subtraction, well known in the social sciences through the notions of "convergent validation," "interobserver reliability," and "data aggregation," whereby everything different about different ways of being in the world (or different ways of seeing the world) is treated as error, noise, or bias, and pure being is the abstraction of those common denominators that make people the same.

Yet "prejudice," "dogma," "illusion," "error," "noise," and "bias" are not the only locutions with which to possess or (as the structuralists would have it) dispossess a tradition, and our ability to recognize each other as pure beings does not necessarily arise out of what is left over after we subtract all our differences.

Anatole Broyard, the American writer and literary critic, once remarked, speaking in a very continental voice, that "paranoids are the only ones who notice things anymore." The essays in this volume are variations on that theme: that our prejudices make it possible for us to see; that traditions not only obscure but also illuminate; that our differences make us real; that while traditions are particularizing (who could *live* by ecumenism alone?), a peculiar existence can be a selective affirmation of pure being; that the freeing of consciousness goes hand in hand with feeling "astonished" by the variety of ways there are to see and to be. In other words, reason and objectivity are not in opposition to tradition, and they do not lift us out of custom and folk belief. Reason may lift us out of error, ignorance, and confusion. Yet error, ignorance, and confusion are not proper synonyms for tradition, custom, and folk belief.

Friedrich Nietzsche once said that he could believe only in a God who could dance. In India, where I do my research, and in other traditions as well, the gods are often desperate for an experience (for a fight, for a good meal, for a romance, for a vacation, for a chance to go dancing). They are eager to assume a human form and to extend themselves into nature, for the sake of a sensible compromise between the purity of a disembodied spirit and the dreary materiality of a disenchanted world. The gods know that when matter rests mindless and spirits float free it is either before the dawn or after the twilight of time and of existing things.

The New Standard Encyclopedia of Universal Knowledge (1931), a pocket-size compilation of tidbits of Enlightenment wisdom—the kind of "culture" one used to be able to pick up in a grocery store (I picked it up at a secondhand book sale)—defines romance as "a passion for adventure, the strange and the marvelous and a tendency to exaggerate the virtues and vices of human nature." It is a superficial definition—sort of like learning a punch line without the joke—and it is quite incomplete, but it will do, as a first approximation. More than one ethnographer of my generation, and of earlier generations as well, went off to the field with visions of the Arabian Nights or the Thief of Baghdad or the Tolkien Trilogy in mind, to adventure beyond the perceived limits of the self, to conduct research on the transformative power of words and deeds—performatives and rituals—and to write up ethnography as a narration of unusual and larger-than-life typifying events or as a record of encounters with exalted persons.

But the definition can be deepened. Romanticism stands out against the view that existence is the negation of pure being, by offering us its alternative, namely, the view that existence is the infusion of consciousness and pure spirit into the material world, thereby narrowing the distance or blurring the boundaries between nature, humanity, and the gods.

Romanticism shares with skeptical empiricism the view that the senses and logic alone cannot bridge that gap between existence and pure being. Left to their own devices, all that the senses and logic can see is a mindless nature, "fallen and dead." Transcendental things are beyond their scope. To make contact with the really real, the inspired (= divinelike) imagination of human beings must be projected out to reality; or, alternatively, the gods must descend to earth.

It is the doctrine of romanticism that existence is best appreciated (that is, understood *and* experienced) as a sensual manifestation of the transcendent, and that time and space, history and local variations in color (and culture), deserve to be examined inspirationally, imaginatively, and artfully for diverse signs of our divinity.

The subordination of existence to pure being has, over the centuries, generated a whole series of other subordinations: of the apparent to the real, of earth to heaven, of the profane to the sacred, of the polluted to the pure, of the body to the mind, of the dirty to the clean, of the pagan to the godly, of the artificial (the "plastic") to the genuine, of the imposed to the chosen, of the exterior to the interior, of custom to individual autonomy, of the superficial to the deep, of rhetoric to logic, of common sense to logic, of cases to principles, of "know-how" to rules, of ambiguity to precision, of the tacit to the explicit, of feeling to calculation, of intuition to reflection, of spontaneity to "five-year plans," of invention to discovery, of art to reality, of the figurative to the literal, of subjectivity to objectivity, of shadow to object, of darkness to light, of engagement to detachment, of the peculiar to the universal, of the sectarian to the ecumenical, of tribe to state, of community to bureaucracy, of the concrete to the abstract, of difference to likeness, of substance to form, of the senses to reason, of image to essence, of observation to meditation, of adventure to quietude, of enthusiasm to dispassion, of what really is not worthy to what really is.

The practical result of romanticism's doctrine is a revaluation of the subordinated pole of each of those oppositions: reality as an achievement of art and invention; objectivity as the extension of imaginative "paradigms" into nature, community and sacred tradition as the precondition of profane knowledge and free criticism; the concrete and the particular ("thick description") as the genuine vehicles of the transcendent; beauty as the figure of truth; logic as a lonely, empty form (there are places where logic alone can take us, but not necessarily where we want to go); feelings and emotions as rational and adaptive ways of being in the world; love as the realization of our veritable nature; language in general, and poetic language in particular, as the divine expressive instruments of the real (hence the trite equation of romance with sentimentality, lyricism, and love); adventure, astonishment, and cultural anthropology as proper responses to the variety of inspiring manifestations of pure being in the world.

Romanticism is routinely disparaged by its critics as mere "emotivism" or "nihilism" or "solipsism" or "paganism" or "perversity" (or, hard as it may be to believe, as "relativism," which is sometimes used as the code word for all of the above). What the critics fear most is that a rebellion in the name of romance against the subordination of existence to pure being will simply reverse the order of domination, leaving us with rhetoric instead of reason, art instead of reality, sentiment instead of calculation, difference without likeness, the idol without the god. What the critics fear most is a world in which the imagination is not inspired but simply intoxicated, a grotesque world in which the fanciful dominates the real, and subjectivity—worse yet, my special egocentric narcissistic sensibility arrogantly claiming to be divine—becomes the measure of all things.

While for every dreaded straw man there are usually several real ones to fear—perversity is not to be denied—as a general evaluation of romanticism the emotivism-nihilism line of criticism is not well founded. For one thing, satire, travesty, and irreverance are regular attendants in the service of reality. Inversions of the order of things rendering this or that world topsy-turvy are the customary instruments of parody, jest, cathartic rites, and Dionysian ecstasy, and of many other deeds corrosive of dogma and thus protective of consciousness. One fears that it is the critics' wholesale disparagement of the techniques of satire and ecstasy that is the real threat to pure being.

More important, the criticism misjudges the true project of romanticism. For the aim of romanticism is to revalue existence, not to denigrate pure being; to dignify subjective experience, not to deny reality; to appreciate the imagination, not to disregard reason; to honor our differences, not to underestimate our common humanity.

The negative intent behind the doctrine of romanticism is to expose the pretense that literal truth is artless. The positive intent is to develop theories about how realism—the experience of transcendent things as direct, transparent, or close at hand—is achieved artfully (see the Conclusion of this volume).

Romantic works aim to portray the infusion of the transcendental into nature. Some romantic texts bridge the gap between existence and pure being through heroic depiction of the descent of the gods, or, alternatively, in a secularized world dubious of discourse about the gods, by self-consciously foregrounding the revelatory role of the imagination. It is not unusual for a romantic text to draw attention to itself as a piece of writing or as a constructed creative act. Clifford Geertz (1973, 1988) writes the way he writes for a good reason. It is part of his point that we should notice what he is doing and how it was done.

Romanticism inclines toward an interest in those inspirations (of religion, of tradition, of individual literary or scientific genius) that take us beyond our senses to real places where even logic cannot go.

Romanticism strives to be a discernible manifestation of its own doctrine and to promote the feeling of astonishment in the face of itself and of many other strange and marvelous things.

———

Astonishment, unlike fear or anger or sadness, is not one of the universal emotions, yet it deserves to be. Victor von Gebsattel, the existentialist and psychiatrist, in a graceful essay half a century ago about the world of obsessive-compulsive patients (1958 [1938]), described astonishment as the experience of "fundamental existential wondering" that arises in the encounter with the differentness of the counterworld of a fellow human being.

Yet there is a deep problem here. I think it was when I heard Mortimer Adler accuse cultural anthropology of ethical incompetence on William F. Buckley's TV interview program, "Firing Line," that I really started to worry about the fate of astonishment, romanticism, and cultural anthropology in contemporary Western society. Adler was supposed to be critiquing Allan Bloom's book *The Closing of the American Mind* (1987), in which the author describes "Make love, not war" as an obscene remark, regrets the lost opportunity to censor rock music before it became popular, and finds it difficult to distinguish Woodstock from Nuremberg.

Bloom's provocative denunciation of the philosophical doctrine of emotivism—the claim that subjective experience is the *only* reality, that beauty is in the eye of the beholder and values merely a matter of taste—is an extended complaint about the romantic intellectual heritage that he holds responsible for the shallowness, even disappearance, of contemporary moral discourse. Today's American college students, Bloom claims, are so morally inarticulate, nihilistic, and tolerant—"to each his own bag"—that they even hesitate to condemn such obvious abominations as suttee (the Hindu practice of cremation, in which a deceased man and his surviving widow are immolated in the same funeral pyre); worse yet, they lack a moral vocabulary for doing so.

In *The Closing of the American Mind* Bloom uses the term *relativism* as a synonym for emotivism (or subjectivism) thereby equating them, in effect linking both relativism and emotivism to permissive and pernicious nihilism. When I first noticed his equation I initially discounted it as a rhetorical flourish. Wherever Bloom wrote "relativism" I read "emotivism" or "subjectivism."

I benefited greatly from Bloom's critique of emotivism (if you do not speak for anything higher than your self, why should anyone listen to you?). Yet, as I pondered his critique, its implications for cultural relativism did not seem very severe. After all, if we live differently in the world we just might live in different "objective" worlds, and not just in different heads. Nonemotive relativism is not an oxymoron (see Chapters 1 and 5); and trying our hand at some version of it is at least one of the games in town, in a town in which many of the players (for example, Goodman 1968; Geertz 1973; MacIntyre

1981, 1985; Putnam 1987; Booth 1988) are able to tell the difference between Woodstock and Nuremberg. There were far more mud and goodwill at Woodstock, and fewer restrooms, than at Nuremberg.

It was somewhat later, when I tuned in to Mortimer Adler in front of a national television audience, ostensibly there to criticize Bloom, pointing his finger at cultural anthropology and adding it to the equation (relativism = emotivism = nihilism = cultural anthropology; "logical positivism" was added to the list as well), that I began to worry about the fate of astonishment in the contemporary world, and to sense that anthropologists have a lot of work to do. This would seem to be the moment to move forward with a new-wave anthropology or cultural psychology that avoids the excesses of the old and tired oppositions monism versus nihilism, reason versus revelation, the absolute public object versus the transitory private subject.

So what is it that makes something like the obsessive-compulsive world encountered by von Gebsattel a true object for "fundamental existential wondering"? What makes it astonishing? The answer is that to answer those questions you must be willing to explicate that world. For if you do explicate a world that is a true object of fundamental existential wonder you will find out what makes it astonishing. You will find yourself wondering about fundamental existential things. (See Chapter 9 for the cognate notion of unpetrified viewing.)

Of course, not every world is a true object for astonishment. Not every world deserves to be spelled out. Yet there are always worlds other than your own that do. In between monism and nihilism there is still plenty of room for the varieties of the really real (and perhaps there is more room than ever, as we have come to appreciate that space). Whatever the perils of experience, to recognize a true object of astonishment you must look at it, and be curious about its peculiarities, so as to see.

The obsessive-compulsive world encountered by von Gebsattel and others (Freud 1959 [1907]; Rapoport 1989), for example, is an astonishing one because it is a world in which the Platonic tension between existence and pure being is acute. It is a world in which the skeptical metaphysical and existential speculations of philosophy and religion have become the stuff of personality. It is a world in which our fellow human beings teach us what it is like to live with an unrelenting nostalgia for the transcendental, for purity, perfection, and peace. It is a world in which we see what it is like to live not just with metaphysical uneasiness but with ontological terror of the "form-destroying powers of existence" (von Gebsattel 1958 [1938]), symbolized by dirt, symbolized by every conceivable danger, symbolized by a myriad of radical philosophical doubts: doubts about the trustworthiness of subjective experience, doubts about the precise and unambiguous meaning of words, doubts about one's control over the ramifying consequences of one's actions, doubts about the possibilities for enchantment in the material world.

The counterworld of obsessive-compulsive patients is an anxious world. It is a world in which we may encounter fellow human beings so captivated by the ideal of logical analysis that they cannot read, because every word must be divided up into its constituent letters; or so uncomfortable with embodiment that they are perpetually disgusted and immobilized by their own body odor and can never cleanse themselves quite enough; or so doubtful of their senses and experiences that they keep checking incessantly to make sure they have locked the door, ever tormented by the method of erasure and the Cartesian insight that their memory of having locked the door could, in principle, be an illusion.

Obsessive-compulsive patients feel "beside themselves" in their anxious counterworld, victims of the idea that existence is the negation of pure being. They live in our world, and they want to be of our world, but they feel abstracted out of it by the formal requirements and impersonal rules of a pure being that obstinately refuses to dance, just because it might sweat or smell or be uncertain about the next step to take. Their obsessive desire, which they experience with the force of a monomania, is to reduce through compulsive rituals and routines the perceived distance between an impure, uncertain, dangerous world and a divine heaven, and to do it by means of a radical subordination of existence to the presumed requirements of pure being. Perhaps a more romantic strategy might help: a dose of Blake, Wordsworth, or Keats, or of some inspiring poetic exaltation on the dignity of dirt or on the exhilaration of a daring adventure and other risky schemes.

The practice of suttee is even more astonishing, because it is so close to the divine. India is a high civilization. As an anthropologist you know you are working in a high civilization when, after you explain your informants' practices to them, they have their own stored-up accounts of what they are up to, and their explanations are often better, and almost always more imaginative, than your own. Alternatively, the locution "primitive" or "uncivilized" might be reserved for those peoples of the world, if there are any, who seem convinced that it is the examined life that is not worth living. Suttee is no "uncivilized" act.

The Indologist Paul Courtright described in a 1988 lecture at the University of Chicago a nineteenth-century eyewitness account by a British officer. Throughout the preparations for her cremation the widow appears jovial. She talks with onlookers. Immediately before her immolation she is handed a mirror. She looks in it and sees her past and future lives, which she narrates to the crowd, a testimonial lending support to the local doctrine of reincarnation. She goes up in flames, without signs of pain. The act seems unforced; no one has bound her to the funeral pyre. The British provide the fire permit.

Now what did the eye witness? Is it an act of heroism or of moral idiocy? And from which world or counterworld should we speak when we praise or blame such a practice? Is it really emotivism ("to each his own bag"; morality is merely subjective preference), as Allan Bloom suggests, that leaves some of us astonished, and tolerant? Is it really the dictates of an autonomous reason that leads others to condemn suttee and legislate against it or to suppose, like Allan Bloom, that it is obviously an abomination?

On September 4, 1987, Roop Kanwar, a beautiful eighteen-year-old college-educated Rajput woman, received national press coverage in India when she immolated herself in front of a large supportive crowd, with her dead husband resting on her lap. Immediately the scene of the event became a popular pilgrimage site. The cremation ground was enshrined as a romantic memorial to an extraordinary act of devotion and as a place in a sacred geography, that could be pointed to as tangible evidence of the reality of the divine and the descent of the gods.

The country was divided in its response. Everyone agreed that no mortal being could voluntarily stay poised on a funeral pyre during immolation and experience no pain or fright. Critics of suttee argued that it therefore could not have happened as reported—Roop Kanwar must have been forced to the funeral pyre, where she must have been agitated and wanted to flee; or, if it did happen as reported, then it could not have been voluntary—Roop Kanwar must have been drugged or hysterical or crazy. Supporters of suttee argued that therefore Roop Kanwar was no mere mortal—she was infused with the spirit of a goddess or she was a goddess.

Both accounts suggest that at the time of immolation Roop Kanwar was, in some sense, "out of her mind" (the expression connotes both insanity and objectivity), but one account validates and dignifies her act, our world, and the events that go in it, while the other disparages them. For which world or counterworld should we speak? For they are different and inconsistently so.

Suttee is a rare and extraordinary act. Viewed as artful realism (literal truth is not artless; see the Conclusion of this volume) suttee works, for those for whom it works, as a representation and confirmation through heroic action of some of the deepest properties of Hinduism's moral world. In that world existence is imbued with divinity. The gods have descended to earth. Since the world is imbued with divinity it is a just world, governed by laws of retributive causation and just retribution for past transgressions and sins. Since the world is a material world it is in transit, an impermanent place through which the divines circulate, at their own rate, in proportion to the limitations of their particular material incarnation and the quality of their moral careers.

Hindu moral doctrine has it that husbands and wives live in the world as gods and goddesses. She is the Laxmi of the house; he is her Narayan. As gods and goddesses their bonds to each other are transcendental and eternal. Yet they are incarnate. They are able to dance and eat and make love and transgress and sin; there is a place for the demonic in a romantic world. And they are able to die, which means that from time to time they must shed their vulnerable human form and be newly born again, male or female, as a lizard, as an owl, as a dog, as a human being. It is the price that must be paid for the romantic possibilities offered by embodiment.

In the Hindu moral world the death of a husband has more than material significance, and its metaphysical meanings run deep. Traditional widows in India spend the balance of their lives absolving themselves of sin (fasting, praying, withdrawing from the world, reading holy texts). In their world of retributive causation, widowhood is a punishment for past transgressions. The fact that your husband died first is a sign telling you that you must now undertake the task of unburdening yourself of guilt, for the sake of your next reincarnation on earth. In such a world the flame on your husband's funeral pyre is appreciated (understood and experienced) as though it was the romantic analogue of the last plane to Lisbon in the movie *Casablanca*. If you are not on the plane it is likely to be a very long time until you see him again, if ever. A shared cremation absolves sins and guarantees eternal union between husband and wife, linked to each other as god and goddess through the cycle of future rebirths.

For those who are in or on the edge of such an inventive world, the extraordinary act of suttee presents itself as an inspiring confirmation of all that metaphysical trafficking between heaven and earth, between humans and gods, between existence and pure being. Indeed, it is conceivable that Roop Kanwar herself understood and experienced her immolation as an astonishing moment when her body and its senses, profane things, became fully sacred, and hence invulnerable to pain, through an act of sacrifice by a goddess seeking eternal union with her god-man.

It is not impossible for us to imagine Roop Kanwar's conception of things. Nor is it difficult to recognize that that particular imaginative conception of things is inconsistently different from our own. The far more challenging issue is whether we can justify the conception of things that I have imagined for her. Can we justify it within the framework of our own rationality, which is the only framework for rationality that we have? Can we *rationally* reject proposition 4 above and endorse the other three? Can we successfully defend the idea (the rejection of proposition 4) that we are rationally justified in our conception of things and that Roop Kanwar is justified in her conception of things, too?

I think we can, and must; yet how we reject proposition 4 will depend, quite crucially, on the conception of reality to which we are committed. How we do it will depend on whether or not we believe that real things (concepts, propositions, gods, the really real) must exist independently of our involvement with them.

If we insist platonically that the very idea of reality suggests something independent of any one of its particular material realizations as a "thing" in time and space, independent of our involvement with it, independent of our verification procedures, of our presuppositions and theories, of our purposes and interests, then to represent suttee as a rational practice we would have to invoke the notions of conditionalized universals and of time-dependent or space-dependent truths. We would have to say things such as "in India souls reincarnate; in the United States they don't." After all, what is true here and now need not necessarily be true there and then, or there and now, or here and then. Perhaps there once were witches in Salem and they have gone away, to the Santa Cruz mountains. Perhaps there is room in Plato's heaven for conditionalized universals; the pure idea of "a witch in the seventeenth century" might qualify as an eternal, unchanging concept.

Yet the positing of time- and space-dependent truths on earth, and of conditionalized universals subsisting eternally in some Platonic heaven, is not the only way to reject proposition 4. One alternative is to insist on an epistemic conception of truth, reminiscent of the late-eighteenth-century romantic view that transcendent objects spring from the imagination and that there is a spiritual alliance between the mind and the world; they make each other up, as Hilary Putnam, has put it (1987, p. 1). Putnam's basic idea is that "there are external facts," and we can *say what they are*. What we *cannot* say—because it makes no sense—is what the facts are *independent of all conceptual choices*" (1987, p. 33).

That romantic conception of an interpenetration or interdependency of objectivity and subjectivity, of pure being and existence, has been variously expressed: as the idea that nothing in particular exists independently of our theoretical interpretation of it; as the idea that our measuring instruments are a part of the reality they measure; as the idea that the world is made up of "intentional" objects, such as "touchdowns" or "weeds" or "commitments" or "in-laws." Intentional objects have real causal force, but only by virtue of our mental representations of them and involvement with them (see Chapter 2). In all the foregoing Platonic (nonepistemic) and (anti-Platonic) epistemic conceptions of what is real, various apparently inconsistent conceptions of things can coexist because they never really meet head on. They are kept apart by contextualization, either by being made time and space dependent or dependent on our theories, verification techniques, and modes of justification, or by being embedded in some intentional world. They are not contradictions battling with each other in the same world. They are arguments in different worlds, whose "weak" (disconnected) inconsistency (Rescher 1988) just might lead us to appreciate those worlds of difference. When you live in the same world all disagreements are matters of error, ignorance, or misunderstanding. When you live in different worlds there is far more to a disagreement than meets the eye.

Some may wish to argue that all conceptions of things, even totally inconsistent ones, must inhabit the same global mind; that such a global mind is latent within each of us, or "subsists" in some Platonic heaven; and that it is some shared right of access to that global mind that constitutes our common humanity. Those are not unappealing ideas, from which it would seem to follow that psychic unity is not what makes us the same (a universally subsisting global mind stocked with a multitude of disconnected ideas has no causal powers to create an existent psychic uniformity); psychic unity is simply that which makes us imaginable to one another.

If psychic unity is what makes us imaginable to one another, then perhaps the really real truth for us mortal beings is that we can never be everywhere at once (even in a global mind), any more than we can be nowhere in particular. As mere mortals or, if you prefer, as embodied gods, we are always somewhere in particular, giving partial expression to our pure being. Because we are limited in that way, the inconsistency between Roop Kanwar's view of suttee and Allan Bloom's (or a feminist's, for that matter) is not something we need to resolve; it is something we need to seek, so that through astonishment we may stay on the move between different worlds, and in that way become more complete.

Others may argue that *any* feeling of this-worldly limitation is a concession to Platonism, and they may be right. Yet that is a concession I am eager to make, for although existence is not the negation of pure being, any particular existence is partial. Of course if you are an "innocent" or a "primitive," convinced that it is the examined life that is not worth living, then you may not be aware that your life is incomplete. But that is precisely why a civilized penchant for transcendence, in the form of a romantic leap into other ways of being, ennobles the spirit and deserves to be in the nature of things.

In the East those natural (and romantic) leaps toward completeness take place on a very long time scale, over many rebirths. In the West, where we think we go but one time around, we are in a bit more of a hurry to take the necessary steps.

———

Romanticism is sometimes thought to be antagonistic to science, but that is a mistake. Romanticism is in tension with only the first of the three major scientific world views sketched by Roy D'Andrade (1986). It is antithetical only to those Platonic approaches to science that proceed as though existence were a negation of pure being (see Chapter 2).

In his discussion of variety in science, D'Andrade defines any good science as one in which the scope and nature of the generalizations developed in any domain are appropriate to the kind of order found in that domain (1986, pp. 26–27). He suggests that different scientists think differently because they imagine different orders to reality. D'Andrade then divides the "good sciences" into three kinds—the physical, the natural, and the semiotic—on the basis of the kind of reality each science imagines it studies and the kinds of generalizations it seeks.

The physical sciences (for example, physics) seek pure or basic or eternal law–like generalizations about a small number of abstract objects or forces whose "interrelations can be stated in quantitative mathematical form." The physical sciences picture a homogeneous universe in which out of "deep necessity" "all generalizations apply equally through all time" (D'Andrade 1986, pp. 20–21).

The natural sciences (for example, geology, biology, economics) seek conditional generalizations about the way concrete historical or evolutionary objects—the human eye, the San Andreas Fault, the World Bank—are put together and work. The natural sciences imagine a "lumpy or patchy" universe made up of "complex contingent mechanisms" (D'Andrade 1986, p. 21).

The semiotic sciences (for example, linguistics, social and personality psychology, cultural anthropology) study things that have meaning to meaning-imposing human beings. They seek contingent generalizations about the regularities that make it possible for people to communicate with each other, with special attention to the learned content—the symbols and meanings—that guide human action. The semiotic sciences imagine a differentiated universe made up of words and categories and presuppositions and propositional attitudes in which different systems of meaning are created, promoted, and spread and become differentially institutionalized in different regions of time and space (D'Andrade 1986, pp. 24, 30, 34) (see Chapters 4 and 5).

As a romantic discipline cultural psychology is a hybrid form of semiotic science and natural science. For it assumes that human consciousness is a complex contingent mechanism whose dynamic functioning is mediated by the system of meaning within which it is embedded (see Chapters 3, 6, 7, and 8). As a semiotic natural science, cultural psychology explores the possibility suggested by Max Weber: that our highest-order systems of meaning—the astonishing world of the Protestant or of the Hindu—have become differentiated into semiotic regions; that as this cultural differentiation has taken place the "contingent mechanism" of human consciousness has undergone shifts in its dynamic functioning (see D'Andrade 1986). Thus, it will come as no surprise to cultural psychology if it should turn out that there are different psychological generalizations or "nomological networks"—a Hindu psychology, a Protestant psychology—appropriate for the different semiotic regions of the world.

———

I believe it was Bertrand Russell who once said that the fact that we each have a mother does not mean there is a mother of us all. On the facing page is the mother of us all, in the South Asian Oriya Hindu

conception of things, and she is not quite what the Western mind might imagine.

It is difficult for a Jew, a Christian, or anyone else unacquainted with Hinduism's narrative traditions to grasp the depiction. The viewer is likely to respond to the image with many powerful interpretations, feelings, and evaluations, but most of these reactions will be revealing of a Western frame of mind.

The Oriya artist has drawn mother-goddess Kali, the ferocious demon-slayer. He has portrayed a famous incident that took place shortly after Kali did battle with a notorious and previously invulnerable demon, who, along with his henchmen, had been terrorizing the gods. Kali has emerged victorious, having taken many demonic heads. Throughout the carnage she has been furiously at work, using her tongue and other implements to keep droplets of blood from touching the earth, for each droplet reproduces another demon. (In one local Oriya folk version of the fight, Kali dances before the demon and then slowly exposes her genitals in a celestial striptease. He watches her, loses his powers, and turns to jelly. She cuts off his head.)

Yet from the ardor of the slaughter Kali has also gone wild. Her husband—the god Shiva, celibate, erotically empowered by the reabsorption of his own semen—comes down from his cave in the mountains, where he has been meditating, to bring her back to her senses. The scene shown here, according to some local Oriya storytellers, depicts the redomestication of Kali and the restoration of her civility. Shiva lies down on the ground as Kali comes stomping along, enraged. She accidentally steps on her husband's chest, a shocking display of disrespect, given the hierarchical order of things. Suddenly she realizes what she has done. A moment before, she was wild; now, startled into re-cognition of her responsibilities as a deferential wife, Kali feels ashamed and fearful. She is about to be subdued. Her facial arrangement as depicted here (tongue out, eyes widened) is occasionally modeled in everyday life in Orissa as a stylized expression for embarrassment, fear, and surprise.

Kali is a symbol for the challenges of any future cultural psychology. How we are involved with the world and react to it depends on our representation of the ambient facts of our reality. Freud taught us mythically that it is the father who is perceived as dangerous by the son, as the son competes with him for their common object of desire, the mother. In India we learn that when we meet the mother of us all we must tame her or be destroyed. She is powerful and dangerous and may be hazardous to our health. Why not let our father have her? A. K. Ramanujan (1983) has even proposed that in India there is a radical inversion of the Oedipus complex. The son does not rebel against the father to get the mother. Instead the father makes the son an offer too good to refuse: give me your virility and I'll give you immortality. The son does it, eagerly.

People live differently in the world of Kali from the way they live in the world of the Virgin Mary. It is a supposition of cultural psychology that when people live in the world differently, it may be that they live in different worlds. It is an appreciation of those different worlds that cultural psychology tries to achieve. As one might have begun to suspect from our brief expedition into Roop Kanwar's world and the land of Kali, the different worlds that are the true objects of astonishment for cultural psychology are worlds in which truths are literal, in a frame-bound sort of way, and in which things follow logically, from powerful imaginative premises that are neither obviously false nor self-evidently true. Perhaps the truly astonishing thing about an astonishing world is that it is both affirmable *and* deniable. It is constructable and deconstructable. There is a sublime or "aweful" (as they say in Indian English) existential wonderment in the recognition that your capacity to affirm some astonishing world or deny it, to construct it or deconstruct it, depends, quite crucially, on whether we take our stand in that world or whether we take our stand in some other equally astonishing world. Or perhaps what is most truly astonishing of all is that when "thinking through cultures" there is no place else, no neutral place, for us to stand.

Part I
Ideas of a Polytheistic Nature

1.

Post-Nietzschean Anthropology: The Idea of Multiple Objective Worlds

Kurt Vonnegut in his novel *Slaughterhouse Five* has some things to say about his education in relativism: "I went to the University of Chicago for a while after the Second World War. I was a student in the department of anthropology. They taught me that nobody was ridiculous or bad or disgusting. Shortly before my father died he said to me—'You never wrote a story with a villain in it.' I told him that was one of the things I learned in school after the war" (1988, p. 8).

The aim of relativist teachings is to give permission to diversity and difference by justifying the permission it grants on the grounds of the coequality or noncomparability of divergent forms. I have tried to imagine myself listening in on a lecture promoting relativism as it might have been delivered by one of Vonnegut's anthropological mentors.

As I imagine it, the mentor approaches his lecture anticipating that within the minds of his highly reflective modern audience resides unconsciously and comfortably a habit of mind called ethnocentrism— the belief that our ways, because they are ours, must be closer to truth, goodness, and beauty than are the ways of others. In Vonnegut's time in academic circles ethnocentrism was thought to be a universal presumption of native thinking. Our mentor enters the lecture hall eager to raise that presumption to consciousness and then to banish it through schooling.

So he begins his lecture with a challenging series of rhetorical questions: What is the proper language for human beings: English, Tamil, Chinese, or French? What is the proper diet for human beings: vegetarian or nonvegetarian? What is the proper mode of artistic expression: the surrealism of Dali, the cubism of Picasso, or the impressionism of Renoir?

It is a strong opening. A modern educated mind, even a relatively ethnocentric one, boggles at the presumptuousness of such questions; for, as our lecturer must have known, when we compare the diverse languages of the world or the diverse modes of artistic expression, we are not typically tempted to make overall judgments about which is better or which is worse. Rather we are tempted to respond that they are just different but in some sense equal, or perhaps that their differences are good for different things, and the different things they are good for are just different but in some sense equal. By stimulating in his audience a few relativistic intuitions the mentor has got his lecture off to a good start.

The lecture, as I imagine it, continues with a fascinating and detailed description of variations in human languages, musical forms, terminological classifications for kinsmen, preferences and aversions and taboos in food, and aesthetic standards and fashions for art, clothing, and hair style.

Finally the lecture concludes with the posit of a moral principle: there are no universally or uniformly valid (objective, binding, constraining, authoritative) requirements for what languages to speak or what foods to eat or what clothes to wear and so on. Others may speak Tamil or eat soured curds or wear kilts, etcetera, even if we do not.

Now I am confident that any thoughtful University of Chicago student in Vonnegut's era presented with that moral principle would have been up all night pondering the "etcetera"; and I suspect that for any thoughtful and liberal student engaged in "etcetera pondering" late at night it must have seemed but a short step to the idea that ethical injunctions, customary practices, and supernatural (that is, metaphysical) beliefs are like the languages, foods, and aesthetic standards of human beings—different but equal. Others may have extramarital sex, circumcise their daughters at adolescence, or believe that "enthusiasm" is a heresy or that there is no random (or accidental) event, even if we do not.

It must have seemed an even shorter step to the conclusion that no one is "ridiculous or bad or disgusting," or wrong or deluded or confused, etcetera.

That conclusion, of course, is fallacious. The fact that there is no single valid mode of artistic expression does not mean that any doodling with paint on canvas is a work of art or is entitled to our respect.

The fallacy can be stated in quite general terms: The fact that there is no one uniform objective reality (constraint, foundation, godhead, truth, standard) does not mean there are no objective realities (constraints, foundations, godheads, truths, standards) at all. The death of monotheism should not be confused with the death of god(s). Ontological atheism or subjectivism is not the only route into relativism. Polytheism or the idea of multiple objective worlds is the alternative.

Over the past several decades the practice of ridiculing with stock counterarguments certain fallacious interpretations and absurd exaggerations of the doctrine of relativism has become a customary recreational activity in a few scholarly disciplines (especially philosophy); and one of the favorite and easy targets is the burlesque claim that nothing is the same across cultures or that nothing can be ruled out as immoral or bad, etcetera. Perhaps the ridicule is deserved, and Vonnegut's teachers should have been more precise and thorough in tracing out the implications of their lectures.

Yet as an anthropologist today I think there may have been something important and valid (and perhaps even subtle) in their message. So by examining two major routes into relativism, ontological atheism (God is dead) and ontological polytheism (monotheism is dead), I am going to hazard to get that message right.[1]

Seeking to get a message right, however, is not necessarily an innocent act; especially so when we live in a conflated world in which for every truth it is possible to serve some political (or personal) interest or end by drawing that truth to our attention or keeping it out of sight. The main aim of relativist doctrine in anthropology is to give permission to diversity and difference, by indicating why and when such permission ought to be granted. The truth in relativism is that there are times—not all times yet some times—when permission ought to be granted to diversity and difference. In drawing our attention to that truth by trying to be clearer about it, anthropology and other modern scholarly disciplines interested in relativism have in fact played a political role.

The Confrontation with Difference

For anthropologists the confrontation with diversity in belief, desire, and practice can be a radical one. Here is a short list of the things we can observe out there in the world of human beings if we look in the right places and with the right clearance: people hunting for witches, exorcising demons, propitiating dead ancestors, sacrificing animals to hungry gods, sanctifying temples, waiting for messiahs, scapegoating their sins, consulting the stars, decoding their dreams, flagellating themselves in public, prohibiting the eating of pork (or dog, or beef, or all swarming things except locusts, crickets, and grasshoppers), wandering on pilgrimage from one dilapidated shrine to the next, abstaining from sex on the day of the full moon, refusing to be in the same room with their wife's elder sister, matting their hair with cow dung, isolating women during menstruation, seeking salvation by meditating naked in a cave for several years, and so on and on.

Let us restrict our observations for the moment to one community in one part of the world. For some years I have been conducting research on moral development and moral reasoning in a Hindu temple town on the east coast of India among various Oriya Brahman sub-castes and among various castes referred to as "scheduled" castes (because they are scheduled for affirmative action programs) by the government of India, referred to as "Harijans" ("children of God") by Mahatma Gandhi, and referred to as *chuuan* (unclean, polluted, untouchable) by the local Brahmans (see, for example, Shweder 1986; Shweder, Mahapatra, and Miller 1987; and Chapters 3, 5, 6, and 9 of this volume).

In all sorts of ways, though certainly not in all ways, Oriya Brahman belief, desire, and practice challenge our own. Eating beef is prohibited. Marriages are arranged. Dating and premarital sexual play are strictly forbidden. Widows may not remarry, and restrictions exist concerning the foods they are permitted to eat and the clothing they are permitted to wear. Menstruating women are not allowed to sleep in the same bed with their husband or enter the kitchen or engage in prayer or groom themselves or touch their children. Adult men prefer to eat their meals at home alone, and it is considered shameless for a husband and wife to eat together. Certain kinsmen—for example, a woman and her husband's elder brother or a man and his wife's elder sister—are not permitted in each other's presence. Children sleep in the same bed with a parent or grandparent (though not with a menstruating woman) until at least the age of six or seven years. Adult women are not allowed out of the house without permission. Untouchables are not allowed in the local temple, and no one can enter the temple for twelve days following a birth or death in the family. The corpse of an adult must be cremated, never buried, with the exception of a holy man, who must be buried, never cremated.

Each of those practices has associated with it a line of argumentation. For example, it is argued by Oriyas that many people, including ancestral spirits, are affected in serious ways by the person you marry. How can the marriage decision possibly be left up to one young, vulnerable person driven by sex, passion, and infatuation?

Or it is argued that the human body is a temple with a spirit (what we call the self or the observing ego) dwelling in it, and it is a proper end in life to preserve the sanctity of the temple and keep it clean and pure. The body of a menstruating woman is impure. Hence she must stay or be kept at a distance from all holy or sanctified ground, including all temples, such as the body of her husband, the household prayer room, and the kitchen.

Each line of argumentation presupposes, makes use of, or culminates in several posits about what the world is like: people have souls, and they transmigrate in proportion to their sanctity; the body is a temple with a spirit dwelling in it; eating food is an oblation; you reap what you sow; nature is just, and received inequalities are a form of just desert; to be born a woman and to survive the death of your husband are indications of previous sin, which should be absolved before you die; ancestral spirits return to your wife's kitchen to be fed, and they will not accept food from your wife unless her caste status is appropriate; and so on. Many residents in the temple town design, organize, and interpret their experiences according to those conceptions of reality.

Confronted with such apparently different conceptions of reality and associated practices, anthropologists have reacted in one of three ways.

Some—let us call them the universalists—have tried to look beyond the differences and search for significant or deeper or more abstract points of similarity, while treating the diversity as merely apparent and the differences as trivial or unimportant or irrelevant.

Some—let us call them the developmentalists—have tried to see within the diversity a continuous or perhaps stagelike process of growth and adaptation, viewed as a battle between reason and superstition, education and ignorance, science and religion, enlightenment and darkness, secondary process thinking and primary process thinking, sophistication and innocence, rationality and irrationality, modernity and traditionalism.

Some—let us call them the relativists—have tried to give permission to the diversity by documenting the significance, relevance, and importance (that is, the genuineness) of the differences between apparently divergent forms, while arguing that not all differences should be ranked into higher and lower levels of development or adaptation.

In the eyes of their respective antagonists the relativists look "soft on superstition," the developmentalists appear "ethnocentric," and the universalists seem "colorless, vacuous, and banal"; the universalists (as the "late" Wittgenstein, an antagonist, might have put it) try to find the real artichoke by divesting it of its leaves.

In this case it is not difficult to see something of value in all three types of responses. Each has its (partial) point within the terms of a well-known and powerful metaphysics of form (or conceptual architecture of likeness and difference).

When it comes to thinking through the metaphysics of form, it is useful to start with the truism that no two things are identical, from which it follows inexorably that in some way any two things are different. The assertion of difference, however, raises the question "different in respect to what?" which presupposes a higher-order likeness. So it also follows that in some way any two things are alike. Any and all two things, it turns out upon reflection, are both different and alike.

Within that tidy conceptual structure for likeness and difference there are separate rooms, each with a view, for universalism, developmentalism, and relativism.

When the differences between things are trivial, unimportant, or irrelevant (that is, when what is true about the functioning of one thing is also true of the other things regardless of their differences), universalism is at a premium, and nonidentical things can, with profit, be treated as equivalent.

Yet sometimes the differences between things do matter, and nonidentical things should not be treated as equivalent. The universals that unite the things are insufficient to explain their functioning: because of their differences the dynamics of their functioning are different, even though in other respects the things are alike.

When the differences between things matter in that way—because of their differences things function differently, even though in other ways they are alike—those differences are sometimes revelatory of progress or advance. This is especially true when the differences represent points or stages in the attainment of some adaptive equilibrium or some proper end state. At such times developmentalism is at a premium.

Sometimes, however, the differences are significant, but neutral with respect to the issue of relative progress. This is especially true when they represent the existence of multiple equilibria or noncomparable end states. At such times relativism is at a premium.

The merit of the relativistic stance is that it gets us to recognize that there are cases of genuine and significant diversity that are not matters for developmental analysis, although not every case is such a case. And by that account it should be possible to construct a version of relativist doctrine resistant to stock ridicule and misunderstanding.

In that version of the doctrine relativism becomes a type of explanation for diversity, in which it is argued that cases exist in which differences are to be expected, because there is no authority worthy of universal respect defining *the* proper way to classify and understand reality or *the* proper ends of life or *the* proper way to design a society, etcetera. As we shall see later, it is possible to differentiate different subtypes of relativist doctrine by examining the reasons and justifications adduced in support of that claim ("different but equal").

This version of relativist doctrine does not prohibit universals, although it does require the absence of any authority simultaneously worthy of universal respect and capable of specifying *the* proper way to understand and experience the world or *the* proper way to live. Relativism is perfectly compatible with the existence of authorities worthy of universal respect (for example, the logical principle of noncontradiction—"a thing cannot both be and not be"; or the moral principle of justice—"treat like cases alike and different cases differently") as long as those universal authorities are insufficient (they may be necessary) for drawing substantive conclusions about what to think or feel and how to live.

What a proper doctrine of relativism does claim is that to derive substantive conclusions of that sort (what to think or feel and how to live) we must *also* appeal presumptively to local authorities (scripture; communally held theories and assumptions about truth, beauty, and goodness) that are not entitled to universal respect. Thus a proper doctrine of relativism must provide an account of the differences between the mandatory and the presumptive (discretionary) aspects of authority. And the doctrine must help us see why both aspects of authority, the mandatory and the presumptive, are necessary if we are to have practical guidance about how to think, feel, and live in the world.

For example, in some relativist accounts mandatory authority is equated with whatever can uniquely be induced from universally available experience or evidence or logically be deduced from undeniable first principles. According to that account there are major aspects of the authority of, say, the Old Testament or Darwin's origin story about the evolution of complex biological forms that are local or presumptive, for their first principles are not undeniable, and the evidence they powerfully interpret by means of their quite deniable assumptions can be powerfully reinterpreted from alternative conceptual starting points; or, at the very least, we must allow for that possibility.

In other words, the doctrine of relativism denies that it is the *sine qua non* of reason that its requirements converge or are uniform across space and time. According to the doctrine it is natural for human beings to be as different from one another as is allowed by their common rationality. Their common rationality is, after all, not all of their rationality but only that part that is common. Any total system of authority capable of giving guidance about what to believe or value or how to live will consist of interacting elements some of which are mandatory, common, or ecumenical and others of which are presumptive, variable, or denominational. In other words, and again, others may have two wives, or believe that all learning is reminiscence, or believe that human beings, "suspended between the angels and the beasts," descended from the angels, even if you do not believe so.

The story of relativism in anthropology, however, is not that simple. Complications arise because there are subtypes of relativist doctrine, each built on a somewhat different conception of the relevant state of mind (for example, pretending that ____, fantasizing that ____, believing that ____) associated with the apparently alien ideas and practices of the "other." And each subtype of relativist doctrine is built, as well, on a somewhat different conception of the relationship between subjectivity and objectivity, interiority and exteriority, fantasy and reality, and imagining and witnessing in the interpretation of symbolic forms.

Rationality, Realism, and the Interpretation of Symbolic Forms

Those complications arise because crosscutting the distinction among universalists, developmentalists, and relativists is an independent issue of interpretation and evaluation concerned with the question of the realism or rationality of symbolic forms. The issue concerns the proper way to attribute states of mind (for example, pretending, believing, wishing) when interpreting and translating the symbolic forms of other peoples. For example, how are we to translate and interpret all those things that people around the world say and do about witches, ghosts, and spirit possession? (See, for example, *Malleus Maleficarum* 1928 [1489]; Trevor-Roper 1967; Obeyesekere 1981; Chapter 9 of this volume.) What state of mind should we attribute to them (knowing? believing? pretending? imagining? wishing? hallucinating?), and why?

The answers given to that question divide the "God is dead" school for the interpretation of symbolic forms from schools of interpretative realism. That division roughly parallels the split between subjectivists and objectivists, emotivists and cognitivists, nonrationalists and rationalists. It is possible to be a relativist or universalist or developmentalist on either side of the divide, although here I shall focus only on the two schools of relativism opposing each other across the emotivist versus cognitivist divide.

Before discussing the two sides of that divide, however, some terms and concepts need to be clarified concerning the interpretation of symbolic forms.

A symbolic form, like many other "appearances" or "sensations" or "experiences" (such as a retinal image or a verbal utterance or a drawing on a pad) is a reality-posit. A reality-posit is a *representation* of a particular state of the world (for example, "There is a unicorn in my garden") that functions as the content, the topic, the object, or the aim for any of the various states of the mind that we designate which such labels as fantasizing (that ____) or wishing (that ____) or believing (that ____) or perceiving (that ____) or remembering (that ____) or what have you. Symbolic forms are the reality-posits that fill in the "that" clause for a state of mind.

Just like many other "appearances-sensations-experiences," reality-posits are symbolic forms because they are about something else. Through their content reality-posits (for example, "There is a unicorn in my garden") refer or point beyond themselves to another realm, that exteriorized framework that we call reality or the world, connecting us to it by positing *of* it (as in fantasy or in memory or in belief) or positing *for* it (as in desire) a particular state of the realm.

A state of mind, on the other hand, is an interpretation or classification of the status (dream, fantasy, imagination, hallucination) of a reality-posit (for example, "There is a unicorn in my garden") as a representational object or symbolic form. State-of-mind classifications are designed to interpret the nature of a reality-posit (for example, seen "as if through a glass darkly"), the conditions of its occurrence (for example, witnessed only while sleeping) or reproduction (for example, brought to mind at will), its degree of availability as an experience to audiences of different kinds (for example, witnessed only by me), and ultimately its source (for example, it's only in the head).

States of mind (believing, fantasizing, wishing) can be postulated, but they cannot be directly viewed or known, which is why one of the most important things up for interpretation in the evaluation and classification of symbolic forms is the state of mind suggested by any particular reality-posit. How is this particular people's particular reality-posit (for example, "people entering into compacts with the devil") to be translated? Is it indicative of a belief, a wish, a fantasy, a desire, and how can one tell? What is the difference, anyway, between, for example, perceiving that ____, believing that ____, imagining that ____, or wishing that ____, and how is it possible, if at all, to distinguish those reality-posits or symbolic forms that are realistic or rational or proportionate to "actual" states of the realm from those that are not?

The issue of the interpretation of the state of mind associated with any particular symbolic form or reality-posit is multileveled. First there is the problem of how to define the proper or ideal ratio of subjectivity to objectivity in reality-finding reality-posits, or in those rational or realistic reality-posits that are thought to be proportionate to or in graceful coincidence with actual states of the world.

Some claim that reality-posits that are rational or realistic or reality-finding are those in which subjectivity has been reduced to zero. That means that perfect rationality or realism (subjectivity set at zero) consists in a perspective-free ("unbiased") witnessing of the world. The idea is one of stepping completely out of our mind, personality, and position in the social order, so as to see the world the way it really is, as a thing in itself, uncontaminated and undistorted by projected traces of our intellectual point of view, wishes, desires, goals, emotions, and interests.

Others agree, but argue that since that is impossible, rationality and realism can never be achieved. As that argument goes, perspective-free perception is a godlike state of mind unattainable by human beings. Others argue that the least we can do is strive to be godlike, correcting for projections and distortions wherever possible. Still others argue that perhaps it is our prejudices that make it possible for us to see; perhaps our prejudices even make it possible for us to see some things as they really are.

Then there is the issue of how to define, label, and classify all the kinds and varieties of states of the mind (see D'Andrade 1987). Every state of mind (for example, believing that ____, wishing that ____, perceiving that ____, remembering that ____, dreaming that ____) carries us through the here-and-now appearance of a symbolic form (for example, the verbal utterance: "There is a unicorn in my garden") into the exteriorized framework (the reality or conceivable world) to which the posit refers.

But what states of mind are there, and how are they interrelated? Some argue, for example, that imagination is opposed to perception, and that it is bad to confuse one with the other. Some argue that perception is a form of imagination (for example, that visual perception is a "construction"), while others argue that imagination is a form of perception (for example, that dreaming is the witnessing of a plane of reality). Still others argue both ways, and dialectically, for imaginative perception and perceptive imagination.

Finally there is the issue of how to identify, interpret, and translate the particular state of mind (wishing that ____, knowing that ____, believing that ____, pretending that ____, imagining that ____) suggested by any particular symbolic form, such as the reality-posit "I am a witch."

What state of mind should we attribute to our neighbor in the sixteenth century when she confesses she is a witch? Is it a case of knowing that ____? Or is it a case of believing ____? or pretending ____? or wishing ____? or dreaming ____? Or is it a case of knowing that ____ because of dreaming that ____? or perhaps of believing that ____ because of wishing that ____? And should that attribution, a sixteenth-century attribution about a sixteenth-century state of mind, be any different from the attribution we should make today about the sixteenth-century state of mind? What if the reality-posit ("I am a witch") came in the form of a confession from our neighbor living today, and we had to make a twentieth-century attribution about a twentieth-century state of mind? Should that attribution be any different, and why?

This example, of course, is hardly random, for there has been within anthropology much controversy over the "witch question," and not surprisingly the issue remains unresolved. The question can be put this way: Cross-culturally and historically, why have so many accused witches confessed, even without torture, and why have so many of them appeared convinced of their own guilt?

Cultural anthropology will probably come to an end when it comes up with an incontestable answer to the witch question. Later I will develop a postpositivist rationalistic conception of so-called supernatural beliefs, which promotes the idea of reality-testing as a metaphysical (= supernatural) act and which implies that we consider answering the witch question this way: because they were witches. Perhaps that answer will help keep cultural anthropology alive for at least another generation.

That crosscutting issue concerning the degree of rationality or realism of the states of mind associated with symbolic forms divides anthropological relativists into two camps.

There are the ontological atheists (subjectivist, emotivist, nonrationalist, "God is dead") who believe that symbolic forms or reality-posits are not uniform or homogeneous around the world because realities are creatively fabricated, invented, or "made up." Culture is interpreted as a case of fancying that ____. Like other products of fancy it is "free" to vary.

Then there are the ontological polytheists (objectivist, cognitivist, rationalist, realist) who think that reality-posits are not uniform or homogeneous around the world because reality is not uniform or homogeneous. Culture is interpreted as a case of perceiving that ____or understanding that ____or appreciating that ____. According to the ontological polytheists the framework of reality is multiplex in disjoint planes, and it makes sense to interpret diversity as though there is more than one objective world.

Of course a third possibility exists. That third possibility is that reality is uniform or homogeneous, and that symbolic forms and reality-posits are not uniform and homogeneous around the world because not everyone is equally in touch with reality (see Spiro 1982, 1984; Gellner 1985). Thus, some peoples, it might be argued, cannot always tell the difference between wishing and believing or between imagining and perceiving, and in certain intellectual domains they confuse fantasy with reality and permit primary-process thinking to become a prominent feature of their mental functioning.

It is the search for an alternative to that third hypothetical possibility (and its developmental and monistic implications) that unites relativists, spanning the divide between the ontological atheists ("God is dead"; reality is a fabrication) and the ontological polytheists ("monotheism is dead"; cultural variety illuminates the multiplicity of objective worlds). The aim of relativism is, after all, to find defensible ways, if there are any, to give permission to diversity.

To write the slogan "God is dead" is to invoke the very much alive spirit of Friedrich Nietzsche, and it is with Nietzsche that any story about ontological atheism ought to begin. Nietzsche was not a *cultural* relativist. He was too much of an existentialist and individualist for that. And we should not forget that it was Nietzsche who once described Asia as a dreamy place where they still do not know how to distinguish between truth, poetry, and other fictions (1982, p. 57). Nevertheless, it is Nietzsche's conception of the nature of cultural things that has set the agenda for modern interpretations of the states of mind associated with symbolic forms. According to Nietzsche's conception reality-posits or symbolic forms have null reference, for the realities they posit do not exist. Thus spake Zarathustra. Ontological atheism was born.

Thus Spake Nietzsche

Friedrich Nietzsche is not an acknowledged founding father of cultural anthropology, yet, far more than is realized, his way of thinking propagated and took over modern anthropology (on the Nietzschean foundations of modern social and political consciousness see MacIntyre 1981). Around 1882 Nietzsche thought he had the answer to the witch question. Many contemporary cultural anthropologists think he was right.

Nietzsche not only suspected (and regretted?) that God was dead. As a protopositivist, Nietzsche had doubts about the realism or rationality of all unperceived or unseen things (including God, witches, souls, sin, necessity, rights, values, and morality).

Positivism is empiricism in its purest form. At the risk of oversimplification, it might be stated that the central doctrine of positivism is that only seeing is believing and that, therefore, one should stick with appearances or experiences, for they are the only reality, while any other claim to knowledge is either tautology or metaphysical non-sense.

Nietzsche put it this way: "Today we possess science precisely to the extent to which we have decided to *accept* the testimony of the senses—to the extent to which we sharpen them further, arm them, and learn to think them through. The rest is miscarriage and not-yet-science—in other words, metaphysics, theology, psychology, episte-mology—or formal science, a doctrine of signs such as logic and that applied logic that is called mathematics. In them reality is not encoun-tered at all, not even as a problem" (1982, p. 481).

Nietzsche's answer to the witch question flows from his no-nonsense positivism: "Although the most acute judges of the witches, and even the witches themselves, were convinced of the guilt of witch-ery, the guilt nevertheless was non-existent." He goes on to say, shock-ingly, "It is thus with all guilt" (1982, pp. 96–97).

Nietzsche gives what might be called a null-reference answer to the witch question. While the reality-posit "I am a witch" has reference to an externalized frame containing "witches" as its content, the re-ality it posits is associated with a state of mind known as fancy and does not exist. Nietzsche then generalizes his null-reference argument to every case in which the following two conditions hold: (1) a sup-posed objective-external yet invisible entity is invoked (for example, natural rights), and (2) with respect to that unseen thing the self is supposed to be subordinate, bound, or guilty.

The gist of a null-reference argument goes something like this: When it comes to God, sin, morality, necessity, and witchery, there is nothing real "out there" in the nature of things to be guilty of or to be bound by. Thus no objective basis exists for the subjective sense of being commanded by God, or for a feeling of sin, or for a pang of conscience, or for a perception of inevitability and necessity, or for the conviction that one is a witch. Such senses, feelings, pangs, per-ceptions, and convictions tell us nothing about the external world but much about phantoms that haunt the human mind.

Nietzsche reasons on. Moral obligations are phantoms, not objec-tive facts out there waiting to be discovered through positive inquiry. As he wrote in his notes of 1880–81: "Being moral means being highly accessible to fear" (1982, p. 74). Similarly, belief in the God-phantom, sin-phantom, conscience-phantom, necessity-phantom, and witch-phantom is little more than slavish susceptibility to cus-tom, suggestion, indoctrination, conformity, reward, or social pres-sure. At best, we believe the things we believe because the expression of those beliefs produces agreeable feelings in powerful or significant others who are the upholders of the phantom order. We certainly do not believe them because they are true, for there is nothing out there for them to be true of.

Enter the *Übermensch* (sometimes translated as "overman"; mocked by George Bernard Shaw as the "superman"), Nietzsche's ideal of the fully developed and mature autonomous individual. "Behind your thoughts and feelings, my brother, there stands a mighty ruler, an unknown sage—whose name is self. In your body he dwells; he is your body" (1982, p. 146).

Thus spake Zarathustra. The self strives to realize its essential, objective, or inherent nature, which is to be self-caused or free. To be self-caused or free is to resist all external constraints, especially phantoms of the imagination disguised as cold necessity or objective truth.

The liberated individual (the *Übermensch*) seeks to rid its self of phantoms. It strives to manifest its deepest nature, the self's will to possess the power of total autonomous self-control (the so-called will to power). The *Übermensch* (who, ironically, in Nietzsche's account seems to be quite godlike) realizes that it is only it who is necessary and real, the creator through reification and projection of what it previously mistook for the discovery of the external constraints of reality.

Thus, according to Nietzsche, men and women are the makers of the reality before which they bow down as its slave. If the self is to authenticate its self and fully realize its nature (essential autonomy or self-creative freedom), apparent realities must be permanently transcended or, at least, repeatedly remade. Just as a "snake that cannot shed its skin perishes," so too perishes the self that cannot shed the "received wisdom" of the past and, so to speak, make its own mind up, for its self.

The *Übermensch* attains this-worldly transcendence. Looking through and penetrating the shroud of tradition, it sees and recognizes a terrible truth. At once aware that much that was supposed to be natural and real is merely a reified phantom of mind, it discards the shackles of convention, disencumbers itself of the yoke of tradition, and sets itself free. There, in Nietzsche's conception of the *Übermensch,* is born, perhaps reborn, existentialism's ego, the idea of a really real plane of ultimate self-determination existing prior to or outside of society, the idea of the creative source behind the phantom of custom-bound constraint. Indeed, Nietzsche used existentialism and positivism reciprocally to define each other.

God Is Dead: The Nietzschean Anthropology of Phantomlike Culture

Nietzsche's answer to the witch question has become, ironically, the conventional wisdom of modern anthropology. Prominent theorists of culture, who are in dispute about almost everything else, share the Nietzschean assumption that tradition-based reality-posits are imaginary phantoms of mind. In general, supernatural entities, moral obligations, and society itself are presumed to have standing only as imposed or projected mental representations or symbolic forms (reality-posits); and the realities that are posited are viewed either as unreal, or as real only as reality-posits.

George Peter Murdock (1980), for example, expresses the now common contemporary Nietzschean view when he states: "There are no such things as souls, or demons, and such mental constructs as Jehovah are as fictitious as those of Superman or Santa Claus (it is not Nietzsche's *Übermensch* he has in mind, but rather the Superman who is able to bend steel in his bare hands). Neither ghosts nor gods exert the slightest influence on men and their behavior" (p. 54).

That Nietzschean null-reference argument is also forcefully reiterated by David M. Schneider (1965).

> There is no supernatural. Ghosts do not exist. Spirits do not in fact make storms, cause winds, bring illness or effect cures. The gods in the heavens do not really make the stars go around and neither do they decide each man's fate at his birth. Since there are no real ghosts, spirits, gods, and goddesses, it follows logically . . . that their real and true nature cannot decisively shape man's beliefs about them or the social institutions related to them. Man's beliefs about ghosts and spirits must be wholly formed by man himself. Whatever unity there is to man's beliefs about the supernatural derives, therefore, from the nature of man himself and not from the nature of the supernatural.   (Pp. 85–86)

Of course, as Schneider was well aware in 1965, that news had not yet arrived in all circles; and over the centuries, in most circles where the news that God is dead had arrived, it had been strenuously resisted. That fact continues to lend great fascination to the problem of interpreting the state of mind associated with so-called supernatural reality-posits and symbolic forms.

Cornelius Loos, for example, had a hard time getting his book published in 1592. The thesis of the book was that the devil did not exist, that there were no such things as witches, and that all those confessions by women throughout Europe stating that they had flown through the night to an orgiastic Black Sabbath were nothing more than products of their imagination. Loos's book was never published; instead he was widely viewed as an enemy of reason and was denounced, imprisoned, and forced to recant. It is sobering to read Hugh Trevor-Roper's brilliant account "The European Witch-Craze of the Sixteenth and Seventeenth Centuries" (1967). For one comes away feeling that it was the promoters of the witch-hunts and witch-burnings who were the guardians of reason and science, while it was the skeptics who seemed to shy away from the reasonable implications of their own conceptual reference points.

One conceptual reference point widely accepted during those two centuries was that the devil, fallen from heaven, had established his own kingdom and that the church was engaged in a mortal struggle against Satan's attempts to regain his lost empire. Rational inquiry was not necessarily incompatible with belief in the doctrine of the kingdom of Satan; and, as Trevor-Roper documents, many of the promoters of witch-hunts were the leading intellectuals of their time, who knew all about the canons of scientific objectivity and logical consistency and applied them to the evidence at hand. A powerful scientific case was developed in defense of the witch-hunts.

The evidence at hand was a corpus of detailed confessions by women, which was scrutinized for its objectivity. Confessions in Scotland were found to converge with confessions in distant Prussia, and certain common themes were identified: a secret pact with the devil to help him recover hegemony, anointment with the fat of a murdered child (so-called devil's grease), an aerial night journey to a sabbath ground, worship of the devil, dancing, macabre music, cold and tasteless food, and a sexual orgy. Aware of the seriousness of a witchcraft accusation, some defenders of the witch-hunts examined the alternative "subjectivist" hypothesis and dismissed it; for if the confessions were all delusions, induced by some subjective state such as melancholia, then why should there be such convergence in reported accounts from separate corners of Europe? The consistencies or common elements in the stories of confessed witches, stories from women who spoke different languages and came from different countries, lent credence to the accounts.

Some defenders of the witch-hunts also entertained the alternative "method effect" hypothesis and dismissed it. The skeptics had argued that the common elements in the confessions of witches could be explained by reference to inquisitors' use of certain standard leading questions and techniques of torture. Skeptics argued that the identity of the elicitation procedures, not the identity of the experience with the devil, explained the similarities in the contents of the confessions. Upon examination, the skeptics turned out to be wrong. Many confessions were voluntary, torture was not used in every country, and even without leading questions the same story unfolded: a pact with the devil, a night flight, a Black Sabbath.

In the face of this onslaught of reason and evidence, the skeptics remained for two centuries on the defensive. For 200 years, the best they could do was advance some wildly speculative claims about the living conditions of the devil (for example, that he had been locked up in hell and could not possibly intervene in human affairs) or else about methodological and procedural issues such as the cruelty of torture or the possibility that some innocent people might be convicted. As Trevor-Roper notes, "To the last the most radical argument against the witch-craze was not that witches do not exist, not even that the pact with Satan is impossible, but simply that the judges err in the identification" (1967, p. 149).

"Malpractice" claims of that sort do not pose a serious threat to the underlying rationality of an ideological region, for they presuppose the conceptual reference points in question. A case in point was reported in *Sudan Notes and Records* (1920). Parents and villagers in a Nubian district of Sudan stood by and watched a female child cease to live while a native healer, by lashing, beating, and choking, tried to cast out of the girl a possessing devil, a "jinn." At the subsequent trial, the healer claimed to have been contacted in a dream and empowered to use his tampura (a mandolinlike instrument) to drive out afflicting demons: "Each devil has its special note. When it is struck the devil speaks, and makes his demands for what he wants, which has to be provided by the friends of the patient, when he is satisfied and leaves the patient." The healer claimed that in this case the devil's requests were refused by the family, and when that happens, the jinn is likely to "break the neck of the afflicted person." The healer claimed to have entered into physical battle with the demon in the girl's body. "My jinn and her jinn entered on a struggle for mastery. Mine in me was throttling hers in her and vice versa . . . Her jinn overcame my jinn . . . Hers killed her because its demands were refused. Mine would do the same to me if I refused its demands."

At the trial it was apparent that for the Nubians involved, if not for the colonial court, this was a potential case of malpractice, which was understood by the participants within the framework of a well-established Islamic theory of satanic beings that no one had reason to doubt. Appearing as a witness was another native healer, a woman, who had originally been consulted by the dead girl's parents: "Azab and Medim brought me their daughter and stayed two nights. Then I told them I could not put her right. They were no ordinary devils [*dsātir*] but malicious jinns who had made her make water on my bed clothes." And the witness told the court that when the accused healer first appeared on the scene and started beating the girl, the witness had said to the girl's father, "There is no medicine for jinns; if you are going to have treatment of this kind [beatings] take her away from my zariba." The witness also revealed that, at the time, the accused healer had told her that the devil was a foreign Christian devil that the witness did not know how to treat.

The father of the girl was cross-examined by the court: "Why did you not stop this cruel treatment?" The father replied, "He told me it would effect a cure and I believed him." A farmer, who observed the beatings, was examined: "How could you stand there and see a girl throttled?" He replied, "It was our ignorance ... [The healer] said, 'Don't say anything. The more you object the more you encourage devils and handicap me.'" The farmer revealed that he himself had tried to tell the healer that if he wanted to drive out devils, there was a way of writing holy passages and a way of smoking demons out of the body.[2]

A striking feature of the trial is that while objections were raised about the competence of the healer, his particular diagnosis, and the procedures used, Nubian theories of illness and cure left open the possibility, and no rational Nubian had reason to doubt, that the girl might have been possessed by a spirit—just as no rational European in the sixteenth and seventeenth centuries could coherently or credibly raise doubts about the existence of the devil (if God exists, then so must the devil). When Cornelius Loos tried to raise such skeptical doubts in 1592, he was punished as a reckless enemy of reason and forced to recant.

A comparable situation today might be that of an evolutionary biologist trying to prevail upon the secular academic community that the evolution of biological forms does not occur by a process of natural selection. He might, for example, try pointing to the lack of transitional forms in the fossil record or to the difficulty of plausibly explaining how highly integrated biological systems or subsystems—which require complex integration among diverse parts to function at all—could exist in incomplete transitional states or be the product of a piecemeal, intermittent, or random process. The biologist might suggest that the facts of natural history are not inconsistent with the idea that all that neatly organized yet increasing complexity is the product of invention and foresight and that it is time to start searching through the galaxies for a possible designer of biological organisms.

Peoples whose symbolic forms posit gods, ghosts, spirits, or witches appear to live under the impression that there is something there for them to be mindful of. Thus their reality-posits have often been interpreted as instances of "believing that _____." Indeed, in those cultures in which such symbolic forms exist the native who posits spirits does not seem indifferent to external reality-referencing questions such as: What makes spirits angry? Can they invade a person's body? How can invading spirits be exorcised? (See Obeyesekere 1981; Nuckolls 1986; Shweder 1986; Chapter 9 of this volume.) And, as we have seen, if we go back not so far in the English and American historical traditions, those who believed in witches went out hunting for them in external reality, where they sometimes found them, occasionally roasting them alive when they had.

In Nietzsche's *Prologue* Zarathustra comes to a forest where he meets "an old man who had left his holy cottage to look for roots in the woods." " 'And what is a saint doing in the forest?' asked Zarathustra." The old man answered: "I make songs and sing them; and when I make songs I laugh, cry and hum: thus I praise God. With singing, crying, laughing and humming, I praise the god who is my god. But what do you bring us as a gift?" (1982, pp. 123–124).

The text goes on as follows: "When Zarathustra heard those words he bade the saint farewell and said: 'What could I have to give you? But let me go quickly lest I take something from you!' And thus they separated, the old man and the man, laughing as two boys laugh. But when Zarathustra was alone he spoke thus to his heart: 'Could it be possible? This old saint in the forest has not yet heard anything of this, that *God is dead*' " (p. 124).

God is dead for contemporary anthropologists. The major measure of his fate is that in contemporary anthropology almost all theory designed to explain the origin and function of other people's reality-posits is made possible by a Nietzschean null-reference assumption. Murdock and Schneider have already been quoted. We can tell that we are dealing with assumptions very deep within the anthropological worldview, very central to its web of belief, when George Peter

Murdock and David M. Schneider end up in agreement. When it comes to the existence of gods, ghosts, witches, and demons, there is agreement.

Melford Spiro (1982, pp. 53–55, 63; 1984), another leading culture theorist, adopts Murdock's and Schneider's identical line of reasoning and, with characteristic clarity, follows it to its logical limit. Spiro argues that precisely because ghosts, spirits, gods, and witches do not exist, the main significance of those ideas is that they are fanciful states of mind analogous to dreams-as-dreamt and other hallucinations in which "stimuli originating in the inner world are taken as objects and events in the outer world" (p. 52), and mental constructs or symbolic forms are taken for external reality. He wonders why it is that "the religious believer does not (like the awakened dreamer) awaken from his religious slumber and recognize that the mythico-religious world exists not in some external reality, but rather in the inner reality of the mind" (p. 55).

As Murdock's, Schneider's, and Spiro's arguments suggest, the received wisdom of the day in anthropology is founded on Nietzsche's null-reference solution to the problem of interpreting the state of mind associated with symbolic forms. Indeed, so commonplace is Nietzschean thinking among anthropologists that it has made its mark on anthropology's central concept, the concept of culture.

According to that Nietzschean conception of culture, posited realities exist outside or externally to us only to the extent that we misperceive them as such. Such reality-posits (for example, of a world in which the ill will of others can make you sick or the spirit of a dead ancestor is a force to be contended with, or in which it is objectively wrong to carry any object more than six feet on the sabbath) are interpreted as mystifying or delusive reifications of our own projections.

In that contemporary conception of culture, reality-posits are theorized to be "constituted" or "constructed" from within a mental zone occupied by such states of mind as fancying, pretending, or wishing. In that mental zone subjectivity predominates over objectivity, and the realities we posit do not exist except as reality-posits. Nothing is objectively or factually good or bad, right or wrong; only falsely believing that it is so makes it seem that it is so.

Contemporary anthropology is very modernist without being self-conscious about it or assuming much responsibility for it. Being modern, most anthropologists are Nietzschean individualists; and being Nietzschean individualists and anthropologists, they are prone to analyze other people's posits about reality, constraint, and obligation as though "reality," "constraint," and "obligation" ought to be put in quotation marks. The received anthropological view of things is that a traditional culture's view of things consists of meanings (aspects of subjectivity) imposed or projected by human beings onto the world, imposed meanings first dignified by each generation as objective knowledge about the world and then passed off as received wisdom from one generation to the next. According to some contemporary theorists of culture, there is always a small elite of philosopher-kings (for example, contemporary theorists of culture) who know that the whole thing is "made up" or a necessary sham or the innocence of Nietzsche's forest saint.

Indeed, I would speculate that one of the appeals of theory in anthropology is that theory in anthropology is atheistic by assumption. There is no need to spend time arguing whether God, sin, or sorcery exists. They are presumed to be fabrications of the mind, figments of the imagination, or imposed meanings whose origin (from within the subject) and ontological status (as a null-reference category) are never in doubt.

Much debate in cultural anthropology thus starts on a common ground of null-reference reasoning—for example, gods and witches (and sin, the evil eye, and so on) do not exist. The common ground then gets divided, often passionately, over a secondary question: Is the native really aiming or intending through his reality-posits and symbolic forms (the idea of a witch) to say something true about states of the world? Is the native's state of mind really a matter of belief?

Those who answer yes to the secondary question (for example, the Marxists or the Freudians) interpret the reality-posits and symbolic forms of other peoples as primary-process thinking or irrational consciousness (false objectivity or reified subjectivity). They are Nietzschean in their interpretation of symbolic forms, but they are not relativists, for their aim is to remove our differences through education rather than permit them.

Those who answer no (for example, the so-called symbolic anthropologists) interpret other people's reality-posits and symbolic forms as some form of poetics or stylistics or drama or pretense or "performative" devoid of any reality-finding intent (or function) vis-à-vis an objective world. They are Nietzschean ontological atheists, and they are relativistic as well.

In either case the reality-posits of the other (for example, the idea of a witch) are assumed to refer to fanciful worlds that do not exist except as reality-posits. In either case the Nietzschean null-reference assumption of the modern liberated individual *qua* anthropologist goes unquestioned and unexamined as it is put to work, but at a great cost.

The Cause That Triumphed: The Cost of Victory

Nietzsche advised: part from your cause as soon as it triumphs; hold suspect all received wisdom and cross-examine it as a prejudice from the past. At this historical moment in the West our received wisdom, obvious truths, and innocent suppositions are Nietzschean: the things to which gods, ghosts, souls, witches, and demons refer exist solely as elements in a fictive or fancied reality; they are posits that human beings impose on the world.

As Nietzsche knew, it is never easy to argue against received wisdom. We always run the risk of being dismissed as passion-driven, as nihilistic, as ridiculous. Yet, if you are a Nietzschean, there is always good reason to try, even when the received wisdom is Nietzschean. In this case there are two good reasons. A null-reference, God-is-dead, phantoms-of-mind conception of culture has two notable consequences, which seem unacceptable to the oversoul I know the best, and which, perhaps, will be judged unacceptable by other oversouls like mine.

The first consequence of a null-reference conception of culture is the degrading of other peoples once the symbolic forms (reality-posits) and states of mind of the other are viewed as alien to the symbolic forms and states of mind of the self. The second consequence is the degrading of society (tradition, custom, ways of life) once society is viewed as alien to nature and to the objective world.

Among anthropologists, as among all other thoughtful people, there are those who feel obliged to go wherever they are led by their preconceptions, while others (and in this case I am one of them) become suspicious when their preconceptions lead them where they do not want to go.

The Other Made Alien to the Self

Because of the prevalence of null-reference reasoning, a characteristic feature of theory in anthropology is the unilateral degrading of other people's (apparently) supposed truths about nature and the world.

Specially targeted for unilateral degrading are those beliefs about natural law that other peoples view as most noteworthy and significant, reality-posits associated with beliefs about wandering or reincarnating souls, witchcraft and sorcery, spirit possession and exorcism, pollution and purity, illness and health, karma and sin, gods and their goddesses, and so on.

The anthropologist, often acting unwittingly or with noble or "liberal" intentions, degrades other peoples' posits about natural law by approaching and analyzing them as though they were supernatural, rhetorical, imaginary, or fantastic. Indeed, it is noteworthy, and perhaps reminiscent of Nietzsche's positivism, that in anthropological theory the notion of the supernatural comes close to meaning null reference, which, if you are a positivist, means metaphysical, which in the language of positivism is a synonym for "nonsense."

It is striking how much the contemporary anthropologist's conception of the native resembles the positivist's conception of the metaphysician. One witty definition of a metaphysician goes like this: "A metaphysician is a man who goes into a dark cellar at midnight, without a light, looking for a black cat that isn't there." How reminiscent of the metaphysical native, on his knees, searching in the inner sanctum of some decrepit temple for a beneficent god.

The received view, then, is that culture consists of received meanings or reality-posits that human beings impose on the world, with the emphasis on the *imposition* of meaning. The meanings that get imposed are assumed to have null reference even when, perhaps especially when, the native is adamant that his ideas about nature and the world are not simply creations or phantoms of mind, but rather conceptions of reality that illuminate experience and take us beyond ourselves to reality.

The more stubborn the native's commitment to his culture's fantastic or metaphysical or supernatural beliefs, the greater the feeling of confidence of the Nietzschean null-reference reasoner. The Nietzschean all along assumed that culture, custom, and tradition exercise their phantom grip over the human mind in direct proportion to the underdevelopment of full and exclusive rationality and individual autonomy. What better evidence of a failure of reality-testing or a confusion of fantasy with reality than the adamant reiteration of the accusation that one's neighbor is a witch, or, worse yet, the neighbor's confession that the accusation is correct?

Accordingly, anthropological theory under the influence of Nietzschean thinking and Nietzsche's philosophy of science has been designed to explain the origin and function of ideas prejudged through positivist null-reference reasoning to be phantomlike, hallucinatory, or fictive.

Not surprisingly, the explanations offered are typically Nietzschean. Hypothesized is some irrational or extrarational process, defined by a diminution or displacement of complete, exclusive, autonomous rational functioning. That irrational or extrarational process is then invoked in order to help explain how so many phantomlike, metaphysical, supernatural, delusionary, and arbitrary reality-posits could have got themselves lodged and stuck inside people's heads.

One type of explanation (culture as conditioned response) argues that human beings impose meanings on the world because human beings are slaves of their culture who believe what they are told. A second type of explanation (culture as defensive mechanism) argues that human beings believe what they wish to be true and that culture is a massive projective system put out there to satisfy their wishes. A third type of explanation (culture as symbolic) argues that human beings, masters of rhetoric, play, sham, and drama, do not, after all, really believe the things we think they believe, or, if they do believe them, they do not literally believe them but rather comprehend them as metaphors or tropes or imaginative creations.

Spiro (1982), for example, only one step removed from Nietzsche through Freud, explains "mythico-religious" reality-posits (for example, the idea of God) as the reified and emotionally motivated projection of one's childhood images and fantasies concerning parents and parental figures. Indeed, the concept of God is interpreted as a need-driven, mixed-up idea of a parent ("Entirely helpless from birth, and absolutely dependent on these beings, young children form highly distorted, exaggerated and even bizarre representations of these parenting figures," which then provide a basis for mental representations of the "superhuman figures of the religious world"; pp. 59, 62), and so-called supernatural beliefs are glossed as primary-process failures of reality-testing, wherein "fantasy is taken for reality" (pp. 52–53).

Murdock (1980, p. 89), who argues Nietzsche-like that the ethical doctrines of other peoples are often arbitrary and devoid of objective justification (he has in mind the fact that among the Semang it is, for example, a sin to comb your hair during a thunderstorm or to tell a joke to your mother-in-law), thinks Nietzsche-like that ethics has its origin in fear of the sanctioning power of a phantom called God—a learning process by which one phantom (God) begets another phantom (sin).

Others point to the weight of history or tradition or social-class position to explain the origin of reality-posits. People believe the fantastic things they believe about the way the world actually is because that is what their teachers told them to believe. And why did their teachers believe it? Because that is what their teachers told them to believe. And why did the first teacher to believe it believe it? Irrational projection. Fear of sanction. Servitude to class interest. Wish fulfillment. Long in advance of research, the Nietzschean anthropologist has ruled out, by presupposition, at least one possibility: that some aspect of experience is actually illuminated by being placed under the description of a god, or a witch, or an invading demonic spirit, or pollution, or karma, or original sin.

Thus, in the end it is a consequence of the Nietzschean anthropology of phantom culture that, wittingly or unwittingly, it represents the "other," the native, the alien, under the aspect of the innocent, the bizarre, the comic, the burlesque, the theatrical, or the absurd, as the history of culture becomes the record of mankind's sometimes staged, sometimes passionate positing and pursuit of things that do not exist.

Tradition Made Alien to Nature

Besides the unilateral degrading of other peoples' ideas about reality, a second consequence of a Nietzschean null-reference conception of culture is the degrading of society, custom, and tradition once they are alienated from nature and set in contrast to the objective world. There is a long history of attempts by theorists to equate customary practice with "convention" and thereby radically separate society from nature. Let us consider only one incident in a much longer story.

Anthropology became the study of phantom reality-posits, in part, because a more general transformation was taking place in our culture's idea of an objective world governed by natural law. Beginning about the time of the Enlightenment, our culture became obsessed with stripping "Mother Nature" of her animus and reinterpreting the concept of what is natural, or a law of nature, as equivalent in meaning to what is mindless, involuntary, and mechanical, without feeling, intention, or plan.

In that enlightened world the designation "natural" science and "real" and "objective" science came to be restricted to those physical and biological disciplines that conceive of nature or the objective-thing-world as a force field of external causal constraints, devoid of any mental or subjective life. Social "science," now a decidedly suspect category, got a reputation for being "soft" and unreal, and for talking in tongues or "jargon."

By the time anthropology first got to know them, society, tradition, and custom had already suffered humiliation through exposure to the Enlightenment. Within the terms of the emerging Western dualism of mindless nature and self-determined minds, physical nature and the natural environment had a legitimate place in the scheme of things, as did individuals, and jointly they typified the really real—but not society, tradition, and custom. It was an achievement of the Enlightenment to cast them out of reality as the heteronomous (that is, authoritarian and arbitrary) impositions of ancient and disposable regimes. Modern anthropology was first introduced to society, tradition, and custom only after they had been denied a rightful and important place in the modern Western scheme of things. Some will say that it is a black and terrible fate, and they will say it with some reason.

That Enlightenment thesis—mindless nature devoid of subjectivity—not surprisingly produced its hypothetical (and nihilistic) antithesis—mindful persons devoid of natural law or objective constraint, for whom "social" constraints were unnatural, hence unreal, and unreal, hence repressive. One hundred years into the Enlightenment, Nietzsche was quite prepared to play both sides of the dualism against any middle.

We have seen how Nietzsche did it: null-reference reasoning pressed to its "enlightened" positive science limit, beyond which there is said to exist a realm of ideal existential freedom. By now the argument is familiar. Nature is mindless, objective, and visible. It is empty of such unseen, unobservable, metaphysical things as god, sin, obligation, value, and morality. If such things exist at all, they exist only as reality-posits in the mind. And if they exist only in the mind, they are not objective and thus ought not be allowed to be constraining. If human beings feel constrained by such things, it is only because, not yet realizing their essential nature (self-determination), they do not distinguish between truth and poetry, confusing, quite irrationally, external reality with what exists nowhere else but in their minds.

Nietzsche is thereby led by his flirtation with positivism to the anticipation of Sartre and many other existentialists, who later try to implement his individualistic and liberationist agenda. Freedom and self-creation are identified as the essential features of self. A finger is pointed at custom, convention, and tradition, which stand accused of being little more than bad faith and self-deception persisting over time, a self-deception founded on the spurious belief that man-in-society is bound by necessary external constraints.

Today, not surprisingly, with our contemporary and now popular Nietzschean consciousness of free individuals and mindless nature, tradition-bound people are widely apprehended as curious or exotic or innocent leftovers who have not yet seen the light. The modern Nietzschean individualist has available a discriminating and impressive vocabulary (innocent, childlike, quaint, simple, primitive, exotic, undifferentiated, misguided, ignorant, uneducated, pious, sentimental, dogmatic, conformist, cultist, brainwashed, authoritarian, fanatical, neurotic, strange, superstitious, and so on) for bracketing or for stigmatizing or for keeping at a distance all those who would insist that it is precisely the strictures and disciplines of their tradition that put them in touch with reality.

To us "moderns" they (for example, the Amish, the Hassidim, or members of the Hare Krishna "cult") seem "out of it," lost in their (quaint or passionate or mindless) illusions off on the peripheries of the modern world we know; whereas the modern world, we know, sits right on top of the pulse of the really real, or, at least, pretty close to it.

The moral of this little parable of "the history of tradition made alien to nature" repeats a central thesis of this essay: anthropology assumed its modern form by stepping into the shadow of a protopositivist, protoexistential Nietzschean vision of reality. Quite naturally, all too naturally, anthropology became, in that Nietzschean world, the discipline for the systematic study and critique of the apparent self-deception and bad faith that is tradition—people hunting for witches that never existed, praying to gods that are dead, sacrificing animals to an empty sky, tormenting themselves with guilt over sins no more substantial than a dream or hallucination; searching in the dark, without a light, for a black cat that isn't there.

An enlightened anthropology just kept things going. Society, tradition, and custom became the objects of a richly elaborated Nietzschean (read "modern") scholarly rhetoric of degradation or displacement. Armed with ever more sophisticated versions of that antisocietal rhetoric, custom became "mere convention" (obligations for which no rational justification can be offered); and it was redefined as either dogma, or as thoughtless habit and routine, or as a quaint relic of outdated ways of doing things; or perhaps, in romantic response, as a somewhat cryptic symbolic code designed to give surreptitious expression to imaginary or fanciful or wistful posits about the world.

As for tradition, it got redescribed in some quarters as arbitrary and oppressive injunction. Arbitrary because the content of its injunctions (for example, no driving of cars on the sabbath day) seemed difficult for reflective individuals to justify through appeals to logic or scientific evidence. Oppressive because, after reason was put aside, the injunction still remained, backed only by power. ("'Shut up!' my father explained," as Ring Lardner put it) and sustainable only by virtue of terrifying or, at least, unpleasant sanctions.

Anthropology is no innocent in the modern world. It has played its proper Nietzschean parts in a reality consisting of (and exhausted by) free individuals and mindless nature, in which tradition has become problematical and has been turned into something burdensome to be overcome or as something fanciful or fashionable to be marketed with "arts and leisure."

Today, anthropology's favorite Nietzschean role is that of the "ghost buster," the enlightened critic who steps outside of and transcends his own tradition. Indeed, many anthropologists spend their time promoting free individualism (rebellion and liberation) through the criticism of social institutions and customary practices and by means of the revelatory unmasking of received wisdom, dramatically exposed as phantom culture. Many phantoms have been added to the modernist's list of things that do not exist except in the minds of their beholders: not only the obvious phantoms such as God, sin, sorcery, witches, and the evil eye but also other phantoms such as childhood, mental illness, sex roles, kinship, sacredness, authority, and even ethnographic writing itself (see, for example, Foucault 1965; Schneider 1984; Clifford and Marcus 1986).

Another favorite Nietzschean role is that of the "psyche analyst." The "God is dead" presupposition presents anthropologists with the apparent problem of having to explain the imaginary reality-posits, primary-process thinking, and phantom culture of others. Hence the intellectual agenda of the psyche analysts in anthropology: to develop a science of other-than-rational or less-than-rational states of mind (for example, wishing, fantasizing, fearing, the motivational integration of culture) to account for the perplexing worldwide distribution of slavish susceptibility to custom and tradition (see, for example, Whiting and Child 1953; Whiting 1959; Spiro 1965, 1982, 1983).

Even those anthropologists who pride themselves on sticking to the study of mindless nature adopt the Nietzschean line about tradition as phantom culture, renouncing as "soft" or "humanistic" the study of society, custom, and tradition, while promoting the "hard" study of genuine external constraints through neurology, biology, demography, or even computer science.

It seems highly likely that occasions exist when the best way to make sense of another person's apparently alien reality-posits is to attribute to him false beliefs, or deficient reasoning, or false consciousness, or to view the reality-posits of the other as intendedly ironical, or hyperbolic, or metaphorical, or comic, or fanciful, or theatrical, or imaginary, and so on. And I am fairly confident there are cases (for example, the American Psychiatric Association's development and dissemination of the diagnostic categories listed in its widely used 1980 DSM-III manual) in which power and self-interest have played a notable part in conferring a sense of realism on fanciful reality-posits.

The "God is dead" school of anthropology has experimented with all of those interpretative possibilities, tracing with much care and sophistication the implications of some seemingly innocent suppositions: the supposition that notions such as God, witch, sorcery, soul, or sin refer to nothing in reality; the supposition that gods, ghosts, souls, and such exist solely as fictive or imaginary elements in psychic (subjective) reality (only "in the head") or as cultural meanings *imposed* by human beings on a constructed world.

Post-Nietzschean Anthropology

To this point I have described the pervasive influence of Nietzschean suppositions in anthropology and identified some of the consequences of Nietzschean reasoning, especially the degrading of custom and tradition, thrown out of the natural world, and the derogation of other people's ideas and practices, made alien to the self and treated as unreal or made up or illusory. Here I outline a post-Nietzschean approach that, it is to be hoped, can avoid those consequences. Two requirements must be fulfilled if that hope is to be realized: the substitution of an alternative philosophy of science for Nietzsche's positivism, and the restoration of dignity to a much-maligned ancient role (the "casuist" and his casuistry), rescripted to be played out on center stage next to the "ghost buster" and the "psyche analyst."

A Postpositivist Philosophy of Science

Nietzsche probably never realized that he was held prisoner by the phantom of positivism. Through its famous (and somewhat notorious) "verifiability principle" and its demand for "operational definitions," the phantom holds that only seeing is believing and that only the data of the senses should be treated as real. With a wave of its antimetaphysical and atheistic hand the phantom of positivism rejects all unseen postulated forces or entities as nonsense that ought never to play a part in our knowledge of the world. The first commandment of positivism is the prohibition on transcendent entities (Gellner 1985), and the first transcendent entity to go is the idea of a reality hidden behind appearances. (Hence the great risk in positivism that it will devolve into solipsism, for how can I ever know for certain if my appearances-sensations-experiences are the same as yours?)

Bewitched by the phantom, yet faithful to its modernist spirit, Nietzsche reasoned himself into a corner. He forced upon himself, within the terms of positivism's conception of objectivity, a rather unfortunate dichotomous choice.

According to positivism either postulated forces and entities are directly verifiable through observation or experience, or else they are unreal. Nietzsche's forced and unfortunate choice was as follows: either classify people's reality-posits about gods, ghosts, witches, and sin as objective, and hence, in principle, directly accessible to the senses of any (reliable? trained? normal?) observer; or else classify people's reality-posits as subjective or imaginary entities with null reference, projected onto the world.

The rub with the first choice is obvious. To argue that God, ghosts, witches, and sin are objective in *that* sense (directly perceptible) is, in the modern world, to run the risk of being branded an enemy of reason and common sense, dismissed, denounced, committed, or forced to recant. With sufficient qualification (and ingenuity) that rub can perhaps be smoothed out. But it would require a good deal of other-than-modern and antidemocratic confidence in the fidelity or veracity of the visions, testimonials, and mystical or miraculous experiences of a self-privileging minority who claim to have special or superior powers to see or experience what no one else is able to observe.

That first choice will, of course, seem both plausible and attractive to those who believe in "seers" and in the extraordinary sightedness of "experts" or "virtuosos" credited with a unique ability to make "contact" and to peer into reality as it really is. The rest of us, however, a diverse collection of modern and postmodern scholars and scientists, admittedly have great difficulty with the idea that knowledge of reality should be established on the basis of "revealed" truths or from the reports of a seer recording his or her visions. Nietzsche's *Übermensch* was not someone with better eyesight, nor was it someone with keener ears, able to listen carefully to voices that no one else could hear.

The second choice, the "God is dead" alternative, was discussed above. As we have seen, it is not difficult to understand what it means to claim that other people's reality-posits have null reference or exist "only in their heads." In evaluating the cogency of the claim the issue is not one of coherency but rather of the plausibility and acceptability of the consequences of certain presuppositions about the reality-posit of the "other."

In the cases with which I am most familiar (that is, orthodox Hindu conceptions of karma and reincarnating souls: Shweder 1986; Shweder, Mahapatra, and Miller 1987; and Chapters 4 and 6 of this volume) all of the following seems to be true of the reality-posits of the other: (1) the other does not view his or her own ideas as arbitrary, conventional, or consensus-based, or as emotive expressions of imagination, desire, or will; (2) the other believes that her or his reality-posits express significant insights into what the world is like and that the reality posited can be used to illuminate or interpret the facts of experience; (3) the other remains convinced that his or her reality-posits are a form of knowledge about the world, even after we explain that he is suffering from a deluded false consciousness or that it is all fanciful or made up; and (4) the other does not reason irrationally with her or his ideas (see, for example, *Malleus Maleficarum,* a closely reasoned treatment of the theory of witchcraft, 1928 [1489]; also Shweder 1986).

The idea is, of course, a familiar one in the modern world that under certain kinds of circumstances certain classes of people may be highly motivated to resist disillusionment and to deny that their consciousness is false. That idea is not incoherent either, and it may even be true in certain fascinating cases. Yet what is the justification for using the idea axiomatically to interpret the long-term refusal of most peoples around the world to abandon their so-called supernatural, phantomlike, metaphysical beliefs (about gods, witches, spirits, fate, and so on)? At this point in the history of modern social science such irrationalist accounts have yet to establish their inherent plausibility through firm empirical backing, and for the most part they have consisted of provocative and sometimes quite spectacular handwaving and much speculation about unseen forces.

Modern thought is also rich in labels ("reification," "naturalization," "naive realism") for the supposed error of taking our "symbols" or reality-posits too directly or too literally, for the supposed mistake of treating our representational scheme as a part of the reality it describes, and for the supposed confusion of conflating the sign with the signified and apprehending our own subjective creation as an objective discovery. Yet, while there are many names for those supposed blunders, there is no convincing explanation for their near universal occurrence. There may even be good reasons to think that the "blunders" themselves are not always blunders (see, for example, Goodman 1968).

Faced with the two unacceptable alternatives posed by positivism's phantom—the choice between reality reduced to perception and the imagination reduced to fancy—a third alternative is to reject them both; or, in this case, to try to struggle free of the phantom's quite special preconception of the idea of objectivity (reality directly observable by means of the senses) found hovering over the alternatives. It should be possible to get free or, in this case, to reconstitute a bond, perhaps an indissociable link, between objectivity and subjectivity without totally destroying either term of their supposed opposition.

Years of postpositivist reflection have yielded an understanding of some of the ways objectivity and subjectivity may need each other and can live together without either's pushing the other out, although it may well be an irony in the history of the philosophy of science that, as Michael Friedman (n.d.) has argued, many postpositivists (Michael Polanyi, Thomas Kuhn, N. R. Hanson, Stephen Toulmin, Paul Feyerabend, I. Lakatos, Mary Hesse, Nelson Goodman) have recapitulated ideas already available in positivist circles (for example, the relativistic conclusions of the Marburg school and the doctrine of "logical idealism").

The main thing to be drawn on in postpositivist reflection is a two-sided idea that can be expressed in variant ways as follows. Although (side 1) nothing *in particular* exists independently of our theoretical interpretation of it (the principle of subject-dependency) and although all theories are inherently underdetermined by the facts (the principle of cognitive undecidability), there still does exist (side 2) the reality and accomplishment of "normal science" operating within the subject-dependent, cognitively undecidable terms of a paradigm.

While, as Toulmin has put it, (side 1) facts are not self-describing, (side 2) neither are theories self-confirming. While (side 1) paradigms may not be fully commensurate or intertranslatable (the principles of holism and incommensurability), (side 2) rationality and a sound reality orientation may not require uniformity or convergence of belief across competent observers. And, by extension, when it comes to the tradition-based reality-posits of the peoples studied by anthropologists, it is the native's success at reasoning with her or his reality-posits and using them to organize and make sense of certain of his or her experiences that lends those theories their authority as accounts of what is natural, real, or objective.

Those, of course, are "big ideas." I cannot argue them here, nor can I undertake to review revisions in the concept of objectivity in contemporary philosophy of science (see Putnam 1981). I cannot even attempt a full-blown explication, much less a systematic defense of the relevant core aphorism for a post-Nietzschean anthropology: reality-testing is a metaphysical (that is, supernatural) act, for *every* account of reality is built up out of assumptions not directly checkable against observable evidence or deducible from undeniable first principles.

In brief, however, the basic line of argument goes something like this. The postulation of our own internal mental constructs as external forces lending intelligibility to the data of the senses seems to be a central and indispensable feature not only of imaginary, fanciful, hallucinatory, and delusional thinking but of scientific thought as well. What Jacques Derrida (1977) calls the "metaphysics of presence," consisting of all those essential asymmetrical contrasts of the signifier to the signified, the sensible to the intelligible, the immediate to the hidden, the apparent to the real, is not something we can do without, for, as Derrida notes all too briefly in a passing remark, "nothing is conceivable" without it (p. 13). Although reality is not something we can do without, neither can it be reached (for it is beyond experience and transcends appearances) except by an act of imaginative projection implicating the knower as well as the known.

For example, there are several hundred million people in that ideological region known as South Asia who believe in the transmigration of the soul and the continuity of identity across lifetimes (see Chapter 6). Let us try to step inside their world for a moment. Perhaps one reason for the near universal acceptance of the idea of the soul is that it helps conceptualize the intuitive experience of what we in our secular culture call the self, that direct contact we all have with our own "observing ego." In South Asia, among Hindus, that observing ego is conceptualized as a soul or spirit, and all sorts of searching questions are asked about where it came from, where it is going, and why it is now occupying the body it happens to occupy (Sivananda 1979). It is at this point in the reflective process that the concept of a reincarnating soul is postulated to exist behind or within experience, and the concept is used to explain or make sense of various facts of life.

Ian Stevenson (1977) has itemized some of the facts of life that can be explained by the concept of reincarnation and the idea of the identity of the soul (self) across lifetimes, and I have added to his list other facts that call out for explanation. The explanation by reference to reincarnation is especially powerful for those who are willing to accept as evidence the pervasive intuitive experience of one's own observing ego and for those who have already adopted a conceptual reference point from which souls exist, for whom reincarnation and the transmission of previous experiences across lifetimes are at least theoretical possibilities. Fact: Identical twins reared together not infrequently display marked differences in personality; for example, one but not the other may become schizophrenic. Fact: The personalities of siblings who grow up in the same family are no more similar to each other than are those of random pairs of people drawn from different families. Fact: Children often have fears or phobias that cannot be accounted for by any known trauma and are not shared by any other members of their family. Fact: Children sometimes have skills or talents, such as mathematical or musical abilities, unlike those of their relatives, abilities that could not have been learned through imitation or instruction. Each of these facts seems resistant to either genetic or environmental explanations or else requires a good deal of handwaving by genetic or environmental advocates. But if the qualities of the self and the record of individual experience in previous lives were preserved over rebirths, the facts could be consistently explained (for example, by reference to musical accomplishment in a former life). Add to these facts several not insignificant questions: Why do I feel as though I've met this person before? (Perhaps you did, long long ago.) Why are some people born into wealth, health, and status and others into poverty and sickness? (Perhaps it is a reward or punishment for conduct in a former life.) What are we to make of those cases in which a child claims to have a memory of a former life in another family at another time and many of the details in the child's account of that family turn out to be accurate? (See

Stevenson 1960 for the documentation of several such cases.) For the believer, the concept of reincarnation is not without explanatory appeal, and in certain communities in South Asia, rationality and objectivity are not inconsistent with its use.

Robin Horton (1967), in effect arguing that there is an indissociable link between science and the metaphysics of presence, aptly makes the point that to construct a scientific theory is to elaborate "a scheme of forces or entities operating 'behind' or 'within' the world of common-sense observation" (p. 51). Except for the radical and flawed attempt by positivists to proselytize a scientific atheism, in which everything unseen, hidden, or beneath the surface is eliminated from scientific discourse, Horton's definition does seem to capture a characteristic feature of reality-finding science.

And, as almost all postpositivists now seem to recognize, the postulation of a world of unseen and unseeable forces or entities operating behind the apparent world is not only an indispensable act of interpretation but also a highly discretionary one, only weakly constrained by the content of experience itself.

An interpretative or hermeneutic or projective element (call it what you will) has long since been incorporated into philosophical conceptions of objectivity-seeking science. Any science must address with great respect all our reality-posits, but it would utterly fail as a science if it ever tried to let all those appearances-sensations-experiences speak entirely for themselves, or if it ever let them by their own authority establish themselves as "observations" or "facts" about reality.

Concepts about dreaming provide an illustration. In our culture, dreams have all but lost their place in our lives, and we treat the events in our dreams as either unreal or fanciful. Interestingly, there is cross-cultural developmental evidence that suggests that even in cultures in which adults believe in the reality of dream events, children become disillusioned with their dreams and, by age ten or so, come on their own to view them as fantasies (Kohlberg 1966, 1969; Laurendeau and Pinard 1972; Shweder and LeVine 1975). Yet despite that universal subjectivism of late childhood, there are many cultures in the world in which adults believe in a spiritual world. In those cultures, the reality of dream events is revived for the disillusioned child through exposure by adults to various theories of soul wandering during sleep (Gregor 1981), communications from guardian spirits (Wallace 1972), visions into the netherworld, or recollections of past lives. Among the Iroquois, for example, dreams were viewed either as expressions of the wishes of the dreamer's soul or as the expressed wishes of some superior spiritual being, and the Iroquois felt under considerable obligation to fulfill those wishes and feared the consequences if they did not (Wallace 1972, p. 69). Iroquois practices were organized (the "Society of the Masks") so as to make it possible to realize that obligation.

It is not all that hard to convert a dream into a perception; sharing a dream will do it. Wendy O'Flaherty (1984, pp. 71–73), in a discussion of the phenomenological status of dream events, analyzes the idea of a shared dream and relates an example from a short story, "The Brushwork Boy," by Rudyard Kipling:

> A young boy dreamed again and again of a girl with whom he rode on horseback along a beach until a policeman called Day awakened him. He grew up and joined the cavalry in India, where he drew a map of the place in his dream. When he returned to his parents' home in England, he heard a girl singing a song about the sea of dreams, the city of sleep and the policeman Day; he recognized her as the girl in his dreams. When he told her of his dream, she told him of the boy she had always dreamed of, in the same dream.

Imagine you have a very detailed dream, with a specific cast of characters, a specific location and setting, and a specific sequence of events. The next day you meet someone for the first time whom you recognize as a character in your dream, and she recognizes you as a character in her dream of the night before and accurately describes, in detail, all the dream events. I suspect it is an experience of that magnitude that would be required to convince the Western skeptic that dream events might sometimes originate from without and not from within. But even that experience might be dismissed as insufficient, coincidental, or just uncanny. Yet for those peoples for whom nature is populated with spirits, gods, and goddesses capable of communication from a world beyond (or, in more mystical cultures, from a world within), evidence of that sort is not required, and it seems eminently reasonable to interpret dream images as blurry perceptions or degraded signals received over a noisy channel. There is nothing irrational about the idea that dream events are real. Most people who believe that dream events are real are quite able in other contexts to distinguish fact from fiction, reality from fantasy, and they themselves, as children, probably once believed that dreams were unreal.

Objectivity-seeking science portrays for us a really real external world so as to explain our reality-posits, but it does so by making use of our reality-posits in a selective, presumptive, and partial way. One reason for this is that there is no authoritative feature of a reality-posit per se that can certify it as a perception or a witnessing rather than an illusion, or guarantee, for example, that dreaming or imagining is not a form of witnessing or that any particular reality-posit is a fact about the world rather than a feature of our state of mind or an artifact of our measuring instruments.

Were we to judge that a particular reality-posit represented a genuine fact about reality we might be led, if it were an anomalous fact, to alter a conception of the world. Yet, were we to judge that that same reality-posit really represented measurement error, we might dismiss it as insignificant and not treat it as sign or indicator of the world outside our symbolic forms.

Since no reality-finding science can treat all appearances-sensations-experiences as revelatory of the objective world, and since, at least for the moment, no infallible way exists to decide which reality-posits are signs of reality and which are not, much is discretionary in every portrait of the objective world out there beyond our symbolic forms. Reality, after all, for all we can ever really know, may be far away, or deep within, or hidden behind, and thus viewable only "as if through a glass darkly"; or perhaps the really real really is available only through a privileged state of mind (such as deep meditation) attainable only by a privileged few. Perhaps, as some peoples around the world have long suspected, the royal road to reality is through the reality-posits that appear before us while we are asleep or in reverie. The idea that dreaming or imagining is a form of witnessing or perceiving or illuminating deeper truths certainly has a noble and common lineage.

Many postpositivist accounts of the history of scientific knowledge conclude that there may not exist self-validating methods or procedures for establishing the realism of the picture we have painted of the unseen and unseeable entities and forces controlling appearance-sensation-experience. Those historical accounts typically, and quite reasonably, treat the institutionalized sciences of our own society as relatively good examples, or at least as the best examples we have, of reality-finding, objectivity-seeking reality-positing. The accounts try to demonstrate that the notable accomplishments of those sciences are not produced by accumulating a vast corpus of directly observable facts (perceiving that ____, in contrast to imagining that ____), nor are they the products of some standardized or automated rules and procedures for gaining knowledge.

For example, the rule of parsimony or simplicity has often been pointed to as a formal standard. for assessing the relative realism or veracity of alternative accounts of what the world is like and for deciding which reality-posits correspond more closely to reality. Yet, as Michael Friedman (n.d.) has pointed out, that standard suffers from deep inadequacies, for "we have no clear account of what such 'simplicity' really comes to nor, more importantly, any assurance that 'simplicity'—whatever it is—is a reliable guide to truth" (p. 18).

The same story seems to hold again and again in the history and philosophy of science. There have been many proposed criteria (reliability or consensus, confirmation through the prediction of other reality-posits, survival through repeated attempts at disconfirmation, parsimony) for assessing the degree of correspondence or realism of a reality-posit to the unseen objective world it purports to represent. Whatever the criterion, there seems to be no way to guarantee that it is a realistic test of similitude. In that regard there is a unity to science, for both the natural sciences and the human sciences lack a standardized or automated methodology.

The postpositivist philosophy of science seems to have two themes, although it is the first theme that has got most, and certainly too much, attention. That celebrated first theme is about the retreat from the idea of a method (the scientific method), which, if diligently and systematically applied, is guaranteed to paint a realistic portrait of the unseen entities and forces controlling the regularities reported through a reality-posit. That theme is about the impossibility of defining, in the abstract, the borders between good science, bad science, nonscience, and imaginary nonsense.

At times the retreat from generalized scientific methodism has had an intoxicating effect. As a consequence of the retreat there has appeared in the minds of some thinkers the specter that objectivity-seeking reality-finding science itself may be false consciousness, totally imaginary, fictive, or delusional, a Nietzschean phantom of mind (see Campbell 1986; Gergen 1986).

There is, I think, a more fruitful path of interpretation to follow, one less cluttered with Nietzschean (protopositivist) prejudgments and far less debunking of the metaphysical or supernatural in science.

At least two responses are possible if we accept the postpositivist claim that physics is indissociable from metaphysics, nature indissociable from supernature, and science indissociable from religion. If you are a positivist, you will respond, "So much the worse for physics, nature, and science." Those Nietzscheans who analyze science as ideology or false consciousness make manifest that positivistic response. The second possible response is "So much the better for metaphysics, supernature, and religion," a response that might serve as a post-Nietzschean's postpositivist retort.

Hence the second theme of postpositivist thinking, the one that deserves far more attention. That theme is about the idea that it is not really cause for alarm that good reality-finding science has important elements that are inextricably subjective or discretionary. Only in a world founded on the presuppositions of positivism will it sound facetious, nihilistic, or ironical to argue that out of respect for Darwin (or Freud) disconfirmability ought to be dropped as a necessary feature of good science, or to argue from the history of successful science that it is not always advisable for scientists to stick to the presumed facts or to strive for agreement on the meaning of core concepts.

In a postpositivist world, or at least in a defensible postpositivist world, that same argument ought to be construed in quite a different way. Postpositivists are no less concerned with what is real than are the positivists, and among sensible postpositivists it is understood that science is good and successful. Yet in a postpositivist world it is also understood that it is possible for us to have important knowledge of the world even if the objective world is subject-dependent and multiplex and even if we give up trying to describe the world independently of our involvement with it or reactions to it or conceptions of it. Hence, the continental chorus singing with Kuhnian overtones that it is our prejudices and partialities that make it possible for us to see, if not everything, then at least something.

Accordingly, it is a core aphorism for the post-Nietzschean position advocated here that the objective world is incapable of being represented completely if represented from any one point of view, and incapable of being represented intelligibly if represented from all points of view at once.

The real trick and the noble challenge for the post-Nietzschean is to view the objective world from many points of view (or from the point of view of each of several prejudices), but to do it in sequence. The proper aim within each point of view is to adopt the stance of what Hilary Putnam has called an "internal realist" ("normal science" operating within the terms of some paradigm), seeing as best one can with the received dogma of the moment. The challenge is always to feel eager to move on to some other worldview, in hot pursuit of the echo of Nelson Goodman's (1984) siren song: "One might say there is only one world but this holds for each of the many worlds" (p. 278).

Mary Hesse, who in her essay "In Defense of Objectivity" (1972) has tried to inform subjectivists and other hermeneutic critics of science that their conception of objectivity-seeking science is about a century out of date, has some stimulating and provocative things to say about divergences in thinking in modern physics. She points out that the description of real-world essences in modern physics has been neither cumulative nor convergent: "The succession of theories of the atom, and hence the fundamental nature of matter, for example, exhibits no convergence, but oscillates between continuity and discontinuity, field conceptions and particle conceptions, and even speculatively among different typologies of space" (p. 282). Other philosophers (for example, Goodman 1984) have recommended for modern physics a policy of "judicious vacillation" between "a world of waves and a world of particles as suits one's purposes (p. 278)." With judicious vacillation one gains access to multiple objective worlds.

There are three implications, as I understand them, to Hesse's observation about divergences in thinking in physics, and none of them is that modern physics has been impeded in its progress or that scientific thinking is a whimsical or nihilistic or ideological process.

One implication is that convergence in imaginative projections about the unseeable or hidden forces lurking behind the evidence of the senses is not an essential element of mature scientific thinking. A second implication is that any established and successful vision of what is real is indissociably linked to judgments that are discretionary and presumptive, and that there is thus legitimate scope for disagreement or divergence in world pictures among quite "hard-nosed" reality-seeking scientists, lay or professional. A third implication is that one of the great challenges for any science is to find some way to represent, describe, and explain the multiplicity of the objective world. Of what does that multiplicity consist?

The message of all this for dedicated Nietzscheans is that it is time to shed our skin and adopt a new philosophy of science. It is time to move from the modern into the postmodern era. In a post-Nietzschean world informed by postpositivist conceptions, objectivity, truth, and reality are inextricably associated with, and are not possible without, something prior contributed by the subject. Nothing intelligible remains of reality once we have "corrected" for all the possible prejudgments or biases of the observer, for all conceptions of reality are, in some measure, irrepressible acts of imaginative projection across the inherent gap between appearance and reality.

In that post-Nietzschean world God is not dead; only positivism and monotheism are dead. Polytheism is alive and well. Its doctrine is the relativistic idea of multiple objective worlds, and its commandment is participation in the never-ending process of overcoming partial views.

Quite rightly there are moderns who will worry about the subordination of the individual with that return of the gods. Yet, in that polytheistic post-Nietzschean world there still remains reason not to be a slave to the received wisdom of tradition. That reason, however, is not that tradition is unreal or fantastic or fictive or empty in its reference. The real reason is that any single tradition is partial, for each tradition is only one piece of reality brought out into high consciousness and enshrined in local doctrine or dogma. The aim for the post-Nietzschean, then, is identical with one of the aims of good anthropology: to be the student and beneficiary of all traditions, and the slave to none.

Perhaps that is a new thing for Nietzscheans: transcendence without superiority, scorn, or cynicism and without the degrading of tradition; and perhaps it is that newness that should recommend it if you are a Nietzschean.

Transcendence without scorn is the kind of transcendence that comes from constantly moving from one objective world to the next, inside and then out, outside and then in, all the while standing back and trying to make sense of the whole journey. It is a state of mind in which there is a detached engagement with each of several traditions, which promotes an engaging detachment from each of one's many selves.

To orthodox Nietzscheans that state of mind of detached engagement will, no doubt, seem far too involved with, and constrained by, the mundane practices of the everyday world, especially in comparison to the state of mind contemplated by Nietzschean ascetics (the ecstatic otherworldliness of the transcendence into pure spirit) or the state of mind contemplated by Nietzschean nihilists (the this-worldly freedom of the transcendence into pure individualism).

Yet, in a postpositivist world that is what an enlightened and noble anthropology ought to be about, at least in part—going to some faraway place where you honor and take "literally" (as a matter of belief) those alien reality-posits in order to discover other realities hidden within the self, waiting to be drawn out into consciousness. In reality the transcendent and the immanent are not that far apart, as polytheistic relativists (and mystics, I am told) come to know.

As for those who fear that if truth is not unitary, then nihilism will reign and that polytheism is merely a code word for anarchy, it is comforting to remind ourselves, again and again, that the fact that there is no one uniform reality (God, foundation, truth) does not mean that there are no realities (gods, foundations, truths) at all.

The Ancient Role of the Casuist

To be a Nietzschean ascetic or liberationist is to be suspicious of pious devotion to tradition or custom. Held hostage, historically, to a positivist conception of reality (only seeing is believing) and a null-reference (phantom) conception of culture, Nietzscheans have not held it legitimate to provide a rational justification for custom or to take seriously the substance or content of other peoples' so-called supernatural or metaphysical beliefs.

The scope for a Nietzschean anthropology is broadened in a post-positivist world, as the rationalization of custom and tradition becomes a legitimate objective, and as there emerges a type of relativist doctrine (ontological polytheism) in which realism and rationality are compatible with the idea of multiple worlds.

For if there is no reality without metaphysics, and if each reality-testing metaphysics (that is, each culture or tradition) is but a partial representation of the multiplicity of the objective world, it becomes possible to transcend tradition by showing how each tradition lights some plane of reality but not all of it. Since each is but a partial representation, it must be transcended. Since each is a representation of reality, it lends itself to a process of rational reconstruction through which it may become an object of respect.

The art of rational reconstruction is an ancient one, sometimes referred to as casuistry, and it is a modern role for the "casuist" that a post-Nietzschean anthropology needs to reconstruct.

It is ironic that in postmodern times the practice of casuistry has retained its medieval stigma of disrepute, connoting a degenerate and deceptive ability through adroit rationalization to justify anything or to defend any exotic practice, act, or point of view. It is ironic because what the medieval church saw as the corruption in casuistry is, in the contemporary world, no longer a sinful thing.

It was in the late Middle Ages that casuistry first got a bad reputation, and ever since it has had terrible press. Blaise Pascal described casuistry as the sophistical evasion of the word of God, and it is not too difficult to understand why.

During the late Middle Ages there was a point of view according to which sadness was thought to be a cardinal sin, as though to be dispirited was an insult to God. In a world with a God so prone to take offense, the practice of casuistry was naturally very risky; for what could be more irritating to a superior being, confident of his own omniscience, than to have some casuist intent on the corrosion of dogma step forward with a nimble defense of some alternative point of view? The supposed corruption in casuistry is its corrosion of dogma, which today, at least in the democracies of the world, ought to be a virtue. Apparently it takes a long time to overcome the effects of a reckless press.

In fact the much-maligned casuists of the Middle Ages were serious scholars at medieval universities who had the temerity to try to come up with a rational justification for tradition and for those seemingly arbitrary ritual observances and ecclesiastical rules that others slavishly accepted on faith or church authority. What made the casuists such a pain in the neck for the medieval church was that eventually the casuists were able to come up with compelling rational justifications for opposition to authority, for disrespect of fixed or formal rules, and for the adoption of alternative traditions and practices.

Perhaps the most famous casuist of the Middle Ages was Peter Abelard (the so-called "Socrates of the Gauls"), the twelfth-century theologian, logician, and canon of Notre Dame, whose passionate life has been immortalized in the love letters of Héloïse. The young Abelard, a master at rationalization, not only talked Héloïse into the virtue of giving up her virginity; he also reasoned his way into several heresies.

Abelard had a knack for infuriating the authorities and promulgators of dogma in the church. He wandered around France wondering out loud how to reconcile divine oneness with the existence of a trinity, and embarrassing his superiors and teachers with puzzles about the one and the many, uniformity and multiplicity, the same and the different, the universal and the particular. He compiled for himself a collection of authoritative, yet diametrically opposed, opinions on points of church doctrine, with the implication that the discrepancies in interpretation could not be reconciled into a single homogeneous truth. Distrustful of any attempt to canonize morality as a set of fixed and general principles, such as "It is wrong to lie," he kept coming up with exceptional cases that did not fit the rule. He reasoned himself to the view that there could be no culpability for sin if we do not intend to transgress; good intentions and personal conscience, he argued, take precedence over deeds and external observances. He nearly turned the church into a debating club, with adversaries outdoing each other with ingenious justifications for the sometimes baffling and seemingly pointless rules and prohibitions set forth in scripture.

Not surprisingly, many twelfth-century ecclesiastics hated Abelard, with a passion. He was persecuted by St. Bernard, who saw madness as the outcome of Abelard's methods—a calculus for heresy. To his critics, Abelard, the apparent nihilist, seemed to be saying that if our conscience does not bother us, we can do whatever we want. As the church viewed it, by the time Abelard finished an exegesis of a sacred text, the words of God had been erased through interpretation. In 1121 his book *Divine Unity and Trinity* was burned at an ecclesiastical council. The pope condemned him and kept him quiet by issuing an injunction against his lecturing. And, as we all know with amazement and perhaps with horror, Héloïse's uncle, a canon of the church, took care of Abelard's manhood—divine emasculation on behalf of an exasperated and tongue-tied God.

It would seem from the example of Abelard that casuistry, at its very best, is antidogmatic and quite risky, surprising and distractive of habitual ways of seeing, agile and on the move against any single fixed point of view or frame of reference. It presses irreverence into the service of reality, in recognition of the idea that it is only by constantly switching frames that we honor the multiplex world.

Abelard, of course, was not the first casuist, for it is an ancient role. There is casuistry in the talmudic commentaries, where for every letter of the law there are always two or more spirits, or rabbis, with quite alternative views of what it all means.

And the Stoics and the Sophists knew of casuistry. I once was told a story (perhaps apocryphal) about a Greek philosopher who was invited to Rome to give two lectures to the imperial elite. Weary of the single-mindedness, smugness, and absolutism of Roman domination, our speaker anticipated Abelard's tactics. In the morning he expounded the thesis that human society is analogous to the societies of ants and bees and other animal societies, and that even monkeys have a military hierarchy and chain of command. A brilliant lecture shedding much light on human behavior that was well received. In the afternoon, refusing to let any one viewpoint of reality reign, he expounded the contrary thesis that human society and animal society are not analogous, and that animals are fundamentally different from people. After all, animals have no language or conscience, and they certainly do not know how to cook. The philosopher, obviously a casuist at heart, found himself imprisoned for irreverence.

It is perhaps fortunate for contemporary anthropologists that irreverence is the first commandment of the postmodern world, and that once again the role of the jester has become an admired one, as we have remembered at long last the importance of living ironically and by our wits. Thus there was no church injunction against lecturing, indeed it was by invitation, when in 1983 Clifford Geertz delivered the annual Distinguished Lecture, titled "Anti Anti-Relativism," to the American Anthropological Association (Geertz 1984). One point of the lecture was to rally anthropologists to the task of challenging the received and unquestioned assumptions and classifications of our own contemporary empire. (I have tried my hand at it here.) Unlike Abelard, Geertz walked off the stage unharmed, to applause. What used to be a medieval heresy is now one of several currents in a contemporary discipline called anthropology, in which, barring the reappearance of a St. Bernard, casuists can now practice their art or alchemy without stigma on the same stage as the ghost busters and psyche analysts.

2.

Cultural Psychology: What Is It?

A discipline is emerging called cultural psychology. It is not general psychology. It is not cross-cultural psychology. It is not psychological anthropology. It is not ethnopsychology. It is cultural psychology. And its time may have arrived, once again. This essay is a preliminary attempt to say, taxonomically and narratively, what the discipline of cultural psychology was, is, and ought to be about.[1] Ultimately it is a story of cyclical return.

In the short run, however, the essay is a story of one of the pitfalls of the "cognitive revolution" of the 1960s, of its failure to develop an adequate theory of the "person," because of the prevailing Platonism implicit in its scientific agenda. It is also a scouting expedition across the boundaries of some very treacherous disciplinary territories in the search to recover an important interdisciplinary identity.

Cultural psychology is the study of the way cultural traditions and social practices regulate, express, and transform the human psyche, resulting less in psychic unity for humankind than in ethnic divergences in mind, self, and emotion. Cultural psychology is the study of the ways subject and object, self and other, psyche and culture, person and context, figure and ground, practitioner and practice, live together, require each other, and dynamically, dialectically, and jointly make each other up.

73

Cultural psychology is premised on human existential uncertainty (the search for meaning) and on an "intentional" conception of "constituted" worlds. The principle of existential uncertainty asserts that human beings, starting at birth (and perhaps earlier), are highly motivated to seize meanings and resources out of a sociocultural environment that has been arranged to provide them with meanings and resources to seize and to use. The principle of intentional (or constituted) worlds asserts that subjects and objects, practitioners and practices, human beings and sociocultural environments, interpenetrate each other's identity and cannot be analyzed into independent and dependent variables. Their identities are interdependent; neither side of the supposed contrast can be defined without borrowing from the specifications of the other.

The basic idea of cultural psychology is that, on the one hand, no sociocultural environment exists or has identity independently of the way human beings seize meanings and resources from it, while, on the other hand, every human being's subjectivity and mental life are altered through the process of seizing meanings and resources from some sociocultural environment and using them.

A sociocultural environment is an intentional world. It is an intentional world because its existence is real, factual, and forceful, but only so long as there exists a community of persons whose beliefs, desires, emotions, purposes, and other mental representations are directed at, and thereby influenced by, it.

Intentional worlds are human artifactual worlds, populated with products of our own design. An intentional world might contain such events as "stealing" or "taking communion," such processes as "harm," or "sin," such stations as "in-law" or "exorcist," such practices as "betrothal" or "divorce," such visible entities as "weeds" and invisible entities as "natural rights," and such crafted objects as a "Jersey cow," an "abacus," a "confessional booth," a "card catalogue," an "oversize tennis racquet," a "psychoanalytic couch," or a "living room."

Such intentional (made, bred, fashioned, fabricated, invented, designated, constituted) things exist only in intentional worlds. What makes their existence intentional is that such things would not exist independently of our involvements with and reactions to them; and they exercise their influence in our lives because of our conceptions of them (Schneider 1968, 1984; D'Andrade 1981, 1984, 1986). Intentional things are causally active, but only by virtue of our mental representations of them.

Intentional things have no "natural" reality or identity separate from human understandings and activities. Intentional worlds do not exist independently of the intentional states (beliefs, desires, emotions) directed at them and by them, by the persons who live in them.

Thus, for example, a weed is an intentional thing. It is an intrusive, interfering, or improper plant that you do not want growing in your garden. Consequently, a daisy, sunflower, a foxglove, or perhaps even a thorny rose that turns up in your vegetable patch might be plucked out as a weed, while one can find intentional worlds in which crabgrass, marijuana, or dandelions are not constituted as weeds at all. Instead they are cultivated as cash crops.

Because a weed is a weed is a weed, but only in some intentional world, there is no impersonal, neutral, "objective," "scientific," independent-of-human-response, botanical, genetic, or "natural kind" definition of plants that can specify *in the abstract* or *in general* which ones count as weeds. The botanical capacity to self-seed bestows on a plant the power to be a nuisance, if the plant is unwanted. Yet the same plant, if it is wanted, has the power to produce abundant harvests. And there are other routes by which a plant might make itself troublesome or become misplaced in your garden, ultimately to be weeded out.

It would seem to follow that in some fascinating and important sense, the weeds in our gardens achieve their reality because we are implicated in their existence, and we achieve our reality, at least in part, by letting them become implicated in ours. Our identities interpenetrate and take each other into account. Without us nature knows little of the existence of weeds. Without the existence of weeds and of all the aims, activities, and practices (Wittgenstein's "forms of life") presupposed by their existence and constitutive of it, there would be less to us worth knowing.

And because a weed is a weed is a weed, but only in some intentional world, what is truly true (beautiful, good) within one intentional world (for example, "That is a 'weed'; therefore, it ought to be plucked out of the ground and discarded") is not necessarily universally true (beautiful, good) in every intentional world; and what is not necessarily true (beautiful, good) in every intentional world may be truly true (beautiful, good) in this one or in that one.

According to the principle of intentional worlds there is no logical requirement that the identity of things remain, fixed and universal, across intentional worlds; while within any particular intentional world (for example, the twentieth-century intentional world of American baseball, or the sixteenth-century intentional world of English witchcraft) the identity of a thing (for example, a "foul ball" or a "witch") can be real and the question of its real identity (for example, was that a "foul ball"? or is she a "witch"?) can be a subject for rational and objective dispute.[2]

(Cultural psychology is the study of intentional worlds. It is the study of personal functioning in particular intentional worlds. It is the study of the interpersonal maintenance of any intentional world. It is the investigation of those psycho-somatic-socio-cultural and, inevitably, divergent realities in which subject and object cannot possibly be separated and kept apart because they are so interdependent as to need each other to be (see Kleinman 1986a; Shweder 1986; and Chapters 1 and 8 of this volume).

Finally, cultural psychology is an interdisciplinary human science. It aims to develop several companion disciplines, especially an anthropology (reunited with linguistics) suitable for the analysis of sociocultural environments (meanings and resources; "forms of life") in all their intentionality and particularity, and a psychology (reunited with philosophy) suitable for the analysis of persons in all their intentionality and historicity.

Answering a "What Is It?" Question

It is a principle of cultural psychology—the principle of intentional worlds—that nothing real "just is," that instead realities are the product of the way things get re-presented, embedded, implemented, and reacted to in various taxonomic or narrative contexts or both. The reality of cultural psychology is no exception to the principle. As a constructed intellectual discipline cultural psychology has a taxonomic and narrative identity whose reality is not independent of our sharing with each other, debating, and acting upon our conception of it.

To say what something is, taxonomically, is to say what it is not, to say what it is a kind of, and to point to instances of it. It is to subsume it as a particular example of something more general and to generalize it, so as to turn something more particular than it into its example.

To say what something is, narratively, is to describe its origination ("once upon a time") and its density (its aim, purpose, or function) and to comprehend its current status, in the here and now, as part of a longer story of strivings, achievements, obstacles, growth, adaptations, failures, dormancy, or never-ending cyclical return.

Placed in its taxonomic context an ideal cultural psychology has qualities that distinguish it from general psychology, cross-cultural psychology, psychological anthropology, and ethnopsychology.

It Is Not General Psychology

First cultural psychology must be distinguished from general psychology.

"People are the same wherever you go" is a line from the song "Ebony and Ivory," by Paul McCartney and Stevie Wonder; that line describes pretty well a basic assumption of general psychology. The assumption is sometimes referred to as the principle of psychic unity of humankind.

General psychology assumes that its subject matter is a central (abstract and transcendent = deep or interior or hidden) processing mechanism inherent (fixed and universal) in human beings, which enables them to think (classify, infer, remember, imagine), experience (emote, feel, desire, need, self-reflect), act (strive, prefer, choose, evaluate), and learn. The aim of general psychology is to describe that central inherent processing mechanism of mental life. Since the central processing mechanism is presumed to be a transcendent, abstract, fixed, and universal property of the human psyche, general psychology has the look, taste, and smell of a Platonic undertaking. For it is that presupposed central and inherent processing mechanism that is the true object of fascination in general psychology and not all the concrete, apparent, variable, and particular stuff, substance, or content that is operated upon by the processor or may interfere with its operation.

It is a necessary step in the general psychology enterprise to distinguish intrinsic psychological structures and processes from extrinsic environmental conditions, to procedurally abstract and analytically withdraw the knower from what he or she knows, and to insist on a fundamental division between the processing mechanism of the person versus his or her personal or group history, context, stimulus and task environment, institutional setting, resources, beliefs, values, and knowledge.

Of course, people are not the same wherever you go. Not even Paul McCartney and Stevie Wonder are the same. And no general psychology is so unworldly as to overlook that fact.

General psychology may be Platonic but it is certainly not thoughtless. The principle of general psychology that "people are the same wherever you go" does not mean that people are the same in *every* respect. It means that transcendently, "deep down" or "inside," where the central processing mechanism lives, people are the same (or, alternatively, what gives people "psychic unity" is what makes them all the same "deep down" or "inside").

All the other stuff—stimuli, contexts, resources, values, meanings, knowledge, religion, rituals, language, technologies, institutions—is conceived to be external to or outside of the central processing mechanism. Observations on Rajput widows in India, motivated by special beliefs and desires, immolating themselves along with their deceased husband on his funeral pyre; or observations on Chinese abacus experts, assisted by special mental representational techniques, solving arithmetic problems "in their head" at a speed several orders of magnitude faster than the rest of humanity—all that may be rich material for humanistic inquiry, journalistic reporting, and literary representation, yet all of it must, given the Platonist impulse, be viewed, in and of itself, as incidental or secondary to the aim of general psychology.

The aim, as noted: to get behind superficial appearances, local manifestations, and external resources to isolate the intrinsic central processing mechanism of the mental life and describe the invariant laws of its operation.[3]

It is that Platonic impulse, one suspects, that was behind the memorable remark from an anthropologist who, upon hearing about Mike Cole and John Gay's research in Liberia (1972), argued to the effect that the thinking processes of West African tribesmen do not differ from our own; only their values, beliefs, and classifications differ, which is why the Kpelle perform so differently on psychological tests (see Cole and Gay 1972, p. 1066).

It is that same impulse, one suspects, that once led Melford Spiro (1955), with his interest in group differences in personality, to express the methodological concern that in demonstrating emotional and behavioral differences across different sociocultural contexts, anthropologists had not demonstrated the existence of *genuine* personality differences at all. They "have merely demonstrated that different stimuli evoke different responses" (p. 257).

The methodological "merely" in Spiro's analysis is revealing. For one might have argued, methodologically and non-Platonically, that the power of a particular stimulus to evoke a particularizing response is not independent of the way a person or people get particularly involved with it psychologically—classify it, reason about it, tell stories about it, appropriate it to their purposes—and that that is what *genuine* personality differences are about. In intentional worlds "stimuli" are not external to or independent of our understanding of them, and those understandings are a large part of what we mean by "personality" (see, for example, Mischel 1973).

In other words, one might have argued, from the point of view of intentional worlds, that the study of genuine psychological differences between ethnic groups should be conceived as the study of how different sociocultural environments become different *by virtue of* the ways they are differently constituted psychologically by different peoples so as to possess different response evocation potentials.

Platonism is an ancient and formidable school of interpretation. It is crucial to recognize that the long-lived and imaginative idea of an inherent (fixed, universal) and central (transcendent, abstract) processing mechanism, a psychic unity to humankind, will never be seriously threatened by the mere existence of performance differences between individuals or populations. Those performance differences can always be interpreted, and should be interpreted, as the consequence of incomparabilities, incommensurabilities, or just some plain differences in all the other stuff; which leaves permanently unsettled and eternally unsettlable the question whether there really is, deep down, an inherent and central processing mechanism hidden behind all the other stuff. Platonism and its alternatives will always be with us, offering different interpretations and competing visions of the nature of the human psyche.

It is equally crucial to recognize that general psychology with its Platonic imagery and premises is not the only imaginative and interpretative game in town for understanding the mental life. If one subscribes to an alternative, non-Platonic principle of intentional worlds, that nothing in particular exists independently of our involvement with it and interpretation of it, it is possible to conceive of the mental life as variable and plural and substantive and constructively stimulus bound.

And it is possible to characterize a large part of the mental life in terms of the particularizing ways peoples constitute and get involved with particulars, thereby giving to those constructed stimuli, task environments, and sociocultural contexts the powers they have to evoke the special responses they evoke.

Nevertheless the aim of general psychology is Platonic, and its Platonic aim is to seek out a presumed central processing mechanism of human beings and to isolate it from all the other stuff.

Given that aim, it is not surprising that general psychology has constructed its own special intellectual standards for knowledge representation (its preferred ontology) and knowledge seeking (its preferred epistemology). Ontologically speaking, knowledge in general psychology is the attempt to imagine and characterize the form or shape of an inherent central processing mechanism for psychological functions (discrimination, categorization, memory, learning, motivation, inference, and so on). Epistemologically speaking, knowledge seeking in general psychology is the attempt to get a look at the central processing mechanism untainted by content and context, and so on.

The main force in general psychology is the idea of that central processing device. The processor, it is imagined, stands over and above, or transcends, all the stuff upon which it operates. It engages all the stuff of culture, context, task and stimulus material as its content.

Given that image, the central processor itself must be context and content independent. That means, in effect, that the processor must be describable in terms of properties that are either free of context/content (abstract, formal, structural properties) or general to all contexts/contents (invariant, universal properties).

Still speaking ontologically, it is that image of an inherent (fixed, universal) and central (abstract, transcendent) processing mechanism—a context/content-independent and omnipresent mental unity—that is the explanation for the great esteem conferred in general psychology upon accounts of the mental life in terms of universal mathematical functions and invariant formal limits or constraints (for example, exponential decay functions mapped in an abstract psychological space for representing the probability of generalization between pairs of stimulus events in any domain for any sensory modality for any species, as in Shepard 1987; or magical numbers, seven plus or minus two, to represent the maximum capacity of the central processing mechanism for distinguishing values, whatever the values, along any single dimension, whatever the dimension, in any single instant, wherever and whenever the instant, as in G. Miller 1956).

Great esteem is also conferred within general psychology upon certain ways of seeking knowledge. Knowledge seeking in general psychology is the attempt to gain direct access to the central processing mechanism without having to become quagmired in all the other stuff.

General psychologists *qua* general psychologists are typically wary of rain forests, swamps, and the complex textures and tones of everyday life, language, and institutional settings. They take comfort in a radically simplifying (some would call it a radically "surreal") article of faith, namely, that the central processor is most likely to reveal its pristine form when lured by meaning-free or unfamiliar or novel stimulus items into a context-free environment.[4]

Nonsense syllables, white coats, and darkened bare rooms may be misguided or monstrous anachronisms for serious researchers in general psychology, yet the experimental lab is still treated as a privileged space, where, quite fantastically and against much evidence, it is conveniently assumed that we can physically enter a transcendent realm where the effects of context, content, and meaning can be eliminated, standardized, or kept under control, and the central processor observed in the raw. The image of a central processing mechanism and the search for a window or a peephole through which to view it naked and pure may explain why in general psychology there has become entrenched the intuition that real scientists do experiments in a lab.

Unfortunately, even if the presumed inherent but hidden central processing mechanism does exist, the psychological laboratory is probably not the mythical enchanted doorway through which we can step straight away into a more fundamental reality. Indeed, one suspects that the sociocultural environment of lab life is not even plausibly equivalent to the physicist's vacuum or the physiologist's X-ray for directly accessing things that are basic, deep, or hidden from view. The ideas of a context-free environment, a meaning-free stimulus event, and a fixed meaning are probably best kept where they belong, along with placeless space, eventless time, and squared circles on that famous and fabulous list of impossible notions. For when it comes to the investigation and examination of psychological functioning, there probably is no way to get rid of all the other stuff, even in the lab.

Of course, nothing I have said argues against studying "stuff" in a lab. If the stuff brought into the lab (or simulated there) is interesting enough stuff to study, and if one can bring it into the lab (or reproduce it there) without spoiling it (those are big "ifs"), then one can certainly study it there, and there may even be very good reason to (see, for example, Milgram 1974). Whether there is a royal road running through the lab to the land of the central processing mechanism of the mental life is, however, quite another issue.

Roger Shepard's recent discussion (published, appropriately, in *Science* magazine) (1987) of "a universal law of generalization for psychological science" is a revealing illustration of Platonist presuppositions in general psychology and the way they guide a research enterprise and structure the interpretation of evidence by even the most brilliant practitioners.

Shepard begins and ends by holding out Newton's mathematical and universal law of gravitation as the standard by which to judge the success or failure of the discipline of psychology. Psychology, Shepard avers, should strive to be the science of the invariant mathematical forms underlying psychological functioning. Three hundred years after the publication of Newton's *Principia* Shepard thinks psychology can finally point to a success, a mathematical law of stimulus generalization which "is invariant across perceptual dimensions, modalities, individuals and species" and which shows that psychology "may not be inherently limited merely to the descriptive characterization of the behavior of particular terrestrial species" or the properties of particular stimulus domains (pp. 1317–18, 1323).

Shepard's "universal law" is basically an abstract spatial representation of an exponential decay function for stimulus generalization likelihoods between pairs of stimuli. The exponential decay function is detectable in several data sets from humans and pigeons, which record for selected domains (for example, consonant phonemes, triangles of different sizes and shapes) the probability that a response learned to any one stimulus within the domain will generalize to any other stimulus within the domain. Shepard believes that this exponential decay function is the central processing mechanism for stimulus generalization in its pristine form—abstract and transcendent (= deeply interior), fixed, and universal (p. 1318).

To have a glimpse at this abstract transcendent processing function Shepard is quite prepared—indeed, feels compelled—to exteriorize, treat as illusory, and withdraw his attention from several levels of reality that play a major part in human classificatory behavior.

First he must withdraw his attention from measurable similarities and differences in the stimulus materials themselves. For it has been shown—he views the relevant findings as "troublesome" and "discouraging"—that there exists no universal mathematical function for predicting the probability of a generalization response from measurable physical characteristics of pairs of stimuli; those mathematical functions seem to vary by stimulus domain (p. 1317). For example, the mathematical function for the color space may differ from the function for tonal scales, and these may differ by species or individuals; and within a particular stimulus domain, such as the color space, a response to a particular color chip may generalize to a distant hue at the opposite end of the spectrum. So if there is to be a universal law of generalization it is not going to be a law of the stimulus environment. It must be a pure psychological function, not a psychophys-ical function (p. 1318). It cannot tell us which stimulus items in any domain will be generalized to, only that the likelihood of generalization across pairs of stimulus items (whichever they should turn out to be) will decay exponentially. To reach the central processing mechanism of stimulus generalization Shepard must get beyond the stimulus environment.

Then he must also get beyond learning processes. For he does not expect his universal law of generalization to describe generalization behavior under multiple learning trials, because "differential reinforcement could shape the generalization function and contours around a particular stimulus into a wide variety of forms" (p. 1322).

Finally he must get beyond reconstructive memory processes. For it is known that the universal law is *not* descriptive of generalization behavior when learning trials are delayed. This Shepard interprets as a failure of the law because of interfering " 'noise' in the internal representation of the stimuli" (p. 1322).

At this point a reader of *Science* interested in similarity and difference judgments might be tempted to ask what we have learned about human classificatory behavior. Having withdrawn his attention from the stimulus environment and from processes of learning and memory, why does Shepard think he is looking at something fundamental such as a central processing mechanism of mind?

The answer is clear and Platonic. Late in his article Shepard points out that, strictly speaking, his universal law is descriptive of stimulus generalization behavior *only* when "generalization is tested immediately after a single learning trial with a novel stimulus" (p.1322).

Here we come to the great and unbreachable divide between general psychology and cultural psychology. Moved by the Platonic impulse (and perhaps by the prestigious image of Newton's gravitational forces operating in a vacuum), Shepard seems to think that something truly fundamental about the mind—an inherent central processing mechanism—can be divined only if we can transcend the noise and clutter of the environment by bleaching it of familiar things and impoverishing it of feedback, and by isolating the mind from its own mental supports.

The alternative interpretation—that of cultural psychology—is that the mind left to its own devices is mindless. From that perspective, Shepard's proposed "universal law of generalization for psychological science" is little more than an extremely unqualified description of the special, restrictive (and, we might add, rather peculiar) effects on similarity and difference judgments of unfamiliar stuff (novel stimuli) examined in one-trial learning environments.

According to the principles of cultural psychology the effects of stuff will not go away, even in the lab, for there is no context-free environment. We are intentional beings who live in an intentional world of constituted and re-presented particulars—domain-specific, concrete, subject-dependent artifactual things. Absolute transcendence is a great and marvelous thing, but not if we want to keep the psyche in psychology.

The implication, of course, is that genuine success for psychological science will come when we stop trying to get beyond the "noise" and start trying to say interesting things about some of the more robust and patterned varieties of it.[5]

That is the challenge for cultural psychology. But I am getting ahead of my story. First we must consider cross-cultural psychology (not to be confused with cultural psychology), which can be very "noisy," perhaps too noisy.

It Is Not Cross-Cultural Psychology

One of the hazards of general psychology as a Platonic undertaking is the inherent difficulty of distinguishing statements about a presumed inherent central processing mechanism from statements about all the other stuff. It is that difficulty that has kept the discipline of cross-cultural psychology in business.

Cross-cultural psychology is a subdiscipline of general psychology that shares with it the Platonic aim of characterizing the inherent central processing mechanisms of the mental life. Practitioners of the subdiscipline carry the general psychologist's tests and research procedures abroad.

Occasionally cross-cultural psychological research replicates some regularity observed in Western-educated subjects (Ekman 1989). The main discovery of cross-cultural psychology, however, is that many descriptions of mental functioning emerging from laboratory research with Western-educated populations do not travel very well to subject populations in other cultures. Thus, although almost all adults in Geneva, Paris, London, and New York display so-called concrete operational thinking on Piaget's conservation of mass, number, and liquid quantity tasks, many adults in many Third World capitals do not (Cole and Scribner 1974; Hallpike 1979).

The definitive problematic of cross-cultural psychology is the struggle, fought in Platonic terms, over how to interpret population-based differences in performance on psychological tests and tasks. Within the framework of Platonic thinking there are only two possibilities. The first possibility is that the performance differences exist primarily because the central processing mechanism inherent in the mind has not yet become fully developed among certain peoples of the world (Hallpike 1979; see Shweder 1982d for a critique). The second possibility is that the performance differences exist primarily because the psychologist's tests and tasks baffle and bewilder certain peoples of the world and deny them a fair opportunity to put on display the extant central processing mechanisms of the mind (Cole and Scribner 1974).

Both interpretations presuppose the principle of psychic unity. According to the first interpretation, psychic unity is the anticipated result of central processor development, but the universal and uniform structures inherent in the mind will mature only under ideal environmental conditions. This leads some cross-cultural psychologists to become concerned with possible external stimulators of growth of the central processing mechanism—literacy, schooling, toys, Socratic dialogue, and so on. According to the second interpretation psychic unity is not just a potential inherent in the mind. Psychic unity has already been achieved. It is there, waiting to be revealed. This leads other cross-cultural psychologists to become concerned with "etics" and "emics" and with the incommensurateness or inappropriateness across cultures of test materials and research tasks; and it leads them to search for more "natural" or "realistic" settings, activities, and institutions in everyday life where central processor functioning goes on unimpeded by the artificial or unfamiliar conditions of psychological task environments.

Cross-cultural psychology has lived on the margins of general psychology as a frustrated gadfly, and it is not too hard to understand why. For one thing, cross-cultural psychology offers no substantial challenge to the core Platonic principle of general psychology (the principle of psychic unity). Moreover, if you are a general psychologist cum Platonist (and a principled one at that) there is no theoretical benefit in learning more and more about the quagmire of appearances—the retarding effects of environment on the development of the central processing mechanism, the "noise" introduced by translation or by differences in the understanding of the test situation or by cultural variations in the norms regulating the asking and answering of questions. Rather, if you are a general psychologist, you will want to transcend those appearances and reach for the imagined abstract forms and processes operating behind the extrinsic crutches and restraints and distortions of this or that performance environment.

Perhaps that is why, in general psychology, cross-cultural psychology has diminutive status, and why its research literature tends to be ignored. Not surprisingly, developmental psychology—the study of age-graded differences in performance on psychological tests and tasks—has suffered a similar fate, and for similar reasons.

It is doubtful that anyone is going to divest general psychology of its fascination with the imaginative idea of an inherent central processing mechanism. And certainly this disenchantment is not going to be produced by merely showing that the regularities observed in the Western lab do not travel well to other contexts, or generalize to subjects from other cultures (or age levels) or to stimulus materials from everyday life (see LeVine n.d.). The Platonist framework for interpretation is likely to remain enshrined in general psychology and definitive of its intellectual agenda. Like the scripture of some great religion of the world, it sets the terms for its own assessment, and it has enormous appeal, especially for those devoted to it to whom it appeals.

A problem with cross-cultural psychology is that it is not heretical enough, even as it raises its serious concerns. It would not be too great an exaggeration to assert that so-called method effects (major variations in research findings as a result of slight variations in research procedure, elicitation technique, wording of questions, description and representation of problems, expectation of examiners, subject population, and so on) are the main effects to emerge out of decades of laboratory research in general psychology. The method effect phenomenon (see Campbell and Fiske 1959; Cronbach 1975; Fiske 1986) is quite consistent with the discovery that generalizations from psychological research on one population do not travel very well across cultural, historical, and institutional boundaries.

Unfortunately, in the face of that evidence most cross-cultural psychologists have been unable to free themselves of the hegemony of Platonistic presuppositions in general psychology. They have continued to assume a psychic unity to humankind and to search for the presumed central processing mechanism in growth-stimulating environments (literate, Western industrialized urban centers) or through culture-fair or everyday stimulus materials.

Cultural psychology is far more heterodox vis-à-vis the canon of psychic unity. For cultural psychology is built out of a fundamental skepticism concerning all those fateful and presupposed distinctions: intrinsic properties of mind versus extrinsic properties of environments, form versus content, the "deep" versus the "superficial," the inherent central processing mechanism (psychic unity) versus all the other stuff.

Cultural psychology offers an alternative discipline of interpretation of the fundamentals of the mind. The mind, according to cultural psychology, is content driven, domain specific, and constructively stimulus bound; and it cannot be extricated from the historically variable and cross-culturally diverse intentional worlds in which it plays a coconstituting part. Consequently, cultural psychology interprets statements about regularities observed in a lab or observed anywhere else, on the street or in a classroom, in Chicago or in Khartoum, not as propositions about inherent properties of a central processing mechanism for human psychological functioning but rather as descriptions of local response patterns contingent on context, resources, instructional sets, authority relations, framing devices, and modes of construal.[6]

It is the aim of cultural psychology to understand the organization and evocative power of all that stuff, to study the major varieties of it, and to seek the mind where it is mindful, indissociably embedded in the meanings and resources that are both its product and its components.

It Is Not Psychological Anthropology

Whereas cross-cultural psychology is a subdiscipline of psychology, psychological anthropology is a province of anthropology; which means that psychological anthropology is less concerned with behavior in laboratories or on standardized tests or with novel stimulus materials and more concerned with other kinds of stuff. The stuff of anthropology includes rituals and folk tales, games and art forms, family life practices and religious doctrines, kinship categories and inherited systems of knowledge. Anthropologists in general like to muck around in the stuff of everyday life and language, and psychological anthropologists are no exception.

It should come as no surprise that psychological anthropology is psychological. Its proper and excellent aim is to understand the way ritual, language, belief, and other systems of meaning function or are put together in the lives and experiences and mental representations of persons.

In recent years many psychological anthropologists have turned to the study of cultural psychology and have revised some of the classic assumptions of the discipline. What I write here applies to psychological anthropology before its more recent reincarnation as cultural psychology. (See Chapter 7 of this volume.)

Classically, psychological anthropology has tended to conceive of the psychological in the general psychology sense, which means that when psychological anthropologists have mucked around in classic form in their favorite anthropological stuff (for example, initiation ceremonies, kinship classifications, origin stories, conceptions of the gods) they have done so with the idea of psychic unity in mind.

Psychological anthropologists of the classic form have gone searching for the transcendental in the world of appearances. They have tried to explain the stuff of culture by reference to the workings of a central processing mechanism underlying psychological functioning. They have tried to use the stuff of culture to characterize or discover a central processing device. Whereas general psychologists search for the central processor by trying to eliminate the "interfering" effects, the "noise" and "distortion" produced by any meaningful stimulus environment, psychological anthropologists have looked for the central processor in the stimulus environment, on the assumption that there is something about long-surviving sociocultural environments that makes them relatively noiseless and distortion free.

The hallmarks of classical psychological anthropology are the sanguine premises that there exists an inherent central processing mechanism for individual psychological functioning and that its powers and influences extend into the sociocultural environment. Therefore, to remain viable any sociocultural environment must be adapted to or expressive of the central processing mechanism's abstract form and invariant constraints.

Psychological anthropology can be taxonomized along received fault lines (body versus mind; affect and motivation versus thought) into two subfields: "culture and personality" and "cognitive anthropology."

Before the recent reemergence of a cultural psychology the subfields of classical psychological anthropology were united with each other, as well as with general psychology and cross-cultural psychology, by the now familiar assumption of the psychic unity of humankind.

The central problematic for general psychology, as we have seen, is to characterize the central processing mechanism inherent in mental functioning by isolating it from the environment and from all the other extrinsic stuff upon which it operates. The central processor is abstract, transcendent (interior, deep, hidden, beyond, somewhere else), fixed, and universal. The central problematic for cross-cultural psychology is to explain the noteworthy performance differences on psychological tests between human populations without renouncing the idea of an inherent psychic unity. Performance differences exist, it is argued in cross-cultural psychology, either because the cultural environment has slowed the full maturation of the central processor in some populations, or because the performance environment of psychological testing has inhibited the central processing mechanism from going on display.

The central problematic of classical psychological anthropology, however, is more imperial—to find expanded into the territory of sociocultural environments the central authority of the psychological processing machine. The imperial premises: that the stuff of sociocultural environments gets shaped or molded by the dictates and constraints of the central processing mechanism into a limited number of possible designs for living; that the central processing mechanism gives structure to a sociocultural environment, either by mediating the relationships between its stuff or by impressing its abstract form upon it.

Thus, in classical psychological anthropology sibling terminological systems might be interpreted as revelatory of a universal and inherent disinclination of the central processing mechanism to engage in disjunctive reasoning (Nerlove and Romney 1967). Cultural origin stories might be interpreted as revelatory of an inherent preference of the human mind for dichotomous categories (Lévi-Strauss 1963). And almost everything from myths to patterns of kinship avoidance and joking to adolescent circumcision ceremonies might be interpreted as revelatory of that famous presumptive psychic universal known as the Oedipus complex (Stephens 1962; Spiro 1983).

Psychological anthropology, classically practiced, is a reductionist enterprise. Unlike Shepard (1987), who searches for the abstract central processing mechanism for stimulus generalization behavior by trying to reach beyond the "noisy," autonomous, and resistant physical constraints of any concrete stimulus domain, principled psychological anthropologists assume that the substantive domains of a sociocultural environment are a relatively pliant content operated upon by, or expressive of, deep and invariant psychological laws or processes of motivation, affect, and intellect.

Cultural psychology is not psychological anthropology.

Psychological anthropology assumes that there is an inherent central processing mechanism.

Psychological anthropology assumes that the central processing mechanism not only stands outside the sociocultural environment as an independent, fixed, and universal given of the human psyche; the central processor also reaches in to the sociocultural environment, leaving its indelible stamp.

Psychological anthropology assumes that the structure and functioning of the central processing mechanism is not fundamentally altered by the content, stuff, material, or sociocultural environment on which it operates.

Psychological anthropology assumes that whatever the differences are between populations in all the other stuff (in religious beliefs, in ceremonial life, in mythology, and so on), those differences can and should be interpreted as just so many products of the deep operations of a psychically unifying central processing device.

Cultural psychology is dubious of all those assumptions; indeed, cultural psychology is psychological anthropology without those assumptions. Many psychological anthropologists today are in fact doing cultural psychology.

It Is Not Ethnopsychology

If cultural psychology is psychological anthropology without the premise of psychic unity, then ethnopsychology is cultural psychology without a psyche at all.

Ethnopsychology is the study of ethnic variations in theories of the mental life. It is the investigation of indigenous representations of mind, self, body, and emotion. Such representations might include biochemical theories linking black bile or tired blood or sluggish neurotransmitters to depression. They might include interpersonal theories of guilt and possessive states conceiving of the mind as populated with the unplacated spirits or shadows of one's ancestors. They might include lay classifications of subjective states (thinking, feeling, willing). They might even include Platonistic theories positing a psychic unity to humankind.

There are many points of similarity between cultural psychology and ethnopsychology, especially a common concern for the psychological categories of indigenous folk. The major point of difference is that ethnopsychology is a subdiscipline of ethnosemantics or ethnoscience. It is primarily concerned with the investigation of mind, self, body, and emotion as topics (along with, for example, botany or kinship) in the ethnographic study of folk beliefs.

Ethnopsychology is thus less concerned with the actual psychological functioning and subjective life of individuals in the cultures whose doctrines about mind, representations of emotions, formal texts about the self, and gender ceremonies are under examination. Ethnopsychology is cultural psychology without the functioning psyche.

For some general anthropologists, especially those who are psychophobic, the focus in ethnopsychology on folk beliefs and doctrines sanitizes its subject matter (mind, self, emotion) and makes it more acceptable for investigation. The person is allowed in to general ethnography safely contained in the form of an idea or an ideology.

Cultural psychology is more person centered and a bit less cerebral; for it is the ethnopsychology of a functioning psyche, as it actually functions, malfunctions, and functions differently, in different parts of the world. Many ethnopsychologists today are in fact doing cultural psychology.

An Origin Story for Cultural Psychology

Taxonomically, as presented so far, cultural psychology is the plural, variable, domain-specific, and constructively "stimulus-bound" psychology of intentional worlds. It is psychological anthropology without the premise of psychic unity. It is the ethnopsychology of the functioning psyche as it actually functions, malfunctions, and functions differently in the different parts of the world.

Cultural psychology tries to synthesize, or at least combine, some of the virtues of general psychology, cross-cultural psychology, psychological anthropology, and ethnopsychology while seeking to disencumber itself of their vices. It should come as no surprise that a vice in the intentional world of cultural psychology turns out to be a Platonist's virtue, and vice versa.

Viewed from the intentional world of cultural psychology, the virtue in general psychology is its concern with the organized nature of the mental life. Its vice is its conception of the mental as a central processing mechanism—abstract, interior (transcendent), universal, fixed, and content free.

The virtue in cross-cultural psychology is its concern with performance differences between ethnic groups. Its vice is its orthodox adherence to the premise of psychic unity.

The virtue in psychological anthropology is its focus on psychological functioning in sociocultural context. Its vice is its subordination of the sociocultural environment to the postulated directives of a central processing device.

The virtue in ethnopsychology is its attention to indigenous or local conceptions of mind, self, body, and person. Its vice is its psychophobia.

There is, of course, much more that needs to be said and worked out about each of those points. Yet there is also another way to "thicken" (Geertz 1973) our appreciation of cultural psychology, which is to treat it not only in a taxonomic context of definition but also in a narrative one.

There are many stories that can be told, at varying orders of magnitude of historical time depth, about ups and downs in the life of cultural psychology. The following tale is a short and very contemporary one, selected from the many that could be told. It is the story of a pitfall of the "cognitive revolution" of the 1960s.

It is probably no accident that the current renewal of interest in cultural psychology is occurring after thirty years of intellectual fragmentation in both general anthropology and general psychology. That fragmentation can be interpreted as a salutary reaction against the Platonism hidden in the agenda of the so-called cognitive revolution of the 1960s (see Shweder 1984b, pp. 7–8).

The cognitive revolution got off to a promising start. Many (and I am one of them) welcomed it as the obvious and necessary corrective to the radical behaviorism that preceded it. The revolution seemed to address a rather serious shortcoming in psychology and anthropology, namely, the lack of a notion of mental representations and intentional states (mind, self, and emotion) in theories of the person and the lack of a notion of mental representations and intentional worlds (subject-dependent objects embedded in constituted "forms of life") in theories of the sociocultural environment.

Unfortunately, the cognitive revolution turned out to be far less than the rediscovery of intentionality and mental representations, and far more than just the displacement of behaviorism. Along with the cognitive revolution came an uninvited *Geist*—the spirit of Platonism—which aroused in psychology, and even in some corners of anthropology, that ancient fascination with formal, mathematical, structural models and an inherent central processing mechanism.

As the cognitive revolution spread through the disciplines, so did Platonism. Although some cognitivists (for example, Roy D'Andrade, George Lakoff, Catherine Lutz) sought to develop the idea of intentionality and mental representations by investigating the specifics of indigenous conceptions of physical, biological, social, and psychological things as those conceptions have a bearing on people's lives (Schank and Abelson 1977; Holland and Quinn 1986), for the most part content got set aside in favor of process, the particular in favor of the general, the substantive in favor of the abstract and the formal. The person and his or her intentional worlds, meanings, and sociocultural resources, like all concrete particulars, somehow got lost in the search for the inherent central processing mechanism of the mind.

Today, thirty years into the cognitive revolution, psychology and anthropology are more fragmented than before. In 1959 it was possible to point to experimental work on animal learning or psychophysics as "real" psychology or to ethnographic field work on social organization, ritual, and kinship as "real" anthropology, and to have some agreement about it. But no longer. When, in 1987, Shepard reported the discovery of a universal law of generalization and compared it favorably with Newton's laws of gravitation, relatively few hearts skipped a beat, and many heads shook in dismay.

To everyone's surprise—some scholars react with delight, others with despair—in 1989 it has become increasingly difficult for leading scholars to reach consensus about the specifications for an excellent psychological research project, or an excellent anthropological one. The criteria for identifying the intellectual core of each discipline have become freely contestable. With the breakup of general psychology and general anthropology, the usual definitional exercises have become strenuous and fruitless. Now when one asks scholars within the respective disciplines to name the prototypical psychologist or the prototypical anthropologist, opinions scatter, with every school of thought fancying a claim to a nonexistent center stage.

Even the recent Platonist nostalgia in some areas of psychology for something abstract and bleached and really real, and the diffuse distraction of attention to the latest intellectual fashion in reductionism and formalism, known as artificial intelligence, has proved to be short-lived. Already other reductive and nonreductive varieties of cognitive science (for example, neural nets and parallel distributed process models) are screaming like demons for their equal time (see the special winter 1988 issue of *Daedalus* on artificial intelligence).

For the sake of developing and liberating a cultural psychology all the commotion and fragmentation has probably been for the good. Too often in the past the wrong hegemonic general psychology has conspired with the wrong hegemonic general anthropology to divide and conquer the realm. General psychology played its part by reducing and diminishing our conception of the person or of psyche to a transcendent and abstract and fixed and universal central processing mechanism. General anthropology, fascinated by all the historical and ethnographic variations and diffusional clusterings of concrete sociocultural institutions, practices, and beliefs, played its part by taking no interest in the person or psyche at all. The two hegemonic intellectual regimes preserved and deserved each other's disciplinary parochialism. Both research traditions made it difficult even to conceive of a meaningful collaboration between anthropologists and psychologists. Culture and psyche were made to keep their distance by defining what they had in common, the person and his or her intentionality, out of both.

Under a Platonist influence most high-status research in the psychological sciences during the 1960s came to be guided by five maxims or research heuristics. Modest exposure to those heuristics produced an instant indifference to the kinds of phenomena (meaning systems, institutional settings, rituals, artifacts, modes of representation, interpersonal power orders, conflicts of motives, goal-setting) of interest to cultural psychology. Those five prescriptions/proscriptions for research went something like this (see Shweder 1984b, pp. 3–4):

Heuristic 1. Search for a central processing system and represent it as an abstract structure or as a pure mathematical form; mere content can be ignored.

Heuristic 2. Language use is epiphenomenal to the true causes of behavior; what people actually say to each other can be ignored. (Note: Grammar and phonology remained legitimate topics for investigation, for they were abstract and structural and perhaps even deep; see heuristic 1).

Heuristic 3. What is really real (the central processing mechanism) is hidden and interior, and exists solely inside the skin of individuals; exterior and extrinsic macrounits such as the sociocultural environment can be ignored.

Heuristic 4. Search for universal (timeless and spaceless) laws of nature; the organization of knowledge in Newtonian physics is the ideal form for all true understanding.

Heuristic 5. Do not think about anything that cannot be controlled and measured in a lab, for the lab is the royal road to the central processing mechanism.

Those were, of course, not the only heuristics widely and wildly promoted by Platonism in psychology during the cognitive revolution. And I would not want to deny that there exists at least one research topic, and perhaps even two or three, for which those heuristics were, and continue to be, quite useful.

During the cognitive revolution, however, those heuristics became reigning ones. Their overextension and prevalence lent credence to epithets defining psychology as the "nonsocial social science." Ironically, right in the thick of the cognitive revolution, the psyche and the person were nowhere to be found in psychology; the discipline designed to study the soul, the subjectivity, the person, the rational strivings of human beings for dignity and self-esteem had turned away from those themes and returned to the mechanistic investigation of automatic processes and deep abstract mathematical forms.

Quite predictably, during the cognitive revolution the person did not succeed at gaining a foothold in anthropology. The local representatives of the revolution, the structural anthropologists (Claude Lévi-Strauss, Sir Edmund Leach), searched for the abstract universal principles of organization (for example, class inclusion, binary opposition) of the central processing mechanism. The ethnosemanticists and ethnoscientists studied classifications of flora and fauna; later they became ethnopsychologists and studied classifications of ideas about emotional states, without studying functioning (or malfunctioning) emotions at all. The culture and personality theorists—the ones who were really supposed to care about the lived experiences of persons in society—either felt disgruntled by the lack of concern for motivation and emotion or played possum; yet they could offer no compelling alternative to the Platonism of the times, since they fully endorsed Platonism's central theme—deep psychic unity. Most anthropologists, however, simply carried on as usual, just more so, documenting ethnographically and historically the diversity of exotic human institutions, practices, and beliefs and taking no interest in the person at all.

Indeed, as if to return (with a vengeance) the compliment of psychology's indifference to the "extrinsic" stuff of culture, society, meaning and context, the hegemonic prototype for research in general anthropology induced among (too) many a motivated state of psychophobia. The more psychology conceived of the person or the psyche as fixed, interior, abstract, universal, and lawful, the more anthropology chose to interpret sociocultural environments as exterior, historically variable, culture specific, and arbitrary and to renounce any interest in psyches or persons, or in the general causes of anything.

The person disappeared from ethnography. The question of why people believe the things they believe or practice what they practice was either begged, tabooed, or trivialized. The question was reduced to questions of conformity or indoctrination or some other variation on the metaphorical theme of robotics or social pressure (see Obeyesekere 1981 and Chapter 9 of this volume).

For three decades a person-free psychology of an abstract invariant human nature conspired with a person-free anthropology of local systems of arbitrary, socially sanctioned coercive practices and meanings to keep a cultural psychology of intentional states and intentional worlds off the center stage.

Fortunately for cultural psychology there were many sideshows, and those sideshows drew an exciting and excited countercultural crowd. If you knew where to look or had the right friends, you could find cultural psychology there all along, doing its unorthodox things outside the main pavilions and the center rings.

Some of the sideshows were dazzling.[7] There was the tent of Lucien Lévy-Bruhl (1910), where exotic ethnic mentalities were put on display in defiance of psychic unity. There was the tent of Ludwig Wittgenstein (1968 [1953]), where Platonism was turned sour and transmuted into a "form of life." There was the tent of Aaron Cicourel (1974) and the "ethnomethodologists," where realities were dissolved, contextualized, infinitely regressed yet still apparently able to reconstruct themselves out of themselves. There was the tent of Roy D'Andrade (1981) and other psyche-sensitive ethnographers of mental representations, where anthropology resisted the Platonism implicit in the cognitivist agenda, on a platform of local or domain-specific territories of meaning.

There was the tent of Clifford Geertz (1973), where there was magic in words and reality in rhetoric, and where manner matters were discussed with such sophistication that the same became the different, the formal became contentful, and the fixed began to move.

There was the tent of Arthur Kleinman (1986a) and the "medical anthropologists," where soma revealed psyche and the body exposed its intentionality, and where all could see that there was more to a "splitting head" or a "broken heart" or "frayed nerves" than the matter of disease. There was the tent of Edward Sapir and the "linguistic relativity" hypothesis, where the barker spoke the ultimate mystery (of cultural psychology): "the worlds in which different societies live are distinct worlds, not merely the same world with different labels attached" (Sapir 1929, p. 209).[8]

So What Is It?

It still remains to be seen what this new age in anthropology and psychology of seeking to conflate ancient antimonies (form/content, process/content, person/environment, interior/exterior, subjective/objective, psyche/culture) will bring.

Cultural psychology, properly understood and practiced, is heretical. Its central theme is that you cannot take the stuff out of the psyche and you cannot take the psyche out of the stuff. Cultural psychology does not presume that the fundamentals of the mental life are by nature fixed, universal, abstract, and interior. It presumes instead intentionality—that the life of the psyche is the life of intentional persons, responding to, and directing their action at, their own mental objects or representations and undergoing transformation through participation in an evolving intentional world that is the product of the mental representations that make it up. Cultural psychology assumes that intentional persons change and are changed by the concrete particulars of their own mentally constituted forms of life.

Those who labor for a cultural psychology must address many difficult analytic, methodological, and substantive issues and overcome many old habits of thinking. Betwixt and between anthropology and psychology in the reoccupied zone of cultural psychology the main agenda item these days is how to minimize, fill in, or bridge the gap created by the Platonist separation of an inherent central processing mechanism from all the other extrinsic stuff. There have been many types of attempts.

First, among those who study formal norms for reasoning (for example, philosophers of science), the Platonist search has largely been abandoned for a universally binding inductive "logic" or "formal scientific method" that might operate on its own or mechanically to draw sound inferences, free of entrenched local systems for encoding and representing and "abducting" events (Putnam 1981; see note 4).

There is also the emergence among psychologists of an interest in "expertise." Among those who study problem solving, the cognition of virtuosos has become a central topic of investigation, and exemplary cognition is increasingly talked about in non-Platonic ways, as knowledge based, constructively stimulus bound, and domain specific or modular. The current turn toward "content" is significant and widespread. Indeed what seems to differentiate an expert from a novice (chess player, abacus user, medical diagnostician, and so on) is not some greater amount of content-free pure logical or psychological power. What experts possess that neophytes lack is a greater quantity and quality of domain-specific knowledge of stimulus properties, as well as dedicated mastery of the specialized or parochial tools of a trade (see Stigler 1984; Stigler, Chalip, and Miller 1986; Stigler and Baranes 1988). It is thus no coincidence that those who study expertise do not equate the mental with the abstract. Instead they interpret the mind as it is embodied in concrete representations, in "mediating schemata," "scripts," and well-practiced "tools for thought."

The idea of tools for thought is an apposite (and self-referring) metaphor for thinking about thinking. It says that thinking is fundamentally interdependent with the traditional intellectual artifacts, representational schemes, and accumulated knowledge of some cultural or subcultural community. It says that as thinking becomes, as it must, metaphorically displaced from the operations of any fixed and central processing mechanism, the life of the mind becomes an extension or an analogue of, or an appendage to, cultural artifacts and their built-in design features.

Jerome Bruner (1966, p. 56), speaking in resistance to the Piagetian notion of a deeply interior and abstract central processing mechanism undergoing progressive development, used to talk of cultural "amplifiers" of thought. His idea was that what we think with (and about) can be decisive for how we think; and that those amplifiers or collective modes of representation, and the role they play in formal and informal education, are proper topics for the psychology of thought.

Of course it is hardly news to point out that one cannot be indifferent to content and still make sense of everyday cognitive, emotional, and conative functioning. From a Platonist point of view everyday cognitive, emotional, and conative functioning is "noise" laden and stimulus bound, which is, of course, precisely why the Platonists believe that the stimulus and task environment must be transcended if pure "psychological" laws are to be discovered (see the discussion of Shepard, above).

What is new (and renewing) in anthropology and psychology is a return of a this-worldly interest in the study of actual functioning and the reemergence of a genuine respect for all that psychocultural, psychophysical, psychosomatic "noise."

Indeed, in the land of cultural psychology all of the action is in the "noise." And the so-called noise is not really noise at all; it is the message.

Notably, in the language of cultural psychology there are no pure psychological laws, just as there are no unreconstructed or unmediated stimulus events. There are intentional persons reacting to, and directing their behavior with respect to, their own descriptions and mental representations of things; and there are intentional worlds, which are the realities we constitute, embody, materialize out of our descriptions and representations of things. Indeed, according to the premises of cultural psychology, even the transcendent realities portrayed by scientists are part of intentional worlds and cannot really take us beyond our mental representations of things.[9] In the world of cultural psychology transcendence and self-transformation are possible but only through a dialectical process of moving from one intentional world into the next, or by changing one intentional world into another.

Every person is stimulus bound, and every stimulus is person bound. That is what it means for culture and psyche to make each other up. That is why a cultural psychology signals an end for the purely psychological in psychology, an end to the quest for the inherent central processing mechanism of mental life, and an end to the Platonist legacy of the cognitive revolution. Cultural psychology is a return to the study of mental representations (emotions, desires, and beliefs and their intentional objects) without the presumption of fixity, necessity, universality, and abstract formalism. And while it may well be true that the constitutive and meaning-laden act of scientific comparison may require the postulation of a standard or universal Archimedean point of view from which to spot differences and talk sensibly about them (difference does presuppose likeness), it should be remembered that such posits of a universal grid for comparison are constructed and deconstructed by us, so as to make our intentional world intelligible. One of the hazards of comparison may be the ease with which the universals that we posit as part of our own intentional activities, in maintaining and enriching our own intentional world, get projected onto some imagined deep and essential structure of the mind.

As interpretative frameworks change, so do perceptions. Thus it is also a sign of the times that the "fundamental" Platonist distinction between "higher"-order and "lower"-order systems (between "deep" structure and "surface" structure) no longer seems quite so easy to sustain.

It is not just that there exist content-rich mediating schemata that bridge the gap between supposed abstract structures and the real-life instances to which they apply. (Platonists have no trouble with that. They view the application of abstract principles to concrete cases as either beside the point or as rulelike and mechanical.) The more difficult problem for Platonism is that once the gap between abstraction and case has been filled in, a general and rulelike distinction between a central processor and its content is not so readily defined.

A deep suspicion has arisen in cultural psychology that so-called strict or intrinsic dispositions for behavior (Putnam 1987) and neat linear relationships between things are the exceptions in a world of local nonlinear dynamic processes with circular or dialectical feedback loops between so-called (and once Platonically conceived) levels of analysis, and between subject and object, text and context, manner and matter, content and form, fact and value, belief and directive force. There seems to be far less distinction in those famous old distinctions than there used to be.

At forums in anthropology and psychology these days someone is bound to say "not so fast" if you blithely presuppose a central processing mechanism consisting of abstract universal underlying structures or laws that impose form on any substance that happens to come along; or if you casually presume a self-evident division between an interior psyche and an exterior sociocultural environment.

Indeed, with the reemergence of a cultural psychology a new aim has been defined for anthropologists and psychologists: to find ways to talk about culture and psyche so that neither is by nature intrinsic or extrinsic to the other.

That aim for cultural psychology is to conceive imaginatively of subject-dependent objects (intentional worlds) and object-dependent subjects (intentional persons) interpenetrating each other's identities or setting the conditions for each other's existence and development, while jointly undergoing change through social interaction. That aim is to develop an interpretative framework in which nothing really real is by fundamental nature fixed, universal, transcendent (deep, interior), and abstract; and in which local things can be deeply embedded, but only for a while; and then, having developed the framework, the aim is to see how far it will go. (It may not go everywhere, but that remains to be seen.) That aim is to bridge the gap between psyche and culture by talking about them in new (or is it in very old?) ways. Here is one new (and very old) way of talking about psyche and culture.

Psyche refers to the intentional person. Culture refers to the intentional world. Intentional persons and intentional worlds are interdependent things that get dialectically constituted and reconstituted through the intentional activities and practices that are their products, yet make them up (see the discussion of weeds, above). Psyche animates her vessels and turns them into persons, leaving them mindful, soulful, willful, and full of goals and judgments.

The breath of psyche is the stuff of intentional states, of beliefs and desires, of fears and fancies, of values and visions about this or that. Psyche refers to patterns of motivated involvement, subjective states responsive to and directed at our mental representations of things. The breath of psyche is the stuff of intentional processes: goal setting, means-ends calculation, reality testing, embodied emotional reactiveness, self-monitoring and self-regulation in the pursuit of personal dignity, and so on. Psyche refers to "already-there" intentional states and processes distributed and organized within a person or across a people, and undergoing change, reorganization, and transformation across the life cycle.

In thinking about culture in new (or very old) ways it is crucial to remind ourselves again and again that a sociocultural environment is a world constituted, occupied, and used by intentional beings (see Sahlins 1976a on the symbolic or intentional uses of food and clothing). For psyche imparts to her vessels that charmed and spiritual quality of intentionality (and the teleology and pursuit after mental objects and final causes that accompanies it): psyche's vessels strive always to keep up appearances, to remain visibly dignified and exemplary of their imagined kind, and to express through their social actions a conception of themselves and of their place in the constituted scheme of things.

Culture is the constituted scheme of things for intending persons, or at least that part of the scheme that is inherited or received from the past. Culture refers to persons, society, and nature as lit up and made possible by some already there intentional world, an intentional world composed of conceptions, evaluations, judgments, goals, and other mental representations already embodied in socially inherited institutions, practices, artifacts, technologies, art forms, texts, and modes of discourse.

It is those inherited conceptions, evaluations, judgments, and goals embodied in cultural things (institutions, artifacts, discourse) about which the intending think, out of which the intending build their lives, and with respect to which the intending give substance to their minds, souls, wills, and directed actions.

Psyche and culture are thus seamlessly interconnected. A person's psychic organization is largely made possible by, and is largely expressive of, a conception of itself, society, and nature; while one of the very best ways to understand cultural conceptions of self, society, and nature is to examine the way those conceptions organize and function in the subjective life of intending individuals (see D'Andrade 1984).[10]

It cannot be repeated enough that a cultural psychology aims to develop a principle of intentionality—action responsive to and directed at mental objects or representations—by which culturally constituted realities (intentional worlds) and reality-constituting psyches (intentional persons) continually and continuously make each other up, perturbing and disturbing each other, interpenetrating each other's identity, reciprocally conditioning each other's existence.

The aim of cultural psychology is to examine the different kinds of things that continually happen in social interaction and in social practice as the intentionality of a person meets the intentionality of a world and as they jointly facilitate, express, repress, stabilize, transform, and defend each other through and throughout the life of a person or the life of a world. There are histories (narratives) that can be written about each, or both—the history of lives and the history of practices and institutions.

Most of the work of cultural psychology is still ahead of us. To achieve its aims cultural psychology must develop an analytic framework for characterizing the relationships between reality-constituting psyches (intentional persons) and culturally constituted realities (intentional worlds) that is at least as rich as the framework developed by behavioral geneticists for characterizing so-called genotype-environment correlations (Scarr and McCartney 1983; Plomin 1986, chapter 6).

As ethnographers, economists, and experimental social psychologists have known for a long time, intentional worlds can be strongly disposing and powerfully promoting of certain intentional states and not of others. They prompt and dispose in a variety of ways—by the way objects and events are represented and described by local guardians of the intentional world (parents, teachers, leaders, experimenters), by the way resources and opportunities are arranged and managed, by the way rituals and routines are performed, by the way sanctions are allocated (see B. Whiting and J. Whiting 1975; Ochs and Schieffelin 1984; Miller and Sperry 1987; Whiting and Edwards 1988); and Chapter 5 of this volume.)

Here is a simple yet vivid example of a strongly disposing (micro) intentional world: an alarm clock ringing loudly from where it was deliberately placed the night before, on the other side of the room, tends to stimulate an intense desire to turn it off, which gets us out of bed (see Schelling 1984, chapters 2 and 3).

For a moment let us borrow from the behavioral geneticists (Scarr and McCartney 1983; Plomin 1986) their analytic framework for talking about genotype-environment interactions, and let us transmute it a bit. Since genotype is irrelevant to the logic of the analytic framework, let us drop it and talk instead about person-environment interactions. Using the Scarr and McCartney framework one can imagine at least six types of relationships between reality-constituting psyches (intentional persons) and culturally constituted realities (intentional worlds). The relationship can be either *positive* (when the intentionality of the world amplifies or supports the intentionality of the person) or *negative* (when the intentionality of the world diminishes or contravenes the intentionality of the person). And the relationship can be either *active* (when the target person himself creates or selects his intentional world), *reactive* (when other persons create or select an intentional world for the target person in the light of that person's intentionality or the intentionality that others anticipate in the target person), or *passive* (when a target person ends up living in an intentional world created or selected by others for others or for themselves). That gives us six types: positive (active, reactive, passive) and negative (active, reactive, passive).[11]

The alarm clock arranged to go off just out of reach is a negative active relationship. The reality-constituting person constructs an intentional world using collective resources to contravene his or her own anticipated preference to stay in bed and go back to sleep. Whistling a happy or confident tune in the dark to alleviate one's fear is a second example of a negative active relationship. Hiding one's face from, or not looking at, or avoiding seductive or attractive things that might tempt you to transgression is a third example. Rituals of transcendence or detachment, such as Buddhist meditative exercises through which a reality-constituting person strives to make his or her own body ego alien by conceiving of it as a bag of feces (Obeyeskere 1985), provide a fourth example.

It is characteristic of the negative *active* relationship that the psyche creates or selects an intentional world to protect itself against itself, often by means of so-called culturally constituted defenses (the alarm clock, the happy tune, and so on).

The negative *reactive* relationship is one in which others intervene to protect you against your own intentionality. The institution of purdah for adolescent females is an example of a negative reactive relationship. Thus, in some intentional worlds girls are not permitted to do at age thirteen what they were permitted to do at age five; whatever desire they may have for autonomy in decision making becomes dangerous with the onset of puberty. Menstruating daughters are kept off the street in that intentional world, for the sake of what is good and true and beautiful in that intentional world. Purdah, too, is a culturally constituted defense, but a reactive one, choreographed by others for the self rather than written by the self for itself.[12]

In contrast, in the negative *passive* relationship the reality-constituting person experiences the meanings and resources of an intentional world created or selected by others for others or for themselves. For example, during the ten to twelve days of death pollution in orthodox Hindu communities in India, family members assist the soul of the deceased in detaching from its corpse and in proceeding on its eternal transmigratory journey. The pollution in the corpse is believed to burden the soul of the deceased and keep it bound to its material vessel. So to assist the deceased his or her living relatives absorb the pollution in the corpse into their own bodies. To facilitate the absorption of death pollution, family members are careful to avoid other kinds of pollutants ("hot" foods, "hot" activities such as sex, and "hot" emotions). They fast. They are abstinent. They stay at home. The mourning period is over when the soul of the deceased has successfully detached itself from its dead body. Family members then cleanse their own bodies of the death pollution they have absorbed. They do so by shaving their hair, cutting their nails, and taking a special bath. They put on new clothes and return to life in the outside world.

It seems likely that for some members of the family, at some point in the life cycle, the experience of the mourning ritual is a negative passive one. Children or other family members may want to go out, play, or eat "hot" foods. Adults may want to have sex. There probably does occur some transgression of the requirements of the intentional world of the funeral practice. Yet because children participate passively and vicariously in the practice and experience its meanings, resources, and sanctions, the intentional world of mourning customs (including the end at which it is aimed—salvation of an eternal transmigrating soul through the help of loyal, devout, and self-sacrificing relatives) comes to be upheld and pursued by precisely those reality-constituting persons whose intentions came to be formed through participation in those very practices.

I will not illustrate or examine all the positive types of relationships between reality-constituting psyches and culturally constituted realities, although instances are not difficult to bring to mind—for example, to mention a positive active type, the gregarious youth who creates dance parties at school.

The main reason for reviewing here a logical scheme for types of person-environment interactions is to suggest that it might be fruitful in cultural psychology to conceive of socialization processes in terms of *at least* those six forms of relationship between intentional persons and intentional worlds. There is a reciprocal and dynamic relationship between intentional persons and intentional worlds, each setting conditions for the other's existence and development. All the relationships are self-transforming and dialectical. At stake in these relationships are both the cultivation of a human psyche suited to the historical context of some intentional world, and the cultivation of an intentional world, capable of cultivating and supporting the human psyche in one of the various forms of its nobility.

The three negative relationships describe "defensive" engagements. Making use of the resources from an already-there intentional world, an already-there personal intention becomes attenuated, modified, or hidden, either through direct self-regulation (active) or through direct or vicarious interpersonal regulation (reactive, passive). The three positive relationships describe "expressive" engagements. Making use of the resources from an already-there intentional world, an already-there personal intention is amplified, reproduced, and displayed, either through direct self-promotion (active) or through direct or vicarious interpersonal subsidization (reactive, passive).

In some orthodox Brahman communities in Orissa, India, for example, there is a positive reactive ritual that takes place in the context of joint family living arrangements the day after a marriage is consummated. Everyone in the extended household knows that the bride has lost her virginity the night before. (Indeed, some of them may have been listening and giggling at her door). She knows that every-one knows it. Everyone knows that she knows that everyone knows it. She feels embarrassed to show her face the next morning; she wants to hide. So she is made to hide. They feel embarrassed to face her. So they are not allowed to face her. The day-after-the-fateful-night-before is explicitly labeled the "day of embarrassment." That day the bride is expected to stay secluded in her room all day or to go away to visit a friend. By means of a positive reactive relationship between a reality-constituting person (yesterday's virgin) and a culturally-constituted world (the "day of embarrassment") the young Hindu bride is protected from humiliation and permitted safely to dramatize her state of mind and realize her intention to hide.

It is tempting but not feasible in this preliminary scouting expedi-tion to view or review the key analytic and empirical contributions of the various intellectual communities that have so much to contribute to a cultural psychology. The territory is too vast.[13] The many insights and refigurations that emerge from those various intellectual com-munities are stimulating (perhaps even breathtaking) in their own terms. Yet they are also suggestive of a possible unification of intellec-tual agendas under the banner of a cultural psychology. Even a very brief consideration of the several varieties (positive versus negative; active, reactive, passive) of continual engagement between intentional persons and intentional worlds should make it apparent that neither psyche nor culture can long be denied by anyone genuinely curious about the functioning and development of either.

The challenge before us is to define more precisely this promising new discipline. How far can we go with an interpretative framework within which, and in whose terms, nothing is by fundamental or in-trinsic nature fixed, universal, transcendent, and abstract? What kind of knowledge can we expect from a cultural psychology?

Those are questions for other occasions. They call for deep rethink-ing and broad discussion across intellectual communities sympathetic to the general framework and aims of a cultural psychology.

It does seem likely, however, that our received images of "real" or honorific science will have to be revised.

A cultural psychology studies precisely those causal processes that go on because of our understanding of and involvement with them. It would seem to follow that the truths to be formulated in cultural psychology are typically going to be restricted in scope, because the causal processes they describe are likely to be embedded or localized in particular intentional worlds. What we are likely to discover are patches of institutionalized regularities, stabilized within culture areas during certain historical epochs, perhaps even for centuries, yet subject to change (see Gergen 1973).

It would also seem to follow that if realities are not independent of our representations of them and involvement with them, then the raising of questions, even "scientific" questions, is no innocent act. Asking people what they want to do is a way of promoting autonomous decision making. Asking about the potential uses of something is a way of constituting it as instrumental. The world of cultural psychology is a world of dialectical feedback loops and dynamic nonlinear relationships between things undergoing transformation. Given such a world, many of our received expectations for, and models of, successful research are going to make less sense. For example, we may not be able to fix or standardize the definitions of concepts. We can do that in a unitary, homogeneous, linear world where things stay put, permitting their presumed essences to be interdefined, but not in the world of cultural psychology.

And we should not expect that the same truths will reappear in every intentional world, or that something more wonderful and fundamental and revelatory has been discovered when and if they do, as sometimes they will (see note 2).

Most important, we should not expect reality to be independent of our participation in it. The likelihood that an event will occur in an intentional world is not independent of the confidence we have that it will occur.

Most normative models for decision making have not yet taken account of that simple truth. There are good metaphors and bad metaphors for the actions of intentional persons in intentional worlds. Most normative models for rational choice are metaphorical variations on the properties of roulette wheels, random-number tables, dice games, and coin flips. Those rather special, peculiar (and ethically controversial) cultural artifacts and technologies have been deliberately designed by us so that their behavior is independent of our attitudes toward them; as a result, they are among the most inappropriate metaphors for intentional action in general. The intentional world is not typically the world of a coin flip. It is more often a world in which our confidence in an event influences the likelihood of its occurrence and in which we not only monitor but also regulate and control deviations from expectation. It is a world in which if we did not have the confidence we have in things occurring, then they might not occur, just because of us! Patterns of decision making that are irrational in Las Vegas may well be rational and constructive in most other intentional worlds.

Thinking Through Others:
Cultural Psychology as an Interpretative Discipline

Among the most celebrated collections of anthropological essays on intentional worlds is Clifford Geertz's *Interpretation of Cultures* (1973). Cultural psychology is an interpretative enterprise in Geertz's senses. Yet just what is it one actually does in the interpretation of (intentional) worlds and (intentional) lives?

The answer to that question has much to do with the process of "thinking through others" (thinking through other cultures, thinking through other lives, thinking through India, thinking through Plato) in at least the four senses discussed in the Introduction: (1) thinking by means of the other; (2) getting the other straight; (3) deconstructing and going beyond the other; and (4) witnessing in the context of engagement with the other.

First, there is "thinking through others" in the sense of using the intentionality and self-consciousness of another culture or person—his or her or its articulated conception of things—as a means to heighten awareness of our less conscious selves.

Orthodox Hindus in India, to select a not so random example, have, as intentional beings, for thousands of years reflected on the relationship between moral action and outcome, on hierarchy, on patronage and paternalism, on sanctity and pollution. The more we try to conceive of an intentional world in their intentional terms, the more their doctrines and rituals and art forms and other modes of representation come to seem like sophisticated expressions of repressed, dormant, and potentially creative and transformative aspects of our own psyche pushed off by our intentional world to some mental fringe. We do not know how to talk about karma or how to comprehend an occasional dread that if we do something bad something bad may happen to us; yet we experience it. We do not know how to justify status obligations and hierarchical relationships, but we live them. We do not quite know how to acknowledge the presence of personal sanctity, yet we feel it.

"Thinking through others" in the first sense is to recognize the other as a specialist or expert on some aspect of human experience, whose reflective consciousness and system of representations and discourse can be used to reveal hidden dimensions of our selves. Some cultures of the world are virtuosos of grief and mourning, others of gender identity, and still others, of intimacy, eroticism, ego striving, and so on.

Ruth Benedict, an ancestral spirit of cultural psychology, with her conception of cultures as selections from the arc of human possibilities, understood well the first sense of "thinking through others."

Then there is "thinking through others" in the sense of getting the other straight, of providing a systematic account of the internal logic of the intentional world constructed by the other. The aim is a rational reconstruction of indigenous belief, desire, and practice. The assumption is that the organization of the psyche is based on a reality principle, whereby culturally constituted realities and reality-constituting psyches are mutually adjusted to one another until some attractive equilibrium is reached—a graceful or proportionate fit between the world as the other has made it out/up and the other's reactions to the world made out and up.

Freud is one of the great champions of the reality principle and the second sense of "thinking through others." In his inspiring defense of nonbiomedical healing practices, "The Question of Lay Analysis" (1962 [1929]), he notes that "if a patient of ours is suffering from a sense of guilt, as though he had committed a serious crime, we do not recommend him to disregard his qualms of conscience and do not emphasize his undoubted innocence; he himself has often tried to do so without success. What we do is to remind him that such a strong and persistent feeling must after all be based on something real, which it may perhaps be possible to discover" (p. 190).

The process of "thinking through others" in its second sense is a process of representing (and defending) the other's evaluations of and involvements with the world—such as a taboo against eating meat or a prohibition against remarriage—by tracing those evaluations and modes of involvement to some plausible alternative intentional world and conception of reality, which, in the ideal case, no rational person, not even Freud, can defeat.

Then there is "thinking through others" in the sense favored by Jacques Derrida and other postmodern deconstructionists. It is the sense of thinking one's way out of or beyond the other. It is the sense of passing through the other or intellectually transforming him or her or it into something else—perhaps its negation—by revealing what the life and intentional world of the other has dogmatically hidden away, namely, its own incompleteness.

It is a third sense, for it properly comes later, after we have already appreciated what the intentional world of the other powerfully reveals and illuminates, from its special point of view. "Thinking through others" is, in its totality, an act of criticism and liberation, as well as of discovery.

And then there is "thinking through others" in the sense of a situated perspectival observer, thinking *while there* in an alien land or with an alien other, trying to make sense of context-specific experiences. It is the sense of Geertz's "I-witnessing" author trying to turn a personal field experience into a "they-picturing" account of the other (Geertz 1988).

In this fourth sense of "thinking through others," the process of representing the other goes hand in hand with a process of portraying one's own self as part of the process of representing the other, thereby encouraging an open-ended self-reflexive dialogic turn of mind.

It seems to me that a genuine cultural psychology, the one we can feel proud of, is the cultural psychology that strives to think through others in all four senses, and more.

Finally, we come to the ultimate question: How far can we go with a cultural psychology? Can it take us all the way?

It is always a good idea to leave ultimate questions for some other occasion. Still, I will express my doubts. I think cultural psychology will take us very far, but not all the way.

I do not think it will take us as far as Nirvana, if there is such a place or state of mindlessness. I think there is such a place. And I think that if we get there we won't have the slightest need for a content- and context-dependent this-worldly cultural psychology. I certainly hope we won't.

Yet who knows; perhaps even Nirvana is really a special state of mind in a special intentional world, which it is the proper business of a cultural psychology to understand.

Part II

Are People the Same Wherever You Go?

3.

Does the Concept of the Person Vary Cross-Culturally?

with Edmund J. Bourne

Anthropologists and psychologists who study other people's conceptions of the person and ideas about the self have documented the prevalence among the peoples of the world of a mode of social thought often referred to as concrete, undifferentiated, context specific, or occasion bound. The folk believe that specific situations determine the moral character of a particular action, that the individual person per se is neither an object of importance nor inherently worthy of respect, that the individual as moral agent ought not to be distinguished from the social status she or he occupies, that, indeed, the individual as an abstract *ethical* and *normative* category is not to be acknowledged. This concrete mode of social thought or occasion-bound way of thinking about social things raises a fundamental question: In what terms should we understand the understandings of other peoples and compare those understandings with our own?

For more than a century anthropologists have tried to make sense of alien idea systems. Confronted with all sorts of incredible and often unbelievable beliefs, as well as all sorts of incredible and often unbelievable accounts of other people's beliefs, they have attempted to translate the meaning of oracles and witchcraft, wandering and reincarnated souls, magical "therapies," unusual ideas about procreation, and all the other exotic ideational formations that have come their way. In doing so they have a tendency to rely on one of three interpretative models for rendering intelligible the apparent diversity of human understandings: universalism, evolutionism, and relativism.

Universalists are committed to the view that intellectual diversity is more apparent than real, that exotic idea systems are really more like our own than they initially appear.

Evolutionists are committed to the view that alien idea systems not only are truly different from our own but also are different in a special way, namely, that other people's systems of ideas are really incipient and less adequate stages in the development of our own understandings.

Relativists are committed to the view that alien idea systems, though fundamentally different from our own, display an internal coherency that can be understood but cannot be judged.

Universalists opt for homogeneity. "Apparently different but really the same" is their slogan. Diversity is sacrificed to equality; equal because not different! Evolutionists opt for hierarchy. Diversity is not only tolerated; it is expected, and it is ranked. "Different but unequal" is their slogan. The relativists, in contrast, are pluralists. "Different but equal" is their slogan, equality *and* diversity their "democratic" aspiration.

Universalism, Evolutionism, and Relativism: Interpretative Standards

Universalists, evolutionists, and relativists all try to process information about alien idea systems following rules tailored to their interpretative model of choice. Indeed, the universalists, evolutionists, and relativists each have their way of processing data to help them arrive at their desired interpretation.

Universalism

There are two powerful ways to discover universals in the apparent diversity of human understandings: (1) emphasize general likenesses and overlook specific differences (the higher-order generality rule); (2) examine only a subset of the evidence (the data attenuation rule).

The higher-order generality rule. Charles Osgood's (1964) investigations of universals in connotative meaning illustrate the application of the higher-order generality rule. Emphasizing the way things are alike and ignoring the ways they are different, Osgood concluded that all peoples appraise objects and events in terms of three universal dimensions: good versus bad (evaluation), strong versus weak (potency), and fast versus slow (activity). These universals were discovered, in part, by moving to a level of discourse so general that "God" and "ice cream" were descriptively equivalent: both were perceived as good, strong, and active.

The tendency to overlook specific differences and to emphasize general likeness is ubiquitous among universalists. Claude Lévi-Strauss (1963, 1966, 1969a, 1969b), for example, rendered the distinctions between voiced/unvoiced (in phonetics), raw/cooked (in the culinary arts), sexual reproduction/asexual reproduction (in the Oedipus myth), and exogamy/endogamy (in marriage systems) equivalent, each an example of a purported human tendency to think in terms of binary oppositions. For ethologists and sociobiologists, conversation (in human primates) and barking (in canines) are examples of a universal "signaling" function of communication systems; for others, the affinities of "marriage" and "pair-bonding," are made much of at the expense of significant differences.

The data attenuation rule. Often the discovery of a universal is the product of a sophisticated process of data restriction and attenuation. Brent Berlin and Paul Kay (1969), for example, discovered universal prototypes for the definition of color categories, and a universal sequence for the emergence of a color lexicon. They began with two applications of the data attenuation rule. First, color classification was equated with the task of partitioning a perceptual space, predefined in terms of hue, saturation, and intensity (thus attenuating the referential range of the color concept as understood by at least some cultures; Conklin 1955). Second, all color categories whose linguistic expression failed to meet certain formal criteria (such as superordination, monolexemic unity) were eliminated from consideration. The consequence of these data attenuation was that 95 percent of the world's expressions for color and most of the world's color categories were dropped from the investigation.

Another application of the data attenuation rule occurred in Sara Nerlove and A. Kimball Romney's (1967) work on universal cognitive processes underlying the formation of sibling terminological systems (for example, in English, the two terms *brother* and *sister*). A major finding of their study was the universal disinclination of the human mind to process disjunctive categories (for example, if a language has two terms for siblings it is rare for it to use one term to refer to *either* older male sibs *or* younger female sibs and the other term for *either* younger male sibs *or* older female sibs). Yet Nerlove and Romney considered only one portion of the referential range of sibling terms, nuclear family referents, putting aside the fact that in many cultures these terms are used disjunctively to refer to *either* full sibs *or* cousins.

———

Universalism's benefits and costs. A major benefit of the universalist stance is the thrill of recognition that comes with identifying a significant point of resemblance. An Azande consults the chicken oracle (see Evans-Pritchard 1937). "Will I be killed on my journey to Z?" The chicken is administered a magical "poison." If the chicken dies it means "yes"; if it lives, "no." The chicken lives. A second chicken is consulted. This time the chicken's survival is taken as a caution to stay at home. But the chicken dies. Reassured, the Azande goes on the journey to Z. He is murdered en route. Do the Azande doubt the veracity of their oracle? No! Instead they explain away the event in one of two ways: counterwitchcraft was being practiced at the time of consultation; or perhaps women, standing too close, had polluted the consultation grounds. Recognizable in these practices are some of the methodological concepts of Western applied science, namely, reliability checks (double consultations), interfering background variables (counterwitchcraft), and measurement error (pollution). The idioms differ, but they are easily overlooked in the light of the recognition that the Azande's search for truth relies on principles not unlike our own.

All too often, however, the pursuit of a higher-order generality is like searching for the "real" artichoke by divesting it of its leaves (Wittgenstein 1968 [1953], paragraph 164). The higher-order sphere is all too often a higher order of vacuity; the air gets very thin.

Consider the concept of justice ("fairness" or "equity"). Stated as a higher-order generality ("Treat like cases alike and different cases differently"), justice is a universal concept. Appreciate, however, the laundered emptiness of this higher-order formulation. As H. L. A. Hart (1961) remarks, the abstract concept of justice "cannot afford any determinate guide to conduct ... This is so because any set of human beings will resemble each other in some respects and differ from each other in others and, until it is established what resemblances and differences are relevant, 'treat like cases alike' must remain an empty form" (p. 155). The fact that Americans deny ten-year-olds the right to vote or to enter into contracts does not violate our abstract concept of justice. Quite the contrary; it indicates that we subscribe to the belief that in certain crucial respects, children are different from adults (for example, they lack the information and judgment to make informed decisions). From a cross-cultural and historical perspective there have been many places in the world where, given received wisdom and without relinquishing the higher-order concept of justice, the difference between male and female, Jew and Christian, Brahman and untouchable, black and white, has seemed as obvious to others as the difference between an adult and a child seems to us. Unfortunately, all these concrete, culture-rich ("thick"; see Geertz 1973) variations in the way people treat each other get bleached out of focus in the higher-order description of justice as an abstract universal. Universality of agreement wanes as we move from higher-order abstract principles to substantive cases.

Application of the data attenuation rule has its costs, as well. These costs are clearly understood by Berlin and Kay (1969), who note: "it has been argued, to our minds convincingly, that to appreciate the full cultural significance of color words it is necessary to appreciate the full range of meanings, both referential and connotative, and not restrict oneself arbitrarily to hue, saturation, and brightness. We thus make no claim—in fact we specifically deny—that our treatment of the various color terminologies presented here is an ethnographically revealing one" (p. 160).

The path traveled by the universalist is rarely the one that leads to ethnographic illumination; only occasionally does it lead to a powerful, context-rich universal generalization. However, when it does it should not be scorned.

Evolutionism

Confronted with the apparent diversity of human understandings, evolutionists rely on a powerful three-stage rule for ordering that variety into a sequence of lower to higher (primitive to advanced, incipient to elaborated) forms: (1) locate a normative model (for example, the canons of propositional calculus, Bayes's rules of statistical inference, Newton's laws of motion, Rawl's theory of justice, Mill's rules for experimental reasoning); (2) treat the normative model as the endpoint of development; (3) describe diverse beliefs and understandings as steps on an ideational Jacob's ladder moving progressively in the direction of the normative endpoint (see, for example, Piaget 1966; Kohlberg 1969, 1971).

The normative model *defines* what it is to have an adequate understanding (for example, given that $P \rightarrow Q$, it is more adequate to conclude $\sim Q \rightarrow \sim P$ than to conclude $\sim P \rightarrow \sim Q$). Variations in thought are ranked in terms of their degree of approximation to the endpoint. The image is one of subsumption, progress, and hierarchical inclusion. Some forms of understanding are described as though they were incipient forms of other understandings, and those other forms of understanding are described as though they can do everything the incipient forms can do plus more (see Figure 3.1a); post-Copernican astronomy replaces pre-Copernican astronomy; experimental logic (Mill's laws of agreement and difference) replaces magical thinking (Frazer's laws of contagion and similarity). If the subsumed, less adequate form of understanding can also be time-dated, that is, linked to early periods in history, to childhood or to both, so much the better.

Evolutionism has its appeal. For one thing, it permits the existence of variety. Instead of searching for higher-order equivalences it takes variety and difference at face value (and tries to assign it a rank). Second, it does provide a yardstick (the normative model) for talking about progress. The vocabulary of the primitive versus modern, adequate versus inept, better versus worse, adaptive versus maladaptive, is highly developed in the evolutionist literature.

However, there is no normative model for many domains of social thought—no way of saying whether one form of understanding is better or worse than another. Which is better: a kinship system in which older and younger brothers are terminologically distinguished, or one in which the distinction is not encoded? The mind boggles at the evolutionary presumption of the question. Which is better: a policy for allocating resources based on the principle "to each equal amounts" or one based on the principle "to each according to his work" (or "to each according to his needs")? There seems to be no *general* answer (see Perelman 1963).

A second difficulty with the evolutionary model is the problem of "presentism," the tendency to perceive the ideas of others through the filter of one's own current concerns. This pattern of perception is diagrammed in Figure 3.1b. It is all too easy unwittingly to rewrite (and distort) the historical and ontogenetic record on others' ideas, dropping out or overlooking problems, ideas, and principles that are no longer of contemporary concern. This is especially true when one's search through the ideas of others is guided by a contemporary nor-

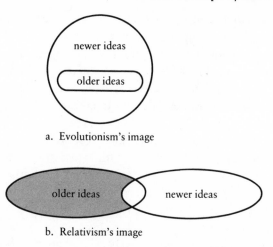

a. Evolutionism's image

b. Relativism's image

Figure 3.1. Evolutionism's and relativism's images of the relationship between historically sequenced ideas (adapted from Feyerabend 1975, pp. 177–178)

mative model. But what if our ideas have succeeded the ideas of others, not through a process of subsumption, betterment, and advance, but merely as a "giving up" on the problems, principles, and concepts of our ancestors (see the hatched-in area of Figure 3.1b). Presentism obscures the historical record, making it appear our ideas can do everything the ideas of our predecessors could do, plus more, when all we may have done is shifted our field of interest and altered the questions to be answered.

Relativism

Confronted with the apparent diversity of human understandings, relativists seek to preserve the integrity of the differences and establish the coequality of the variegated forms of life. Relativists typically process evidence according to two rules: (1) the contextualization rule and (2) the principle of arbitrariness.

The contextualization rule. A primary goal of the relativist is to seek, and display, more and more information about the details of other peoples' objectives, premises, presuppositions, standards, knowledge, meanings, and so on; so much detail that the ideas and conduct of others come to make sense *given* the context (premises, standards).

Thus Ruth Benedict (1946), in her classic analysis of Japanese culture, took bits and pieces of Japanese conduct in World War II—their lack of respect for national sovereignty (for example, the invasion of China and attack on Pearl Harbor), the suicide bombings, the "mistreatment" of American prisoners of war, and so on—and placed them in a conceptual framework (the Japanese understanding of the advantages and necessity of "taking one's proper place" (p. 21) in a domestic, national, and international hierarchy of individuals, groups, and nations) *within which* "militaristic expansionism" was redescribed as an obvious remedy for international anarchy and the "atrocities" of the camps redescribed as a valorous contempt for materialism and scorn of "damaged goods" (p. 39).

The principle of arbitrariness. A closely related goal of the relativist is to show that equally rational individuals can look out on the "same" world and yet arrive at different understandings; the relativist must find a way for reason to leave us a free choice. To the extent that no rule of logic and no law of nature dictates what is proper or necessary for us to believe or value—that is, to the extent there is an element of arbitrariness or free choice in our understandings—to that extent reason is consistent with relativism. Socrates may have been right that the concept of truth implies one, not many, but there are many points in a cognitive structure where questions of truth and falsity, validity, error, and so on are simply beside the point.

Hence the relativist's passionate interest in the types of ideas underlying *non*rational action, ideas that fall beyond the scope of scientific evaluation, such as constitutive presuppositions (Collingwood 1972) (for example, "All behavior is motivated by a desire to maximize pleasure and minimize pain"; what could possibly count as a disproof?), performative utterances (Austin 1962) (for example, "You're fired," "I dub thee . . ."; in such cases the problem of getting one's words to correspond to, or match, reality does not seem to arise) and other declarative speech acts (Searle 1979) (for example, various acts of "definition"), categorical judgments of value (Hempel 1965) (for example, "Killing is evil" and other avowals or expressions of a commitment to a norm of conduct), and, of course, Vilfredo Pareto's "sentiments" (1935).

Hence the relativist's rejection of both the "innocent eye" ("we classify things as we do because that's the way things are") and the "absolute given" ("we classify things the way we do because that's the way people are") (Goodman 1968; parenthetical quotations from

Volney Stefflre, personal communication). For the relativist, knowledge, at its limits, is without foundation; what is of value and importance is a matter of consensus; social "facts" are created, not discovered. The world of the relativist is a world in which objects and events are not classified together because they are more alike than other things; quite the contrary, the relativist argues, objects and events seem to be alike because they have been classified together (Goodman 1972). And why have those people classified things together in that way? That, the relativist will retort, "depends on their purposes." And why do those people pursue the purposes they pursue? That, the relativist will say, is a question for the historian.

Relativism's benefits and costs. Relativism, like universalism and evolutionism, has distinctive benefits and costs. Relativism is consistent with a kind of pluralism or cognitive egalitarianism—a definite benefit, at least for some observers. Relativists provide us with a charitable rendition of the ideas of others, placing those ideas in a framework that makes it easier to credit others, not with confusion, error, or ignorance, but rather with an alternative vision of the possibilities of social life.

Ironically, however, despite its egalitarian intentions relativism lends support to a world based on intellectual domination and power assertion. The relativist views the understandings of others as self-contained, incommensurate, ideational universes ("paradigms"): *across* these universes there is no comparability, no common standard for rational criticism (for example, Rorty 1979). Consequently, people's changes of ideational worlds (which do happen) can be explained by the relativist only in terms of domination, force, or nonrational conversion. And for disagreements between two or more peoples (which often happen) the only means of adjudication is force of arms—there is nothing to discuss. When consensus is the final arbiter of what is real, numbers count, and the powerful and/or the masses have their way.

An Alternative Concept of the Person: The Phenomenon

Many Western observers of some nonwestern peoples have noted a distinctive apperceptive style or mode of social thought that has been variously described as concrete, nonabstractive, nongeneralizing, occasion bound, context specific, undifferentiated, situational.

Robert Levy (1973) illustrates this "concrete style" of social thinking by reference to one of his Tahitian informants, Poria. Poria is asked to define the word *hoa*, which Levy glosses abstractly as "friend." Poria, however, responds by enumerating a list of restricted, context-dependent conditions: "A hoa—we love each other—I come and get you to go to my house so that we may eat together. Sometimes we go and stroll together on the path. Sometimes I go to your house to eat. Sometimes I want you to help me with my work. Sometimes I go to help you. Sometimes we joke with the girls" (p. 24).

Levy notes that "much of village behavior having to do with personal and social description" is marked by an emphasis on "contexts and cases" and is "oriented to richness of detail" (pp. 262, 268). He believes that Poria's thinking and the thinking of most Tahitian villages involves "a calculus in which terms are understood on the basis of a large number of contextual factors" (p. 262). Numerous other observers in Africa, Central America, New Guinea, and Central Asia (for example, Werner and Kaplan 1956; Bruner, Olver, and Greenfield 1966; Piaget 1966; Horton 1967; Greenfield 1972; Luria 1976) concur in the observation that certain cultures perceive things (for example, "an apple found in a store" and "an apple found on the ground") in terms of unique contextual features (for example, time, place, coterminous objects, concurrent events) while failing to generalize across cases or to equate things in terms of cross-contextual invariances (such as the fact that both are apples; see Price-Williams 1975, p. 28). Informants either respond to questions about how things are alike by enumerating the ways in which things are different, or else emphasize the way objects and events fit together in functional complexes or actions sequences, without abstracting a common likeness.

This same style of concrete, contextualized, nonabstractive, apparently undifferentiated thinking is found in various cross-cultural reports about the concept of the person. What is noted is a tendency *not* to abstract a concept of the inviolate personality free of social role and social relationship—a tendency not to separate or distinguish the individual from the social context. Clifford Geertz, for example, asserts that "the Western conception of the person as a bounded, unique, more or less integrated motivational and cognitive universe, a dynamic center of awareness, emotion, judgment, and action organized into a distinctive whole and set contrastively both against other such wholes and against a social and natural background is, however incorrigible it may seem to us, a rather peculiar idea within the context of the world's cultures" (1975, p. 48).

There is, he notes, in Bali

a persistent and systematic attempt to stylize all aspects of personal expression to the point where anything idiosyncratic, anything characteristic of the individual merely because he is who he is physically, psychologically or biographically, is muted in favor of his assigned place in the continuing, and, so it is thought, never-changing pageant that is Balinese life. It is dramatis personae, not actors, that endure; indeed it is dramatis personae, not actors, that in the proper sense really exist. Physically men come and go—mere incidents in a happenstance history of no genuine importance, even to themselves. But the masks they wear, the stage they occupy, the parts they play, and most important, the spectacle they mount remain and constitute not the facade but the substance of things, not least the self. (P. 50)

Twenty years earlier, in a brilliant discussion of morality and personhood, Kenneth Read (1955) spoke in similar terms about the Gahuku-Gama of New Guinea. The Gahuku-Gama conception of man "does not allow for any clearly recognized distinction between the individual and the status which he occupies" (p. 225). The Gahuku-Gama do not distinguish an *ethical* category of the person. They fail "to separate the individual from the social context and, ethically speaking, to grant him an intrinsic moral value apart from that which attaches to him as the occupant of a particular status" (p. 257). The Gahuku-Gama recognize "no common measure of ethical content which would serve as a guide for the moral agent in whatever situation he finds himself" (p. 260). For the Gahuku-Gama, people "are not conceived to be equals in a moral sense; their value does not reside in themselves as individuals or persons; it is dependent on the position they occupy within a system of inter-personal and intergroup relationships" (p. 250). What this means is that for the Gahuku-Gama being human per se "does not necessarily establish a moral bond between individuals, nor does it provide an abstract standard against which all action can be judged" (p. 261). Rather, the "specific context," the particular occasion, "determines the moral character of a particular action" (p. 260). For example, the Gahuku-Gama believe it is wrong to kill members of their own tribe, "but it is commendable to kill members of opposed tribes, always provided they are not related to him. Thus, a man is expected to avoid his maternal kinsmen in battle though other members of his own clan have no such moral obligation to these individuals" (p. 262).

Louis Dumont's (1970) observations on India sound almost redundant. He warns us against "inadvertently attributing the presence of the individual to societies in which he is not recognized" (p. 1), and he points to a relational, contextualized "logic" in which justice con-

sists primarily in "ensuring that the proportions between social functions [and social roles] are adapted to the whole [that is, society as a
primary, not derivative, object]" (p. 94).

Geertz, Read, and Dumont contrast Bali, New Guinea, and India
with a Western mode of social thought in which the individual is abstracted from the social role, and the moral responsibilities of this
abstracted, inviolate individual are distinguished from his or her social responsibilities and duties. Read puts it this way: In the West "the
moral duties of the person are greater than any of the duties which
the individual possesses as a member of society. His moral responsibilities, both to himself and others, transcend the given social context,
are conceived to be independent of the social ties which link him to
his fellows" (1955, p. 280).

In the West, as Lionel Trilling so aptly remarks, the person, inviolate in his self-image, supposes that he is "an object of interest to his
fellow man not for the reason that he had achieved something notable
or been witness to great events but simply because as an individual he
is of consequence" (1972, p. 24).

How are we to interpret this widespread mode of social thought in
which the individual is not differentiated from the role, and in which
the person achieves no abstract, context-independent recognition?

The Person in Context: Evolutionary and Universalist
Interpretations

The Evolutionary Account

In keeping with their respect for intellectual variety and their desire
to rank diverse forms along a scale of progress, evolutionary theorists
argue that concrete, occasion-bound thinking (in both the social and
nonsocial domains) is unequally distributed across cultures and can
be explained by reference to one or four types of cognitive "deficits,"
namely, the absence of (1) cognitive skills, (2) intellectual motivations,
(3) pertinent information, or (4) linguistic tools.

Deficit 1: Cognitive skills. Alexander Luria's (1976) work illustrates
the evolutionary emphasis on the absence of cognitive skills. He argues that "for some people abstract classification is a wholly alien
procedure," and he suggests that illiterate, unschooled peasants in the
Uzbekistan and Kirghizan regions of Central Asia lack the *skill* to
"isolate (abstract) a common feature" of things "as a basis for com-

parison" (pp. 60, 80–81). Luria credits schools with fostering the ability to abstract, to generalize, and to think scientifically (see also Bruner, Olver, and Greenfield 1966; Greenfield 1972; Goody 1977).

Lawrence Kohlberg (1969, 1971) adopts a similar approach. His evolutionary scheme for the ethical category of the person would account for the occasion-bound, socially contextualized person concept of the Balinese, Gahuku-Gama, and Hindu by locating it as a stage in the evolution of an adequate moral orientation in which respect for the abstract person transcends social roles. Thus, for example, the Gahuku-Gama view that the moral value of life cannot be separated from the social status of a person, and the cognate view that in a "catastrophe" important people, people of status, should be saved first, would be interpreted by Kohlberg as an early, childlike form of understanding, an initial step on the ladder ascending to the more mature recognition of universal respect for the value of life per se. For Kohlberg, movement through the stages of his evolutionary scheme is ultimately explained by reference to the development of certain cognitive processing skills, such as the abilities to differentiate, to take the perspective of another, and to generalize.

Deficit 2: Intellectual motivation. Levy's (1973) work illustrates the evolutionary emphasis on intellectual motivation instead of cognitive skill. Levy interprets concrete thinking as an adaptation to life in a "cultural cocoon." Tahitian villagers, he argues, are deeply "embedded" in their own mundane daily contexts. They are not *motivated* to reflect upon the alternative cultural practices that surround them (for example, the Chinese), nor do they have any *need* to locate their own customs conceptually in a more general comparative framework. Levy speculates that such contextual embeddedness is "not conducive to science [and abstraction]" (pp. 269–270).

Deficit 3: Pertinent information. Robin Horton's (1967) evolutionary interpretation explains concrete thinking by reference to informational limitations. Contextual embeddedness, he argues, is primarily a cognitive concomitant of living in a "closed intellectual predicament" (p. 155), one too limited in opportunities to become aware of alternative visions of reality. Informational opportunities wax with the development of external trade, literacy, and urbanization, and thus these three conditions, Horton argues, are conducive to the development of abstract modes of thought. Super, Harkness, and Baldwin (1977) also discuss the informational conditions favoring abstract thought and conclude that cultures that are "materially simple will rarely require [abstract] categorical organization" (p. 5).

Deficit 4: Linguistic tools. It has occasionally been suggested that concrete thinkers are speakers of impoverished languages, that is, languages lacking general terms as a symbolic resource (for example, Jesperson 1934). Thus, in Tasmanian each variety of gum-tree and wattle-tree has a name, but there is no equivalent for the expression *a tree,* while in Bororo (the classic illustration) each parrot has its special name, but the general lexical entry *parrot* is absent. Deficient in their symbolic resources, lacking general terms, speakers of such languages are said to be prone to overlook the likenesses between things; hence the failure to abstract.

The Universalist Account

Whereas evolutionary theorists argue that some peoples are distinctively concrete in their thinking, as a result of deficits in cognitive processing skills, intellectual motivation, pertinent information, or requisite tools, universalists are skeptical of the claim that some peoples are concrete thinkers, others abstract thinkers. From the perspective of the universalist, attributions of differential concreteness (or abstractness) by one people about another are illusory and amount to little more than an indication that the category system of the observers fails to align with the category system of the people observed.

There are three claims implicit in the universalist interpretation of concrete and abstract thinking. First, it is argued that apparent evidence of concrete and abstract thinking is *equally* present in all cultures (concrete versus abstract thinking is not a variable that can be used to distinguish one culture from another). Second, it is argued that the attribution of concreteness or abstractness to other people's thinking is the inevitable result of the confrontation between uncalibrated conceptual systems. More specifically, the universalist argues, we describe other people's thinking as concrete when they overlook likenesses or truths that we emphasize; we describe their thinking as abstract when they emphasize likenesses or truths that we overlook. Finally, it is argued that since no one conceptual system can take note of, or encode, all possible likenesses or record all possible truths, where conceptual systems clash there will always be areas of *both* apparent concreteness and apparent abstractness. The works of

Alfred Kroeber (1909) and Charles Frake (1962) illustrate the universalist interpretation.

Frake's (1962) universalist argument was advanced against the evolutionary view of Jens Jesperson (1934) that the mind of the "primitive" is concrete (overlooks likenesses) in its classification of flora and fauna. Ironically, Kroeber's (1909) universalist argument was advanced against the opposite evolutionary view (Morgan 1871) that the mind of the "primitive" is excessively abstract (overlooks differences) in its classification of kinsmen (for example, a father-in-law and a grandfather are similarly labeled in the Dakota language).

It would be a mistake to conclude from this irony that primitive terminological systems are concrete when it comes to plants and animals yet abstract for kinsmen. Rather, the main point of the universalist interpretation is that the contrast between concrete and abstract systems of classification is an *illusion* that

> has its origin in the point of view of investigators, who, on approaching foreign languages, have been impressed with their failure to discriminate certain relationships [for example father-in-law and grandfather] between which the languages of civilized Europe distinguish, and who, in the enthusiasm of formulating general [evolutionary] theories from such facts, have forgotten that their own languages are filled with entirely analogous groupings or classifications which custom has made so familiar and natural that they are not felt as such [for example, the difference between cousins older and younger than oneself]. (Kroeber 1909, p. 77)

Frake (1962) made a similar point. He remarked that there is "no necessary reason" for other people to heed those particular attributes that, for the English-speaker, make equivalent all the diverse individual organisms that she or he labels "parrots" (p. 75; see Findley 1979). As Frake noted, any comparison of unaligned category systems will reveal cases in which others' thought seems quite concrete (they overlook likenesses that we emphasize) *as well as* cases in which their thought seems quite abstract (they emphasize likenesses that we overlook).

Having described the "logic" of universalist, evolutionary, and relativist understandings of other people's understandings and characterized the evolutionary and universalist interpretations of concrete, context-dependent, occasion-bound thinking, we now focus on a specific example of concrete thinking, that is, occasion-bound *social* thinking, more particularly, the concept of the context-dependent person. In presenting the results of a cross-cultural study of person description in India and the United States, we display our reasons for rejecting the evolutionary and universalist interpretations of the context-dependent person concept. According to our alternative, relativist interpretation, the context-dependent concept of the person is one aspect of a broader sociocentric "organic" (or holistic) conception of the relationship of the individual to society. Holistic thinking considers that "units" (organs, body parts, groups, individuals, and so on) are necessarily altered by the relations into which they enter (Phillips 1976). We argue that concrete thinking (as a general phenomenon) is a by-product of the commitment to a holistic world view, and we discuss the implications of the sociocentric organic conception of the individual-social relationship for the developing ego's view of its self.

Contexts and Cases: A Study of Person Description in India and the United States

It is by reference to contexts and cases that Oriyas in the old town of Bhubaneswar (Orissa, India) describe the personalities of their friends, neighbors, and workmates. These personal accounts are concrete and relational. Oriyas tell you what someone has done; behavioral instances are often mentioned. They tell you where it was done. They tell you to whom or with whom it was done. The descriptive attention of Oriyas is directed toward the behavioral context in which particular behavioral instances occurred; for example, "Whoever becomes his friend, he remembers him forever, and will always help him out of his troubles"; "has no cultivable land, but likes to cultivate the land of others"; "when a quarrel arises, cannot resist the temptation of saying a word"; "will talk right in the face of even a British Governor"; "comes forward whenever there is an occasion to address a public meeting"; "behaves properly with guests but feels sorry if money is spent on them."

This concrete-relational way of thinking about other people differs from the abstract style of our American informants. Americans tell you what is true of a person's behavior (for example, "He's friendly, arrogant, and intelligent") while tending to overlook behavioral context. As we shall see, the striking tendency of Oriyas to be more concrete and relational than Americans does not readily lend itself to evolutionary interpretation in terms of relative amounts of formal schooling, degrees of literacy, relative socioeconomic status, the presence or absence of abstract terms in one's language, the absence of skills of abstraction among Oriyas, or relative awareness of alternative behavioral contexts or variations in behavior. The concrete-relational style of Oriya social thought seems unrelated to variations in cognitive skill, intellectual motivation, available information, and linguistic resources. By elimination, we are led to consider the way a culture's world view and master metaphors per se influence the relationship between what one thinks about and how one thinks. We consider differences in Indian and American conceptualizations of the relationship of the individual and society with special reference to the sociocentric organic versus egocentric reductionist view of "person-in-society."

Methodology

INFORMANTS

The seventeen informants in the American sample came from three separate groups: counseling psychologists (three women, two men), a college fraternity (six men), and nursery school teachers (six women). Members of each group had known each other for at least one year. Their ages ranged from nineteen to forty-seven, and all had received or were about to complete a college education. All lived in or around Chicago and were predominantly middle-class.

The seventy Indian informants resided in the old town of Bhubaneswar, Orissa. They were selected on the basis of caste criteria as part of a general inquiry into household composition and caste interaction patterns. Thus, the full range of the local caste hierarchy was represented. All but two of the Oriyas were males, and they spanned a wider age range (eighteen to seventy) than the Americans. Educational variability was also greater, ranging from no formal education to a master's degree. Seventeen informants had no education at all. Eighteen were illiterate.

Caste, formal schooling, and literacy were not unrelated in the Indian sample. Informants from the lower castes tend to be less educated and illiterate, but a number of informants from the upper castes were literate but relatively unschooled. The confounding of caste, literacy, and schooling in the sample is less worrisome than it might at first appear. The cultural differences in concrete-relational thinking, reported below, are stable across the entire Indian sample and do not vary by caste, education, or literacy. Unschooled, illiterate untouchables and highly educated, literate Brahmans differ from Americans in the same way and do not significantly differ from each other.

THE TASK

Informants in both populations responded to the task of describing a close acquaintance. However, in the Indian group each informant described up to three friends, neighbors, or workmates, whereas in the American group each described the other four or five members of his or her group. There were also slight differences in the instructions and format of the descriptive task between the two cultures, an inevitable consequence of the fact that they had originally been associated with independent studies. Indian informants were presented with the instructions (in Oriya): "Tell me in depth about so-and-so's character, nature [personality], and behavior," whereas Americans were asked: "How would you characterize so-and-so's personality?" Indians could respond in as many or few ways as they chose (they averaged seven to eight descriptive phrases), whereas Americans were asked to provide twenty descriptive sentences or phrases. Finally, Indians responded orally while Americans wrote out their description.

Because these procedural differences could have interacted with the cultural difference observed on the various dependent variables (see results section), the following *ex post facto* study was done with a sample of ten Americans. Informants were divided into two groups and given one or the other of the two instructions mentioned above. In each of these groups some informants were permitted to make as many responses as they wished, the others told to give twenty responses. All responses were given orally. While the different instructions had a slight, statistically nonsignificant effect on the tendency of informants to give concrete or abstract descriptions, this effect was nominal in comparison with that associated with cultural differences, as reported in the results section.

THE CODING OF DESCRIPTIONS

To facilitate coding, all descriptions were broken down into constituent sentences. A compound or complex sentence was further broken down into units, each of which contained no more than one subject-predicate-object sequence. These units were subsequently referred to as descriptive phrases. Each descriptive phrase was typed on a three-by-five-inch card. In this fashion a total of 3,451 descriptive phrases for both cultures was obtained.

A coding system was developed to enable judges to decide on the presence or absence of a number of features related to concrete thinking, in particular (1) descriptive reference to abstract traits; (2) descriptive reference to concrete action; (3) descriptive incorporation of contextual qualifications.

An abstract trait reference (abbreviated T) was operationally defined as any attribute that answered the question "What kind of person *is* the ratee?" The judgment was made independently of the presence or absence of contextual qualifications in the descriptive phrase. Thus "She is stubborn" or "She is stubborn about family matters" would both be coded T, although the final coding for the two phrases would differ in the specification of additional contextual qualifiers.

An action reference (A) answered the question "Is this something the ratee does?" This judgment also was made independently of the presence or absence of contextual qualifiers. Thus, "She uses dirty language" and "She uses dirty language when her friends give her advice about family matters" would both be coded A, although they differ in the specification of additional contextual qualifiers.

Pure emotive-evaluative terms (TE) such as "He is a good man" were not considered traits (T) in our final analysis. One reason for drawing the distinction was the reference to (moral) character in the Oriya instructions. This tended to elicit a ritualized initial response from most informants. They would first say, "He is a good man" or "He is not a good man," and then go on with their description. TE phrases in both the American and Oriya descriptions were dropped from the analysis discussed below. The total number of descriptive phrases actually analyzed numbered 3,209 (1,524 Oriya, 1,685 American).

Contextual qualifications were coded under the following categories:

Personal Reference:

reference to a specific individual, often denoted by a proper or common noun (for example, "He gets angry with his father"), coded $P1$

reference to a specific group of others (for example, "He makes fun of his family"), coded $P2$

reference to people or others in general (for example, "He is honest with others"), coded $P3$

reflexive reference to the person being described (for example, "He gets angry with himself"), coded SR

reference to the rater (for example, "He gets angry with me"), coded RR

Qualification:

temporal: statement of when or how frequently the attribute occurs (for example, "Last year he did favors frequently"), coded "time"

locale: statement of where or in what location the attribute occurs (for example, "At school she puts on a front"), coded "place"

general qualification: any statement of the conditions under which an attribute occurs or obtains (for example, "He gets irritable if provoked"), coded "qual"

inferential qualification: statement of the conditions under which the *rater* makes the attribution (for example, "judging from what others say, he is reserved"), coded "inf"

any phrase that states an action, trait, and so on *without* qualification, coded "Noqual."

A coding category called "Miscellaneous Types" allowed us to make more refined judgments about the presence or absence of references to traits or actions:

Miscellaneous Types:

what the ratee likes (L or LA)

wants, seeks, or desires (D or DA)

experiences (E or EA)

feels (F or FA)

is interested in (I or IA)

is capable of or able to do (C or CA)

values (V or VA)

what type of person the ratee is (for example, "He's a joker. "He's a friend) (R)

the social role the ratee fills (for example, "He's a leader," "He's a teacher") (R social)

the physical characteristics of the ratee (Phys)

The coding system provided explicit criteria, with positive examples, for the identification of all the preceding categories. Phrases that were refractory to any of the categories were coded "questionable" (?). Here are two examples of a descriptive phrase and its coding according to the system above: "He jokes with his friends" (A, P2); "She is stubborn" (T, Noqual).

Two composite categories consisting of combinations of those listed above were also defined, arranged along two dimensions of abstractness/concreteness. Following Levy (1973), we labeled them "Cases" and "Contexts."

> *Cases:* The contrast between trait-type references (*T, R,* or *R*Social) (for example, "He is a leader") and action references (*A, LA,* or *DA*) (for example, "He lends people money").
>
> *Contexts:* The contrast between context-free references ("Noqual) (for example, "He is verbally abusive") and context-dependent references (*P1, P2, P3,* time, or place) (for example, "He is verbally abusive to his father-in-law whenever they meet at his home").

RELIABILITY AND THE DETERMINATION OF
CONSENSUAL CODINGS

Four judges, all graduate students, were trained to use the coding system. At least two judges independently coded all 3,451 phrases comprising the basic data. In a majority of cases three or all four of the judges coded the phrase.

Judges were originally asked to provide a first, second, third, or more alternative codings of a phrase in cases in which they felt some ambiguity about the correct coding. Only the first coding of each judge was used in our study. If anything, this reduced intercoder agreement (reliability) from what it would have been if the "closest" codings of a phrase among all of the two, three, or four judges' several alternatives had been used.

For the final data analysis it was necessary to arrive at a single, common coding for each phrase. Two alternative procedures suggested themselves at this point: (1) judges might discuss the discrepancies among their independent codings for each phrase and achieve a consensus, or (2) a mechanical procedure could be used to derive a "consensual coding" from among the two to four alternatives for each phrase. The latter procedure was chosen, both in order to save the time that would be involved in having judges reconcile their differences for each of the 3,451 phrases, and to ensure that an identical impartial procedure would be applied to each set of alternative codings for a phrase.

A computer program was devised to consider the alternative codings for a particular phrase and include in the final, consensual coding any category (trait, action, personal reference, and so on) that occurred in all or a majority of independent codings (two out of two or three, three out of three or four, and four out of four). Thus, if four judges' codings of a particular item were (1) *T, P3*, time, qual; (2) *T, P1*, qual; (3) *R, P3*, qual; and (4) *T*, qual, the consensual coding would be *T*, qual.

Out of a total of 3,451 phrases, this procedure achieved a consensual coding for 3,290 phrases, or 95 percent of the corpus. This result in itself suggests a relatively high level of interjudge agreement. Interjudge reliability was measured more precisely, however, by determining how many of the judgments of any of the coders were represented in the consensual coding. Thus, in the example above the two categories comprising the consensual coding—*T* and qual—occur seven times among the various alternative codings. Since the total number of instances of all categories among the alternatives is 12, it follows that 7/12, or approximately 58 percent, of the alternative codings are represented in the consensual coding. In brief, this particular reliability index estimated the proportion of variance among the alternative codings that was "common" or consensual.

Over the interjudge reliability estimates for the total of 3,290 phrases for which consensual codings were obtained, the mean estimate was found to be 77 percent. This level of agreement seems both satisfactory and surprising, given the difficulty the judges reported in applying the coding system.

DATA ANALYSIS

With the consensual codings of phrases available, it was possible to compare the frequency and proportion of occurrence of any category between the two cultures or among caste, literacy, or educational groups in the Indian sample. This constituted the first step of the data analysis.

Chi-square tests were performed to test the significance of the difference in frequencies observed for each comparison from the expected frequency. The major results are reported in the following section.

In the second step of the data analysis we examined the relationship between the two composite categories representing the "cases" and "contexts" dimensions of abstraction. Each dimension was dichotomized. The "cases" dimension was scored 1 or 0 depending upon whether a particular phrase contained a trait, type, or social-role attribution (*T, R, Rsocial*) or any of the action attributions included under the composite category (*A, LA, DA*). The "contexts" dimension was scored 1 if the phrase contained any instance of the categories P1, P2, P3, time, or place, and 0 if it contained no qualification (coded Noqual).

Results

CONTEXTS

Oriyas are more likely to say "She brings cakes to my family on festival days." Americans are more likely to say "She is friendly." Contextual qualifications having to do with personal reference ($P1$, $P2$, $P3$), time, and place each occur significantly more often in Oriya descriptions of personality ($p = <.001$ for all five variables). American descriptions are noteworthy for the frequency of descriptions that are entirely unqualified by context (Noqual) ($p = <.001$). There are two exceptions. Americans use more self-referential qualifiers (SR) (for example, "She is beginning to accept herself," "He is hard on himself") than Oriyas ($p = <.001$). Americans also use more inferential qualifiers (inf) (for example, "Judging from what others say, he is very reserved") ($p = <.001$).

Measured in terms of the composite "contexts" variable (P_1, P_2, P_3, time, place, vs. Noqual), the ratio of context-free to context-dependent phrases is 3 to 1 in the American descriptions and 1 to 1 in the Oriya descriptions.

CASES

Oriyas tell you what someone has done (for example, "He curses at his neighbors"). The emphasis is upon behavioral occurrences or "cases." Americans tell you what is true of what someone has done (for example, "He is aggressive and hostile"). Americans describe personality by means of trait (T) (for example, "friendly") and type (R) (for example, "a friend") concepts ($p = <.001$). Oriyas describe personality by reference to actions (A, LA, DA) ($p = <.01$ for all three variables). The only time Americans are more likely than Oriyas to mention what someone does is when they describe a person's capabilities (CA; $p = <.05$) or interests (LA; $p = <.01$).

Measured in terms of the composite "cases" variable (A, LA, DA versus T, R, $RSocial$), the ratio of abstractions to actions is 3 to 1 in the American descriptions but only 1 to 1.8 in the Oriya descriptions.

CONTEXTS AND CASES

Case reference and context reference are not entirely independent descriptive acts, although their associational relationship, while statistically significant ($p = <.001$), is only weak to modest (phi $= .30$ for the Oriyas and .18 for the Americans). The relationship can be summarized as follows: There is a greater tendency to contextualize descriptions that make reference to a behavioral case. One is more likely to contextualize "He curses" [his mother-in-law] than "He is aggressive" [to his mother-in-law]. "He is aggressive" is more likely to stand alone.

Discussion

Oriyas are more concrete than Americans in their descriptions of personality. Eighty percent of Oriya descriptions are either contextually qualified ($P1$, $P2$, $P3$, time, place) or make reference to a behavioral instance (A, LA, DA) (in contrast to 56 percent for the Americans). Forty-six percent of American descriptions are *both* context free (Noqual) and abstract (T, R, $RSocial$) (in contrast to 20 percent for the Oriyas). This result compares favorably with the findings of Susan Fiske and Martha Cox (1979). When American informants were asked to describe someone "so that someone else would know what it's like to be around this person," 40 percent of the items were abstract traits. Trait attributions were twice as frequent as references to behavioral patterns.

How is this cross-cultural difference in the thinking of Americans and Oriyas to be explained? We believe that each of the following plausible evolutionary hypotheses is *not* supported by the evidence.

Hypothesis 1: The Oriyas have less formal schooling than the Americans. Therefore, they are more concrete.

Formal schooling is often viewed by evolutionary theorists as a condition for the development of skills of abstraction (for example, Bruner, Olver, and Greenfield 1966; Luria 1976). Considered as an aggregate, the Oriyas are less educated than the Americans. Twenty-four percent of the Oriya descriptive phrases came from informants who had never been to school; 65 percent came from informants with less than three years of schooling. Nevertheless, the relative concreteness of the Oriya personality descriptions is not related to this difference in education. Table 3.1 shows that the descriptive phrases elicited from Oriyas with an educational level comparable to the Americans' (beyond high school) are more concrete than the American descriptive phrases. In the Oriyan sample, concreteness does not significantly vary across educational levels for either "cases" or "con-

Table 3.1 The relative emphasis on contexts and cases in the descriptive phrases of all Americans, all Oriyas, and various subgroups of Oriyas

	All Americans	Oriyas						
		All Oriyas	Beyond high school	No school	Literate	Illiterate	Brahmans	Bauris
Contexts								
Context-dependent (*P1, P2, P3,* time, place)	28.3%	49.6%	48.3%	51.8%	48.4%	53.2%	50.6%	50.4%
Context-free (*Noqual*)	71.7%	50.4%	51.7%	48.2%	51.4%	46.8%	49.4%	49.6%
N =	1685	1505	215	357	1135	370	494	244
Cases								
Actions (*A, DA, LA*)	25.4%	64.8%	58.8%	66.7%	64.6%	65.5%	66.1%	70.1%
Abstractions (*T, R, RSocial*)	74.6%	35.2%	41.2%	33.3%	35.4%	34.5%	33.9%	29.9%
N =	1333	1194	117	282	901	293	392	201

texts." Concrete thinking in the personality domain transcends variations in formal schooling experience. (See Table 3.2.)

Hypothesis 2: The literacy level of the Oriyas is less than the Americans'. Therefore, they are more concrete.

Literacy is often cited by evolutionary theorists as a condition for the development of skills of abstraction (for example, Greenfield 1972; Luria 1976; Goody 1977). The overall literacy level of the Oriyas is certainly less than the Americans'; 25 percent of the Oriya descriptive phrases were elicited from entirely illiterate informants. Nevertheless, this relative difference in literacy levels does not explain the relative concreteness of Oriya descriptions of personality. Literate and illiterate Oriyas do not significantly differ in the relative concreteness of their personality descriptions for either "cases" or "contexts." Concrete thinking in the personality domain transcends variations in literacy in Orissa. Moreover, if the illiterate Oriya informants are eliminated from the sample, the difference in concrete thinking between Americans and literate Oriyas continues to be significant. (See Table 3.1.)

Hypothesis 3: The Oriyas are of lower socioeconomic status than the Americans. Therefore, they are more concrete.

Social and economic impoverishment is sometimes cited by evolutionary theorists as a condition retarding the development of skills of abstraction (for example, Luria 1976). Considered as an aggregate, the Oriya sample is probably of lower socioeconomic status than the American. We say "probably" because the notion of relative socioeconomic status is difficult to apply in a comparison of India and the United States. A high-status Brahman can be relatively impoverished without serious threat to his or her caste position. Wealthy and powerful informants can come from middle-level or even relatively low-status castes. However, since 16 percent of the descriptive phrases came from Bauris, an untouchable caste "scheduled" by the government for affirmative action, and since these informants were uniformly impoverished, it seems safe to conclude that by most standards the Oriyas, as an aggregate, are not as high status as the Americans.

Socioeconomic status, an elusive cross-cultural yardstick, does not seem to explain the relative difference in concrete thinking in the personality domain between the two cultures. In Orissa, concrete thinking does not vary by caste status for either "cases" or "contexts." A

Table 3.2 The relative emphasis on contexts and cases across Oriya educational levels

	Formal schooling				
	None	1–3 years	4–7	8–11 years	Beyond high school
Contexts					
Context-dependent (P_1, P_2, P_3, time, place)	51.8%	50.0%	48.2%	49.6%	48.4%
Context-free (Noqual)	48.2%	50.0%	51.8%	50.4%	51.6%
N =	357	328	455	125	215
Cases					
Actions (A, LA, DA)	66.7%	62.5%	68.2%	64.4%	58.8%
Abstractions (T, R, RSocial)	33.3%	37.5%	31.8%	35.6%	41.2%
N =	282	259	349	104	177

comparison of Brahman informants with American informants continues to reveal a cultural difference in concrete thinking. Brahman informants differ little from the overall Oriyan sample. In fact, the truly remarkable feature of Tables 3.1 and 3.2 is the stability of the evidence of concrete thinking across all the Oriyan subsamples. In Orissa the concrete style of personality description transcends variations in education, literacy, and caste.

Hypothesis 4: Concrete-abstract thinking is a global cognitive process variable that distinguishes Oriyas from Americans. Oriyas lack the skill to abstract or generalize across cases.

Hypothesis 5: The Oriya language lacks general terms with which to refer to individual differences in behavior. Therefore, Oriyas are deficient in linguistic resources for generating abstract descriptions of personality.

An investigation carried out by Shweder (1972) makes it apparent that hypotheses 4 and 5 are not very helpful. The study concerned the influence of preexisting conceptual schemes and taxonomic structures on judgment and included a subset of descriptive phrases elicited from Oriya informants. The results revealed the ability of these informants to generate and intellectually manipulate abstract behavioral descriptions, and to recognize and utilize conceptual likenesses among them.

Ninety-nine representative descriptive phrases were written on cards and presented to forty-three Brahman informants from the community whose concrete style of personality description we have been discussing. Most of the phrases were concrete; that is, they were either case-specific or contextually qualified or both (see Shweder 1972, pp. 56–60, for a complete list). Each informant was asked to sort the descriptive phrases into piles, placing together in the same pile items that might "go together" in the same person. Each informant was then asked to name or label the piles he had created. Informants were free to make as many piles as they liked and to place as many descriptive phrases in each pile as they wished. After making an initial sorting and labeling their piles, informants were asked to collapse their piles into fewer, more general piles and to name or label the new piles. This process of collapsing groupings of phrases and naming new groupings went on as long as the informant was willing to produce fewer and fewer piles, with more and more descriptive phrases in each.

The sorting task successfully generated abstract and general terms (trait and type concepts) for describing personality from every informant: 420 different abstract trait and type terms were generated. English translations of 81 of these terms are shown in Figure 3.2 (see Shweder 1972, pp. 65–66, for the original Oriya terms). A casual perusal of G. C. Praharaj's seven-volume lexicon of the Oriya language (1931–1940) should dissuade anyone who believes that the Oriya informants speak a language that lacks abstract personality trait and type concepts.

Oriya informants have no difficulty recognizing and arranging things in terms of overarching conceptual likenesses. This was most clearly revealed by a second sorting task study. Eighty-one personality trait and type concepts (see Figure 3.2) were selected to represent the 420 terms that had been generated in the first sorting task. They were written on cards and presented to twenty-five Brahman informants in the community. The sorting task was identical with the one described above, except that informants were also asked to indicate which items in each pile were exemplary instances of the concept suggested by the pile. After an initial sorting they were asked to construct progressively abstract hierarchies or taxonomies by collapsing the initial piles into progressively smaller numbers of general categories. Each time they were asked to label (or describe) the categories. (See Shweder 1972, appendix 1, for the hierarchies of all twenty-five informants.)

A measure of association between all possible pairs of eighty-one terms was calculated on the basis of sorting task data. The particular measure has been described by Michael Burton (1968, pp. 81–84). It is a normal variate score that is sensitive to three indices of "proximity" between a pair of terms. The primary index of proximity is the number of times two terms are placed together in the same pile. This simple frequency count is adjusted to the number of terms in the pile in question (the larger the pile, the less proximate the two terms) and the total number of piles made by the particular informant (the fewer the piles, the less proximate the two terms). The final measure of association is a Z score. It was calculated by using each level in the hierarchy of each informant as if it were the sorting task of a different informant. The measure was thus based on seventh-three partitionings of the eighty-one terms into piles. Subsequent analysis revealed that a simple frequency count of the number of times two items appear together in a pile over each of the hierarchical levels of each of the informants correlates .98 (Pearson r) with the Z score used in our analysis.

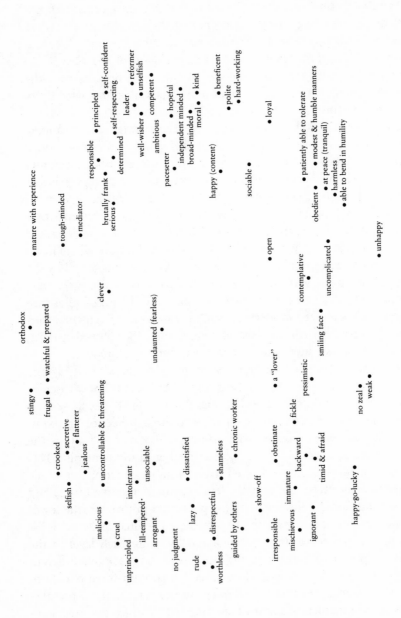

Figure 3.2. Two-dimensional scaling solution for Oriya personality terms

The matrix of association among all possible pairs of eighty-one terms generated from the second sorting task was scaled in two-dimensional space by using the multidimensional scaling program (MDSCALE) devised by Donald C. Olivier. A two-dimensional spatial representation of the associational relationships among the eighty-one terms is shown in Figure 3.2.

The scaling solution demonstrates that the Oriya informants consistently classified the terms on the basis of two independent underlying conceptual likenesses that they abstracted from the eighty-one terms. The vertical axis in Figure 3.2 is interpretable as a "dominance vs. submission" (or "power") dimension. The horizontal axis is interpretable as a "social desirability" dimension. In its abstractness, generality, and dimensional content the Oriya scaling solution in figure 3.2 is comparable to the conceptual organization of the personality domain discovered in America (see, for example, Leary and Coffey 1955; Lorr and McNair 1963, 1965; also see White 1980 on the possible universality of the scaling solution in Figure 3.2). Figure 3.2 suggests that the concreteness displayed by the Oriya informants when they freely described personality or answered a request for information about someone's character, personality (nature), and behavior is *not* an indication of a deficit in the cognitive skills of abstraction and generalization. Hypotheses 4 and 5 must be rejected.

Hypothesis 6: Oriyas live in a "closed" intellectual environment in which they never have to confront alternative customs, behavioral styles, or viewpoints. Abstract thinking (the search for likenesses between diverse phenomena) presupposes that one has access to information about variant phenomena and different perspectives. Oriyas, lacking such information, are disinclined to abstract or generalize across cases.

Hypothesis 6 can be construed at a global level or at a level that is specific to the way Oriyas freely describe personality. At a global level it might be argued that Oriyas are so culturally insulated that they ought to display concrete thinking in all domains. We have already discussed the evidence that has led us to reject the notion that Oriyas lack the ability to abstract (hypothesis 4). There are also a number of features of life in the old town of Bhubaneswar and India in general that make it difficult to entertain seriously the hypothesis that Oriyas live in a "closed" informational environment.

There are twenty-four Oriya castes (including five major Brahman subcastes) represented in the residential wards and quarters of the old town of Bhubaneswar. There is considerable consensus concerning the relative status position of these castes, a judgment that takes into account the relative "purity" of the customs and behavior of a caste community. The concept of a caste hierarchy itself presupposes (1) an awareness of the diverse life styles of interdependent communities (for example, do they eat meat, let their widows remarry, cut their own hair, wash their own clothes?); (2) the ability to evaluate and rank caste communities in terms of the common yardstick of purity (see, for example, Dumont 1970). India is a land where diversity has always been accommodated by means of the sophisticated device of explicit hierarchical interdependence. Oriyas, evolutionists to the core, encourage diversity and rank it.

Caste disputes over relative status are common events in Orissa. Whenever they occur, one has the opportunity to observe social cognition in action over matters of importance to the participants. What one sees is a keen sensitivity to behavioral variations and to the way those behavioral variations will be judged from a third-person perspective, for example, by a particular outside community or by the general community.

A characteristic pattern of Oriyan social thought surfaces in disputes over the relative status of caste communities. Consider a typical instance. Three untouchable castes are involved in a dispute over the relative status of the two lowest. The issue at stake is simply, "Who is the lowest of the low?" In order of relative purity the cast of castes includes community A (washermen), community B (agricultural laborers), and community C (scavengers, basketmakers, and drummers). A's wash other people's dirty linen. The "unclean" nature of this work guarantees their untouchable status. Nevertheless, A's are unquestionably higher in rank than either of the other two communities; their relative superiority is asserted and in part constituted by their refusal to wash B or C clothing. B's and C's are too impure even for the A's. The A's are the highest of the untouchable castes. Their superiority was never assailed in the dispute that arose between the B's and C's. In fact, the competitive status claims of the B's and C's could be resolved only because both communities accepted unquestionably the A's perspective on matters of purity. At the time the dispute surfaced, the C's were generally thought to be the most "polluted" of all the castes. Their caste position was asserted and in part constituted by their traditional activity of cleaning the latrines (and thus handling excrement) in the wards of other castes. But then events got underway.

1. The status ploy by the C's. They refuse to clean the latrines in the B ward, thus symbolically asserting their superiority. The move is effective. The B's have a serious dilemma. Either the B's must let their ward latrines accumulate excrement, thereby polluting their neighborhoods, associating themselves with filth, confirming their untouchable status, and aggravating an already unpleasant living condition, or else they must clean their own latrines, thereby sacrificing the one taboo or restraint they have to their credit that distinguishes them from the C's in the eyes of outside communities. What to do?

2. B–A status negotiations. B representatives approach representatives of the A community. They seek a trump card to use against the C's. In fact, they seek no less than to convince the A's to wash their clothes. "Impossible," assert the A's. "Your linen would pollute us and disgrace our community." The B's persist. They remind the A's that without the B's, A weddings could not take place. B's blow the conch shell at A weddings; they threaten to withdraw. The ploy is effective. Either the A's must cease marrying their children (which is no option) or else they must blow the conch shell themselves or find someone else to do it (Would it really be a wedding?).

3. B–A compromise. A compromise is struck. The A's will wash B clothing. Not all B clothing. Not even most B clothing. They will wash the ritual clothing that B performers wear in one particular religious ceremony on one particular day. It is reasoned that ritual cloth is not polluted even if worn by a B. The B's are pleased. At least the A's wash their clothing on some occasion. They never wash the C's clothes (as the C's are soon to be informed, and redundantly reminded). The A's are pleased. They can continue marrying their daughters at no cost to their community's status. And the C's? They go back to cleaning the latrines in the B ward. The absence of diversity and the nonrecognition of alternative perspectives is just not an Indian problem.

However, hypothesis 6 might be construed narrowly. It might be argued that Americans are more likely to experience their intimates in diverse behavioral settings, and thus are more likely to abstract a common feature of their behavior for personality diagnosis. We can only suggest that the situation with our Oriya and American informants may be the reverse of that supposed by hypothesis 6. Ethnographic observation suggests that our Oriya informants experience their intimates in a relatively small and standard set of contexts: at work, in family affairs, in ritual contexts, at public meetings, and so on. They also have much secondhand knowledge via gossip and rumor. However, the number of settings in which teachers in a nursery school, college students in a fraternity, and psychologists in a counseling center experience one another may be even less. Hypothesis 6 does not seem relevant to the cultural differences we have discovered in the concrete versus abstract way in which Oriyas and Americans describe individual differences.

We seem to be left in an explanatory void. In their free descriptions of personality Oriyas are more concrete than Americans. They describe their intimates by reference to behavioral instances (cases) and they qualify their descriptions by reference to contexts. These differences hold up even when one is comparing Americans with literate Oriyas, educated Oriyas, and high-caste Oriyas. Within the Oriya community, the concrete style of describing individual differences is stable across castes and across educational and literacy levels. The difference cannot be explained in terms of the "intellectual predicament" of the Oriyas. They are aware of alternative behavioral styles. It is not a reflection of a deficiency in skills of abstraction. In sorting tasks, Oriyas display a facile ability to think abstractly. The difference has little to do with education, literacy, socioeconomic status, or language. It seems to be a cultural phenomenon, and it is perhaps as a cultural phenomenon that we should try to understand it.

A Relativist Theory of the Context-Dependent Self: Holism and Its Cognitive Consequences

As we have seen, Oriyas are less prone than Americans to describe people they know in abstract, context-free terms. Instead of saying so-and-so is "principled" they tend to say "He does not disclose secrets." Instead of saying so-and-so is "selfish" they tend to say "He is hesitant to give away money to his family." While this difference in person perception is only a tendency (46 percent abstract, context-free descriptions from Americans, 20 percent from Oriyas), it is a pervasive tendency, stable across Oriya subsamples, a tendency significant enough to allow us to reject a universalist interpretation of context-dependent thinking.

Our results also lend little support to an evolutionary interpretation. Oriya informants do not lack skills of generalization and abstraction. They are aware that the behavior of someone who "does not become partial while imparting justice" and "does not disclose secrets" can be described as "principled"; they recognize that there are likenesses that link such very different behavioral occurrences as imparting justice and keeping secrets. If asked to select from a corpus of concrete behaviors those that generally "go together" in people, Oriyas, like Americans, will utilize conceptual likenesses to assist them in the task ("all those are principled behaviors"; see hypothesis 5 above; also D'Andrade 1965, 1973, 1974; Shweder 1972, 1975, 1977a, 1977c, 1980a, 1980b, 1982b; Shweder and D'Andrade 1979, 1980). Similarly, our results suggest that the concrete mode of person perception of the Oriya informants cannot be explained by reference to deficient information, motivation, or linguistic resources (see hypotheses 1–6 above). Why, then, are Oriyas more prone than Americans to describe their intimates by reference to cases and contexts?

A Relativist Interpretation of Concrete Thinking

Relativists acknowledge that concrete, contextualized, occasion-bound thinking is unequally distributed across human cultures. However, it is the position of the relativist that the prevalence of context-dependent thinking in some cultures tells us little about underlying deficits in cognitive processing skills, intellectual motivation, available information, or linguistic tools. The trick for the relativist is to acknowledge diversity while shunning the evolutionary notion of cultural deficits. How can this be done?

THE DISTINCTION BETWEEN IDEATIONAL PRODUCTS AND INTELLECTUAL PROCESSES

Why are Oriyas more prone than Americans to describe their intimates by reference to cases and contexts? Relativists answer this question by drawing a sharp distinction between intellectual *process* and ideational *product*. The relativist hypothesizes that cultures differ less in their basic cognitive skills (for example, generalization, abstraction, reversibility) than in the metaphors by which they live (Lakoff and Johnson 1980a), the world hypotheses (Pepper 1972) to which they subscribe, and the ideas underlying their social action. Thus, according to a relativist account, the Oriyas, Balinese, and Gahuku-Gama are perfectly competent information processors, not unskilled at differentiating, generalizing, and taking the perspective of others. What really distinguishes them from us is that they place so little *value* on differentiating (for example, person from role), generalizing (for example, "treat outsiders like insiders"), or abstracting (for example, the concept of humanity); and, the relativist is quick to point out, they show so little interest in such intellectual moves because Oriyas, Balinese, and other such folk live by a metaphor and subscribe to a world-premise that directs their attention and passions to particular systems, relationally conceived and contextually appraised. Indeed, a central tenet of a relativist interpretation of context-dependent person perception is that *the metaphors by which people live and the world views to which they subscribe mediate the relationship between what one thinks about and how one thinks.*

HOLISM: A MEDIATING WORLD PREMISE

Holism is a mode of thought elaborating the implications of the "part-whole" relationship, namely: (1) what is true of, or right for, the whole is not necessarily true of, or right for, any or all of the parts of the whole (for example, "An arm can throw a football" and "An elbow is part of the arm" does not imply that "An elbow can throw a football"); (2) diverse parts of the whole are not necessarily alike in any crucial respects (for example, while different "kinds of" canines, say terriers and spaniels, are alike in some characteristic ways, different "parts of" a body, say fingernails and red blood cells, or different "parts of" an automobile, say the axle and the fan belt, need not commune in any way whatsoever); (3) each part is defined by the particular relationships into which it enters within the specific whole of which it is a part (for example, try defining "tongue" or "brake" without functional, relational, or contextual references). For a holist, "unit" parts are necessarily altered by the relations into which they enter (Phillips 1976).

From a holistic perspective unit parts (for example, an elbow) change their essential properties when isolated from the unit wholes (for example, an arm) of which they are a part. Thus, the holist concludes, it is not possible to understand or appraise an entity in isolation, in the abstract. The holist is prone to seek contextual clarification before making a judgment; the holist is disinclined to examine or judge things *in vacuo.*

THE BODY: "A METAPHOR PEOPLE LIVE BY"

All societies are confronted by the same small set of existential questions, and some societies even try to answer them. A minimal set includes:

1. The problem of "haves" versus "have-nots." It is a fact of life that the things all people want are unequally distributed in any society. Have-nots must be told in convincing terms why they have not.

Haves must have confidence that their privileges are justifiable and legitimate.

2. The problem of our way of life versus their way of life. Diversity of custom, value, belief, and practice is also a fact of life. Why should I live this way and not some other way? "There but for fortune goes you or goes I" is not a satisfying answer.

3. The problem of the relationship of nature to culture. Are we merely "naked apes" or, better yet, "rational featherless bipeds" or, still better, "the children of God"?

4. The problem of the relationship of the individual to the group, to society, to the collectivity. There seem to be relatively few "solutions" to this last problem; the "sociocentric" solution subordinates individual interests to the good of the collectivity, while in the "egocentric" solution society becomes the servant of the individual; that is, society is imagined to have been created to serve the interests of some idealized autonomous, abstract individual existing free of society yet living in society.

Holistic cultures seem to embrace a sociocentric conception of the relationship of individual to society, a sociocentric conception with an organic twist. Some Indologists (see Dumont 1960, 1970, pp. 184–86; Marriott 1976), for example, have noted that the concept of an autonomous, bounded, abstract individual existing free of society yet living in society is uncharacteristic of Indian social thought. A person-in-society, for Indians, is not an "autonomous, indivisible, bounded unit" (Marriott 1976, p. 111). Like most peoples, Indians do have a concept of a person-in-society, but a person-in-society is not an autonomous individual. He or she is regulated by strict rules of interdependence that are context specific and particularistic, rules governing exchanges of services, rules governing behavior to kinsmen, rules governing marriage, and so on.

The idea that man-in-society is not an autonomous individual is not unique to India. Henry Selby's (1974, 1975) discussion of Zapotec culture in Oaxaca, Mexico, makes this apparent. Selby argues that the "folk explanatory model that puts responsibility for morality and cure on the individual" is "deeply rooted in Western thought"; it is "as old as Thucydides, who wrote 2,400 years ago and was rediscovered and glorified in the Renaissance and Reformation" (1974, pp. 62–66). Indeed, in the West, the fact that good works (for example, scientific discoveries) are often the products of base motives (for example, envy) is treated as a glaring insult to our faith in the individual as the ultimate measure of all things. It is otherwise among the Zapotecs. Selby explicates the Zapotec expression "We see the face, but do not know what is in the heart" as follows: It is "not an expression of despair. They [Zapotecs] do not have to know what is in the heart, because it isn't defined as being very interesting and it shouldn't have anything to do with human relations" (p. 63). With regard to perceptions of deviant behavior, Selby notes that Zapotecs "do not, therefore, have to overcome their own prejudices about the character of people who go wrong. They know their own society and how it works, and they are aware of the sociological nature of deviance. They have no need to peer into people's heart and minds." (ibid.). Selby presents case material indicating that even blatantly deviant acts (for example, murder) do not elicit characterological attributions.

Oriyan culture is not Zapotec. Indians do peer into one another's hearts and minds; Indians, unlike the Zapotecs, do have a concept of autonomous individualism. But an Indian, to be an autonomous individual, must leave society. The autonomous individual is the holy man, the renouncer, the sadhu, the "dropout" (Dumont 1960, 1970). Yet even here the goal is not to find one's distinctive identity but rather to merge one's soul with the soul of others. When Indians peer into one another's hearts and minds they are more likely than most peoples to look for the ultimate universal, the ground of all things, God.

What makes Western culture special, then, is the concept of the autonomous distinctive individual living in society. What makes Indian culture special is the concept of the autonomous nondistinctive individual living outside society. When it comes to a person-in-society, Indian views are not unique (indeed, their views are prototypical and lucid expressions of a widespread mode of social thought), but they do diverge considerably from the "natural man" tradition of Western social thought. In America, people-in-society conceive of themselves as free of the relationships of hierarchy and exchange that govern all social ties and are so central to theories of the self in Orissa.

The sociocentric conception of the individual-social relationship lends itself to an organic metaphor. Indeed in holistic sociocentric cultures like India's the human body, conceived as an interdependent system, is frequently taken as a metaphor for society (and society, conceived as an organic whole, is sometimes taken as a metaphor for nature).

The human body is a pregnant metaphor. It has its ruler (the brain), its servants (the limbs), and so on. Political affairs, interpersonal dyads, family organization are all easily conceived in accordance with a model of differentiated parts arranged in a hierarchy of functions in the service of the whole.

What follow from a holistic world view and sociocentric organic solution to the problem of the individual-social relationship are some of the features of the context-dependent, occasion-bound concept of the person: (1) no attempt to distinguish the individual from the status she or he occupies; (2) the view that obligations and rights are differentially apportioned by role, group, and so on; (3) a disinclination to ascribe intrinsic moral worth to people merely because they are people. To ask a holist "Is killing wrong?" is like asking a morphologist or physiologist to assess the value of a body part or organ without knowledge of, or reference to, its function in the interdependent organic structure of this or that particular species. Indeed, with their explicit cultural recognition and even deification of obligatory, particularistic interdependence, Oriyas would seem to be culturally primed to see context and social relationships as a necessary condition for behavior.

By contrast, in the West, as Louis Dumont (1970) notes, each person is conceived of as "a particular incarnation of abstract humanity" (p. 5), a monadic replica of general humanity. A kind of sacred personalized self is developed and the individual *qua* individual is seen as inviolate, a supreme value in and of itself. The self becomes an object of interest per se. Free to undertake projects of personal expression—personal narratives, autobiographies, diaries, mirrors, separate rooms, early separation from bed, body, and breast, of mother, personal space—the autonomous individual imagines the incredible, that he or she lives in an inviolate region (the extended boundaries of the self) where he or she is free to choose (see Friedman and Friedman 1980 for the purest articulation of this incredible belief), where what he does is his own business.

More than that, the inviolate self views social relationships as derivative matters, arising out of consent and contract between autonomous individuals. Society is viewed as mere association (see Dumont 1970). It thus hardly seems surprising that despite much evidence to the contrary (Hartshorne and May 1928; Newcomb 1929; Mischel 1968; D'Andrade 1974; Shweder 1975; Nisbett 1980; and Chapter 7 of this volume), our culture continues to promote the fiction that within the person one can find a stable core character. Nor is it surprising that this abstract individual, person-as-voluntary-agent, is protected by deeply enshrined moral and legal principles prescribing privacy and proscribing unwanted invasions of person, property, and other extensions of the self. Americans are culturally primed to search for abstract summaries of the autonomous individual behind the social role and social appearance.

FROM CONCRETE THINKING IN PARTICULAR TO CONCRETE THINKING IN GENERAL

We have argued that concrete, cases-and-contexts person perception is an expression of a holistic world premise and sociocentric organic conception of the relationship of the individual to society. But what of concrete thinking in other domains? For example, what about the evidence on "functional complexes," that is, the tendency of informants in some cultures to respond to requests about how things are alike by linking the things in an action sequence or activity structure? Consider one of Luria's (1976) Central Asian informants. The informant is presented with four objects (hammer, saw, log, hatchet). He is asked: "Which of these things could you call by one word?" He is told: "One fellow picked three things—the hammer, saw, and hatchet—and said they were alike." The informant responds: "A saw, a hammer, and a hatchet all have to work together. But the log has to be there too . . . if you have to split something you need a hatchet" (p. 56).

To interpret this type of finding within a relativist framework one might speculate that from the point of view of a holistic thinker it makes no sense to ignore the functional interdependencies among objects and events. Indeed Luria's illiterate, unschooled peasants repeatedly try, in vain, to explain to him that it is "stupid" to ignore the way objects and events fit together in action sequences (for example, 1976, pp. 54, 77). One is reminded of Joseph Glick's (1968) Kpelle informant who insisted on grouping objects into functional complexes while commenting, "A wise man can do no other." Only when asked, "How would a fool group the objects?" did he give the Westerner what he wanted, a linguistically defined equivalence structure.

Is it farfetched to imagine that holism, the sociocentric conception of the individual-social relationship, and the organic metaphor have a generalized influence on cognition? Perhaps. But one should not overlook the following fact about the cultural organization of knowledge. Although in our culture it is the "natural" sciences that have an elevated position, in many nonwestern cultures (see Fortes 1959; H. Smith 1961; Durkheim and Mauss 1963; Horton 1968) much of the intellectual action is in the arena of social thought. For us it is the organization of knowledge in physics and chemistry that is adopted wholesale as the ideal for social understanding. More than a few social scientists are busy at work searching for a "periodic table" of social elements. Many more have been enamored of physical metaphors (forces, energy, mechanisms, and so on). In the West, the physical world has become the model of the social world. Why should not a reverse extension—take the social order as the model of nature—take place in other cultures? Metaphors, deliberately selected to guide our thinking, often have generalized effects on how we think.

Privacy and the Socialization of the Inviolate Self

We have sketched the outline of a relativist interpretation of both cases and contexts person perception in particular and concrete thinking in general. The concept of the context-dependent person is one expression of a broader sociocentric organic view of the relationship of the individual to society which in turn is an aspect of the holistic world view adopted by many cultures. The holistic model, the sociocentric premise, and the organic metaphor focus one's attention on the context-dependent relationship of part to part and part to whole; the holist, convinced that objects and events are necessarily altered by the relations into which they enter, is theoretically primed to contextualize objects and events, and theoretically disinclined to appraise things *in vacuo,* in the abstract.

To the question "Does the concept of the person vary cross-culturally?" our answer is obviously "yes"; we have tried to identify two major alternative conceptualizations of the individual-social relationship, namely, the egocentric contractual and the sociocentric organic. Neither of these conceptualizations of the relationship of the individual to society has the epistemological status of a scientific category. They are not inductive generalizations. They are not the discoveries of individual perception. Quite the contrary, the egocentric and sociocentric views are creations of the collective imagination. They are ideas, premises by which people guide their lives, and only to the extent that people live by them do they have force.

How do people live by their world views? It is instructive to reflect, for example, on the socialization of autonomy in the West.

We find it tempting to argue that Western individualism has its origins in the institution of privacy—that privacy promotes a passion or need for autonomy, which, for the sake of our sense of personal integrity, requires privacy (see Trilling 1972, p. 24). Socialization is terroristic. The young are subject to all sorts of invasions, intrusions, and manipulations of their personhood, autonomy, and privacy. Where they go, when they sleep, what they eat, how they look—all the intimacies of the self are managed for them, typically without consent. Heteronomy is the universal starting point for socialization; it may or may not be the endpoint.

It is sobering to acknowledge that our sense of personal inviolability is a violatable social gift, the product of what *others* are willing to respect and protect us from, the product of the way we are handled and reacted to, the product of the rights and privileges we are granted by others in numerous "territories of the self" (Goffman 1971) (for example, vis-à-vis eating, grooming, hair length, clothing style, when and where we sleep, who we associate with, personal possessions). Arnold Simmel (1968) notes that "the right to privacy asserts the sacredness of the person" (p. 482). And where are these "assertions" redundantly (even if tacitly) reiterated? Well, the assertion is there in the respect shown by a parent for a child's "security blanket." It's there when an adult asks of a three-year-old "What do you want to eat for dinner?" and again in the knock on the door before entering the child's personal space, his or her private bedroom, another replica of the assertion.

The ego's view of its self is the product of the collective imagination. In the West, the messages implicit in many of our child-handling practices may well socialize deep intuitions about the "indecency" of external intrusions, regulations, or invasions of our imagined inviolable self. Practices cultivate intuitions, intuitions about what is decent, which then support such Western notions as freedom to choose (Friedman and Friedman 1980), autonomy in decision making, sanctuary, and "my own business" (see the literature on privacy law, for example, Bostwick 1976; Gerety 1977).

Of course not all cultures socialize autonomy or redundantly confirm the right of the individual to projects of personal expression, to a body, mind, and room of one's own. To members of sociocentric organic cultures the concept of the autonomous individual, free to choose and mind his or her own business, must feel alien, a bizarre idea cutting the self off from the interdependent whole, dooming it to a life of isolation and loneliness (Kakar 1978, p. 86). Linked to each other in an interdependent system, members of organic cultures take an active interest in one another's affairs and feel at ease in regulating and being regulated. Indeed, others are the means to one's functioning, and vice versa.

It is also sobering to reflect on the psychic costs, the existential penalties of our egocentrism, our autonomous individualism. There are costs to having no larger framework within which to locate the self. Many in our culture lack a meaningful orientation to the past. We come from nowhere, the product of a random genetic accident. Many lack a meaningful orientation to the future. We are going nowhere; at best we view ourselves as machines that will one day run down. The social order we view as the product of our making—an association based on contract and individual consent. In our view, society is dependent on us. And what are our gods? Personal success and wealth; "the tangible evidences of financial success have come to symbolize . . . the whole expectancy of ego satisfaction" (M. W. Smith 1952, p. 398). Cut adrift from any larger whole, the self has become the measure of all things, clutching to a faith that some "invisible hand" will by sleight of hand right things in the end.

Of course what we have just said about egocentrism and autonomy in the West could easily be rewritten in terms of psychic benefits, and we should not forget that sociocentrism also has severe costs. Perhaps the real point is that the costs and benefits of egocentrism and sociocentrism are not the same (*pace* universalism), nor are the benefits mostly on one side and the costs mostly on the other (*pace* evolutionism).

Conclusion

In 1929 Edward Sapir remarked that "the worlds in which different societies live are distinct worlds, not merely the same world with different labels attached" (p. 209). Here we have tried to show not only that different peoples adopt distinct world views but also that these world views have a decisive influence on cognitive functioning.

People around the world do not all think alike. Nor are the differences in thought that do exist necessarily to be explained by reference to differences or deficits in cognitive processing skills, intellectual motivation, available information, or linguistic resources. It is well known in cognitive science that what one thinks about can be decisive for how one thinks (for example, Wason and Johnson-Laird 1972). What is not yet fully appreciated is that the relationship between what one thinks about (for example, other people) and how one thinks (for example, contexts and cases) may be mediated by the world premise to which one is committed (for example, holism) and by the metaphors by which one lives (Lakoff and Johnson 1980b).

4.

The Social Construction of the Person: How Is It Possible?

with Joan G. Miller

According to Volney Stefflre (personal communication) theories of category formation can be divided into three general kinds: (1) realist theories, which argue that "people categorize the world the way they do because that's the way the world is"; (2) innatist theories, which argue that "people categorize the world the way they do because that's the way people are"; and (3) social construction theories, which argue that people categorize the world the way they do because they have participated in social practices, institutions, and other forms of symbolic action (for example, language) that presuppose or in some way make salient those categorizations. The "constructive" parts of a social construction theory are the idea that equally rational, competent, and informed observers are, in some sense, free (of external realist and internal innate constraints) to constitute for themselves different realities; and the cognate idea, articulated by Nelson Goodman (1968, 1972, 1978), that there are as many realities as there are ways "it" can be constituted or described (see also Nagel 1979, pp. 211–213). The "social" parts of a social construction theory are the idea that categories are vicariously received, not individually invented; and the cognate idea that the way people divide the world into categories is, in some sense, tradition bound, and thus transmitted, communicated and "passed on" through symbolic action.

The following pages explore a social construction theory of category formation, with special attention to cross-cultural variations in conceptualizations of the person. An ethnographic account of traditional Hindu conceptualizations of the relationship between the individual, the moral-social order, and the natural order introduce the distinction between duty-based and rights-based moral codes and the cognate distinction between those cultures in which it is believed that social roles are the fundamental building blocks of the social order and those cultures in which it is believed that the social order is built up out of self-interested individuals in pursuit of their wants and preferences. A cross-cultural analysis of America and India in terms of person descriptions and explanations of individual actions indicates that duty-based and rights-based conceptions of the person have different cognitive consequences. A realist theory of category formation is contrasted with the social construction approach. Both theories are employed to explain why some categorizations of the world seem "natural" while others seem artificial.

Oriya Conceptions of the Person, Society, and Nature

The following account of traditional Hindu views is based on twenty-seven months of field work between 1968 and 1984 in a community of Brahmans and temple priests in the old temple town of Bhubaneswar, Orissa. Many features of the conceptions of the Oriya community are typical of traditional Hindu culture.

The Natural Order Is a Moral Order: The Idea of Karma and the Just World Hypothesis

Oriya adults do not subscribe to a mechanistic-physicalist conception of nature. Rather, they believe in a natural process or principle known as karma: the natural order is viewed as a moral order in which events happen for an ethical purpose, namely, to promote an equitable distribution of rewards and punishments. The facts of life are emblems of virtue, and the moral quality of one's life, past and present, is written all over the trials, tribulations, and rewards of this world. Thus, for Oriyas, there are no accidental, random, or morally insignificant events. Rebirth is a sign of prior sin. Rebirth as a woman is a sign of prior sin, as is giving birth to a daughter, dying a widow, or suffering a lingering death. It is a sign of prior sin to be ugly or malformed or disfigured or handicapped. It is a sign of prior sin to die prematurely or suffer any major calamity. Oriyas believe that, in the long run, nature punishes vice and rewards virtue. Every informant can cite cases from personal experience. A man kicked his father; later the man's leg became crippled. A relative went to Assam and unwittingly ate beef. He died a long-drawn-out and painful death. And, in support of the idea of karma, informants are adept at citing the cases recorded in the vast "historical" corpus of the Hindu scriptures.

For orthodox Hindus in the old temple town of Bhubaneswar, a major way to prove a point is to cite or recount a historical or personal narrative, and a central body of evidence about what the world is like consists of the "historical" experiences narrated in the Hindu Puranas and Epics. For orthodox Hindus the actors of history include gods, demons, and hermits, who through meditation and self-denial gained extra-ordinary insight into the past and future as well as the ability to dominate the material world mentally. Although orthodox Hindus are perfectly capable of distinguishing fact from fiction, and will tell you without hesitation that the events portrayed in a Hindi film at the local cinema are not necessarily true, they do not treat the stories of the Puranas and Epics as fantasies, allegories, or poetic flights of the imagination. What we might view as myth or fairy tale they view as a solid factual account. They believe that the recountable experiences of their forefathers recorded in those stories are a reasonable guide to reality; thus, most expositions about what the world is or should be like begin, "Let me tell you a story."

Let me tell you a story. Once Laxmi (the goddess of wealth) and Narayan (the god Vishnu, Laxmi's husband) were talking with each other. Laxmi, spotting a beggar, said, "Look at that wretched man. He is suffering and he is not getting any food. Now look at the man in that house. He is getting a lot to eat: ghee, milk, butter. And he is not giving anything to the hungry beggar." Narayan replied: "The beggar has nothing in his karma." Laxmi would have nothing of it. "You are everything," she said. "You are all in all. Creator, doer, destiny, and fate. You are always telling me that no one is superior to you. Many times I have heard you say, 'Whatever is done or is going on, I am doing it all.' If that's so, then why is that beggar wandering and going hungry? Why are you troubling him?" Narayan replied: "He has done nothing virtuous and therefore deserves nothing." Laxmi said: "You please give him something!" Narayan said: "Okay. Go and tell the beggar that I will put some money over there near that tree. But he must go there and get it." So Laxmi visited the beggar in his dreams and told him: "God has kept money for you near the palm tree. Go early in the morning and you can get it." The next morning the beggar awoke and set off in search of the palm tree. But it was not in his karma to find it. Just as he neared the tree he shut his eyes and walked like a blind man, missing the money. Then Narayan said to Laxmi: "Have you seen that? It is not in his karma."

That story, narrated by a thirty-seven-year-old male resident of Bhubaneswar, was meant to prove the point that nature is fair if not merciful and that even the gods are bound by an inexorable natural law of justice called karma. We could perhaps argue whether the story is about a natural *law* of justice, which the gods have no choice but to obey, or about a natural *canon* of justice, which the gods, out of fairness, are morally obliged to enforce. By either interpretation the story is explicit and unambiguous in its reference to one purported fact of nature: you reap what you sow. Oriyas in this old temple town draw from the story an even deeper, perhaps implicit meaning: *Only* if you do bad things will bad things happen to you. And they do not overlook the logical implication: If bad things happen to you, you must have sinned.

A blind widow, an eighty-three-year-old high-subcaste Brahman, lost her husband five years ago. A year later she lost her eyesight, and a year after that her eldest daughter died. Interviews with the blind widow were conducted by Candy Shweder over several months, yielding about twenty hours of transcribed material. Thirty seconds into the first interview:

Blind widow: You must not be feeling the cold at night. (Reference to the fact that the interviewer has a husband to sleep with at night.)
Interviewer: No, I'm not cold. I have two children. Where do you think they came from?
Blind widow: I've put a screen on my eyes. My husband is dead so I have put a screen on my eyes because I may get tempted by the husbands of others if I look at them.

In fact the widow does believe she is responsible for her blindness. Several weeks later, without the levity of the first interview, indeed, amidst tears, she recounts how her life is marked with signs of prior sin: "I was born a woman. I gave birth to a daughter. My daughter died. My husband died before I did. Suddenly my vision disappeared. Now I am a widow—and blind." She weeps: "I cannot say which sin I have committed in which life, but I am suffering now because I have done something wrong in one of my births. All the sins are gathered near me."

In fact for several years the widow has been concerned with almost nothing but the mitigation of her sins. The precise nature of her sin is unknown, probably unknowable, but from her point of view the evidence of prior sin, her current suffering, is undeniable. She experiments with every local form of expiation: fasting, isolation, meditation, prayer, confession, offering donations, feeding Brahmans, ritual baths, worship of the Tulsi plant (a basil plant, which has mythological and ritual significance for Hindus). She fears for her family and for herself: "I will take rebirth after death. But I do not know what type of birth I will take; it may be an animal or beast."

For the blind widow, historical and personal narratives support the idea that life's events are ethically meaningful, that suffering is deserved and expiation possible. Moving back and forth between historical narrative and personal narrative the widow tells the story of how the god Lingaraj (the resident deity of the major temple of Bhubaneswar; a form of the Hindu god Shiva) committed the sin of killing a cow, and then she relates Shiva's sin to certain events in the life of her husband's elder brother. According to the widow:

> Once Lingaraj went for a bath in the tank. He brought with him a bundle of holy grass, which he placed by the side of the tank. When a cow swallowed the holy grass Lingaraj became angry and threw one of his wooden sandals at the cow's face, breaking the side of the cow's jaw and its teeth. To this day cows have no teeth on the side of their jaws. The cow died. Lingaraj was polluted by his sin. Even now, once a year, he must take a purifying bath and beg forgiveness from Yama, the god of death.

(Indeed, both those events, the bath and the confessional, do occur in the annual cycle of ritual events at the Lingaraj temple. Thus, on his way home from visiting his sister's temple, on that one day a year called Jama Dutiya in late October or early November when brothers all over Orissa make a ceremonial visit to the home of their married sisters, Lingaraj stops at the temple of Yama, the god of death, and begs forgiveness for his sin.)

Sin and suffering are closely associated in the Oriya mind. That association is reminiscent of Jean Piaget's (1965 [1932]) account of the idea of "immanent justice" in five- and six-year-old Swiss children. According to Piaget, the child conjectures that nature is just. From the child's point of view the physical and biological worlds function like a judge, guaranteeing that transgressions do not go unpunished (p. 257) and that for every fault of conduct there is some physical catastrophe that serves as its punishment (p. 258). Indeed, so deep is the child's faith in just desert that like other "simple souls" the child "would rather assume some hidden fault to explain a neighbor's misfortune than admit the fortuitous character in the trials that befall mankind (p. 262)." Piaget himself does not believe in immanent justice. He argues that "experience shows that wickedness máy go unpunished and virtue remain unrewarded" and that "the greater the child's intellectual development the more clearly he will see this" (pp. 261, 262). He claims that the belief in immanent justice wanes with age and experience (p. 253) and that among adults the belief in immanent justice persists only among "primitives," "simple souls," and "those who never learn from the facts" (p. 262).

To scholars of South Asian thought, Piaget's account of immanent justice will seem both uncanny and naive. The account will seem uncanny because the Swiss child's idea of immanent justice corresponds remarkably well to the traditional Hindu idea that nature is just (the idea of karma), and those issues about which Piaget claims the child lacks conviction (for example, by what process is just desert guaranteed?) are analogous to those issues about which Hindus waver and speculate. Piaget's account will also seem naive. For scholars of South Asian civilization routinely encounter "sophisticated souls" of considerable intellectual power who are convinced that the physical and biological world is ethically meaningful and who are able to interpret many of the facts of experience, especially the unequal distribution of health, wealth, and status, as signs of prior sin. Indeed, contrary to Piaget's developmental hypothesis, in India at least, faith in a just world does not decline with age, experience, and mental development; and on a worldwide scale the association of illness with prior sin is one of the more popular ideas among adults. According to George Peter Murdock (1980), for example, 80 percent of the world's cultures subscribe in some degree to the belief that illness is directly caused by a transgression of some social taboo or moral injunction. Murdock discovered in his study of 134 societies that violations of injunctions concerning food and sex are most likely to be associated with subsequent illness. Perhaps not too surprisingly, the tendency of thought that links sexual transgression with suffering persists (albeit in primordial form—just below the surface) even in our own culture, where the AIDS epidemic is sometimes portrayed as a punishment visited upon the homosexual community and the herpes virus seems to many of its victims like just desert for promiscuity.

Oriyas believe that nature punishes vice and rewards virtue. It is but a short inferential step to the idea that the Hindu social order is a natural order; that there is a set of objective obligations reflected in Hindu social arrangements; that Hindu society as a moral order is in tune with the requirements of nature. Or as one informant put it: "If you obey every custom you will be free of pollution and you will not suffer from any diseases." Hindu dharma as recorded in the corpus of Hindu scriptures is believed to be an account of those natural, objective obligations.

The Moral Order Is a Natural Order: Hindu Dharma and Natural Law

Oriyas not only believe that nature is ethical; they also believe that ethics are natural, and that the most natural of ethics is Hindu dharma, as described in their sacred scriptures (the Vedas, the Puranas, and the Epics) and as embodied in their social institutions and traditional practices. What makes the Hindu scriptures sacred to Oriyas is that they reveal the truth; not "revealed truth," but a truth arrived at over millennia in a world that kicks back. Oriyas believe that Hinduism, being a very ancient religion, has come closer to the truth than any other religion, and they view their social institutions and practices as reasonably well adapted to the ethical demands of nature. They believe that their distant ancestors gained salvation, and that as long as they follow the practices of those ancestors they will not suffer. A temple priest and local tailor comments: "We will be punished by God if we violate our customs—bad will come." A young newlywed, the youngest daughter-in-law in a large joint family, comments: "We feel that something bad might happen if we don't perform a ceremony—even if we don't feel like doing it."

For example, it is traditional practice to change clothes after defecation. The prescription is important for married women because it is the wife's duty to offer food to returning spirits of dead ancestors; for this she must be pure. After defecation and before entering the kitchen a married woman *must* wash and change her clothes. Were she to violate the prescription, terrible things would happen: the ancestral spirits would refuse to eat, Laxmi (the goddess of wealth) would leave the house, and ruin would descend on the family.

Traditional practice also requires that a woman avoid her husband's elder brother. A woman may not eat with her husband's elder brother or talk directly to him or even wash the plates on which he eats. The Oriya kinship term for husband's elder brother means one-

and-one-half fathers-in-law. Were a woman to violate this proscription terrible things would happen: she would die from a fatal disease and be reborn as an owl. (There are also strong avoidances between a woman and her husband's father and between a man and his wife's elder sister. Conversely, there is a joking relationship, and a sexy one at that, between a woman and her husband's younger brother and between a man and his wife's youngest sister.)

For Oriyas the moral order is a natural order; almost every justification of social practice is given in objective terms. Consider some of the justifications offered by informants for their cultural practices. It is natural to have arranged marriages: "A marriage is something that affects so many relatives and friends. How can you leave it up to one person, blinded by lust or passion, to make the decision?" It is natural for five-year-old children to sleep every night with their parents.

> Children should sleep with their parents because they may be afraid of something and not be able to express it. He may be afraid to urinate alone but he cannot express his fears. Even though a child of five can speak, he may not be able to speak immediately or know what to say. We are observing in our home that a four-year-old girl gets up and cries suddenly for no reason.

It is natural for a married son to inherit most of the father's estate and for a married daughter to inherit little:

> Parents live with their married sons, not their married daughters. It is the son who must care for the parents in their old age. He must bear the financial burden and arrange the funeral rites. Married daughters have received a dowry and left the family. The needs of the son are greater.

It is natural for widows to wear white saris:

> If a widow is fair-complected and wears a black sari, then she will look attractive. White color is the best way to symbolize a simple life. If you see a woman wearing a white sari you will not be tempted to look her over. To eye a widow is a very great sin and will cause you harm. If widows in every country would wear white saris instead of colored saris then the age of truth [Satya Yuga] would prevail.

It is natural for widows to avoid fish and meat: "Meat, fish, eggs are all hot foods. They heat the body and stimulate the senses. Rice, dal (lentil sauce), milk, bread, vegetable curry are cool foods. If you eat hot food the sexual appetite increases. This is the reason widows are denied hot foods." It is natural to eat with your hands:

> We can eat more food than you when we eat with our bare hands. Eating with your hand has some advantages. It is good for your health; your five fingers touch your food and after eating you suck your fingers, which creates saliva, which helps digestion.

It is natural for the eldest son to refrain from eating fish or meat for ten days after the death of his father: "If the eldest son ate chicken the day after his father died, the deceased father would not eat the food offered to his soul and consequently the father would not get salvation." It is natural for a menstruating woman to be isolated and secluded, to be kept out of the kitchen and to be prohibited from sleeping in the same bed with her husband:

> Menstrual blood is poisonous. If the husband cohabits with his wife he will be destroyed. His beauty will vanish. He will become ill and after some days he will die. For four days an evil soul is inside the woman, making her inferior to an untouchable, so no one should touch her. A menstruating woman takes the form of the goddess Kali; so no one should look at her face. If she enters the kitchen the deceased ancestors will not come again to the home for seven generations.

Oriyas are sensitive to the real or imagined consequences of conformity to or deviations from the moral order, and they believe that if you violate natural law, nature will let you know.

> Women do not plough the land. They can go to the field, sow the plants, arrange the plants in a row, but they may not plough. People will not let her plough because if she does, Laxmi will leave her house. If she touches the ploughing iron, something bad will happen. There may be an earthquake or the hills may split into pieces. Something will be destroyed—the oxen, houses, something."

The idea of natural law is not alien to the Western mind, and it still holds a respectable place in our moral and legal codes, especially in discussions of natural "rights." For what we think is natural about natural rights is that the obligations they place on us (for example, to respect the civil liberties of others) are objective obligations, and thus inalienable. The idea of natural rights is arguably a fiction, but as it has been conceived it places certain rights (free speech, privacy, travel) beyond the realm of the subjective, out of the reach of majority vote, above convention and consensus. Of course, a government or state may fail to realize its objective obligations and may not grant to its citizens any rights at all. But, according to those who believe in natural rights, the obligation is there nonetheless; being objective, it does not go away for having been misperceived.

If you ask an American or an Oriya whether it is all right for a brother and sister to marry each other, both will say no. They will tell you it is a very serious transgression. They will tell you it is wrong for brothers and sisters to marry even if it were done secretly and no one knew about it. They will tell you it is wrong even if the women were infertile and could not have children. They will tell you that the practice of brother-sister marriage is wrong even if it is approved of in other societies, and that societies that condone the practice, if there are any such strange places, would be better societies if they did not. They will tell you that it would be wrong to engage in brother-sister marriage even if most people wanted to marry a sibling and even if a majority voted to make the practice legal. They will tell you that brother-sister marriage should not be allowed, and anyone who engages in it should be reprimanded, fined, or punished. What is intimated by this pattern of responses is the perception that brother-sister marriage is an unnatural act even when regularly practiced, and that the law that forbids it is a natural law, objectively binding on all those to whom it applies—in this case, all humankind. And, being an objective obligation, it is binding on those to whom it applies regardless of their individual wants or collective subjective preferences. There is no issue here of rights; willing, consenting adults are forbidden to marry their siblings even when no third party is harmed. There is an issue of duty, a role-bound restriction on one's conduct that is supposed to be natural. Brothers and sisters do not marry! Nor do members of the same sex, and so on.

Natural rights are not all there is to natural law. As the duty-bound taboo on incest suggests, the idea of natural law is more general than the idea of natural rights. Thus, to the extent that rights and duties are not the same thing, it is always best to keep separate the idea of the natural from the issue of what is natural: rights, duties, or something else.

A natural law is an objective obligation. What it is that is objective is an obligation, an imperative that tells us what we must do or must not do regardless of what we feel like doing. And that obligation is an objective thing; for example, incest is wrong whether or not it is recognized as such. The wrongness of incest is perceived as an external fact of life. Engaging in incest does not make it right, precisely because incest is an "unnatural" act.

Perhaps the simplest way to think about the idea of natural law is to imagine that there are certain standards to which social practices, man-made rules (so-called positive law), and personal desires must conform if those practices, rules, and desires are to be valid. Those standards of validity are natural laws. They are held out as natural laws because, if followed, they are thought to, *in fact,* promote certain ultimate, important, and categorical ends of life, ends that take precedence and are thought to be in no need of justification by those whose ends they are—ends such as liberty, justice, safety, salvation, and the elimination of suffering.

It is not hard to see why the idea of natural law is indispensable for designers of society. For it is the idea of natural law that is presupposed whenever we speak of a discrepancy between what is and what ought to be. What would American revolutionaries have done in 1776 without the idea of the natural rights of man? What would Iranian revolutionaries in 1978 have done without the idea of natural duties such as veiling, purdah, and so on?

The idea of natural law also does a lot for those of us who want to get others to do what we want. It is quite unreasonable to expect others to do the things we want simply because we want them to, and it raises all sorts of nasty problems of coercion, how to mount enough power to force them to our will, and so on. In contrast, it is not unreasonable, and requires no power at all, to expect others to respect the "facts of life," especially if those facts of life promote ends of life that are undeniably important to those whose ends they are. By an appeal to natural law, the weak can control the strong and the few can control the many. Indeed, it is the appeal to natural law that makes *rational* moral discourse possible in the first place. Without the idea of natural law all that would be left of the moral order is the strong or the many imposing their subjective preferences, tastes, or desires on everyone else.

What one culture views as reasonable is not always the same as what is viewed as reasonable in another culture. What is thought to be natural on one side of the Indian Ocean is not always thought to be natural on the other. The Oriya practice of arranged marriage and the various restrictions on widows—the prohibition against remarriage, against wearing ornaments or colored saris, against eating onion, garlic, fish, or meat—are viewed with dismay and disdain by Americans as violations of natural law. Americans believe there is a natural right to free choice in such matters, a natural right that, being factual, cannot be taken away, given up, or alienated. Oriya Brahmans, however, view the American practice of communal family meals with shock, horror, and disgust as a violation of natural law. Such American meals are sometimes prepared by menstruating women who join in and sit at the same table with everyone else! Seated at the same table might be a woman and her father-in-law or husband's elder brother, or a man and his wife's elder sister! Toward the end of such a meal a man might eat leftovers off his wife's plate or off the plates of his children! For Oriyas all those are unnatural acts. Natural law requires that pollutants and polluted persons be kept at a safe distance, that differences in sanctity, and hence status, be respected, and that those who are sanctified, and hence superior, be neither fed discarded food like hungry dogs nor insulted by a presumption of "free" affiliation.

Oriyas believe in natural law. They call it Hindu dharma. A sixty-five-year-old blind hermit speaks as though he had been reading ancient Greek texts: "Only man has the power to reason, and by virtue of this he is able to understand good and bad." A young former holy man takes a more empiricist view:

> Suppose we say that everything in the Puranas is false. You can make a trial of it. You try having sexual intercourse on the Sankranti day [first day of each fortnight] or the Ekadasi day [eleventh day of each fortnight]. You will know yourself why the hermits have prohibited such things at certain times.

What everyone believes is that it is reasonable to learn from experiences recounted in the Puranas and Epics—and what is recounted there reveals Hindu dharma—valid standards for judging social practice and individual conduct adapted to a natural world in which you reap what you sow. Why repeat the suffering of others? Hindu dharma is that objective ideal, and it is used in judgment of what is.

Duty-based versus Rights-based Codes

Ronald Dworkin (1977) distinguishes among rights-based, duty-based, and goal-based ethical codes. It is Dworkin's point that, whereas all ethical codes have some place for social goals, individual rights, and individual duties, ethical codes differ in the scales over which goals, rights, and duties range and in the priority given to goals over rights, rights over duties, and so on. For example, in a goal-based ethical code, some goal such as "improving the general welfare" is taken as fundamental. In a rights-based ethical code, a right such as "the right of all men to the greatest possible overall liberty" is taken as fundamental. In a duty-based ethical code, a duty such as "the duty to obey God's will as set forth in the Ten Commandments" is taken as fundamental.

According to Dworkin's conceptualization, rights and duties are not merely different ways of talking about the same thing. It does seem likely in the Oriya case that there are duties without correlative rights; for example, that the duty of the householder to feed a guest is owed to some third superior force or party such as God or Hindu dharma, without the implication that a guest has a right to be fed. It is Dworkin's argument that, in many cases, rights and duties are not correlative because

> one is derivative from the other and it makes a difference which is derivative from which . . . there is a difference between the idea that you have a duty not to lie to me because I have a right not to be lied to, and the idea that I have a right that you not lie to me because you have a duty not to tell lies. In the first place I justify a duty by calling attention to a right; if I intend any further justification it is the right I must justify, and I cannot do so by calling attention to the duty. In the second case it is the other way around. (1977, p. 171)

Ethical codes differ in terms of whether they take rights or duties as more fundamental. According to Dworkin it is a difference that makes a difference. Duty-based codes are concerned with the moral quality of individual action, with the conformity of individual action to a code of proper conduct. The code itself takes precedence over individuals, their appetites, wants, or habits. In a duty-based culture, the individual must conform to the code "or be punished or corrupted if he does not" (p. 172). Duty-based cultures enshrine some blueprint for how people should live (for example, Hindu dharma with its emphasis on natural roles and duties); such duty-based cultures stick to the principle that one is not free to deviate from the plan or to call on others to do so.

Rights-based codes, in contrast, "protect the value of individual thought and choice" (Dworkin 1977, p. 172). Individuals, their appetites, goals, and habits, take precedence over any conception of either the "proper" ends of life or the way it is "natural" for people to arrange themselves in society. As long as one does not harm others or violate their right to pursue their own chosen wants freely, one is at liberty to do or live as one wants; and in a rights-based culture it is the liberty of the individual to do and live as he or she wants that is protected and takes precedence. Between "consenting adults" almost anything goes—although not incest.

It has been said of ancient Indian ethics (O'Flaherty and Derrett 1978) that it "knew nothing of rights, only of duties" (p. ix). Contemporary Oriya culture does know something of rights; there is a term for it in the language—*adikara*. But rights are typically subordinated to duties, and it is the duties (of a son to his father, of a householder to his guest, of a wife to her husband) that receive the most elaborate treatment in local scripture and doctrine. It is the performance of duty in the face of adversity that stimulates feelings of righteousness and dharma.

Parallel to the distinction between rights-based and duty-based ethical codes is the distinction between person-centered and role-centered societies. It remains to be seen whether, on a worldwide scale, the two sets of distinctions run parallel, overlap, or are independent. In Orissa, at least, a duty-based ethical code has converged with a role-based conception of society. More generally, we speculate that those who believe that society is built up out of individuals in pursuit of their interests and satisfaction of their desires will prefer to rationalize the moral order in terms of natural rights, while those who believe that society is built up out of statuses and roles will prefer to rationalize the moral order in terms of natural duties.

Of course, the social order is built up out of both individuals (who always have interests and desires) and roles, and both are necessary conditions for social action. Nevertheless, cultures display considerable variation in what they take to be more basic, fundamental, or real—individuals or roles—facts about personality or facts about social status. Not surprisingly, in most sociocentric role-based societies (for example, East Africa) it is sociology, not psychology, that thrives as an academic discipline. In other, more individualistic cultures (for example, the United States) it is psychology that flourishes at universities and popular bookstores, while sociology has an uneasy relationship to a public that finds sociological discourse to be unreal and laden with "jargon."

Clifford Geertz (1975) evokes this dimension of cultural self-conception in his discussion of the Balinese concept of the person. There is, he notes, in Bali

> a persistent and systematic attempt to stylize all aspects of personal expression to the point where anything idiosyncratic, anything characteristic of the individual merely because he is who he is physically, psychologically or biographically, is muted in favor of his assigned place in the continuing and, so it is thought, never-changing pageant that is Balinese life. It is dramatis personae, not actors, that endure; indeed it is dramatis personae, not actors, that in the proper sense really exist. Physically men come and go—mere incidents in a happenstance history of no genuine importance, even to themselves. But the masks they wear, the stage they occupy, the parts they play, and, most important, the spectacle they mount remain and constitute not the facade but the substance of things, not least the self. (p. 50).

From Conceptions of the Person to Social Cognition

Both rights-based and duty-based ethical codes represent society as a natural object of a certain kind. In rights-based societies it is the individual that is fundamental and real and the passions, tastes, and preferences of the individual and his or her liberty to pursue them that are made salient. In duty-based societies it is the organization of social roles that is fundamental and real and role-based obligations that are made salient. In traditional Hindu society the social order *qua* natural order is thought of as an organization of roles and duties. Justifications of social practice and prescriptive arguments move from purported facts of life—for example, hot foods stimulate sexual appetites—to role-bound duties—for example, "the duty of a widow not to eat hot foods such as fish or meat; and from derivative role-bound duties (the duty of the widow not to eat fish or meat) to more fundamental role-bound duties—for example, the duty of women to remain chaste. And why should a woman remain chaste? Well, almost everyone will have a story from personal experience or from the scriptures—suffering will be linked to deviation from role expectations. Nature will be shown to approve of traditional practice.

The traditional Hindu moral code is duty-based and focused on social roles. The American moral code is rights-based and focused on individuals. Duty-based codes direct attention to the moral quality of individual action, to the fit between a specific action and the code of proper conduct (for example, Hindu dharma). Rights-based codes direct attention to the value of individual choice and appetites, tastes, and preferences that the individual chooses to pursue. Recent comparative and developmental research (J. G. Miller 1984; Chapter 3 of this volume) on social cognition in India and the United States shows that each culturally conditioned saliency factor distinctively affects how persons are represented and described and how behavioral events are explained. As we saw in Chapter 3, adult informants in India and the United States described the behavior, characteristics, and nature of someone they knew well in very different ways. The Indian informants displayed a strong tendency to focus on the behavioral act, what someone actually did, and to situate the act in time, place, and by reference to specific dyadic relationships. The Americans displayed a strong tendency to focus on what the person was like, not what he or she actually did, to decontextualize behavior and to describe the person by reference to abstract, situation-free personality traits. Indians were more likely to say, "She brings cakes to my family on festival days." Americans were more likely to say, "She is friendly." The tendency of Indians to perceive others in terms of contexts and cases and of Americans to perceive others in terms of underlying dispositions of the person reflects a general cultural difference. Indian informants who radically differed in education, social status, and literacy displayed a common style of interpersonal perception that distinguished them from American informants.

Joan Miller (1982, 1984) examined the developmental acquisition of cultural conceptions of the person in research conducted in Chicago and in Mysore, a city in southern India. American and Hindu children (ages eight, eleven, and fifteen) and adults were asked to explain everyday deviant and prosocial behaviors. The results documented the existence of culture-specific age changes in explanation. Little difference in social explanation was observed among the youngest American and Hindu informants. With increasing age, however, Americans gave increasing weight to general dispositions of the agent (for example, the personality traits of the individual), whereas increasing age brought no significant increase along such a dimension among Hindus. In contrast, Hindus gave greater attributional weight to contextual factors, with no such shift in such references occurring among Americans. This evidence suggests that the observed trends reflect individuals' acquisition of conceptions of the person emphasized in their culture, rather than differences in individuals' cognitive capacities or objective adaptive requirements. The results highlight the importance of processes of social communication in the acquisition of person concepts. They indicate that initiation into a cultural tradition is a dynamic process, with shifts in individuals' culturally derived conceptual assumptions occurring gradually over development.

Most of the cross-cultural differences in social explanation observed among older informants resulted specifically from differences in attributions to personality traits and to aspects of the social/spatial/temporal location—a category encompassing references to social roles and interpersonal relationships (for example, "She is my aunt") as well as references to the placement of persons, objects, or events in time or space. Indians tended to focus on social role expectations and interpersonal relationships, whereas Americans focused on the agent's character. These cultural differences are illustrated below in explanations of the same deviant behavior offered by a Hindu informant and by an American informant:

Deviant behavior cited by Hindu adult subject:
This concerns a motorcycle accident. The back wheel burst on the motorcycle. The passenger sitting in the rear jumped. The moment the passenger fell, he struck his head on the pavement. The driver of the motorcycle—who is an attorney—as he was on his way to court for some work, just took the passenger to a local hospital and went on and attended to his court work. I personally feel the motorcycle driver did a wrong thing. The driver left the passenger there without consulting the doctor concerning the seriousness of the injury—the gravity of the situation—whether the passenger should be shifted immediately—and he went on to the court. So ultimately the passenger died.

Interview question:
Why did the driver leave the passenger at the hospital without staying to consult about the seriousness of the passenger's injury?

Explanation by Hindu adult subject:
It was the driver's duty to be in court for the client whom he's representing [context—social/spatial/temporal location].
Secondly, the driver might have gotten nervous or confused [agent-specific aspects].
And thirdly, the passenger might not have looked as serious as he was [context—aspects of persons].

Explanation by American adult subject:
The driver is obviously irresponsible [agent—general disposition].
The driver was in a state of shock [agent—specific aspects].
The driver is aggressive in pursuing career success [agent—general dispositions].   (Miller 1984, p. 972)

While both subjects attributed the driver's behavior to affective considerations, the Hindu informant also cited contextual reasons for the behavior, whereas the American informant also made reference to personality factors. The contextual factors—that is, the driver's role obligations as a lawyer and the passenger's physical condition—were explicitly mentioned in the Hindu informant's event description. The American, however, overlooked such available information and instead emphasized dispositional properties of the agent, which could only be inferred. The evidence suggests that such cross-cultural attributional differences reflect both descriptive and prescriptive differences distinguishing theories of the person stressed in the two cultures. In particular, the American's explanation appeared based, in part, on the culturally derived premise that agents possess enduring generalized dispositions and constitute the primary locus of moral responsibility. The Hindu's focus on contextual factors, in contrast, appeared informed by a culturally derived view of persons as highly vulnerable to situational influences and of the social role as the basic normative unit.

Miller's coding scheme is based in part on a system for analyzing human motivation developed by Kenneth Burke (1969). The scheme identifies global distinctions that, it may reasonably be assumed, are universal. Designed for use in cross-cultural developmental research on social explanation, the scheme permits exhaustive coding of subjects' free responses. Major distinctions are made between reasons referring to: (1) the agent, including the agent's general dispositions (for example, "Agent A is insecure") and specific aspects (for example, "Agent A felt hungry"); to (2) the context, including the social/spatial/temporal location (for example, "He was the oldest brother"), aspects of persons other than the agent (for example, "Agent A's friend was feeling tired"), and impersonal aspects of the context (for example, "The sidewalk was icy"); and to (3) acts or occurrences ("He walked outside"; "It started to rain"). Simultaneous references to the agent and to the context are encompassed under a combination category (for example, "They [the agent and his sister] were pleased by the news"). Three additional categories exist to accommodate remarks that do not mention a reason for the behavior being explained. These include categories of rejected or mitigating reasons (for example, "It wasn't because she is kind"; "He helped even though she was a total stranger"), extraneous comments, and questionable remarks.

Social Construction: How Is It Possible?

In our social construction approach to the analysis of cross-cultural variations in concepts of the person, we have argued that the way individuals perceive, describe, and explain each other's behavior is decisively influenced by received conceptualizations of the person in relationship to the moral-social order and the natural order. We have assumed that even though each society viewed its own moral code—whether duty-based and role-based or rights-based and individual-based—as "natural," there is no logical, prudential, or evidential grounds for selecting one type of moral order over the other. Societies, we have implied, are "free" to construct themselves in one way or the other, history being the only constraint. We have also implied that we conceptualize the person the way we do, not because that is the way the person intrinsically is, not because that is the way we intrinsically are, but because that is the kind of conceptualization of the person that is presupposed by our social order and a requisite for its functioning (see Shweder 1984a for an extended discussion of the nonrational foundations of society).

The social construction theory, however, is not the only theory of category formation. In recent years a powerful alternative approach has been proposed, in the form of a naive realist theory of "natural" categories. In the following pages we examine and critique that alternative.

Natural versus Artificial Categories

The most fundamental challenge for any theory of category formation is to explain why some categories seem natural while others seem artificial. Not every category is a natural one. Not every pair of things that are alike in some way—for example, a black cat and the eightball in billiards—are thought to be two of a "kind." Some groupings of like things ("things that are black"; "things that you see on the ground") feel like artificial contrivances. The distinction between a "kind" and a "contrivance," or between a natural classification and an artificial classification, is fundamental; yet it remains the source of controversy and much misunderstanding.

Every classification, whether it is a classification of plants or a classification of mythological figures such as witches, unicorns, fairies, or gods, is natural in the sense that there is some ostensible thing that is classified. In the case of witches, unicorns, fairies, or gods, what one classifies are representations, and representations such as pictures, words, icons, or descriptions are as real and material as plants, organisms, or furniture. We see no rational grounds for claiming that the product of a flower (for example, its pollen) is natural but the product of a human (for example, a picture of a god) is not. The distinction between what is natural versus artificial lies elsewhere.

It is best to illustrate the difference between kinds (natural categories) and contrivances (artificial categories) before trying to understand the nature of the difference. Consider the following natural categories: "Americans," "promises," "females," "Third World countries," "touchdowns," "southerners," "blondes," "Buddhists," "fish," "fowl," "fairies." Compare them with the following artificial categories: "botanists whose fathers had beards" (Gilmour 1951), "adults who were born with the umbilical cord draped around the neck," "football games in which no points were scored in the last two minutes of the third quarter," "cousins who are the daughters of a brother of one's mother."

It is intuitively obvious that there is some type of difference between these two sets of categories. It is also apparent that "Buddhists," "fairies," and "touchdowns" (for example) are kinds (natural categories) even though they refer to cultural and historical creations, whereas "adults who were born with the umbilical cord draped around the neck" is a contrivance (an artificial category) despite the fact that it refers to a biological happening. But wherein lies the difference between the category "touchdown" and the category "botanists whose fathers had beards"? What makes the first a kind and the second a mere contrivance? To this question the Adansonian school of taxonomists (Michael Adanson was an eighteenth-century French botanist) has proposed an answer that is the antithesis of our own (see Jevons 1920, pp. 679–685; Gilmour 1937, 1951; Sneath 1961; Sokal and Sneath 1963; Sokal 1974). A similar answer has been advanced by Elinor Rosch and her associates (Rosch 1975, 1978; Rosch and Mervis 1975; Rosch et al. 1976).

Adansonian Realism: A Critique

The Adansonian approach to natural categories can be summarized in terms of four principles (Gilmour 1937, p. 1041; 1951, p. 401).

1. "The particular classes we construct (e.g., 'hot things' and 'things that hurt') always arise in connection with a particular purpose (e.g., the avoidance of suffering)."
2. "There cannot be one ideal and absolute scheme of classification for any particular set of objects . . . there must always be a number of classifications, differing in their basis according to the purpose for which they have been constructed."
3. "The *primary* function (or purpose) of classification is to construct classes about which we can make inductive generalizations (e.g., 'hot things' are 'things that hurt')" [emphasis added].
4. A natural classification is one "founded on attributes which have a number of other attributes correlated with them, while in an artificial classification such correlation is reduced to a minimum." In other words, a classification becomes more and more natural "the more propositions there are that can be made regarding its constituent classes."

From a social construction perspective the first two Adansonian principles seem promising, although they call out for exegesis, expansion, and extension, while the last two provocatively highlight the differences between a naive realist and social constructionist approach to category formation. (See the Conclusion of this volume, where social construction becomes *artful* realism.)

The first two Adansonian principles state that purpose determines attribute preference, that human purposes are various, and that, therefore, there is no truest or absolute pattern of relative likeness and difference frozen into reality waiting to be encoded.

One implication of these principles is that estimates of likeness or similarity are variable judgments. Goodman (1972) illustrates the point as follows:

> Suppose we have three glasses, the first two filled with colorless liquid, the third with a bright red liquid. I might be likely to say the first two are more like each other than either is like the third. But it happens that the first glass is filled with water and the third with water colored by a drop of vegetable dye, while the second is filled with hydrochloric acid—and I am thirsty. Circumstances alter similarities. (P. 445)

A second implication is that estimates of relative likeness are a product of the way we classify, not the source of those classifications; and that we judge two things to be alike because we have classified them together, not vice versa. That second implication is, in fact, one of the foundation stones for a social construction theory of category formation, and is derivable from the cornerstone principle of a social construction theory, *the principle of logical equidistance among objects.* The basic idea is that the mere counting of common or distinctive properties has little to do with our judgments of similarity, because from the point of view of the number of features that are shared all things are equally alike and equally different. Goodman (1972) puts forth the principle in the following terms:

When, in general, are two things similar? The first response is likely to be: "When they have at least one property in common." But since every two things have some property in common, this will make similarity a universal and hence useless relation. That a given two things are similar will hardly be notable news if there are no two things that are not similar.

Are two things similar, then, only if they have all their properties in common? This will not work either; for of course no two things have all their properties in common. Similarity so interpreted will be an empty and hence useless relation. That a given two things are similar in this sense would be notable news indeed, but false.

By now we may be ready to settle for a comparative rather than a categorical formula. Shall we say that two things *a* and *b* are more alike than two others *c* and *d* if *a* and *b* have more properties in common than do *c* and *d*? If that has a more scientific sound and seems safer, it is unfortunately no better; for any two things have exactly as many properties in common as any other two. If there are just three things in the universe, then any two of them belong together in exactly two classes and have exactly two properties in common: the property of belonging to the class consisting of two things, and the property of belonging to the class consisting of all three things. If the universe is larger, the number of shared properties will be larger but will still be the same for every two elements. When the number of things in the universe is n, each of two things has in common exactly $2n-2$ properties out of the total of $2n-1$ properties; each thing has $2n-2$ properties that the other does not, and there are $2n-1$ properties that neither has. If the universe is infinite all these figures become infinite and equal. (P. 443)

The principle of logical equidistance states that in terms of the number of properties that things have in common all things are equally alike and equally different. (Satosi Watanabe 1969 has given a formal proof that *insofar as all properties have the same weight* "there exists no such thing as a class of similar objects in the world" [p. 376]. Watanabe points out that "if we acknowledge the empirical existence of difference classes of similar objects, it means that we are attaching non-uniform importance to various predicates, and that this weighting has an extra-logical origin" [ibid].)

Social construction theorists assume that reality does not dictate how it is to be categorized or represented. Hence the assumption that the counting of common or distinctive properties has little to do with our judgments of similarity. Indeed, imagine the two very peculiar ways the world would have to be experienced if judgments of similarity were based on a property-counting procedure.

On the one hand, if likenesses were enumerated, since all things are equally alike, we would experience reality as a continuum of merging forms. On the other hand, if differences were enumerated, since all things are equally different, we would experience reality as a scatter of unrelated points. Benjamin Lee Whorf (1956), who understood the principle of *logical* equidistance, referred to reality as a "kaleidoscopic flux of impressions" (p. 213). This is exactly the way the world would have to be perceived if perception was based on a property-counting procedure (where all properties had equal weight). Of course, we experience reality in neither of these ways. Instead, as Whorf recognized, the world is understood categorically and by reference to types of things.

Then, how are such categories and types created? Why is it that, in the face of an indefinitely large number of ways in which any two things are alike (and an indefinitely large number of ways in which they are different), some things are judged more alike than others? The answer, social construction theorists argue, has nothing to do with the sharing versus nonsharing of properties (all things share some property) or with the relative number of properties shared (all things share an infinitely large and thus, in effect, equal number of properties). What the answer does have to do with is the content and purpose-dependent saliency (relevance, weighting, or importance) of the attributes that are shared. Goodman (1972) concludes his "seven strictures on similarity" as follows:

More to the point would be counting not all shared properties but rather only *important* properties—or better, considering not the count but the overall importance of the shared properties. Then *a* and *b* are more alike than *c* and *d* if the cumulative importance of the properties shared by *a* and *b* is greater than that of the properties shared by *c* and *d*. But importance is a highly volatile matter, varying with every shift of context and interest. (P. 443)

Any theory of judged similarity must explain the differential and variable salience of that particular subset of properties (out of the indefinitely large number of properties two things have in common) that have been selected for categorization and description. According to Adansonian taxonomists (principles 1 and 2 given earlier) the salience of a particular property corresponds to its judged relevance, and judged relevance is a purpose-dependent and context-dependent estimate.

The first two principles of the Adansonian approach seem valid. Purpose determines property preference. The steel mill classified according to the capitalist is not the same as the steel mill classified according to the ecologist. The library collection classified according to the card catalog is not the same as the library collection classified according to the accountant (Goodman 1968, p. 6). "A study of the relationship between female authorship and murder stories calls for a different classification of books than a study of American publishers and limited editions" (Gilmour 1951, p. 401).

But are there not certain properties, for example, color and size, that are differentially salient (prepotent) simply by virtue of biological or innate inheritance? We believe that there are. We consider it established fact that on a task in which the only purpose is to list the properties that one notices, certain properties (for example, color) will be universally mentioned before other properties, and some properties will not be spontaneously mentioned at all. We also believe that this established fact carries no general implication for a theory of category formation.

We have maintained that classifications are created for a purpose, and that only properties that are relevant to that purpose will be selected and used to group things in categories. Relevance in this sense has little to do with the biological prepotency of a property. First, "Aunt Vera's cat" and "the highway between Nairobi and Mombasa," "Batman's emblem," and "the eightball in billiards" are not two of a kind even though they are members of the category "things that are black." An eyelash and a paper clip, an ant, and a postage stamp are not two of a kind even though they are members of the category "things that are small" (see Stiles and Wilcox 1974). The biological prepotency of a property (for example, color) is not *sufficient* to turn two things that share the property into two things that are two of a kind, or members of a natural category. Second, the biological prepotency of a property is not *necessary* to turn two things that share the property into two things that are two of a kind (for example, "two glasses of water"). Our classifications of things typically overlook biologically prepotent properties (for example, color) because those properties are irrelevant to our classificatory purposes. As Willard Quine (1969) notes: "The remarkable fact, which has impressed scientists and philosophers as far back as Galileo and Descartes, is that the distinctions that matter for physical theory are mostly independent of color contrasts" (p. 127).

The crucial point is that biologically prepotent properties are often overridden in context (thus, in Goodman's "liquid" example, color becomes irrelevant). Property relevance depends upon context and purpose, and this fact holds for properties that are biologically prepotent as well as for those that are not. Context and purpose can encompass a biologically prepotent property and transform it into one that is hardly noticed. In context, properties that are not biologically prepotent (for example, whatever it is that distinguishes an "insult" from a "joke") are often amplified to a point where they will not be overlooked.

On the other hand it is important to emphasize that, with regard to particular instances, the three types of theories of category formation (realist, innatist, social construction) are not necessarily mutually exclusive. At least some categories may be acquired because that is one of the ways the world is *and* because that is the way people are *and* because those are the categories displayed in social practice and communication. In other words, for certain cases, the realist, innatist, and social construction theories may each be a description of one of the multiple necessary conditions for the acquisition of a category. Consider the rhesus monkey's categorization of snakes as phobic objects (Mineka, Keir, and Price 1980; Mineka and Keir 1983; Cook, Mineka, Wolkenstein, and Laitsch, 1985). Eighty to 90 percent of rhesus monkeys reared in the wild exhibit dread of snakes, whereas rhesus monkeys reared in the laboratory experience snakes with little trepidation. Nevertheless, laboratory monkeys rapidly acquire the fear upon witnessing snake distress in another member of the species. Once acquired, the snake phobia is difficult to extinguish, even though the laboratory monkey has had no direct aversive experience with a snake or snakelike object. It seems reasonable to conclude that all three types of theories of category formation have something to contribute to our understanding of the rhesus monkey's categorization of snakes as objects of fear. In the wild a green mamba is a realistic threat to a monkey's survival; that is one way the world is. But there is more to it than that. Monkeys are predisposed to associate distress with snakelike objects, even in the absence of direct trauma; that is the way monkeys are. Nevertheless, and despite the innate predisposition, without social communication via observational learning the fear might not be acquired at all.

Although Adansonian taxonomists and social construction theorists agree about the role of purpose in classification, social construction theorists reject principles 3 and 4 as expressing a naive realist perspective.

Adansonian taxonomists assume that "the primary function of classification is to construct classes about which we can make inductive generalizations" (for example, "hot things" are "things that hurt") (Gilmour, 1951, p. 40). They imagine that the world is "a scene of recurrent kinds of events and changes which exemplify certain regular connexions" (Hart, 1961, p. 184). Adansonians believe that taxonomies are tools for acquiring knowledge of these regularities. In other words, Adansonian taxonomists assume that classifications exist primarily to serve the needs of "man as scientist." This inductive theory of classification is then extended to the problem of natural categories (kinds).

The Adansonian theory of natural (vs. artificial) categories (kinds vs. contrivances) is well illustrated by Peter Sneath's observations (1961):

A librarian can arrange books in many ways. If arranged alphabetically by authors, then it is only good for one purpose, which is to find it quickly if you know the author's name. It is quite useless as a guide to its size, color, or subject matter. It is a special arrangement for a special purpose, and the analogy in taxonomy is an arbitrary division on a single character, such as dividing vertebrates into four-legged and two-legged. Such divisions do not in general create the kind of entity we call natural taxonomic groups. But one can also arrange books in a *general arrangement*, by employing a summary of all their properties, and this leads to a classification which is primarily by subject matter, since the printed statements in the book will greatly outnumber the other attributes. This is the *best arrangement for general purposes*, because we will usually find what we want in the books of the appropriate subject, although we will never be certain to do so . . . There is therefore a general arrangement best for general purposes, but perfect for none . . . what we call "natural" classification is precisely a general arrangement for general purposes. (Pp. 120–121)

Sneath's procedure for arriving at the natural classification of things, the classification that is best over all possible purposes yet best for no particular purpose, is to: (1) use as many properties as possible, (2) assign equal weight to all the properties, and (3) construct classes on the basis of the proportion of all the properties that any two things have in common (see also Sokal 1974; Sokal and Sneath 1963, p. 50). Consequently a natural classification is said to be one "founded on attributes which have a number of other attributes correlated with them, while in an artificial classification such correlation is reduced to a minimum (Sneath, 1961, p. 121). In other words, Adansonian taxonomists argue that a classification becomes more and more natural the more propositions there are that can be made regarding its constituent classes. Thus, Gilmour (1937) asserts that "a classification of mankind on a basis of nationality is more natural than one based on the initial letter of surnames, because more propositions can be made regarding an Englishman (for example, that he probably speaks English, knows 'God Save the King,' has a white skin, etc.) than about a man whose name begins with E" (p. 1041).

Adansonian taxonomists might advance a similar argument to explain our intuition that the category "mammals" is a kind while the category "black things" is a contrivance. Earlier we noted that Adansonians correctly reject the notion that there is some "ideal or absolute scheme of classification for any particular set of objects." Unfortunately, Adansonian taxonomists reintroduce the notion of an ideal classification or "literal transcript" of reality in their approach to natural classifications, in the guise of correlated attributes or the proportion of properties that objects share.

The first difficulty with the Adansonian theory of natural categories is that if we were actually to follow Adansonian procedures we would arrive at no taxonomy at all. Contrary to Sneath's claims, an arrangement of books that faithfully tried to summarize *all* their properties would have to classify books on the basis of the number of vowels, letters, syllables, words, sentences, paragraphs, pages, and so on, in the text, the quality of ink used in printing, the initial letter of the fifth word on page 17, the presence or absence of stray markings in the columns of even-numbered pages except page 24, and so on, ad infinitum. There is an infinite number of sets in which any two books are coelements; on the basis of a mere property count all books would be equally alike and equally different. Or, as Goodman notes (1968): "To admit all classifications on equal footing is to make no classification at all" (p. 32).

The second difficulty with the Adansonian theory of natural categories is that not all classifications are inductive in their intent or designed to serve the inferential purposes of "man as scientist." "Man as rulemaker" has a very different purpose; a primary function of classification is to construct classes of things the behavior to (of) which can be regulated or governed by prescriptions, recommendations, and taboos. For example, "dogs" are potentially eatable animals that one should not eat. "Siblings" are potentially sexy people with whom one should not have sex. One function of classification is to tell the world how it ought to behave, and since most human behavior is rule governed, many, perhaps most, of our categories serve this function, at least in part. For example, *Modern Etiquette in Private and Public* (1872) (see Douglas 1973, pp. 216–218) tells us something about the category "fish." At a dinner party it is to be served directly after the soup, and "you must eat it with a fork, unless silver knives are provided." As for the category "soup," you always eat it from the side of your spoon, "you should make no noise in eating it," and "you should beware of tasting it while too hot, or of swallowing it fast enough to make you cough." To construct classes for the sake of drawing inductive generalizations is to pursue only one of the major purposes served by a taxonomy. Thus, any scientific (or descriptive) classification (in contrast to a prescriptive classification) is in this sense a special classification for a special purpose.

The third difficulty is that the differential weighing of properties cannot be avoided; inevitably most of the properties of an object are unconsciously excluded as irrelevant. Those that are selected are differentially weighted by the act of selection itself.

Adansonians want to construct a classification that will generate the highest average number of true statements about objects across a finite number of fields of inductive generalization (for example, physiology, morphology, ecology, genealogy). Given that purpose and given their belief that the scientific goals of the morphologist are no less important than the goals of the ecologist, it is reasonable to assign equal weights to all the properties one has selected. But, that is a weighting decision recommended only by the rather special purpose Adansonian taxonomists happen to pursue.

The Adansonian theory of natural categories (kinds) is a fine theory for cases in which one's purpose is to draw probabilistic inferences across a variety of preselected fields of generalization. In fact, the Adansonian theory of natural categories is really a statement of what the best classification would be, *given that purpose*. Our own theory of kinds (or natural categories) is more general, and it has the advantage of not tempting us to imagine a single system of kinds or natural categories, out there, fixed in reality, waiting to be discovered by means of property-counting procedures or correlational analysis.

Our view is as follows: The difference between a kind (a natural category) and a contrivance (an artificial category) is the degree of "psychological availability" of some purpose and context with respect to which the things grouped together in the category can be seen as relevant. By the psychological availability of a context and purpose we mean the ease with which a purpose or context can be brought to mind when the category is mentioned (see Tversky and Kahneman 1973, 1974).

Natural categories have a place in our purposes; artificial categories do not. Thus, it seems artificial to group together a puddle, a mushroom, and a utility hole cover despite the fact that they are all "things you see on the ground." We have difficulty imagining a context in which we might make use of the things collected together by such a property. On the other hand, it seems perfectly natural to talk of such kinds as "tooth fairy," "uncle," "small slam," "port tack," or "ironic comment" despite the fact that the numbers of true propositions one can make about them are no more or less numerous than those we can make about "things we see on the ground." Some categories have a place in our "forms of life" (Wittgenstein 1968 [1953]); others do not. In other words, the category "botanists whose fathers had beards" would remain a contrivance even if it were the case that such botanists were more likely to have been born with the umbilical cord draped around the neck, tended to marry their mother's brother's daughters, and displayed a preference for football games in which no points were scored in the last two minutes of the third quarter. None of these correlates plays a part in our purposes (unless we are Adansonian taxonomists).

Our theory of natural versus artificial categories is a theory about the psychological availability of a culturally appropriate context or purpose within which the things grouped together in a category can be seen to have a place. Is there anything we can say about the conditions influencing the psychological availability of an appropriate purpose or context? The psychological availability of a context tends to be greatest when it is occupied. The psychological availability of a purpose tends to be greatest when it is being pursued. Thus, in context, it seems natural to distinguish "balls" from "strikes" (I am pitching in the World Series), or "mother's brother's daughters" from "mother's sister's daughters" (I am an Ojibwa Indian looking for a wife; cross-cousin marriage is preferred), or "daughters with a fair complexion" from "daughters with a dark complexion" (I am an Oriya Brahman arranging a marriage; the darker the skin of my daughter the greater the dowry I will have to accumulate. It's a black-and-white issue.)

In the wrong context *any* distinction can seem contrived. Females over here. Males over there. "Wait a minute," bellows the judge. " 'Plaintiffs' and 'defendants' don't sit together in my court room. And get that 'jury' back together!" Out of context, the psychological availability of a form of life probably has no direct relationship to the frequency with which that form of life is pursued, although the more cultural activities there are in which a category plays a part, the more things there are that informants have to say about the category. For example, the category "female" plays a part in many of our purposes. In this respect, the category "female" contrasts with the category "four bids in a major suit" (which to our knowledge is relevant only in bridge play, bridge books, bridge columns, and bridge conversation). But—and this is our main point about "out-of-context" thinking—it is not apparent that the numerous forms of life associated with categories such as "female," "competition," "questions," "contracts," "middle class," "in-laws," "corporations," and "democracy" are any more psychologically available than the less frequent forms of life associated with "tooth fairy," "solitaire," "best man," "small slam," or "jibe." All these categories are natural. All these categories have been picked out for description and representation, and the mere mention of the label brings to mind the appropriate forms of life. Distant contexts are made available to us by means of our language. In this sense, "nature is a product of art and discourse" (Goodman 1968, p. 33).

5.

Determinations of Meaning:
Discourse and Moral Socialization
with Nancy C. Much

This essay explores social communication and its power to represent and transmit moral beliefs. Moral beliefs have their ontogenetic origins in the messages and meanings implicitly conveyed through talk, conversation, discourse, and customary practice. Children are continually assisted by local guardians of the moral order in constructing their notions of right and wrong, and the inferences they draw about both the moral (its form) and what is moral (its content) are personal reconstructions recreated within a framework of tradition-based modes of apperception and evaluation represented in everyday discourse.

A scheme of concepts (communicative array, indexicality, instantiation, background knowledge) accounts for the construction of meaning in discourse. We focus on the way a picture of the moral order is indexed and tacitly conveyed through speech, and we outline a method of discourse analysis based on the expansion or unpacking of what is said to reveal propositions about the moral order that remain unsaid yet are nonetheless effectively communicated through everyday speech. This method of expansion implements our theory of how meaning is constructed in discourse: since speakers always mean and convey more than they say, meaning is revealed by making explicit the relationship between the said and the unsaid.

We apply our theory of meaning and method of expansion to one part of the text of a moral dilemma interview (Kohlberg's Heinz dilemma; see appendix to this chapter, page 229) conducted with an orthodox Hindu informant in India. Lawrence Kohlberg himself classifies the unexpanded text as an instance of stage 3/4 conventional reasoning. Not until the text is expanded or unpacked to explicate implicit meanings is it possible to recognize the postconventional reasoning of the informant, who, unlike Kohlberg, represents the Heinz dilemma as a problem in the irrationality of committing a sin rather than as a problem of rights, justice, or life versus property. From this analysis it seems clear that codings of unexpanded moral development interview protocols, based exclusively on propositions explicitly stated in an interview, are likely to misrepresent the moral beliefs of informants.

In trying to make sense of the widespread academic phobia for studying everyday talk and its power to represent and transmit moral beliefs, we are led to rethink the terms of the destructive debate over whether moral judgments ("that's wrong;" "that's bad") are cognitive or noncognitive (emotive). Both cognitivists and emotivists have unfortunate conceptions about the relation between moral judgments and natural or objective entities. Emotivists tend to view moral judgments as entirely subjective, and to dismiss moral discourse or argumentation as pretense, or as a mock or illusory rhetoric disguising an underlying pragmatic function (for example, to preserve privilege or power). Cognitivists tend to search for the objective foundations of moral judgments in an abstract-formal-logical realm far removed from everyday thoughtful talk. Our neorationalist approach shares with cognitive approaches the assumption that natural or objective moral entities exist and that moral understandings are a form of knowledge about some objective moral world. Our neorationalist approach is defined by three distinctive assumptions: that genuine objectivity can be, in some measure, subject dependent; that the existence of moral facts and moral knowledge is compatible with the existence of multiple objective moral worlds and alternative forms of postconventional moral reasoning; and that each of those several objective moral worlds is found in, and maintained through, the ordinary conversations of everyday life.

Discourse and the Framing of a Moral Universe

During the last several years we have been conducting research on moral development in India and the United States (Shweder 1982a,

1982c; Shweder, Mahapatra, and Miller 1987; and Chapters 4 and 6 of this volume). The research in India has been carried out in a Hindu temple town on the east coast of India among various Oriya Brahman subcastes and among various castes referred to as unclean or "untouchable" by the local Brahmans.

In Orissa, arguments favoring or defending a practice are often presented in the form of a narrative account. Indeed, for orthodox Hindus a major way to prove a point is to recount a historical or personal narrative, and a central body of evidence about what the causal structure of the world is like consists of "historical" experiences recorded in the Hindu scriptures, especially the Puranas and the Epics (the *Ramayana* and the *Mahabharata*). Orthodox Hindus believe that the experiences of their forefathers recorded in the scriptures are a reasonable guide to the causal structure of reality. Thus, most expositions about what the world is or ought to be like begin, "Let me tell you a story."

Let me tell you a story about stealing. Once some sadhus [wandering mendicant holy men] came to a poor man's house. He and his son were the only members of the family. The sadhus wanted this man to be their host for that night. Holy men never ask for credit. They never steal. They have only what they earn from begging alms, which they cook and eat.

The sadhus arrived at the man's house as guests, and as guests they were considered as a god. So the man and his son pawned whatever belongings they had and arranged dinner for the sadhus. Before going to their dinner the sadhus said that ghee was essential for their dinner. [Ghee, or clarified butter, is classified in the native theory of foods as a "cool" food. Unlike "hot" foods, such as onions, garlic, fish, or meat, cool foods do not stimulate the senses or draw the consumer's attention to such bodily or organic process as taste or digestion. Thus cool foods are conducive to the quest of the sadhu, which is the distillation of the spirit in an attempt to transcend this worldly and momentary material existence.] Both the father and the son pondered again and again where to get the ghee. They were really "in a stew."

They went to the sadhu of a nearby monastery to get some ghee. But the sadhu refused to give them ghee. So they made a hole in the wall and the son entered the storeroom of the monastery. It was full of wealth, but the son picked up only the ghee pot. While he was halfway through the hole, suddenly the sadhu got up and caught hold of the son's two legs. But outside the father was pulling the son's hands. So a tussle went on for some time. The son told the father to take the pot of ghee and offer it to the sadhu guests. He also told his father to cut off his head and take it away so the sadhu of the monastery would not be able to recognize him. The father did this and threw away his son's head.

The father did such things only because he wanted to help the sadhus. After he offered ghee to his guests the sadhus were satisfied. The next morning the father bode them farewell, and they asked, "Where is your son? He is not seen." The father started to cry. The sadhus asked him why he was crying. So he told all the details and facts, and said it was nobody's fault.

The sadhus said, "You have made a mistake. Okay. If you have done it only to satisfy us, if you had no evil intention under it, if you had no temptation for the wealth, and if your son died only for this, then we will pray to God for his life." They asked, "Where is your son's head?" They wanted to show God the decapitated head. The father took the head of the son to the sadhus. They sprinkled some Tulsi water on the head. [Tulsi is a basil plant. The leaf of the plant in water produces a substance believed to have various potent causal powers. Among orthodox Hindus there is a well-known story about how Tulsi became a basil plant. In brief, Tulsi was the loyal, chaste, and devoted wife of a demon. Her husband was very successful at terrorizing the gods. He could not be killed unless he was weakened, and the only way to weaken him was to violate the chastity of his wife; her chastity made him strong. So the Hindu god Vishnu disguised himself as Tulsi's husband and slept with her. The demon was killed. When Tulsi discovered the treachery she cursed Vishnu and told him he would turn into a log or piece of wood. In fact Vishnu is today represented as a log in the Temple of Juggernaut in Orissa. Vishnu, however, blessed Tulsi and made compensation to her by turning her into a holy plant, which he always keeps with him, and which is today worshiped by wives and widows all over India. In the courtyard of every Brahman household is a Tulsi plant.] So the son returned to life.

This story was narrated in the Oriya language to Shweder during an interview concerning whether a man should steal a drug to save the life of his wife. The interview, based on Kohlberg's Form A (the Heinz dilemma), was modified in trivial ways to eliminate obvious culture-specific or ethnocentric features (for example, Heinz was re-named Ashok). (See the appendix to this chapter for the full text of the interview.) It is only one of many stories the informant told to support his position that Ashok should not steal.

The text above incorporates in brackets a minimal explication or expansion of elements of Hindu life that are obviously opaque to a Western reader (for example, what a sadhu is, why it is important for sadhus to have ghee for dinner, and what Tulsi is). There are, however, many other things in the text that are opaque without being obviously so, and there are many unstated propositions that must be made explicit if an uninformed reader is to appreciate the compelling nature of the case that is being advanced by the informant against committing the sin of stealing. At this point we merely note the characteristic Oriya form of moral argumentation: telling stories related to precedents recorded in scriptures that reveal truths about the causal structure of reality as a natural-physical-moral order.

One of the more striking findings of our moral development research in India and America (Shweder, Mahapatra, and Miller 1987) is that by age five Oriya children are very Oriya and American children are very American. When it comes to judgments about what is right and what is wrong there is virtually no correlation between the judgments of the five-year-olds in the two cultures. That is also true of the moral judgments of older children and adults in the two cultures. Thus while there are some areas of agreement between the five-year-olds in the two cultures (for example, that it is wrong to break a promise, destroy a picture drawn by another child, kick a harmless animal), there are just as many areas of disagreement. Oriya (but not American) five-year-olds believe it is wrong to eat beef or address one's father by his first name. American (but not Oriya) five-year-olds believe it is wrong to cane an errant child or to open a letter addressed to one's fourteen-year-old son. Moreover, while the obligations (whatever they are thought to be) associated with each of those issues are conceived by five-year-olds in both cultures to be natural or objective obligations (that is, unalterable and, in most cases, universally binding), the Americans, but not the Oriyas, represent those obligations in terms of natural rights and in terms of values associated with liberty, equality, and secular happiness. On the other hand, the Oriya concept of dharma and sin and the concept of the moral authority of custom or tradition are alien to the moral sensibilities of secularized American informants.

Finally, the evidence of Shweder and colleagues (1987) suggests that, within each culture, those moral judgments that are common to both cultures (for example, that it is wrong to engage in arbitrary assault, break promises, destroy property, commit incest) are learned at about the same rate as those that are distinctive of each culture (for example, in America, that it is wrong for a husband to beat his wife if she repeatedly leaves the house without permission; or, in India, that it is wrong for a widow to remarry or eat fish or meat or wear jewelry). This evidence of a roughly equal rate of acquisition for culture-specific and universal moral content indicates that both the universal and the culture-specific aspects of a moral code may be learned by means of the same process.

Children five years of age and older in orthodox Hindu India and secularized America have orthogonal judgments about what is right and wrong, conceive of obligations in somewhat divergent terms (for example, it's my right; it's a sin), and achieve an understanding of the culture-specific aspects of their moral code at the same rate as they achieve an understanding of those aspects of their moral code that are shared with other cultures. Our social communication approach to moral development is an attempt to identify that unitary process of moral socialization.

Our basic (and perhaps commonsensical) notion is that children develop the moral ideas they have because local guardians of the moral order (parents, teachers, peers) re-present and convey to children powerful morally relevant interpretations of events. Those interpretations are conveyed, we believe, in the context of routine, yet personally involving, family, school, and social life practices (practices having to do with eating, sleeping, grooming, possessing objects, distributing resources, and so on). They are conveyed through the verbal exchanges—commands, threats, sanction statements, accusations, explanations, justifications, and excuses—necessary to maintain routine practices. We assume that morally relevant interpretations of events are got across and made salient, as well, by the emotional reactions of others; for example, anger or disappointment or "hurt feelings" over a transgression. Finally, we assume that moral interpretations of events are expressed through and are discernible in the very organization of routine practices (a separate bed for each child, a communal meal, lining up—first come, first served—to get tickets). In sum, it is our view that children's emerging moral understandings are the product of continuous participation in social practices (the mundane rituals of everyday life), and those socially produced and reproduced understandings are the grounding for later attempts reflectively or self-consciously to reconstruct their own moral code.

It is an axiom of our social communication approach to moral socialization that local guardians of the moral order persistently and powerfully trace for children the boundaries of a normative reality and assist the children in stepping into the frame.

Because language is perhaps the most powerful means of social communication, we focus on the analysis of discourse. The data corpus available to us consists of conversations between children (ages four and five) and adults in situations of accountability in an American preschool (Much and Shweder 1978; Much 1983). Our route to understanding those symbolic forms is by way of what Clifford Geertz (1973) has called "thick description." While what is said in everyday discourse in preschool settings may seem "thin" and obvious, what is implied, suggested, got across, or accomplished by what is said is "thick" and often surprising. Implicit in or presupposed by what is said is a conception of an objective moral universe.

INCIDENT 1: ALL THE CHILDREN ARE FRIENDS IN SCHOOL

It is "rug time." Children are seated around Mrs. Swift on the rug. Emily sits just to the left of Mrs. Swift and Andrea sits next to Emily. Vicki leaves her seat and approaches them.

1. *Vicki:* I want to sit next to Emily.
2. *Mrs. Swift:* There's no room and you stay where you are. [Vicki would have to place herself between Mrs. Swift and Emily or between Emily and Andrea in order to sit next to Emily.]
3. *Vicki:* Emily . . . my friend.
4. *Mrs. Swift:* All the children are friends in school.
5. *Vicki:* Yeah, but some children say they're not my friend.
6. *Mrs. Swift:* Well, then you try to make them your friend.

INCIDENT 2: THE VALUE OF FRIENDLINESS.

Mr. Price and some children are sitting in the back playroom. A teacher from another classroom appears at the door with a child from her unit. Alice (a four-year-old) addresses them.

1. *Alice:* What are you doing in our class?
2. *Teacher:* Well, we came up the stairs and we didn't know where we were going and here we are.
3. *Alice:* Get out of our class.
4. *Teacher:* That's unfriendly of you.
5. *Mr. Price:* That's not very friendly.
6. *Mr. Price:* You should be friendly to visitors.
7. *Mr. Price:* Sometimes you go up and visit their classroom.

In both incidents local guardians of the moral order trace for these four-year-olds the boundaries of a moral universe and help the children step into the frame. In incident 1 Vicki presses for the privilege of affiliating with Emily on the grounds that Emily falls into a certain category of person, "my friend" (utterance 3). Mrs. Swift, however, will not allow Vicki to treat this category as an exclusive class; she introduces a norm including all classroom members in the category "friend" (4). Mrs. Swift's proposition (4) may appear to be a factual proposition, but it is used to deliver a moral message; it describes the way things ought to be, not the way they are. Whether in this instance Vicki understood the normative force of Mrs. Swift's utterance is ambiguous; Vicki's next utterance (5) introduces a contrary fact, which calls into question Mrs. Swift's implication. This suggests that Vicki either interpreted Mrs. Swift's utterance (4) as a factual proposition or understood its normative implication yet tried to evade its normative force by conveniently "misreading" it as a statement of fact.

But notice how carefully Mrs. Swift monitors the uptake of her own messages. Vicki's factual objection is met not by further factual reasoning, but by another statement of a normative proposition (6), which is a prescription for appropriate action. Vicki has objected to Mrs. Swift's reasoning on the grounds that Mrs. Swift's words do not describe the classroom as Vicki knows it. Mrs. Swift, however, proffers a norm, making it unambiguous to the children that she expects them, through their actions, to get the world of the classroom to line up with her words. The conversation portrays for these young children a moral world based on free or at least nonexclusive affiliation.

In incident 2 ("get out of our class") the child, Alice, tries to understand the event in terms of rights (what is ours and not yours) (1, 3) and the attendant privilege of imposing one's own intentions (3). However, adults in the episode are interested in instructing Alice in the expectations of free and nonexclusive affiliation. They represent for Alice and call her attention to a moral universe in which three evaluative criteria compete with Alice's one-dimensional evaluation of the event in terms of who holds rights. The norm of "friendliness" is introduced and prescribed (4, 5, 6) along with a category, "visitor" (6), which is supposed to classify the outside teacher as a person with whom one is expected to affiliate. A rationale for affiliation is expanded in utterance 7 by reference to the actions of the outside teacher relative to the actions of members of Alice's class; that is, a norm of reciprocity is represented and applied. The message is that rights are not the only or most important consideration bearing upon the event, and that in the moral universe in which we are going to live together rights must be weighed or balanced against other values.

Everyday conversation and social interaction between adults and children involve a relentless process of representation and rationalization making salient certain powerful belief conclusions about the nature of experience. At home and at school young children are (to borrow an apt metaphor from Judith Dunn) continually "bathed" in verbal evaluations and discourse-based representations of a moral universe. The discourse indexes, or points in the direction of, a conception of a moral world that has been worked on over many generations. That collectively evolved conception of a moral universe is a complex network of ideals, supposed facts, maxims, presuppositions, and much more, which not only specifies the kinds of persons and events that exist in that moral world but also places limits on what is going to count as a sensible argument in defense of the rationality, objectivity, and hence legitimacy of that moral world. One goal of our analysis is to make explicit that network of objectifying knowledge.

Yet there is more to it than that. In constantly monitoring and assisting them as they go about describing and evaluating events, American middle-class adults not only treat children as novice recipients of knowledge and insights into the objective nature of the moral order. American adults also expect young children to uphold the moral order, to care about upholding the moral order, and to become their own local moral guardians. Through discourse an objective moral universe is not only represented; it also comes to be reproduced.

INCIDENT 3: THE FOUNDATION OF RIGHTS, OR "I HAD IT FIRST AND I'M USING IT"

Clifford is seated at a table, using a felt-tip marker to color a wooden dinosaur he has built. Mrs. Swift stands nearby. Sean enters the room and comes to the table.

1. *Sean:* Hey Clifford. I need this [indicating the marker].
2. *Clifford:* Yeah, but I got it first.
3. *Clifford:* You mean it's yours?
4. *Sean:* Yeah.
5. *Clifford:* Did you take it home? [meaning: bring it from home?]
6. *Sean:* No.
7. *Clifford:* Were you using it before?
8. *Sean:* Yeah.
9. *Mrs. Swift:* He was using it before he went downstairs.
10. *Clifford:* Well, I was just using it.
11. *Mrs. Swift:* Well, but you should ask.

This conversation reveals not only Clifford's emerging competence (and sophistication) in representing events in terms of who holds rights, but also several features of the way rights are conceived in the moral universe undergoing reconstruction in the mind of the four-year-old American child.

First, when Sean wishes to claim an article in Clifford's possession he objectifies his claim by oblique reference to some purpose or constraint. Sean's utterance "I need this" (1) implies an intention to use the implement for some purpose. Whether such a purpose is actually present "in Sean's mind" is a separate question that, in this context, is of little importance. Nursery school children have learned the advantage of using "I need" where "I want" could also be used; it lends an air of legitimacy to a demand or request. While the usage certainly does not guarantee the success of the claim, it does tell us something about the norms for making a legitimate claim on communal resources. Purposiveness has become a reasonable basis for personal removal of resources from the common pool.

It is noteworthy that Sean extends a justification by reference to purpose to account for a claim to an implement already in the possession of another child. Sean's reasoning represents the standard justification among preschool children for demanding or requesting rights to material resources in another's possession or use. Here Clifford meets the demand-request with an assertion of his own rights to the implement on the basis of a widely recognized principle for establishing temporary personal claim to communal property, namely, priority (2). But Clifford rechecks Sean's meaning (3); Clifford wants to know whether Sean's claim was also supported by established rights. Sean indicates that it was.

A sequence follows (5–8) in which Clifford tries to determine the basis of Sean's rights. Clifford begins by testing the hypothesis that the implement is Sean's private property, that Sean has brought it from home. This would constitute the strongest kind of claim to rights that Sean could have. But, as Sean indicates (6), this is not the case. The next principle Clifford checks is priority (7)—was Sean using the implement even before Clifford was? Sean assents to this condition as the basis of his claim, and Mrs. Swift (9) swiftly, and with considerable weight, enters to support his contention.

The argument thus far has been concerned with determining who has established rights over the implement, a not uncommon type of argument in the nursery school. Once the basis of Sean's rights has been established, apparently to Clifford's satisfaction, Clifford not only submits to Sean's claim but also accounts for his own actions with a constituting denial (10).

A constituting denial disclaims the blameworthiness of an action by defining it in such a way that the action as described does not breach the norm in question; typically a contrast is implied between the action as defined and another possible definition of the action that would make it appear as a breach. That move may be accomplished with the use of "only" or "just" ("I was just using it"; "I was just seeing it") or by substitution with the alternative definition ("You stole my chair!" "No, nobody was in it and I sat in it").

What is noteworthy about Clifford's constituting denial (10) is that he recognizes his potential liability to some blame, although it is unclear whether that recognition is the result of his reasoning or the result of the teacher's intervention, or both. In his constituting denial (10) he defines his action in such a way as to disclaim intent to infringe upon Sean's rights; Clifford seems to be saying that what he did was not really bad because he did not know the marker was already claimed.

In the closing utterance (11) Mrs. Swift, a guardian of the moral order acting on her didactic agenda, seizes an opportunity to teach Clifford a principle: you should ask before using something. This is a fascinating admonition. Does Mrs. Swift really intend that Clifford conduct a systematic inquiry for establishing prior rights every time he wants to use an article of communal property? She certainly does not. What she probably does intend is to make salient for Clifford a general responsibility to anticipate possible rights of others over resources even when prior claims are not immediately evident. How incessantly yet delicately we trace for each other the boundaries of our moral universe, and our responsibilities to it and within it.

Socialization and the Construction of Meaning in Discourse

Our theory about the acquisition of moral beliefs is a theory about how meaning is constructed in discourse. Recent work on the analysis of discourse and conversation has made it axiomatic that ordinary talk means far more than it says and carries information about cultural beliefs and knowledge systems that transcends the grammatical and referential aspects of language (Labov and Fanshel 1977; Longacre 1983).

For example, in the utterance "Oh dear, I wish I were taller" at least three things are happening (Ervin-Tripp 1976). The speaker is explicitly stating a proposition regarding an intentional state (wishing to be taller). The speaker is implicitly requesting a service ("Please get the dishes down for me"). The speaker is implicitly communicating something about her relationship to the interlocutor (that he is familiar, that he may be expected to have a solicitous attitude toward the speaker, that he is taller than the speaker). In ordinary conversation what is said is never a complete representation of what is implied or suggested or got across by what is said.

One way to state the axiom is that what is said carries *indexical* meaning—it points beyond itself to implications and suggestions whose connection to what was said is inferential. The meaning and coherence of any stretch of conversation are dependent upon processes of inference that tie the utterance to features of the context in which it is embedded, and to various unstated background propositions. A corollary of the indexicality axiom: In drawing inferences from what was said to what was unsaid, participants need to be informed, and in fact become informed, about things that were never mentioned.

A second axiom is that for an inference to occur in the construction of meaning the recipient or observer of a communication must have sufficient prior knowledge to infer the implication or suggestion that is the meaning of what was said. The basic idea is that prior knowledge (knowledge of categories, propositions, maxims, contexts, intentional states, logical relations, and so on) is the most powerful factor in generating further knowledge (the meaning of what was said).

A corollary of the prior knowledge axiom is a principle of intersubjectivity that states: (1) participants in conversation address utterances to listeners who are assumed to have sufficient prior knowledge to understand them; (2) participants monitor the uptake or comprehension of their utterances and watch for indications that they may be wrong in their assumption that the listener has sufficient prior knowledge; and (3) conversation is a self-corrective process in which an equilibrium is sought between what is said and the prior knowledge needed to comprehend it.

That self-corrective process can be thought of as a progressively constrained dialectic that proceeds iteratively in two directions. From one direction prior knowledge consisting of unstated propositions is brought to bear in interpreting what was said; to the extent the interpretation "works" it gives a sense of reality or objectivity to the unstated propositions. This is sometimes referred to as the *instantiation* of beliefs—the utterance is seen as an instance of an unstated general proposition that is already known.

In the other direction what is taken as known is used to draw inferences beyond itself, as part of an effort to make sense of what was said and to search for a propositional content that is not yet known but is implicit in what was said. Again, in forcing participants to draw inferences from what was said to what was unsaid, discourse has the power indirectly to inform participants (for example, children) or observers (for example, ethnographers) about things that were never explicitly mentioned.

A third axiom of discourse analysis is that the relevant unit of analysis is the entire communicative array linking by means of knowledgeable inference what was said to what was meant. A communicative array is a set of coexisting elements—speech (what is said), context, and background knowledge—in which the three elements bear a mutually constraining relationship. Thus to construct the meaning of discourse in a communicative array, as either a participant or an observer, involves referring the explicit content of speech (what was said) to two indexed levels, the context and all the relevant prior background knowledge needed to make sense of what was said. Indeed, everyday discourse is abbreviated, condensed, and implicit (indexical) precisely because participants count on each other to count on (and can count on each other to take account of the other's counting on) context and a (presumed) shared body of prior knowledge to contribute the knowledge needed to draw a reasonable inference from what was said to what was meant.

A corollary of the communicative array axiom is that objective determinations of meaning are possible. That is not the same as saying that there are formal, logical, deductive, or structural principles that can be mechanically, automatically, or routinely applied to an utterance to arrive at a determination of what it means; if the meaning of an utterance is indexical there is no formal or structural feature of the utterance per se that determines what it means, yet the utterance may still have a meaning that can be determined objectively.

Thus given sufficient prior knowledge of context, background assumptions, usage, and so on, it is possible to distinguish between valid and invalid inferences about what an utterance means; to recognize improper or implausible deductions about what was left unstated, presupposed, or assumed in the communication; and so on. The process of determining the meaning of an utterance in a communicative array is somewhat like solving a hermeneutic jigsaw puzzle, but if you have enough pieces in place it becomes easy to see how the rest should be filled in. The following analysis shows how the process works.

INCIDENT 4: "THAT IS NOT A PAPER CUP"

Alice (age four years) is seated at a table. She has a glass full of water. Mrs. Swift (the teacher) approaches and addresses Alice.
1. *Mrs. Swift:* That is not a paper cup.

The episode contains two more utterances, but for the moment consider only the initial one. It is noteworthy that while there is no formal, abstract, or logical feature of the utterance that marks it as an "accusation," the context, the discourse, and certain background knowledge make the teacher's utterance readily identifiable as such.

It is also noteworthy that at the time of recording the episode the observer (Much) had not yet learned of the classroom rule that children are supposed to use paper cups and not glasses (except at snack time with the teacher's supervision). However, from Mrs. Swift's utterance (1) the rule could be immediately inferred or constructed, at least as far as "children are supposed to use paper cups and not glasses." Indeed, it is only because of that rule that the utterance "That is not a paper cup" is the kind of speech act it is at all—an accusation.

In other words, the rule, a context-specific and unmentioned entity, is crucial for the very constitution of the speech act. Yet a listener who did not previously know about the existence of the rule is able not only to understand the speech act (as an accusation) but also to infer the rule and become informed of its existence from the very fact of its functional presupposition. A hermeneutic dialectic is at work, and it operates rapidly, unconsciously, and effectively.

This episode illustrates the principle that if we have enough pieces of the puzzle we can fill in the missing ones. We recognize expressions of belief and desire through voice and action cues in context, and those tell us how to interpret or go beyond the surface content of what was said. We are assisted by our general knowledge of cultural belief propositions concerning the relevant differences between glasses and paper cups (the former break and the latter do not) and the anticipated competences of children three to five years old (who, we believe, might knock things over and get hurt). Even though lacking a formal procedure or generalized coding instruction for identifying accusations as accusations, knowledgeable observers of the communicative array have little difficulty reliably classifying utterance 1 as an accusation. The utterance has a meaning that can be objectively determined.

The episode continues:

2. *Alice:* I want to put it down [broken, whimpering voice].
3. *Mrs. Swift* (taking the glass away from Alice): No, that's just for snack time when the teacher is at the table.

It is ambiguous from utterance 2 whether Alice had prior knowledge of the rule that constitutes the accusation. The fact that Mrs. Swift initially engaged in an indirect indication of the rule (1) suggests that she thought it was something the child already knew; in other words, Mrs. Swift expected Alice to recognize the rule even though it was only implicit in what was said. Alice's utterance (2), however, is not a definitive confirmation of Mrs. Swift's expectation. Alice seems to appeal to some intention that she believes mitigates the breach (if I put it down rather than hold it in my hand I won't be breaking any rule).

What is clear is that Alice recognizes Mrs. Swift's speech act and the intention behind it. Alice knows that she is being told that she is doing something wrong. This is confirmed by her plaintive tone and her effort to "repair" the situation. Mrs. Swift, in utterance 3, seems to express doubt that Alice has fully comprehended utterance 1 or correctly inferred the rule implicit in it. This can be inferred from the fact that Mrs. Swift responds to Alice by giving the rule further explicit formulation in utterance 3, telling Alice that the glass is just for snack time when the teacher is assisting.

It is clear from this illustration that determining the meaning of a stretch of discourse (as either a participant or an observer) is no formal or mechanical matter, yet it is objectively constrained. It calls for a good deal of prior cultural knowledge, and it is through the process of determining the meaning of a symbolic form that more cultural knowledge is acquired by both the child and the outside observer. Of course in interpreting the meaning of discourse one is always trying to make sense of what was explicitly said, and that is a major constraint on attributions of meaning. But there are other kinds of constraints as well.

One constraint is the way language gets used indexically. Mrs. Swift's utterances, though quite condensed, powerfully summarize the cognitive-normative core of the event and point the child in the direction of understanding it. Though abbreviated, the utterances crystal-lize and transmit the moral meaning of the event. The utterance "That is not a paper cup" is basically a category contrast, meaning "That is not a paper cup, it is a glass." It refers the meaning of the event to what is assumed to be known about the relevant differences between paper cups and glasses (a potential for harm through break-age), focusing the meaning of the event on the issue of potential harm. Although the teacher's utterances never explicitly mention the issue of harm, the child seems to understand it, as she shows by her offer to "put it down" (so that she will be less likely to break it?).

The teacher's final utterance gives additional normative content to the event and corrects the child's partial misunderstanding. Glasses in the classroom are used only for snack time and only when a teacher is supervising. The teacher's utterances (1, 3) leave a lot unsaid. No one has actually stated that paper cups are different from glasses be-cause glasses break, that glasses are dangerous when broken, or that young children (you, Alice) are insufficiently competent or conscien-tious to be trusted with the unsupervised use of fragile and potentially harmful materials.

Nor has anyone mentioned the "obvious" moral proposition be-hind this: that teachers should take responsibility for protecting young children from classroom activities in which they are likely ac-cidentally to injure themselves. All of that propositional content re-mains unspoken, and all of it is necessary for a true and objective understanding of the episode.

However, what is spoken points to or implicates that material so powerfully that anyone to whom those belief propositions are famil-iar will connect them with the event—the event will instantiate the beliefs. And an observer or participant who did not have prior knowl-edge of those propositions would, at the very least, be alerted to search or query for them; to anyone trying to comprehend what was going on it would be obvious that something of importance was miss-ing—that is, one would wonder *why* the teacher wanted Alice to use a paper cup instead of a glass except at snack time.

A second constraint on the interpretation of the meanings implicit in a communicative array has to do with the monitoring of the partic-ipants' expressed state of mind. Expressed intentions are important as evidence of the uptake of an utterance. In incident 4, Alice's rather plaintive reply (2) and her offer to put the glass down instead of giv-ing it up suggest a rather partial recognition of the teacher's meaning. Senders of messages about cultural propositions (for example, Mrs.

Swift) tend to be alert to indications of the uptake of their messages, and any expression of only partial recognition generates even more explicit message content.

In other words, guardians of the moral order often respond to what they themselves consider to be evidence that an inference or construction of meaning has not taken place. The child's responses, verbal and nonverbal, to attempted regulation often function as queries or probes for further explication of content. What is not understood gets clarified with supplements to the prior knowledge base, thus revealing indexical meanings and moving the conversation in the direction of an intersubjective equilibrium point where what is said is understood because there is sufficient prior knowledge. Whether one is concerned with the acquisition of moral beliefs by children or the interpretation of moral beliefs by an outside observer, several sources of evidence converge to constrain the extraction of indexical meaning from a communicative array.

Unpacking the Babaji Interview: Heinz in Orissa

The discourse in moral development interviews is often processed and coded as though what was explicitly said were a complete repesentation of what was meant or being argued. By expanding or unpacking one part (about 30 percent) of the text from a single interview and identifying its implicit argument structure, we raise some doubts about the ability of current coding and classification procedures accurately to represent the moral reasoning of an interviewee. If discourse is to be the measure of moral understanding and reasoning, then we must be concerned not only with what was said but also with what was presupposed, implied, suggested, or conveyed by what was said; and we need a theory of how meaning is constructed in discourse to help us go from what was said to what was meant.

An interview conducted by Shweder at his residence in Orissa, India, with the Babaji, a male in his thirties, gives expression to a central concept in the Hindu worldview, the concept of dharma (religion, duty, obligation, natural law, truth).

The Babaji, as a young child, was betrothed to a goddess to protect him from various misfortunes predicted by an astrologer, and he was raised in a village monastery. As a young adult he was returned to the everyday world, where he got married and became a father. Though not a Brahman, he is a member of a high-status "clean" caste. His formal education is limited to approximately five years of primary school. He is literate. His knowledge of automobiles, how to drive them and how to fix them, helps him earn a living. Shweder, who has known the Babaji for many years, views him as an articulate and highly intelligent participant in the devotional, meditative, and mystical aspects of Hinduism as they apply to the management of one's personal life.

Our analysis of the expanded text of the interview raises several issues, in need of further discussion among moral development researchers, concerning (1) the proper meaning of postconventional moral reasoning, (2) the comprehensiveness of Kohlberg's stage scheme, and (3) the hazards of interview scoring procedures that operate exclusively on unexpanded texts and code only explicit utterances that come in propositional form. In our text expansion we assume that the interview text per se (the totality of recorded and transcribed utterances) is only a fragmentary representation of its own meaning, that the text points beyond itself to a network of ideas about social and cognitive events, which co-constitute what the interviewee is trying to get across through the utterances inscribed in the interview text.

That assumption was exemplified in incident 4; the meaning of the utterance "That is not a paper cup" could be determined only with reference to its context, plus certain background knowledge instantiated in the episode. The context included, among other things, a teacher approaching a child holding a glass of water, and a classroom rule. The background knowledge included, among other things, beliefs about the relevant properties of glass objects, the competences of young children, the probabilities of harmful consequences, and the responsibilities of teachers. It was not the surface text alone, but all of those things, and more, that constituted the meanings that were conveyed by what was explicitly said ("That is not a paper cup").

If we are to use ordinary language to investigate moral reasoning or moral understanding, we must have some way of taking account of the implicit meanings of utterances. One way of doing that involves giving explicit propositional form to the implicit material that co-constitutes the meaning of an utterance. The procedure is illustrated by Labov and Fanshel (1977), who give it the name *expansion*.

The relevant implicit meanings, to be drawn out and stated in propositional form, might have various kinds of referents. Propositions might refer to observations ("It is raining"), rules (Thou shalt not steal), beliefs or assumptions (If a man sins, he will suffer), roles, statuses, or other social identities (wife, holy man, untouchable), and so on. Some propositions might be quite specific to the situational context (a child is holding a glass in a nursery school classroom). Other propositions might have a more general content that happens to be instantiated by this or that event (young children are apt to have accidents with breakable glass objects). To expand an utterance or stretch of text is to unfold its meaning by bringing its implicit meanings forward in explicit propositional form, as if they had occurred on the same plane as the text itself.

In our analysis of the Babaji interview we limit ourselves to two orders of expansion. In the first-order expansion of the text we make explicit various assumptions, rules, and beliefs of the interviewee, which lend meaning to what was stated but were presupposed, taken for granted, or otherwise left unstated during the interview. In the second-order expansion we try to highlight the "logical" or "rational" organization of the first-order expansion, to reveal its coherence as a form of reasoning. As it turns out we have not been able to maintain a neat division between the first-order and second-order expansions, although we believe the distinction is helpful even if not neat. What we refer to as the second-order expansion of the text involves drawing out the logical, rational, or inferential relations (*since, therefore, insofar as, although, because, if . . . then,* and so on) that organize into a reasoned argument in support of a particular conclusion the propositional content of the first-order expansion. In drawing out some of the inferential relations implicit in the interview text we have been greatly assisted by Longacre's (1983) classification of basic logical relations expressed in natural language discourse. (The reader will benefit from reading the appendix beginning on page 229.)

Interviewer: Should Ashok steal the drug?

Babaji: No. He is feeling desperate because his wife is going to die, and that's why he is stealing the drug. But people don't live forever, and providing her the drug does not necessarily mean she will live long. How long you live in not in our hands but in God's hands. And there are other ways to get money, like selling his landed property, or even he can sell himself to someone and can save his wife's life.

First-order expansion: Ashok is feeling desperate because his wife is going to die. It is his desperation that impels him to steal the drug. Because he is desperate he overlooks the fact that stealing is wrong, insufficient, and unnecessary. If he were not desperate he would recognize that there is a natural limit to (a given) human life; that providing his wife with the drug will not necessarily prolong her life; that it may be this woman's destiny to die at this time; and that if that is the case the drug will not prolong her life. It is God's intention and not human intervention that ultimately determines matters of human life and death. It follows that providing the drug is neither a sufficient nor a necessary condition for saving the woman's life. From the human point of view the result of providing the drug is unpredictable.

Moreover, other means are available to raise needed money. Ashok could sell his property or, if need be, sell himself into indentured servitude in order to raise the money. Since those alternative means exist and have not been exhausted, stealing is not a necessary condition for obtaining the drug.

Since the drug itself cannot be assumed to be effective in determining the course of events, and since one can assume the existence of alternative means to obtain the drug, there is no justification for stealing it.

Second-order expansion: The argument attributes the intention to steal to confusion deriving from desperation, in contrast to a well-considered and informed motive. The argument locates the ultimate efficient cause (including necessary and sufficient conditions) for human life and death with divine agency rather than with human intervention in events. The understanding is that human destiny is an expression of divine intention, and that human destiny is an actual plan given to an individual by God. The implication that follows from that proposition is that any specific human intervention is neither a necessary nor a sufficient condition in the determination of life and death.

Having set forth that implication in the first part of this piece of reasoning, the Babaji then changes the focus of logical evaluation to a different locus in the causal structure of events. Having first dealt with the question of necessary and sufficient conditions and the ultimate causal course determining matters of life and death, in the latter part of his response he considers causality from the viewpoint of possible human interventions.

The argument takes administering the drug as the proposed intervention, which presupposes, that the drug must be obtained. That goal then becomes the focus of evaluative reasoning. The argument asserts, in essence, that, even if one were to assume that administering the drug is the best intervention, stealing the drug is not a justifiable means of obtaining it; there are other ways to raise the money to buy it at the asked price. Assuming, for the sake of argument, that the goal is to obtain the drug, the argument contrasts stealing to obtain the drug with an alternative causal or instrumental sequence (sell one's property or oneself), with the additional meaning that the alternatives are to be preferred.

In essence the Babaji's response states that if Ashok steals it is because he has become confused in his desperation and lost sight of reality, and not because stealing the drug is a defensible solution. There are no informed grounds for concluding that one ought to steal the drug, and this is why:

Interviewer: He has no other way out. He has neither money nor anything.

Babaji: Stealing is bad. He has made a mistake.

Interviewer: But his wife is going to die!

Babaji: There is no way within Hindu dharma to steal even if a man is going to die.

Interviewer: But doesn't Hindu dharma prescribe that you try to save a person's life?

Babaji: Yes. And for that you can sacrifice your blood or sell yourself, but you cannot steal.

Interviewer: Why doesn't Hindu dharma permit stealing?

Babaji: If he steals it is a sin, so what virtue is there in saving a life? Hindu dharma keeps man from sinning.

Interviewer: Why would it be a sin? Isn't there a saying, "One must jump into fire for others"?

Babaji: That is there in our dharma—sacrifice, but not stealing.

First-order expansion: The act of stealing is wrongful and not virtuous. It is prohibited by Hindu dharma (religion, duty, obligation, natural law, truth). If a man commits such an act he makes a serious moral and spiritual error, which, because of the nature of cause and effect, will divert him further from virtue and wisdom and in the direction of ignorance and suffering.

Dharma prohibits such acts even at the cost of human life. The purpose of dharma is to instruct humans in how to live a virtuous life that will spiritually benefit themselves and others; its purpose is to keep individuals from committing grave errors that will lead to spiritual degradation and suffering. If a man steals he commits a grave sin;

even if he saves a life in doing so the outcome is not virtuous. According to Hindu dharma, it is virtuous to save a person's life. Dharma instructs that one may endure extreme hardship or even sacrifice oneself in order to help others. But even though the dharma condones extremes of personal self-sacrifice in order to help others, it does not condone actions such as stealing. As a means to help others, stealing is an unvirtuous action that goes contrary to the natural order.

Second-order expansion: The Babaji classifies stealing as a sinful and unvirtuous action and asserts that such actions are always wrong. He does not tell us, at this point, why it is always wrong to commit a sin, yet two considerations seem to be involved. First, the Babaji seems to hold that those actions classified as sins by dharmic law are wrong independently of circumstance, good intention, or apparent outcome; sins are by nature wrongful actions.

Second, a further expansion of the concept of sin could be proposed, based on general Hindu belief as it is explicitly expressed by the Babaji later in the interview: Actions classified as sins have certain natural consequences as part of their inherent causality. The Hindu concept of sin, in fact, entails causal implications. In general, actions that are sinful tend to lead persons to situations or conditions that are still more desperate than the one they were trying to get free of in the first place. In those desperate situations a person is likely to become confused and commit even more errors. Sinful actions lead an individual away from virtue and wisdom and into ignorance and suffering.

In essence the Babaji argues that the purpose or end of instruction in dharma is to enable human beings to distinguish virtuous actions from sinful ones, so that they will be able to avoid the latter. The reason for avoiding sinful actions is that they have destructive consequences, for they lead people into degraded forms of existence in which both suffering and ignorance are greater and in which it becomes still more difficult to distinguish truth from falsity and illusion. In addition, specific instruction with regard to the act of stealing is attributed to dharma. From that the Babaji derives an obligation: a man should not steal, for if a man steals he commits a great sin.

But there is more to it than that, for the nature of sin entails something further. What is apparently the ultimate conclusion of the argument is expressed in the Babaji's interpretation of dharma concerning the relationship of moral polarities at the means-ends loci of a causal structure. That is, if a sin is committed (for example, stealing) the action is considered sinful and not virtuous even though it may be for a virtuous purpose (for example, to save a life).

The argument implies that the moral value of the ends locus does not exert important, or at least decisive, influence on the evaluation of the means locus. Rather, the important moral influence operates in the reverse direction. To save a life is virtuous only if it is accomplished by virtuous means. If it is accomplished by sinful means, it becomes a sinful act; seemingly, it becomes a different act altogether.

It seems possible, given what we know about the Hindu world view as expressed by the Babaji in this and numerous other interviews, that the Babaji's reasoning is based on distinctions concerning God-given constraints on human action that have the force of natural law. As long as a man exerts his efforts in accordance with dharmic law, he can feel that he served God and dignifies human existence. However, if he commits sinful actions such as stealing, even in the interest of a virtuous purpose, he has overstepped the constraints on human action according to natural law and God's design. His action, therefore, offends God and nature and risks obstructing divine intention or divine order. Nothing truly good can result from such an act, because (1) acts congruent with the will of God (helping others) cannot be achieved with acts that are forbidden by him (stealing); and (2) sinful actions always have evil as their consequence, if not immediately then in the long run. No lasting good can be achieved through sinful actions. A maxim would seem to follow: Do one's dharma; that above all else!

In the final part of his reply the Babaji comments on the moral implications of the means adopted for attaining an apparently virtuous end. Again the moral values are attributed directly to the laws and teachings of dharma. As he has argued previously, to commit sinful actions in the service of a virtuous purpose is to act in a way that is sinful and not virtuous. The true moral course of action in any situation is quite otherwise. It is to exert maximal and even heroic effort toward virtuous ends, but only through such courses of action as are defined as virtuous, or at least permissible, by divine law. The moral course of action is to be followed regardless of how any fallible individual (mis-) perceives the apparent contingencies or projected outcomes of sinful versus virtuous action.

In understanding the Babaji's reasoning it is important to recognize that he is arguing that a virtuous means of conduct is the *only* conceivable efficacious route to an end. One cannot cheat divine or natural law, for it simply will not work. The functioning of natural moral law is not dependent on one's goodwill, intentions, or knowledge. If one jumps off a roof, one is going to fall to the ground. If one seeks to attain an end by means of unvirtuous actions, the result, in the long run if not in the short run, will simply not be satisfactory. The Babaji ends with a contrast between the virtuous means given by dharma through which one may aid others, and sinful acts such as stealing that are forbidden even though done in the service of a virtuous purpose. The purpose under consideration (saving a life) is assumed to be virtuous as long as it is achieved within the rightful limits of human action.

Interviewer: But if he doesn't provide the medicine for his wife, she will die. Wouldn't it be a sin to let her die?

Babaji: That's why, according to the capabilities and powers which God has given him, he should try to give her shamanistic instructions and advice. Then she can be cured.

Interviewer: But that particular medicine is the only way out.

Babaji: There's no reason to necessarily think that that particular drug will save her life.

First-order expansion: Yes, it would be wrong for a man not to do what he could to save the life of his wife. But he must act in recognition of the limitations of man's rightful place in the natural order, and he must act within the constraints on virtuous conduct set forth in the dharma. For example, according to the capabilities and powers God has given him, he should try to give his wife shamanistic instructions and advice. It is conceivable that she could be cured that way. But it is our moral duty to pursue right ends by right means, as set by dharma, and it is not human action that truly decides the fate of other persons or the outcome of events. The actual outcome does not rest solely in our hands. Nor can such things be attributed to any one particular material causal factor; there is no reason to think that the drug in question would be necessary or sufficient to save the woman's life. Consequently, there is no reason to neglect other courses of action and pursue only that one.

Second-order expansion: Here the Babaji separates two aspects of the causal structure of the original dilemma, two aspects that Kohlberg presupposed to be fused in the context of the dilemma as presented.

According to the Babaji, given his understanding of the causal structure of nature, saving the woman's life is not to be equated with providing her with the drug. Providing the drug is neither a necessary nor
a sufficient course of action for saving the woman's life, even if it
should turn out that in this case human intervention can influence the
outcome. By separating aspects of the causal structure that we might
fuse, the Babaji creates an additional issue around which a proposed
solution is argued.

Indeed for the first time in the interview it becomes clear that the
Babaji believes that there is a moral obligation to make an attempt to
save the woman's life. The fact that a person's God-given or natural
destiny is decisive in matters of human life and death does not relieve
an individual from personal responsibility to act on behalf of another.
It would be a sin simply to let her die if there is anything one *can* do
to save her life. The Babaji's arguments, in fact, suggest that somewhat heroic measures might be expected. What the Babaji says one
can do, however, is in some ways expanded and in other ways restricted relative to the predominant Western world view. On the one
hand, the range of efficacious actions (including ritual and prayer)
through which the woman might be cured is greater than what is
allowed for in the original dilemma. On the other hand, the domain
of possibility is held to be constrained by the limits of the opportunities and capabilities that exist for action in accordance with dharma.
Action that is sinful should be regarded as simply impossible.

The Babaji here and elsewhere perceives no conflict between what
is effective and what is moral; indeed, the efficacy of action is viewed
as proportionate to its moral value, and thus what Kohlberg views as
a moral dilemma (preserving life versus upholding the law) is not a
dilemma, given the Babaji's view of the world. Within that view of
the world it is as if the contingencies of action were functions of interrelationships in a consistent system of natural order in which physical and social contingencies are but one further manifestation of
moral law.

Interviewer: Let's suppose she can be saved only by that drug, or else
    she will die. Won't he face lots of difficulties if his wife dies?
Babaji: No.
Interviewer: But his family will break up.
Babaji: He can marry other women.
Interviewer: But he has no money. How can he remarry?

Babaji: Do you think he should steal? If he steals he will be sent to jail. Then what's the use of saving her life to keep the family together?

First-order expansion: It is false to believe that Ashok's family will suffer great hardships if his wife dies, for he can marry another woman to take her place in the family. Even if he were unable to remarry, it would be foolish to steal in order to preserve his family, because if he steals he will end up in jail, which would be as disruptive to his family as the death of his wife. In that case the good of his family would not have been served by saving her life.

Second-order expansion: In this argument the Babaji once again demonstrates the uselessness of an act such as stealing. Here the interviewer introduces the question of the possible social and domestic consequences to Ashok and his family if Ashok's wife were to die.

In reply the Babaji offers a causal argument concerning the uselessness of stealing as a means to avoid such consequences. If Ashok steals, his family will suffer hardship on account of that, and no one will be any better off. It would be better simply to remarry or to suffer the loss of the spouse. The argument becomes a warning against stealing, in the form of a comparison of the uselessness of stealing with the preferable implications of other possible courses of conduct, including simply bearing the loss of his wife.

To this point in the interview the overall sense of the argument is that unvirtuous courses of action do not bring about satisfactory results. There is nothing to recommend unvirtuous action, even from a mundane instrumental point of view. Because of the evil consequences it bears at every level, unvirtuous conduct defeats even its own purposes.

Viewed in the broader context of other arguments in the interview, this last stretch of discourse is a restatement, this time at the level of immediate social causality, of the belief that from an objective point of view "sin does not pay." At every imaginable level, actions that are sinful fail to bring about the desired result. If there is any way at all to achieve something (and there may not be), sin is never the only way. Intelligent action and virtuous action are the same. No genuine benefit can come to anyone through unvirtuous action; and things will appear to be otherwise only to those ignorant of the true laws of cause and effect.

Babaji: She enjoyed the days destined to her. But stealing is bad.

First-order expansion: A person comes into the world with a certain destiny, which can be attributed to God's plan or purpose for that person in that particular life. It may be that this woman has enjoyed the days destined for her and it is time for her to go to her next life. If that is the case, it is useless to interfere. Her death at this time is the fulfillment of divine intention or natural law. Her death is right and good. But to steal is bad and goes against God's law and natural order. If that is her destiny, it is better to let her die than to commit sinful acts in a desperate attempt to save her.

Second-order expansion: Here the Babaji is challenging the end that is presupposed in the original dilemma. He implies that the rightness of the proposed goal (that the wife's life should be saved) is questionable, at least as an absolute value. In his view it is possible that it may be right or even best that the woman die, because it may be time for her to end this particular life and go on with her journey of the spirit through its various rebirths. In his view, allowing her to die may be the action most consistent with a concern for her well-being.

The Babaji does not take this conclusion lightly. He does not assume that, because such things are destined, an individual has no responsibility to intervene in another's illness or imminent death. Quite the contrary; even to the point of great personal sacrifice, one must do all one can to help another. It is rather that the Babaji's view allows for the possibility that the woman is meant to die at this time. That possibility enters as a consideration that has a bearing on reasoned action. But it is not something that can be known directly or assumed to be the case. Therefore, the mere possibility that it is the case does not relieve one of the responsibility to act.

Indeed, it would seem that the way to discern such issues of destiny is to act in whatever way one can within the constraints of dharmic law, and then observe the outcome; the fact that a given end could not be accomplished in that way is evidence that the outcome was destined to be what it was. If one tries aggressively to intervene in events by means of actions that violate dharmic law, then one is trying to force the outcome to one's own will and is neither respecting the destiny of others nor honoring the intentions of God.

On the other hand, if one neglects the actions that one could take in accordance with dharma, then one is neglecting to take one's rightful or intended place in the outcome of events, for it might also be the case that one had a destined or intended role to play in the event. That view seems to rest on a notion of coincidence just the opposite of our view of chance or accident. It is assumed that the way that things come together in any particular situation is meaningful and morally instructive, an expression of natural moral law or divine intelligence. Accordingly, what is moral coincides with what is efficacious and what is beneficial or advantageous.

According to that view, conflict between motivational domains (what is right versus what is advantageous) is merely apparent, the result of our ignorance of the reality underlying events and the totality of circumstances involved. What is right or wrong in any situation is not a matter of subjective judgment but rather an objective process; but, since one's personal ability to discern what is right or good in a situation is limited, it is an objective process of which one typically has only a partial view. Through instruction in dharma one has been given certain guidelines for acting in situations without overstepping the boundaries of what is humanly knowable. Given the known limitations of mortal judgment there is good reason to respect those guidelines.

Babaji: Our sacred scriptures tell that sometimes stealing is an act of dharma. If by stealing for you I can save your life, then it is an act of dharma. But one cannot steal for his wife or his offspring or for himself. If he does that, it is simply stealing
Interviewer: If I steal for myself, then it is a sin?
Babaji: Yes.
Interviewer: But in this case I am stealing for my wife, not for me.
Babaji: But your wife is yours.

First-order expansion: Our sacred scriptures tell of cases in which stealing is considered a virtuous act condoned by dharma. In order for that to be the case the act would have to be completely unselfish, involving absolutely no personal gain for the person committing the act. For example, if I were to steal to help a stranger who had no personal relationship to me, that might be an act of dharma. This would be particularly true if the act were committed in the service of a holy man or individual who could be regarded as particularly god-like, close to God, or in some significant way equivalent to God. In such cases it is as if one were acting directly in God's service.

But stealing for selfish motives is not an act of virtue. A person cannot rightfully steal for himself or his wife or his children. A man's wife and children belong to him. They are complementary to and interdependent with him. So he has a selfish interest in them. If a man steals for himself or for those who belong to him it is not a virtuous act; it is ordinary selfish stealing. What distinguishes stealing as an act of dharma from ordinary stealing is the complete absence of any self-serving motive.

Second-order expansion: Here the Babaji proposes a variety of apparent exceptions to the generalizations he has already advanced about the inherent wrongfulness of stealing. Later he specifies more precisely the nature of such apparent exceptions in six dramatic narratives or stories to clarify and defend his conceptions of natural moral law. The apparent exceptions are attributed directly to the scriptural record of historical experience and are not presented as personal opinion or subjective interpretation. The narrative that comes later (the story of the father and son who steal ghee in order to have the right food to serve their sadhu guests) illustrates the customary nature of the type of apparent exception being drawn by the Babaji, and it suggests that it is not an exception at all but rather the kind of case that proves the rule of dharmic consequences for sin, including bad consequences for even selfless stealing.

Basically the Babaji argues that there is a point of view from which stealing could be seen as a virtuous act. This is true even given what has already been said about how such an act would be wrong for the sake of saving the life of one's wife. The Babaji's argument once again focuses on the ends presupposed by the causal structure of the original dilemma. Earlier the Babaji has considered the moral value of ends (stealing the drug in order to make it available to the woman) from the point of view of outcomes: the degree of likely benefit to the recipient of the action and the general harmony of action with the natural moral order. Here the Babaji considers the moral value of the end in relation to the motives of the actor.

The Babaji proposes that it would be an act of virtue if one were to steal for the benefit of a stranger (or, as we shall soon see, a holy man). That is virtuous because such an act is devoid of mundane self-interest. But to steal for one's wife or one's child is just like stealing for oneself; it is ordinary selfish stealing. One's wife and children are part of one's household, and their contribution to one's life and proximity to one's identity are so great that their life and death could not possibly be considered independently of one's own mundane advantage or personal attachment. Because of the purity of its motive, an act done out of compassion with no relation to personal gain or even to personal duty or personal responsibility has an exceptional status (and that is so even if the act is intrinsically a sin and is not to be recommended). Further explication of that position follows in our expansion of the Babaji's first dramatic narrative. The interview continues:

Interviewer: Doesn't Ashok have a duty or obligation to steal the drug?

Babaji: He may not get the medicine by stealing. He may sell himself. He may sell himself to someone for, say, 500 rupees for six months or one year.

Interviewer: Does it make a difference whether or not he loves his wife?

Babaji: So what if he loves his wife? When a husband dies the wife does not die for him, or vice versa. We have come into this world alone, and we will leave it alone. Nobody will accompany us when we leave this world. It may be a son or it may be a wife. No one will go with us.

Interviewer: For whom do you feel one should steal? Let's say it is not his wife but a holy man or a stranger. Would it have been better if he had stolen for them?

Babaji: Stealing is bad. It is not right according to Hindu dharma, but if he stole for himself the degree of sin would be more.

Interviewer: Is it important to do everything one can to save another's life?

Babaji: Yes. But that does not mean stealing. You can borrow from someone. You can go without eating. You can give your food to others, or you can sell yourself.

Interviewer: Suppose Ashok had come to you, told you his situation, and sought your advice whether or not to steal. What would you have told him?

Babaji: I would have asked him not to steal. We have a practice in the villages. Everyone would have decided to give him the required money from the village common fund, or they would have collected some donation. But he should be advised not to steal.

Interviewer: But shouldn't people do everything they can to save a life?

Babaji: One should try to save another's life. Because, after all, he is a human being. But you should not do it by virtue of stealing.

By this point, we hope, it is unnecessary to expand the text or unpack its underlying consistencies and reiterations. Instead we shall examine in some detail the very next moment in the interview, when the Babaji adopts a traditional Oriya mode of moral argumentation, summarizing and justifying his conception of natural moral law with the first of six historical narratives.

Interviewer: Is it against the law for Ashok to steal?
Babaji: Yes. It's against the law.
Interviewer: Are the laws always morally right? Do you feel all laws are right?
Babaji: Let me tell you a story about stealing. Once some sadhus came to a poor man's house . . . [Here the Babaji narrates the story about the father and son who stole the ghee pot. The reader should now reread that story.]

Second-order expansion: Let me tell you a story about an incident from which you can see for yourself the consequences of committing a sinful action such as stealing, even in one of those apparently exceptional cases involving selfless motives. A primary implication of the story is that although the man stole for righteous motives devoid of self-interest, the action nonetheless bore the dharmic consequences of sin, involving him in further sin and greater suffering.

The story focuses on the host-guest relationship between ordinary men and holy men. In the Hindu world view the way one treats a guest is a test of one's relationship and attitude to dharmic truth (the divine), and when the guests turn out to be holy men that issue is especially salient.

The Babaji begins by pointing out that holy men, who are certainly more aware of dharmic truth than we are, never steal or ask for credit. They are able to meet all their needs by simply begging, and no one ever hesitates to give them what they need. The implication is that if Ashok had lived a more noble or holy life he would not find himself contemplating theft (this interpretation is borne out later in the interview); throughout his life Ashok must have been swimming against the dharmic current.

In any case the host, an ordinary man, stole only in order to honor the godliness represented in his guests. That is the purest of ends, yet his action resulted in disaster because he foolishly believed that the end could justify any means. His guests asked for ghee, a food suit-

able for holy men because it is a "cool" food and is one of the products of the holy cow (or holy mother). The man stole the ghee only
after exhausting all other means available to him. He had already
sacrificed his worldly possessions to provide the meal. He had begged
the sadhu at the monastery to give him the ghee. Surely this is an
exceptional case, far more compelling than the case of Ashok, who
has not exhausted every possible dharmic means and only wants to
save his own wife. If stealing is foolish and hence unjustified in this
case, certainly we must judge it to be foolish in the case of Ashok.
Look at what happened to the man and his son and learn from it!

The man set in motion a chain reaction of cause-and-effect relations
that escalates into disaster. Having determined to steal the ghee, he
caused his son to commit the act. Because the son was in the storeroom stealing he was apprehended. It did not matter that he left all
the treasures of the monastery and was not stealing for himself.
Things just kept getting worse; because father and son were desperate
to deliver the ghee and escape the humiliation of capture, the son's
life was sacrificed through decapitation, thus causing the father intense suffering.

The Babaji's point in retelling this incident is to show a chain of
events in which purposes intertwine with arising circumstances in
such a way that once one is headed in the direction of sin (the "downward path," as it were) circumstances conspire to embroil one in increasingly desperate situations.

The basic idea is that the moral and the physical order are not
separate domains, and punishment and reward in this world are not
dependent merely on the legal processes of society. Reward and punishment follow automatically, though not always immediately, from
the nature of action. To commit sinful actions in order to free oneself
from difficult circumstances is only to become further entangled in
increasingly desperate circumstances. Not only does sin not pay, but
what better way is there to determine which actions are sinful than to
learn from the historical record of the suffering of others?

Even the holy men told the ordinary man that what he had done
was wrong; the tragic consequences were the result of his error. Yet
his action, while foolish, is exceptional, because his sin had been committed for the sole purpose of serving the sadhus and without any
trace of self-serving motive or personal gain. Because of the purity of
the motives of the father and the son, the sadhus were willing *through
dharmic means* (prayer and ritual upon the severed head of the son)

to reverse the natural consequences of the sin and to instruct the father and son in the truths of dharma. Where theft had failed, dharmic means (prayer and ritual) worked, even to restore a dead person to life. The message is to avoid sin, even when, unlike Ashok, you have motives that are pure and meritorious.

This expansion or unpacking of the beliefs and arguments implicated in part of an interview text suggests that the analysis of such material must be informed by a theory of how meaning is constructed in discourse. If we attempt to understand the moral reasoning and beliefs of a "subject" by merely coding propositions explicitly mentioned in the surface structure of the text and matching them against a list of proposition types in a standard coding manual, we have commited ourselves to a view of language in which what is said is a complete and isomorphic representation of what is meant. How defensible is that approach to language and the analysis of interview texts?

One practical way to answer that question is to ask: How shall we classify the Babaji's moral reasoning? How would it be stage-classified following Kohlberg's standardized coding procedure, in which the surface structure of the interview text, consisting of explicit propositionalized judgments, is matched to criterion statements set out in a coding manual? How would it be classified if we analyze, as well, the expanded text and its implicit argument structure?

Kohlberg (1981) classifies moral reasoning into three developmental levels, each divided into two stages. At the lowest, "preconventional," level (stages 1 and 2), subjects define the meaning of rightness and wrongness in terms of subjective feelings and interests. If the self likes it, it is right; if the self does not like it, it is wrong. There are no higher obligations. Egoism and self-interest reign. At the intermediate, "conventional," level (stages 3 and 4), a consciousness of the collective emerges, and, although subjects continue to define the meaning of rightness and wrongness by reference to feelings, now the collective feelings of others are what matter. The idea of obligation is equated with the authority of the group (the commands of parents, interpersonal expectations concerning proper role behavior, the laws of legislatures). If one's reference group likes it, it is right; if one's reference group does not like it, it is wrong. Conformity and consensus reign. At the highest, "postconventional," level (stages 5 and 6 in Kohlberg's earlier formulations, stage 5 in more recent formulations; Kohlberg, Levine, and Hewer 1983), rightness and wrongness are defined by reference to objective universal principles that stand above the feelings of either the self or the group. Those principles are justice, natural rights, and a humanistic respect for all persons, and a post-conventional reasoner can appeal to them to criticize social institutions and personal preferences.

The Babaji interview was analyzed and stage-classified by two expert coders (Lawrence Kohlberg and Ann Higgins) following the procedures detailed in the *Standard Issue Scoring Manual* (Colby et al., 1987), whereby coding is restricted to what is explicitly stated in propositional form in the interview text. Kohlberg (personal communication) makes several observations about the interview and the coding process. He notes that "much of the material [in the interview] was unscorable." One reason some of the material was unscorable was that it involved "spontaneous elaborations by the informant in the form of stories or allegories and references to Hindu mythology." Fortunately, however, according to the coders, "there was enough scorable material to match to manual points even though many interesting points could not be fit to the manual."

Not surprisingly, Kohlberg comes up with several perceptive informal observations on the interview. He notes that for orthodox Hindus society seems "to be defined by a mixture of custom and tradition and religious dharma as distinct from legal and political rules and systems." He also notes that orthodox Hindus seem "less oriented to individual rights and to interpersonal balancing of feelings through role-taking and more oriented to custom." He notes that the interview material "fit our manual much less easily than the Turkish and Israeli data on which I have personally worked. When the Turks invoked religious references it was either to straightforward divine command and punishment or to following the norms of being a good Muslim as a defined religious group" (personal communication).

Kohlberg wonders whether the distinction between convention and morality would hold up for orthodox Hindu adults (it does not; see Shweder, Mahapatra, and Miller 1987) and notes that while orthodox Hindus seem to "make much of the distinction between the legal and the religious . . . the religious encompasses the conventional and the moral for them." Kohlberg classifies the Babaji's orientation to religious dharma as "essentially stage 4, though somewhat unlike American law oriented or American religious-law oriented stage 4. American stage 4s seem to use a more clear social systems perspective when explaining or using their religious codes." Kohlberg and Higgins give the Babaji interview a global stage score of 3/4. Kohlberg remarks that "scoring by the manual fit our clinical intuitions as to stage, though our ignorance of the Hindu culture made us somewhat uncertain about our own clinical intuitions." Having found the interview "very interesting," he notes that he is somewhat surprised that it ends up with the score of an "average American adult"—stage 3/4.

By coding only propositions explicitly mentioned in the surface structure of the interview text, Kohlberg and Higgins ignored the entire narrative content of the interview and were unable to take account of the implicit argument structure in the text. They were methodologically doomed to end up with a stage classification that deforms the moral reasoning of the informant, assimilating it to the requirements of an a priori interpretative scheme while leaving us with very little insight into the Babaji's view of the moral order. Was the Babaji really trying to say that obedience to social consensus is a goal in its own right (a stage 3/4 doctrine)? Did he really deny the stage 1/2 doctrine that what is right is closely related to obtaining desired practical consequences for oneself? Did he not give strong expression to the stage 5/6 doctrine that there are nonrelative objective values, including respect for the dignity of human beings, that must be upheld in any society and regardless of majority opinion?

Kohlberg is quite right when he notes that the interview does not easily fit the manual. But perhaps, instead of trying to assimilate the interview to the requirement of the stage scheme and the coding manual, we should try to accommodate the coding procedures and our classification of forms of moral reasoning to the requirements of the interview. Surely it would be instructive to interpret not only what the Babaji explicitly said in propositional form, but also what was implicit in what he said, regardless of how he said it (dramatic narratives). What does the expanded text and its implicit argument structure reveal about the Babaji's form of moral reasoning?

In the Babaji's version of the orthodox Hindu view of the moral order, moral laws are no less objective than the laws of physics. Moral cause and effect is as real and concrete as material cause and effect, while having the subtlety of social and psychological cause and effect. The laws of morality are completely independent of personal or group opinion. According to the Babaji's view, however, certain persons have greater knowledge about the truths of moral law; and one of the best guides to natural moral law is the historical experiences recorded in the Hindu scriptures. A thoughtful person will also take into account the authority of certain customary practices, many of which, it may be assumed, are relatively good adaptations to the requirement of objective moral law.

In the orthodox Hindu view moral decisions have their own natural causality, and there is a direct interplay between moral causality, material causality, and social causality. Thus the consequence of a sin may be disease or a bad marriage.

Let us consider a few salient features of the Babaji's view of the moral order. In Western academic circles we sometimes perceive a conflict between what is the morally right thing to do and what is the expedient or personally beneficial thing to do; and for us moral acts are not thought to be directly linked to material and social consequences. In the Babaji's orthodox Hindu view, what is moral coincides with what is expeditious for personal well-being. The conflict is only apparent; the perception of conflict results either from ignorance of the laws of moral cause and effect or from limited human understanding of complex circumstances. The Babaji believes it is arrogant to presume that we know which outcome is truly in the best interests of any or all persons involved, for those individual interests extend far beyond this life and are not usually knowable to us as ordinary mortals.

The Babaji believes that certain kinds of actions (for example, stealing, killing) are inherently sinful and other kinds of actions (for example, giving alms, sacrificing) inherently virtuous. Those qualities of sin and virtue belong to the actions themselves; intentionality and circumstances do not create sins or eliminate them. The act is sinful even if it is done unknowingly. In that view circumstances "out of one's control" are regarded as one's own fault; they are the manifestations of prior sinful actions. In that view wrongful action is not a breach against society or other people; it is sin against dharma, an attack on God and the natural order of things. And it is destructive not of society or other people, but of the person's own eternal spirit, the essence of the person that is most godlike. To sin brings degradation to your truest self; and because this self is connected to all living beings, it is a sin against the whole of existence. The implication of that view of sin is that man should strive to be perfectly godlike, to be so enlightened or omniscient that no act is unintentional, to have no motive corrupting of dharmic choices for action, and have no circumstance out of control.

In his arguments the Babaji understands Ashok's point of view, but he is more concerned with Ashok's spiritual well-being than with his worldly or social well-being or even with the prolongation of this particular incarnation of Ashok's wife. The Babaji applies the same rigorous rules to Ashok that he would apply to himself. He achieves a moral and objective point of view by being impartial in exactly that way.

The Babaji also takes the perspective of Ashok's wife, but again from the point of view of her spiritual well-being rather than from the point of view of one particular worldly life. His assertion on behalf of Ashok's wive is that she has her own spiritual journey, which has been arranged for her by God, seemingly in a very personal and individual manner. Since a person's spiritual path quite reasonably entails matters concerning when one life situation is to be ended and another begun, the time of one's death can be regarded as part of a beneficent plan. For Ashok to cling desperately to the life of his wife is selfish, not empathic or compassionate; it may even obstruct rather than benefit her spiritual development—like keeping a child from entering school because one would rather have him or her at home.

The Babaji has a clear hierarchy of spiritual and material goals, and he argues that there is a relationship between spiritual and material well-being. He does not deny the value of human life; quite the contrary, it is the supreme value of the material world. But it derives its value and sacredness from its relationship to the spirit or soul, of which material life is a manifestation. For that reason material well-being is not privileged over spiritual well-being. Spiritual well-being is fundamental because the condition and degree of purity of one's soul have a decisive influence on the particular state of one's body (male or female, healthy or sickly) in successive rebirths.

For the Babaji, human beings are responsible agents in the extreme for events within the domain of their authority to act, yet that domain has certain limits. He recognizes that his own human position is neither omniscient nor omnipotent within the scheme of moral-physical causality, and he does not consider his own intelligence to be the highest or most perfect intelligence acting upon human events. It is for the Babaji a matter of objective fact to acknowledge the limits of his own understanding and efficacy. In the West a large residue of causal determinacy is written off to "chance." In India the universe is thought to be fully determinate, and given that there are serious spiritual consequences associated with any course of action, the boundaries for legitimate action are greatly respected.

That does not mean that human beings are impotent, or even that the limits on human action and accomplishment are narrow by Western standards. The Babaji does not view human beings as powerless or constrained to enact a limited set of obligatory roles or routines. Extraordinary and heroic effort is possible and may accomplish extraordinary ends. In the accounts and narratives presented in the interview, one finds possibilities for altruism that achieves its end through almost unthinkable sacrifice, knowledge that can cure the sick and bring the dead back to life through prayer and ritual and other dharmic techniques, repentance by a world conqueror moved by a moment of imparted insight into the divinity of life, and disciplines that lead to prescience of the course of the divine plan. Indeed, the range of possible solutions to human problems is much greater than the one we are accustomed to think of in our own pragmatic terms. While there is a respect for the limits of human knowledge, heroic efforts are possible, and, if those efforts run with, instead of against, the current of dharmic law, extraordinary things may be accomplished. Such efforts make a human being more godlike; one cannot defeat the mind of God, but one can share in it.

One of the remarkable features of the interview is that the Babaji does not represent the dilemma in terms of rights or justice or life versus private property. He represents the dilemma in terms of the cause-and-effect relations associated with human action, and he argues that it is irrational to commit a sin once the laws of cause and effect and the interdeterminacy of moral and material events are properly appreciated.

It seems impossible to deny the informant an interest in abstract universal principles. In fact, abstract universal considerations dominate the interview (for example, dharmic virtue over material life).

Perhaps most significantly, the Babaji seems to view the dilemma in terms of a causal structure that is not at all coincidental with the causal structure that is presupposed, and thus unwittingly privileged, by those who composed it as a dilemma. The causal structure as understood by the Babaji is as follows:

1. *Agency.* One cannot assume human agency to be the only agency operating in the event. Considerations of divine intention place limits on human authority to act.
2. *Separation of fused causes.* It cannot be assumed that administering the medicine will save the woman's life; it will not save her if it is her destined time to die. It cannot be assumed that the medicine is the only way to intervene, or even a superior form of treatment. It cannot be decisively determined that to save her is the responsible and compassionate thing to do. Since such things are not fully open

to our view they require sensitive testing by rightful action and observation of the consequences. Failure to save her life by taking every morally permissible action is evidence that her dying at this time is part of her destiny.

3. *Consequences of action.* Sinful actions never fulfill their purposes, at least not in the long run. Sinful actions have such disastrous consequences that no thoughtful person would use unvirtuous action as a route out of trouble. Those consequences pertain least of all to legal or societal punishment or to matters of social consensus; rather they pertain to mental, physical, and social well-being in this and future lives.

It is a sign of prior sin and negligence that Ashok finds himself in such a desperate situation. A householder who lives a life of dharma and attends to his responsibilities typically has a little money or property or credit or can raise money if he is in need. It is likely that Ashok is already blameworthy, and further acts of moral desperation (such as stealing) will only lead him further along the path of sin and spiritual degradation.

There is a common illusion that what is personally beneficial does not always coincide with what is virtuous. The wise understand that if a result cannot be accomplished by virtuous means then the result is not as beneficial as it may seem to be from the limited viewpoint of ordinary persons.

Presumably Kohlberg and Higgins coded the Babaji interview as stage 3/4 (conventional) because the informant does not weigh the value of life against property or speak about rights and justice, but rather refers repeatedly to a norm (dharma) construed *by the coders* as a social norm. There are several problems with classifying the interview as stage 3/4. Indeed, Kohlberg's stage scheme seems unable within its own theoretical terms to represent accurately the orthodox Hindu view of the moral order. Here are some of the problems:

1. The Babaji views dharma not as a social norm, but rather as an independently existing and objective reality—somewhat like the laws of physics.
2. The Babaji argues that the moral-physical world is such that wrong actions lead to suffering and spiritual degradation; thus, if one understands the laws of cause and effect, committing a sin is irrational. Again, social consensus has little to do with it.
3. Although his concept of objective obligations has nothing to do with justice and rights, the Babaji adopts a hyperrational perspective on morality. There is no strain of subjectivism or egotism run-

ning through the interview, and moral obligation is understood to be entirely independent of individual or group preference or opinion.

4. There is no hedonistic orientation in the interview. There is no motive to avoid pain or maximize personal pleasure in this world. Indeed there is an expressed willingness to undergo painful sacrifice to help others. While there is a strong motive to avoid actions that bring degradation to the spirit or soul and cause suffering in future rebirths, to call that hedonism is to equate hedonism with the principle that spiritual cleansing is the highest possible value.

From expanding the Babaji interview text and identifying its implicit argument structure it seems apparent that the interview gives articulate expression to an alternative form of postconventional reasoning that has no place in Kohlberg's stage scheme. In a sense the stage scheme is exploded by its own inability to classify adequately the moral reasoning of the Babaji. One may also begin to wonder how many other moral development interviews coded as stage 3/4 would turn out to be alternative forms of postconventional reasoning, if only we permitted ourselves to move from what is said to what is unsaid, to expand the interview text and identify its implicit argument structure.

Neorationalism and Divergent Rationalities

Ordinary conversations not only carry in condensed form a vision of the moral order, they are also the vehicles by which we reproduce the moral order by describing and evaluating events. Given the power of everyday conversations to transmit moral beliefs to children, why have moral development researchers taken so little theoretical interest in the moral world view indexed in and through everyday talk? Verbal interview protocols are, after all, a primary source of evidence in moral development research. Yet every well-known school of thought dealing with moral development quickly moves away from any sustained reflection about the nature of ordinary language use. Thus psychoanalytic researchers, with an interest in the development of conscience, focus on children's intrapsychic conflict anxieties and on defensive processes leading to identification with powerful, envied, or feared others. Cognitive structuralists limit their attention to children's purported efforts to construct for themselves the formal features of moral reasoning. Social learning theorists do examine social communication, but they have bleached it of all implications or message content except reward and punishment, approval and disapproval; and they have kept their field of vision narrow, focusing on the process of modeling or mimicking significant others. No one has taken seriously the substance, content, or meaning of what children and adults say and do to each other. Few have taken to heart the idea that moral development is, in large measure, a problem in the acquisition of moral *knowledge* through the inferences embedded in social communications.

There has been a long and destructive debate in philosophy and in the social sciences over whether moral judgments (that is right or wrong; that is good or bad) are cognitive or emotive judgments. In our view one of the main victims of that debate has been research on the moral arguments embedded in ordinary conversations in everyday life. The moral noncognitivists or so-called emotivists (including social learning theorists and psychoanalysts) premise their research on the idea that rightness and goodness are not real or natural or objective qualities of things. Since, the emotivists argue, rightness and goodness do not describe anything objective in the external world, moral judgments cannot appropriately be said to be either true or false, nor are moral judgments capable of justification through argumentation or other rational means. And since from the point of view of the moral noncognitivists there is nothing really out there to be described with such terms as *right* or *good,* the only thing that is real in moral discussions is their pragmatic use in nondescriptive ways— to express opinions, to command or commend, to dominate and control, to preserve privilege, to resolve intrapsychic conflicts, and so on. Not surprisingly, the moral noncognitivists emphasize the pragmatic use of moral discourse and, for the most part, display little interest in either the semantic content of the moral universe suggested by a moral judgment or the reasons, grounds, warrants, or arguments in support of a moral judgment advanced implicitly or explicitly in moral discourse.

The moral noncognitivist or emotivist viewpoint has been driven by two very special and probably false assumptions about what a truly cognitive-scientific discipline is. The first is the positivist's assumption that any term or concept that plays a part in the production of knowledge must be verifiable either by logical interdefinition or by empirical means. The relevant terms or concepts in the moral arena are terms such as *right* or *good;* since moral concepts cannot be verified in that way, it follows that there cannot be genuine moral facts or objective moral knowledge. The second questionable assumption is that real objective knowledge implies convergence in beliefs; and thus that in any genuine cognitive-scientific discipline disputes get resolved over time. The moral noncognitivist's conclusion: Since disputes over what is right or wrong (abortion, capital punishment, polygamy, arranged marriage, adolescent circumcision) do not go away, moral judgments cannot be a form of objective knowledge.

Ironically, the moral cognitivists (including Kohlberg and other cognitive structuralists) share with the moral noncognitivists precisely those two assumptions about the nature of genuine objective knowledge. The moral cognitivists, however, actually think they can achieve that kind of objective knowledge in the moral domain. Given that goal, it is understandable that the moral cognitivists are not interested in the pragmatic uses of moral discourse or in nonrational processes (imitation, modeling, identification, reward and punishment, indoctrination, genetic inheritance) for reproducing moral judgments in the next generation. Instead, they set themselves the task of defending the objectivity and rationality of moral judgments in terms of those very two assumptions about genuine objectivity and rationality mentioned earlier. Thus the moral cognitivists have launched themselves on various projects to establish that moral disputes (all moral disputes? some of them? at least one of them? the disputes *defined* as moral?) could be resolved by the methods associated with (what they view as) genuine science, by inductive inference from indisputable facts or by deductive reasoning from undeniable premises.

The moral cognitivist's goal is to build an abstract airtight moral system whose rational appeal will be universally obvious to any *competent thinker* (a slippery notion), whether that thinker is a Hindu priest, a Chinese mandarin, an African Bushman, or a Radcliffe undergraduate. In practice the competent thinkers usually turn out to come from a small pool of philosophers, mostly Western, and even they never seem to be able to agree on what is rationally appealing. It is small wonder that the moral cognitivists have taken so little interest in the parochial and context-bound moral discourses of everyday life, where premises are always deniable, terms are rarely explicitly defined, and a complete and consistent account of the entire moral order is never forthcoming.

A second reason for the lack of attention to everyday moral discourse in the child development field may have something to do with the history of high-status research in the psychological sciences. Laboratory experimental research programs on perception, memory, learning, and decision making (the traditional high-prestige topics) have made some progress by relying on a small set of research heuristics: (1) be indifferent to content; process and structure are primary; (2) language is epiphenomenal; it can be ignored; (3) what's really real is inside the skin; the individual is the only relevant locus of analysis; (4) search for universals, study automatic processes, or both; if psychology is to be a genuine science it must uncover highly general laws; (5) don't think about anything that can't be measured.

Whatever the explanation for the survival power of those heuristics in the history of American psychology, they are widely diffused, institutionally entrenched, and deeply intuitive for many psychological researchers. Thus it is not surprising that there has been resistance to the study of the semantics of everyday moral discourse. To study meaning is to study content. To study discourse is to study language. To study language is to shift the locus of study beyond the individual to the communicative array, a collective product. It is to credit as much importance to what is local and special as to what is general and universal. And it is to recognize that objective knowledge is possible even in the absence of a formal, general, or standard measuring device.

Our own interest in the socialization of moral beliefs by means of inferences and arguments implicit in, and carried by, everyday discourse is related to our view that it is time to displace the tiresome terms of the traditional dispute between cognitivists and noncognitivists. It is also time to replace some of our research heuristics, especially in the study of moral development.

That displacement is today conceivable thanks to several important insights from the philosophy of science. In effect we are now in a position to "soften" (David Wong's apt expression) our view of the real hard-knowledge-producing disciplines. It turns out that convergence may not be a defining feature of a genuine cognitive-scientific enterprise, and paradigm conflicts do not always go away, even in physics (Hesse 1972; Pinch 1977). It turns out that not all respectable concepts or terms can be verified by logic or direct observation; knowledge systems are presuppositional, analogical or metaphoric, and holistic. And not only can theories not be proved (by now a commonplace piece of received wisdom); it may turn out that they cannot be disproved, either; measurement error and anomaly may not be distinguishable on any formal grounds.

In another context (Shweder 1986) this neorationalist approach has been identified with the idea of "divergent rationalities" and with the attempt to broaden the notion of rationality to include not just inductive and deductive logic but several other cognitive elements as well: the presuppositions and premises from which a person reasons; the metaphors, analogies, and models used for generating explanations; the categories or classifications used for partitioning objects and events into kinds; and the types of evidence viewed as authoritative—intuition, introspection, external observation, meditation, scriptural evidence, evidence from seers, prophets, or elders, and so on.

One effect of all this softening up of the hard sciences is that it is now possible to "harden" our view of the soft sciences and disciplines and to define a more realistic rationalist agenda for studies of morality and moral development. For example, it is possible to argue that moral concepts and judgments refer to natural or objective entities in the world, as long as it is understood that the existence of moral facts and objective moral knowledge is not incompatible with the existence of irreconcilable moral disputes, and that there can be more than one valid moral universe, just as there can be more than one valid physical science representation of the nature of light.

The Babaji interview presents us with an alternative version of an objective postconventional moral world. Given a neorationalist conception of objective knowledge, there is no longer any necessity to deny that it is rational or postconventional. The objective moral world is many, not one; or, as Nelson Goodman (1984) has put it: "One might say that there is only one world but this holds for each of the many worlds" (p. 278).

Appendix: The Babaji Interview Using Kohlberg's Interview Form A (Modified)

A woman suffered from a fatal disease. To cure her, doctors prescribed a medicine. That particular medicine was available in only one medicine shop. The pharmacist demanded ten times the real cost of the medicine. The sick woman's husband, Ashok, could not afford it. He went to everyone he knew to borrow money. But he was able to borrow only half of the price. He asked the pharmacist to give him the medicine at half price or to give it to him on credit. But the pharmacist said, "No I will sell it at any price I like. There are many persons who will purchase it." After trying so many legal ways to get the medicine, the desperate husband considered breaking into the shop and stealing the medicine.

Should Ashok steal the drug?
No. He is feeling desperate because his wife is going to die, and that's why he is stealing the drug. But people don't live forever, and providing her the drug does not necessarily mean she will live long. How long you live is not in our hands but in God's hands. And there are other ways to get money, like selling his landed property, or even he can sell himself to someone and can save his wife's life.

He has no other way out. He has neither money nor anything.
Stealing is bad. He has made a mistake.

But his wife is going to die!
There is no way within Hindu dharma [religion, duty, obligation, natural law, truth] to steal even if a man is going to die.

But doesn't Hindu dharma prescribe that you try to save a person's life?
Yes. And for that you can sacrifice your blood or sell yourself, but you cannot steal.

Why doesn't Hindu dharma permit stealing?
If he steals it is a sin—so what virtue is there in saving a life? Hindu dharma keeps man from sinning.

Why would it be a sin? Isn't there a saying, "One must jump into fire for others"?
That is there in our dharma—sacrifice, but not stealing.

But if he doesn't provide the medicine for his wife, she will die. Wouldn't it be a sin to let her die?
That's why, according to the capabilities and powers which God has given him, he should try to give her shamanistic instructions and advice. Then she can be cured.

But that particular medicine is the only way out.
There's no reason to necessarily think that that particular drug will save her life.

Let's suppose she can be saved only by that drug, or else she will die. Won't he face lots of difficulties if his wife dies?
No.

But his family will break up.
He can marry other women.

But he has no money. How can he remarry?
Do you think he should steal? If he steals, he will be sent to jail. Then what's the use of saving her life to keep the family together? She has enjoyed the days destined for her. But stealing is bad. Our sacred scriptures tell that sometimes stealing is an act of dharma. If by stealing for you I can save your life, then it is an act of dharma. But one cannot steal for his wife or his offspring or for himself. If he does that, it is simply stealing.

If I steal for myself, then it's a sin?
Yes.

But in this case I am stealing for my wife, not for me.
But your wife is yours.

Doesn't Ashok have a duty or obligation to steal the drug?
He may not get the medicine by stealing. He may sell himself. He may sell himself to someone for, say, 500 rupees for six months or one year.

Does it make a difference whether or not he loves his wife?
So what if he loves his wife? When the husband dies, the wife does not die for him, or vice versa. We have come into this world alone, and we will leave it alone. Nobody will accompany us when we leave this world. It may be a son or it may be a wife. No one will go with us.

For whom do you feel one should steal? Let's say it is not his wife but a holy man or a stranger. Would it have been better if he had stolen for them?
Stealing is bad. It is not right according to Hindu dharma, but if he stole for himself the degree of sin would be more.

Is it important to do everything one can to save another's life?
Yes. But that does not mean stealing. You can borrow from someone. You can go without eating. You can give your food to others, or you can sell yourself.

Suppose Ashok had come to you, told you his situation, and sought your advice whether or not to steal. What would you have told him?
I would have asked him not to steal. We have a practice in the villages. Everyone would have decided to give him the required money from the village common fund, or they would have collected some donation. But he should be advised not to steal.

But shouldn't people do everything they can to save a life?
One should try to save another's life. Because, after all, he is a human being. But you should not do it by virtue of stealing.

Is it against the law for Ashok to steal?
Yes. It's against the law.

Are the laws always morally right? Do you feel all laws are right?
Let me tell you a story about stealing. Once some sadhus [wandering mendicant holy men] came to a poor man's house. He and his son were the only members of the family. The sadhus wanted this man to be their host for that night. Holy men never ask for credit. They never steal. They have only what they earn from begging alms, which they cook and eat.

The sadhus arrived at the man's house as guests, and as guests they were considered as a god. So the man and his son pawned whatever belongings they had and arranged dinner for the sadhus. Before going to their dinner the sadhus said that ghee was essential for their dinner. [Ghee, or clarified butter, is classified in the native theory of foods as a "cool" food—one of the foods eaten by holy men]. Both the father and the son pondered again and again where to get the ghee. They were really "in a stew."

They went to the sadhu of a nearby monastery to get some ghee. But the sadhu refused to give them ghee. So they made a hole in the wall and the son entered the storeroom of the monastery. It was full of wealth, but the son picked up only the ghee pot. While he was halfway through the hole, suddenly the sadhu got up and caught hold of the son's two legs. But outside the father was pulling the son's hands. So a tussle went on for some time. The son told the father to take the pot of ghee and offer it to the sadhu guests. He also told his father to cut off his head and take it away so that the sadhu of the monastery would not be able to recognize him. The father did this and threw away his son's head.

The father did such things only because he wanted to help the sadhus. After he offered ghee to his guests the sadhus were satisfied. The next morning the father bade them farewell, and they asked, "Where is your son? He is not seen." The father started to cry. The sadhus asked him why he was crying. So he told all the details and facts, and said it was nobody's fault.

The sadhus said, "You have made a mistake. Okay. If you have done it only to satisfy us, if you had no evil intention under it, if you had no temptation for the wealth, and if your son died only for this, then we will pray to God for his life." They asked, "Where is your son's head?" They wanted to show God the decapitated head. The father took the head of the son to the sadhus. They sprinkled some Tulsi water on the head. So the son returned to life.

In the story the sadhus brought the son back to life because he had stolen for others. Likewise Ashok is doing this for his wife, isn't he?
The relationship between a wife and husband and between a man and a holy man are quite different. Suppose a river is flowing. This idea is also from our sacred scriptures. Pieces of wood are all tied together in a bundle and floating down the river. They are tied perfectly. Slowly the tie loosens. After some time individual pieces of wood leave the flow and stop on the bank of the river. They become changed. They could not be together as they were before. This world is like that. The son will go his way. We will go our way. If you think only of the truth, if you obey Hindu dharma, then stealing is not allowed. Maybe we are together, five souls [literally, "hearts"] are joined and we are sitting here. You will go to your home. I will go to my home. No one has the power to detain anyone. So anyone who has faith in God, he will not try to steal to detain his wife's journey.

Don't people steal in certain circumstances?
Yes, people are stealing, and we cannot know what punishment they get for this. If you understand how you have come into this world you will not steal. Stealing is a great sin.

Which is a greater sin, to kill a man or to steal?
Both are great sins. You must have gone to Dhauli [the battlefield where King Ashoka slaughtered hundreds of thousands of Oriya Kalinga in battle—the place where in repentance for the slaughter Ashoka converted to Buddhism, later to spread Buddhism to Southeast Asia]. When Ashok conquered Kalinga, a monk came to him and said, "You are defeated." Ashok said, "What? I have already conquered Kalinga, killed thousands of people, and with their blood the water of the river Daya has turned red. What do you mean 'I am defeated?'" The monk said, "You are born as a man. You proclaim that you are a great man." Ashok said, "You please come with me, so you can see how many persons are beheaded, how many dead bodies are lying down there. You see my sword. I have killed many persons with this sword."

The monk said, "It is by killing hundreds of thousands of people that you have failed. If you can give life to any one of these then I will say you are great. Their wives and children, those who depend on them, how they are crying. You are only killing. You have not recognized the atman [soul, divinity] in them. How have you conquered?" So Ashok, the butcher, changed. He threw down his sword and begged forgiveness from the monk.

Isn't the husband killing his wife by not stealing the drug?
No, he is not killing. If something is with me and I do not give it, then it is my fault. The husband must have some homestead land, or some vehicle. If he has nothing then he has at least his self, which he can sell.

No, Ashok has nothing. He is poor.
He can sell himself. We have the tradition of Havis Chandra—the king who sold himself to give remuneration that he owed. It is a time when God puts you to a test. At such a time you can sell yourself. Suppose I earn 7 rupees a day. I can borrow 500 rupees on a condition to serve the man for five years. Alternatively, when the wife is going to die, he can die in her place. He will die in sorrow anyway.

But had he stolen the drug, he would have saved her.
Definitely it will be a sin. Thinking in terms of dharma he cannot steal. This is a fact. If I steal it's my dharma that's involved. My wife will not be sent to jail. I will be sent. Dharma is like that—I will be at fault. There's a story I want to tell you. During the age of the *Mahabharata* [the Indian epic] Kali [the goddess of destruction] came to earth and Dahadebu tied her up. She was bound. That was during the age of Satyayuga [Truth]. A peasant was ploughing the land of a Brahman. Once while he was ploughing he found a golden armlet in the earth. So he went to the Brahman and said, "Here, take this golden armlet since I have found it on your land." The Brahman said to the tiller, "It's yours to take since you ploughed the land." So they quarreled with each other, each trying to give the golden armlet to the other. When one gives it to the other the latter says, "Why should I commit a sin?" So no one took the armlet.

Both of them went to the king, Yudhisthira. It was the tradition in those days to give such disputed things to the king. The king said, "Our time of rule is over, and we are going to the Himalayas. We cannot stay here, and there is no use of taking such property with us to the Himalayas." So Yudhisthira told them to ask Sahadeba to judge the dispute. Sahadeba was a man capable of seeing both the past and the future. So do you know what he did? He freed Kali! He let her loose. Immediately the Brahman claimed the armlet. Then the tiller claimed the armlet because he got it while ploughing. The fighting continued between them. Everything depends on the age, whether it's the age of Kali or the age of Satya. This is the age of Kali.

Do you know any laws that are morally wrong?
Family planning. According to dharma it is wrong.

What's wrong with it?
The operation and the sterilization. They are murdering through abortion.

Is the law forbidding dowry morally wrong?
Dowry is not part of our dharma. But it's in practice nowadays. One should give voluntarily.

What about the law permitting untouchables to enter the temple? Is that law morally wrong?
There is a history of touchable and untouchable. It's not a sin if a Hadi [an untouchable caste in Orissa] touches a Brahman or a Karan [a clean caste in Orissa] or visits the temple. But there is a reason behind the idea of untouchable. Suppose you have taken your bath and I have not. Untouchables do not keep their own sanctity. Human being means all are equal. God has created the hierarchy among them so that they will work according to their duty. Untouchables can enter the temple but they should be cleaned. They should perform their daily duties like bathing properly.

If they perform their daily duties properly can they enter then?
Yes. No restriction. Even God has not restricted them. You know what the goddess Laxmi [goddess of wealth, consort of Vishnu] has said: "From Hadi [sweeper] to Chandala [another untouchable caste] all will touch prasad [a holy food] on their head."

What about the law requiring equal inheritance between son and daughter? Is that law morally wrong?
Both son and daughter are equal; they are born to the same father, and for him everyone is equal. But the thing is that the daughter gets married and becomes part of her husband's family. It is the son who takes care of his parents. They live with him. And it is the son who performs all the death rituals and, after the parents' death, other rituals for the ancestors as well. That's why we do it: 60 percent for the

son and 40 percent for the daughter. If both of them were unmarried and the brother did not finance the sister's marriage, then as in the government's law, it ought to be 50/50.

But the law says that even if the son and daughter are married they must share equally. Is that morally correct?
The son has many duties to perform for ceremonies and other occasions. They are costly. If he manages all these duties then the daughter cannot take an equal amount. Thinking in terms of dharma the government law is wrong.

Can you think of any Indian custom or tradition which is morally wrong?
Eating with your younger brothers' wife is against our custom. It's not wrong according to dharma; it's not bad. But you will feel guilty if you do it—you will feel that you have made a mistake.

Foreigners are not allowed in Juggernaut temple. Is that morally right?
They are not allowed because they do not believe in the Hindu religion. They are all Christians.

Suppose the foreigner had converted to Hinduism?
If he were a Hindu he would be allowed to enter. If he believes in the Hindu religion he will be allowed.

Untouchables are not allowed in the temple. Is that morally correct?
I told you before about touchability and untouchability. Suppose we were untouchables. We would be feeling guilty. Because we have not taken our bath or washed our dress we do not enter the temple. Untouchables do not perform cleansing rituals—they don't keep to habits of purification. So they are not allowed in sanctified places.

Are all the practices, customs, and traditions of Hinduism right?
The traditions of the Hindu religion are not bad but good.

The Indian population is increasing. Suppose the government passed a law that no family can have more than three children. Otherwise the child should be killed. Would that law be okay?
No. Such a law should not be obeyed.

Why should it not be obeyed?
Suppose a child is born. There is no way within the context of Hindu dharma to kill him. Take, for example, the case of a tree studded with

fruit. It is a great sin to cut down that tree. If it is an obstacle or if it harms or gives some kind of pain then we are bound to cut it down. Otherwise one should not cut the tree. If we see it bending down on us, then we cut it. Imagine the government saying, "You have five or six children but you may not keep them!" There's a lot of difference between the age of the gods and our age, between the age of the epics and the present age.

Why do you think that stealing is forbidden in Hindu dharma?
If one steals, in the next life who knows what form he will take? Any man who realizes this will not steal. That's why it is restricted.

Are the punishments the same for different kinds of stealing?
Yes.

What about someone who steals to save a life?
His punishment should be less. But it is a matter of dharma. We cannot steal, and it is not us who gives punishment. God is considering their case. There was once a king. He was always offering things to Brahmans—he offered hundreds of thousands of cows as donations to Brahmans. Once one of the donated cows "played hookey" and returned to the king's cowshed. The king was not aware of this fact. So by mistake he again donated that particular cow to a different Brahman. Soon the first owner of that donated cow saw that cow while the second Brahman was taking it with him. He recognized the symbols on the cow's tail and the turmeric spot. So he proclaimed that the cow had been a gift of the king to him. He told the second Brahman to go to the king. When the king saw them coming he shivered. He wondered why the two Brahmans had come to him with a cow. Both of them put forth their claim. The king told the second Brahman, "You see I have already donated this cow. You return it to the first Brahman and I will donate a hundred thousand cows to you." But the second Brahman said, "No. I must take this cow because you have donated it to me." So both of them started quarreling with each other over the ownership of the cow. The quarrel lasted so long that at last the cow died.

But even though the king had unknowingly redonated the cow he had to shoulder the sin. On the other hand, the king had donated hundreds of thousands of cows and even golden-made cow horns. When Yama [the god of Death] saw him, he said, "This king has done so many virtuous things and but one vice—unknowingly redonating that cow. So his mistake is only one percent. Still, he has to undergo the effect of sin." Yama asked the king, "Would you like to enjoy first the sin or first the virtue?" The king said, "I have not done this knowingly. Still, since I have committed a serious mistake, I will first experience the sin and then the virtue." Then Yama uttered the word *kukulash* [lizard] and threw the king into a well in the jungle. How can the king be saved? When Krishna goes to that place, then only will the king get salvation. Otherwise no one can remove him from the well. So even if we do something unknowingly, it can be wrong—from the point of view of dharma it is a mistake.

(Ashok did break into the store. He stole the drug and gave it to his wife. Ashok was arrested and brought to court. A jury was selected. The jury's job is to find whether a person is innocent or guilty of committing a crime. The jury finds Ashok guilty. It is up to the judge to determine the sentence.)

Should the judge give Ashok some punishment, or should he let him go free? Why?
According to law—when he has stolen he should be punished. Ashok has created a family in this world. God gave him hands and legs, yet he has not saved money by working and laboring. Now he has no money and cannot buy the medicine or cure the disease. With all his lethargy he did not think of his wife's getting ill before. So if he steals now, he has to bear the punishment.

Thinking in terms of society, should people who break the law be punished?
It is written in our Hindu sacred scriptures that whatever may be the religion, be it Muslim or Christian, it is wrong to denigrate or blame other religions. God has not said I have one particular name. Whoever prays to him in any name—one should not think him wrong. But if someone is about to destroy Hindu dharma or break Christian dharma, then he should be punished. The destruction of Hinduism is not the point; it's the destruction of any dharma.

How does this apply to how the judge should decide?
The case should be considered. He was involved in stealing. On the other hand we have to look carefully at the law. Why was that pharmacist demanding fifty rupees for a drug that cost five rupees? So, the pharmacist has done wrong. He should get punished.

Ashok acted out of conscience. Should a lawbreaker be punished if he is acting out of conscience?
Yes. He should get punished.

Should he get the same punishment from the judge as the person who steals for his own benefit?
Yes, the same punishment. It is our law that one cannot forcibly enter into another's house.

One man steals for himself, and another steals to save a life. In the next life will they be reborn in the same way? Will God give the same kind of punishment for both offenses?
They'll get different kinds of punishment.

Then why shouldn't the judge give less punishment to the person who steals to save a life?
What's the same is that they get punished—the means is the same. The degree can differ. One person gets fined two rupees for taxation punishment. Another is fined five rupees. Not everyone gets six months' imprisonment. Some get one year. The judge will consider the type of stealing in deciding on the punishment. Suppose I kidnapped a girl, and another person, being hungry, stole away some black-gram cutlets [a type of grain fried as a cutlet; in this case a trivial theft]. In both cases it is stealing, but there is a difference between the degree of stealing. Before the creation of the world the Formless One created these three—Brahma, Vishnu, and Siva. During that time there were demons in the world. The Formless One decided to kill the demons and create the world. The world was full of water all around. Seeing this, Vishnu plucked a hair from his body and threw it away. It created a mountain on the earth. This trinity, Brahma, Vishnu, and Siva, lived on the mountain and created a flower garden. They thought about all the things they would create. Meanwhile, many days passed, and the Formless One wondered where the three had gone and why they had not returned. He told this to the First Mother and asked her to go and see what the three were doing. When she reached the mountain Brahma and Vishnu had gone somewhere; only Siva was there, alone. The garden was all decorated. Seeing the First Mother, Siva became excited and starting have sexual intercourse with her. Brahma and Vishnu returned and saw it all. They abused the First Mother—so she cursed them and told them they would suffer after being born in the womb of the mother they

were now abusing. Being cursed this way, Brahma and Vishnu went to the Formless One and told him all the facts. Hearing about it, the Formless One cursed the First Mother and made her take birth as a cow on earth.

So the First Mother has sinned. Lingaraj [the reigning deity of Bhu-baneswar] and other gods and goddesses have also sinned from time to time. But has the First Father done any sin?
No. He has never sinned!

Is there anything more valuable than life?
No.

Then if Ashok can save a life by stealing, what is the harm of it?
He should have saved her life by virtue of labor. Whatever may be, he should not steal. It is a wrong to steal, and you will get punished. Ravana [the villain of the epic *Ramayana*] was a great learned man before he kidnapped Sita [Ram's wife in the *Ramayana*]. When he stole away Sita he sinned. He was cursed for it, and he was killed for it. Saving a life by means of stealing is not the only way out.

6.

Menstrual Pollution, Soul Loss, and the Comparative Study of Emotions

There are three general questions in the comparative study of emotions: (1) What is an emotional life? (2) With respect to which aspects of emotional functioning are people alike or different? and (3) How are these likenesses and differences to be explained? This essay is concerned with all three questions, with special focus on the second.

To ask whether people are alike or different in their emotional functioning is really to pose several more specific questions: Do people vary in terms of the type of feelings felt (the taxonomic question), the situations that elicit those feelings (the ecological question), the perceived implications of those feelings (the semantic question), the vehicles for expressing those feelings (the communication question), the appropriateness of possessing or displaying certain feelings (the social regulation question), and the techniques or strategies used to deal with feelings that cannot be directly expressed (the management question)?

To speak of the emotional life is to talk about *felt* experiences. Three-year-olds, Ifaluk islanders, and psychoanalysts (in other words, almost everyone, except perhaps the staunchest of positivists) recognize that emotions are *feelings*. To understand the emotional life of a person is to understand the types of feelings (anger, envy, fear, depersonalization, shame, joy, love, homesickness, and so on) felt by that person, the distribution and frequency of those feelings across time and context, the kinds of situations that elicit them, the wishes and fantasies that occur with them, and the action tendencies set off by them.

Now, it is true that feelings cannot be seen; the only feelings we have direct experience of are our own. I do not feel your feelings as you feel them, and indeed I have no way of knowing with certainty that you have feelings at all. I know that you move your face in complex ways and change your posture and utter words such as *pain* and *anger*, but faces, postures, and words are not feelings—and it is the feelings that interest us, though they cannot be seen. For some, that fact marks the end of the study of emotions. Positivists, for example, committed to the view that only what is perceivable is real, have confined themselves to reportage of that which can be observed—facial movements, heartbeats, and hormone levels. Most of us, however, are willing to live with assumption, inference, and conjecture, for the study of facial movements, heartbeats, and hormone levels takes on interest only if they can be used to draw inferences about things that cannot be observed—namely, how other people feel.

Conjecture plays a large part in our understanding. Some of our most fundamental ideas—that contiguity in time and space implies causation, that objects continue to exist in the absence of an observer, that what you see is what I see—are conjectures. It is a conjecture that other people have an emotional life, and it is a conjecture that trees and plants do not. Without conjecture there could be no understanding, and there would hardly be any point to studying emotions if we were unwilling to conjecture that other people's feelings, though unseen, are nevertheless there.

There are several aspects of emotional functioning and many distinct but compatible questions we can ask about the emotional functioning of a person or people. Six are listed below.

1. There is the *taxonomic* question: What types of feelings do these people experience? The first step in any study of emotions is to document the range and types of feelings felt. Lexical studies can be quite misleading in a taxonomic investigation, for there are documented cases (for example, Robert Levy's Tahitians) of people who talk a lot about an emotion (for example, anger) yet rarely experience it, or experience an emotion (for example, guilt) yet have no word for it and rarely speak of it (Levy 1973, pp. 273–288; 1984). A people's

lexicon for emotions is a rather poor index of their emotional functioning.

It is a challenging fact about emotional functioning—a fact about which I shall have more to say later—that very young children display *situation-appropriate* facial expressions for a diverse set of discrete emotions. If you hold a cookie just out of reach of a six-month-old or confine his arms to his sides, he will show the face of anger. Not the face of pain or the face of distress, but the face of anger. The inference is nearly irresistible that by eighteen months of age, that is, before language learning, children experience and know the difference between anger, surprise, distress, interest, fear, and disgust. By the age of thirty months they experience jealousy, and by the time they are four years old they are quite competent at expressing a wide range of such emotions through face, language, voice register, and posture (Charlesworth and Kreutzer 1973; Paradise and Curcio 1974; Van Lieshout 1975; Emde, Gaensbauer, and Harman 1976; LaBarbera et al. 1976; Hiatt, Campos, and Emde 1979; Sroufe 1979; Izard et al. 1980; Ochs 1982; Cohn and Tronick 1983; Stenberg, Campos, and Emde 1983).

It is also a fact about emotional functioning—and I shall return to this fact as well—that the type and range of emotions in the experiential repertoire of young children are not necessarily the same as the types of emotions experienced by adults. Eskimo and Tahitian six-month-olds are probably capable of feeling anger and may well experience it more frequently than Eskimo and Tahitian adults (Briggs 1970; Levy 1973).

2. There is the *ecological* question: What are the emotion-laden situations for these people, and which emotions are elicited by which situations?

Obviously there are many culture-specific or person-specific elicitors. Not everyone finds the same situations emotion laden or experiences them in the same way. Being offered help, being told what to do, being "mothered" elicits anger in some people but deference, respect, dependency, and gratitude in others. Being the center of attention elicits embarrassment and fear in some, self-satisfaction and pride in others. In matters of love and loss, the Samoans experience what has been called a "generalized nonchalance," whereas Americans feel agitated and distressed (H. Geertz 1959).

One should not, however, rule out the possibility that there are some universal elicitors. The more we look at the emotional life of young children around the world the more it seems that certain situations are emotion laden in the same way, at least in the first few years of life. Loss (for example, your mother or caretaker disappears, leaving you with a stranger) is experienced as distress. Frustration (a cookie is kept from you just out of reach) or confinement (someone forcibly keeps you from lifting your arms) is experienced as anger. Unexpected events (for example, a sudden sound, the popping up of a jack-in-the-box) are experienced as surprise. The "visual cliff" (an apparatus used by experimental child psychologists to test whether infants will crawl into an apparent abyss) elicits fear (Campos et al. 1975; Hiatt, Campos, and Emde 1979). In the first few years of life certain events seem to be interpreted in similar ways and experienced or felt in the same way by almost everyone. There are probably fewer universal elicitors for adults than for young children, yet even with adults one should not rule out the possibility that certain ideas are widely shared and certain emotions widely experienced. For example, the idea of natural law or sacred obligations may be a universal idea, and so may be the experience of shame-guilt-terror associated with the transgression of sacred obligations. And, while irreversible loss may imply or suggest different things to different peoples, certain of these implications or suggestions do have a worldwide distribution. There is a common thread of meaning to bereavement; as Paul Rosenblatt, Patricia Walsh, and Douglas Jackson (1976) discovered in an examination of mortuary rites in seventy-three societies, in all but one society crying is a featured mode of emotional display and expression at funerals. Bali is the notable, and ambiguous, exception.

3. There is the *semantic* question: What do the feelings imply? Studying the meaning of emotions is not the same as identifying the lexical labels (happy, sad, angry) that are used to refer to emotions, and such lexical study per se is relatively uninteresting and probably unrevealing. To study what something means is to study what it entails, implies, or suggests to those who understand it (Hirsch 1967, 1976; Solomon 1976, 1984). To say that I love my "dog" is to entail logically that I love an animal. To say that the ball is "hard" is to imply that heads may be cracked by it. To say that one of my grandparents was a "surgeon" is to suggest it was a grandfather, although that meaning ("*male* grandparent") is neither entailed nor implied by the concept "surgeon."

Sometimes the meaning of something seems to be *in* the thing itself. "It's square" implies that it won't roll. "She's your mother" seems to imply that she ought to care about your health. Sometimes the meaning of something seems to be more in our head than in the thing itself. "He's your father" does not imply that secretly he wants to mutilate or castrate you or remove you from the scene, but that is what it means to some people. When the ideas suggested by something are widely shared, those suggestions become *implications*. When the suggestions are not widely shared, they remain suggestions or "free" associations. Nevertheless, whether we study what has been called "meaning-in" or "meaning-to," things often carry with them entailments, implications, suggestions, and free associations, and that is what the study of meaning is about.

Emotions have meanings, and those meanings play a part in how we feel. What it means to feel angry, indeed what it feels like to feel angry, is not quite the same for the Ilongot, who believe that anger is so dangerous it can destroy society; for the Eskimo, who view anger as something that only children experience; and for working-class Americans, who believe that anger helps us overcome fear and attain independence (Briggs 1970; Rosaldo 1980, 1984; P. Miller 1982).

Some emotions imply action tendencies. Surprise implies focus. Fear implies flight. Other emotions suggest certain wishes or fantasies. Anger suggests explosion, destruction, and revenge. Shame suggests exposure and banishment. Guilt suggests reparation, absolution, reintegration, and forgiveness. Sadness suggests withdrawal, self-criticism, loss, and the idea of being helped. These implications may or may not be universal. In any study of ethnosemantics, some implications will be widely shared and others will not. Jealousy takes on a special meaning for those who believe that illness and death are the result of the envy of others and that to wish someone ill is to practice witchcraft against that person. Loyalty, respect, deference, and dependency do not have the same associations for autonomous, egalitarian Americans as they do for interdependent, hierarchical Indians. Shame does not have the same meaning for Americans, who tend to think they have a right to be let alone to do their own business and who have nearly reduced shame to embarrassment and blushing before the public eye, as it has for more tradition-bound people, who believe that most of what they do is governed by natural law and who view with shame any action that discredits their standing in the natural order of things. The life of the emotions itself takes on a special meaning if we believe that emotions, *if unexpressed,* are dangerous and do not go away, or alternatively, if we believe that emotions, *if expressed,* are dangerous and do not go away.

4. There is the *communication* question: How are feelings expressed, or what are the vehicles for communicating an emotion?

There are many vehicles of emotional expression and communication—the face, voice register, body posture, words, and so on. Some expressive symbols we know how to read or interpret without much training or instruction. There is a common language (an "Esperanto") of the face, voice register, and body posture that is understood by nearly everyone, young and old, and I for one have little difficulty with the idea that there is "prior" knowledge of the code for reading *some* emotional expressions. Most three-year-olds can tell from certain common features of the voice, face, and body when someone is happy, sad, angry, or surprised; and even some of the metaphors for emotional expression ("down," "empty," "blue") may have a universal reading. Roy D'Andrade and Michael Egan (1974), for example, found that the colors associated with different emotions are very similar for Tzeltal-speaking Mayan Indians and English-speaking Americans. The way the visual experience of color is mapped onto or used to express concepts of emotion (happiness, worry, sadness, fright, anger) may not be all that variable either historically or cross-culturally. And even some of the notable, and often noted, exceptions to the rule (for example, widows in India wear white, not black) may disguise a deeper similarity (the absence of gay hues or attractive colors). The association, for example, of red with anger and black (or white) with bereavement is no historical accident; very different kinds of peoples know how to translate the color-affect code, and they translate it in a similar way.

Obviously, not all aspects of the code for communicating emotions involve prior knowledge. The language of deference and respect, for example, is highly developed in some cultures, and there is simply no way to know the correct terms of address or reference without training or instruction. And not everyone bangs his head against the wall to express grief or knows what it symbolizes when someone else does it. And certainly some facial expressions are culture specific and difficult to read without acquired knowledge of the code. For example, Oriya women in Bhubaneswar, India, use a facial expression in which the tongue extends out and downward and is bitten between the teeth, the eyebrows rise, and the eyes widen, bulge, and cross. It is the face of surprise-embarrassment-fear, a combination of feelings that might be felt by an American graduate student if she were to shout vulgar abuse at a passing motorist only to discover that the driver was her thesis adviser. That face of surprise-embarrassment-fear appears on pictorial representations of the Hindu goddess Kali (see page 21). Tongue out, eyes bulging, she is shown stepping on the chest of her consort, Shiva. The representation is often misinterpreted by Western observers, who tend to see in Kali's face only ferocity and demonic rage and not the shock and shame she conveys to Oriya observers. It is noteworthy, nevertheless, that even many of the culture-specific aspects of emotional communication codes seem to get learned rapidly and early in life. Elinor Ochs (1982), for example, has examined the diverse ways in which affect is encoded in the Samoan language (via special-affect particles, pronouns, and so on). Her important finding is that with the exception of the respect vocabulary, all the affect features are acquired by Samoan children during the first four years of life.

Language is a very powerful means of emotional expression and communication. Most ordinary language utterances tell us how to feel about the things being discussed (Labov and Fanshel 1977; Searle 1979; D'Andrade 1981, 1984; Much 1983). Among the less emotive aspects of ordinary language are the terms for emotions. There is nothing particularly "hot" about such words as *happy, sad, angry,* or *surprised.* They are far less evocative than saying of someone's wife that she is "past her prime" or talking about "little things that squirm in the night," or simply uttering "'Twas brillig, and the slithy toves / Did gyre and gimble in the wabe." Nevertheless, despite variations in emotional intensity, there are very few ordinary language phrases that are without feeling tone, and even the most innocent descriptions ("She's my friend," "She's my mother," "She's my lover") tell us how to feel.

5. There is the *social regulation* question: What feelings or emotions is it appropriate or inappropriate for a person of a particular status to feel or display, or both?

Both the possession and the display of certain feelings are subject to social regulation (Hochschild 1979). Social roles and role relationships, for example, carry with them a certain obligation to feel and express certain feelings and not others. One is not supposed to have sexual feelings toward blood relatives or express hatred toward a friend, and the emotions that get displayed have many implications for relationships. Respect is what inferiors express to superiors, not vice versa. Gratitude binds equals. Empathy links members of one's own kind.

In thinking about the social regulation of emotions, it is useful to employ the often-used metaphor of the theater. To view life as a stage. To view society as an arrangement of roles. To view social interactions as the enactment of role-based scripts. To view the communication of this or that feeling as quite distinct from the actual experience of that feeling. The performance or spectacle we call society requires of its actors only the skillful, or at least competent, public display of appropriate feelings (for example, empathy, seriousness, respect, loyalty), not the private experience of them. Consider the private experience of feelings of intimacy or closeness among various family members in Oriya Brahman households. Informants were asked to rank the eight nuclear family dyads in terms of closeness or intimacy. As reported by married women and men, the most intimate relationship is between husband and wife. Next on the scale of intimacy or closeness come the four parent-child dyads (mother-son, father-daughter, father-son, mother-daughter); the relative ordering of these dyads varies by informant. The least intimate relationships are the three sibling dyads (sister-sister, brother-brother, brother-sister); again, the relative ordering of these three dyads varies by informant.

It is tempting, even if hazardous, to speculate that there might be a universal patterning of intimacy across the eight nuclear family dyads such that in all societies there is an ordering of private feelings of intimacy: spouse>child>sibling. The ordering of those dyads by Oriya Brahmans is, after all, quite similar to orderings given by Americans despite the obvious and substantial differences between kinship and family in Orissa and America. At some very general level there may well be something about the marital bond, the filial bond, and the sororal-fraternal bond that organizes feelings of intimacy into a common pattern.

What is more relevant here, however, is that in Oriya Brahman families the public display of intimacy does not coincide with the private experience of intimacy. Indeed, among Oriya Brahmans the husband-wife relationship is scripted for mild avoidance. Spouses may not eat together. They do not address each other by name. They never touch or display affection to each other in public. They move through social life separately; women stay at home and do not, for example, go to the marketplace or even attend the ear-piercing ceremony of their sons. Husband and wife rarely present themselves or appear in public as a "couple."

Thus choreographed displays of avoidance or aloofness of the type standardly reported in ethnographies (for example, J. Whiting and B. Whiting 1975) are not necessarily indicative of the underlying private feelings of the actors, and it seems hazardous to interpret ritualized avoidance in terms of the psychodynamics of the actors. Oriya Brahman couples are far more likely to spend the night together in the same bed than to eat together. Bedding down together occurs in a realm defined as private, a realm in which feelings of intimacy can be expressed. Eating occurs in a realm defined as public. The avoidance script applies—and there may be witnesses and gossip.

On stage, social actors communicate role-appropriate feelings; they do not necessarily experience those feelings, and they certainly do not convey everything they do feel. If social actors conveyed everything they actually felt, and only what they actually felt, the performance called society, or at least the spectacle called civilization, would be very difficult to mount. On stage, how you actually feel is far less relevant than how you act, far less important than the role appropriateness of the feelings conveyed by your actions. An Oriya Brahman feels "close" to his or her spouse, but he or she cannot show it in public.

Avoidance and its presumed opposite, the joking relationship, are classic topics in anthropology (Tylor 1889; Radcliffe-Brown 1940). Despite several noteworthy attempts at explanation and interpretation (Stephens and D'Andrade 1962; Driver 1966; Sweetser 1966; Witkowski 1972; LeVine 1984), the problem remains unsolved (see Levinson and Malone 1980, pp. 117–127). The area is rich with challenges.

For the most part, anthropologists have examined avoidance and joking in the context of kinship relations. The more provocative findings (Murdock 1971; Goody and Buckley 1974) can be summarized as follows. In most societies of the world (80–90 percent), the mother-in-law/son-in-law and father-in-law/daughter-in-law relationships are marked by avoidance-respect-formality. In most societies of the world (roughly 80 percent), the relationship between a man and his wife's younger sisters or between a woman and her husband's younger brothers is marked by informality, joking, or sexual license. The affect-display script for each of these relationships is pretty much the same across quite diverse societies, and the script for each seems to transcend societal variations in descent system, residence pattern, religion, economy, political system, and so on.

In contrast, the brother-sister script is a bit more variable cross-culturally (although worldwide it tends in the direction of avoidance-formality-respect), while the scripts for a woman and her husband's older brother and for a man and his wife's older sister are highly variable from society to society. Societies with a matrilineal or bilateral descent system seem to promote avoidance-respect-formality between a brother and a sister; you do not joke around with your brother in societies in which your children are going to inherit his property. Societies with patrilineal descent systems seem to promote avoidance-respect-formality with the wife's older sister and the husband's elder brother.

What to make of all this? Any unifying theory of kinship avoidance has a lot of explaining to do. Why, for example, within a single community, must a man treat his sister with informality, joke around with his older brother's wife and wife's younger sister, yet avoid his younger brother's wife and wife's older sister? And why are the scripts for the display of emotions to a brother or husband's older brother more *variable* from culture to culture than are the scripts for a father-in-law or a husband's younger brother? A unifying theory should help us understand the meaning or function of any particular mode of affect display (avoidance versus deference versus informality versus joking versus abuse) and should help us relate each mode of affect display (for example, avoidance versus joking) to the underlying dynamics of the role relationship. By the underlying dynamics, I mean the mix of necessary cooperation and unavoidable competition in the relationship, the relative balance of power or status, and the potential consequences or costs of a struggle or conflict over desired but limited resources. At the moment there is no unifying theory. Displays of emotions are socially structured and socially regulated; we still have much to learn about the dynamics of the choreography.

6. There is the *management* question: How are those emotions that are not expressed handled? We know, for instance, that certain feelings such as anger or emptiness or envy are not displayed or directly expressed in some cultures, and it appears that the techniques for handling them vary widely from denial to displacement to projection to somatization (LeVine 1973, chapter 17; Kleinman 1982).

The management of emotions question is, of course, a central one for culture and personality theorists (see, for example, Whiting and Child 1953; Roberts and Sutton-Smith 1962; J. Whiting 1964, 1977; Spiro 1965, 1983; and Chapter 7 of this volume). It is the main tenet of many culture and personality theorists that myths, rituals, games and religious beliefs, practices and symbols are "projective systems," that is, indirect ways of vicariously satisfying repressed wishes, disguised means for reducing anxiety or expressing deeply felt but forbidden desires. If the culture and personality theorists are right, many cultural practices—from prayer to head-hunting, from monastic retreat to adolescent circumcision, from obedience to the Ten Commandments to professional football—exist, or at least persist, as cultural practices for the sake of managing emotions (dependency, hostility, latent homosexuality, anxiety over sexual identity, and so on) and for the sake of providing them with a safe outlet.

The fate of felt-but-unexpressed emotions is still poorly understood. It is plausible to imagine that certain emotions are functionally interconnected: to imagine, for example, that sexual arousal lowers the threshold of anger or aggression; to imagine that certain emotions (for example, anger) will not go away until they are expressed or "acted out"; or to imagine that if they cannot be acted out in one way (for example, by killing your father) they will be acted out in a less dangerous way (by directing the hostility against "outsiders") or transformed into something else (such as depression; see, for example, Silverman 1976, which presents evidence that the subliminal presentation of hostile or aggressive imagery magnifies feelings of depression in depressed patients). The problem is that it is just as plausible to imagine the opposite: to imagine, for example, that anger, if unexpressed, slowly dissipates and ultimately disappears. Our knowledge in this area is so limited that in the 1980s it was still possible for Michelle Rosaldo (1984) and Melford Spiro (1984) to disagree about whether Freudian defense mechanisms are a generic property of the human mind.

Rosaldo (1984) examines emotional functioning among Ilongot head-hunters in the Philippines. Adopting the position that culturally constituted ideas have a decisive influence on mental processing, she argues against the notion of a psychic unity to mankind, against the notion of a generic human mind. On the basis of her observations she notes that the Ilongot "did not think of hidden or forgotten affects [for example, anger] as disturbing energies repressed; nor did they see in violent actions the expression of a history of frustrations buried in a fertile but unconscious mind" (p. 144). Rosaldo holds out the possibility that feelings work among the Ilongot differently from the way they work in our own culture; that, for example, among the Ilongot anger is not repressed and displaced, that defensive processes are the product of a Western way of constructing a self. Spiro (1984) argues for a generic human mind and an inherent mental machinery, including repression, displacement, and projection. It is also imaginable of course that defensive processes are not automatic defense mechanisms (inherent in the machinery) but rather habitual defensive strategies, and that the strategy of choice (for example, denial or projection versus sublimation or intellectualization) may vary with a culture's construction of a self. Blame-externalizing defenses such as projection may be disapproved of in some cultures but not in others.

Undoubtedly there are universals and cultural specifics with regard to each of these six aspects of emotional functioning. It is ludicrous to imagine that the emotional functioning of people in different cultures is basically the same. It is just as ludicrous to imagine that each culture's emotional life is unique.

The Lost Soul: A Phenomenology of Depression

In the following semantic approach to emotions, I attempt to explain the meaning of depression and to identify what depressed feelings are about.

I try to unify reports about what it feels like to feel depressed (for example, Jackson 1980; Leff 1980) and what these feelings imply about the self and the world.

The idea of soul loss helps to make sense of the subjective experience of depression and some of its associated symptomatology (see, for example, Beck 1976; Orley and Wing 1979; Marsella 1980; Mezzich and Raab 1980; Mathew, Weinman, and Mirabi 1981; Gada 1982; Kleinman 1982). When you feel depressed you feel as though your soul has left your body. You feel empty, and a body emptied of its soul loses interest in things, except perhaps its own physical malfunctioning as a thing. The phenomenon of soul wandering is widely acknowledged among the world's cultures, and the phenomenology of soul loss has been a topic of theoretical and practical concern for millennia. A sophisticated and nearly universal doctrine has emerged which has it that the body is routinely emptied of its soul at the time of death and while sleeping or dreaming. Despite all the historical and cross-cultural variations in theories of the soul, most religious and cultural traditions associate death and sleep with soul loss. Against this background of common understanding it is perhaps not too surprising that when a fully conscious, awake person loses his soul, he finds it difficult to (is afraid to?) sleep or dream, and he spends much of his now-extended waking time fantasizing about death and wondering why his soul has been withdrawn at such an uncanny time—while he is awake and still alive.

Emptied of a soul, some people fear they are "under desertion by

God" (Jackson 1980, p. 63). Others conclude that they are bad or evil people and that this is their just desert. Some imagine that the world is a "rotten" place in which it is impossible to have or keep the things one wants, a place booby-trapped with unlooked-for disappointments, a place where striving is fruitless. Still others think there is an amine or a gene that has done it to them and that there must be some "thing" wrong with any "body" that cannot hang onto its soul. Some find comfort in the thought that it is the body and not the self that is to be blamed for suffering. Others wonder why such an unfair thing, a genetic deficiency, should have happened to them, and despair over the thought that life is absurd.

When your soul leaves your body you feel empty. Emptiness is a dark concept with many implications or connotations. It has spatial dimensions: to be empty is to be down (versus up), low (versus high), cut off (versus connected), hemmed in (versus free). It has a tactile feel: to be empty is to be dry and cold, not moist and warm. It has a familiar visual aura: to be "blue" or black. The idea of emptiness is rich in associations. It is passive and weak, sluggish and cheap, fragile, inert, and headless. There are all too many testimonies to the felt implications of emptiness: to be empty is to be down, low, blue, cold, dried out, weak, cut off and alone, isolated without energy and without hope. It is to feel "depressed," to feel the blood stagnate in your veins. It is to have "tired blood" (is Geritol a magical therapy for women with the "blues"?).

It remains to be seen whether these implications or suggestions are universal. It would not be surprising if they were. Charles Osgood, William May, and Murray Miron's (1975) cross-cultural analyses of affective meaning in twenty-one societies find that adjectives such as "empty" (versus "full"), "dark" (versus "light"), and "low" (versus "high") are widely experienced as bad or unpleasant; and it is not unlikely that there are synesthetic or associative connections among those and other concepts. There is also good reason to suspect that the metaphorical meanings of a basic orientational dimension such as down (versus up) ("I'm on top of the situation"; "Things are looking up") are not arbitrary, and that vertical (up/down) imagery is put to similar use in many societies. The human head is up. The gods are up. The heavens are up. The mighty are up. Control is up. What's good is up (see Lakoff and Johnson 1980a, 1980b; B. Schwartz 1981). We should not, of course, rule out the possibility that with deliberate effort (for example, by means of the meditative disciplines of various religious traditions) intuitive feelings about the meaning of "low," "dark," "down," and "empty" might be reversed or denied. It is also possible that in certain contexts the connotations can shift, perhaps radically. The relevant context of use for the present discussion, however, is the feeling of emptiness associated with soul loss, and soul loss, as we know, is widely associated with death and vulnerability. Of course, even death and vulnerability can, with effort, be infused with positive connotations, although typically that does not occur. People cry at funerals.

When you lose your soul you lose interest in things—basic things such as food, sex, other people, and life's projects. You stop eating and you stop sex. You lose weight and you lose sleep. During soul*ful* functioning there is a constant, even if barely noticed, perception of self and others as "spirited," as a dynamic center of initiative and free will organized around an "I" (the observing ego). That "I" is transcendental: it is more than or other than a list of body parts or an assemblage of muscle and blood and skin and bones. It is the "I" that looks out at the world and out at the "me" in the mirror. It is that sense of pure yet distinctive subjectivity that makes it coherent, even if somewhat fantastic, to conjure up the image of retaining identity while dwelling in someone else's body. During soulful functioning, that "I," that dynamic center of initiative and free will, works in concert with the senses, reason, imagination, memory, and body. When the soul is lost, that changes. The "dispirited" body and mind do not function very well without will and initiative. You feel listless and tired. The brain goes. You have headaches. You can't think straight. You forget things. The senses go: your vision blurs, and you feel dizzy. The body goes: your gut aches; your back hurts; you feel weak, shaky, and short of breath. To function effectively, a mind and a body require a soul. There must be psychosomatic unity.

Emptiness gets expressed (or discussed) in different ways in different cultures, and there appear to be three ways to convey the feeling of soul loss: by the language of *causal responsibility,* the language of *concomitant mood metaphor,* and the language of *physical consequences.* Emptied of your soul you can either dwell on the "why" of it all (Am I under desertion by God? Did I inherit this from my mother? Why can't I keep the things I love?), or generate concomitant mood metaphors (I feel as though I'm in a cold, dark room on a winter's night, down, dried up, blue, cut off, "made of glass"), or focus on what is left, a dispirited body depleted of its normal appetites.

The cross-cultural literature on depression has a lot to say about the somatization of depression (Climent et al. 1980; Mezzich and Raab 1980; Kleinman 1982). To somatize depression is to talk about the perceived physical consequences of emptiness—loss of sleep, weight, energy, the appetites; headaches, back pain, dizziness, blurred vision, stagnating blood; and hunger for air. Some populations do it more than others.

People are more likely to focus on the perceived consequences of emptiness if they are nonwhite, non-Protestant and nonmale. Catholic women somatize more than Protestant women, West Africans and Taiwanese more than in Minnesota. That there are individual and cultural differences in whether people dwell on the causes, on the mood state, or on the physical consequences suggests that there are individual and cultural differences in the perceived implications and consequences of displaying a feeling (social regulation) and in managing one's moods and emotions. For example, it is tempting to speculate that somatization is more likely when the direct expression of felt emotion is thought to be threatening to one's social status and disruptive of social relationships with others. It is also tempting to speculate that the belief that the expression of felt emotions is dangerous is more common among those who believe that society is constructed of interdependent social roles and less common among those who believe that individuals in pursuit of their wants and desires are the fundamental units of society. The less "personal" the society, the more dangerous it is to expose anything so subjective as one's emotions; and the more personal the society, the more it will be viewed as healthy to emote. As Mr. Rogers has told many American preschool children: "Everyone has a history. Everyone has a name. Everyone has a story. No one's story is quite the same." Personal biography and affect display go together.

The idea of soul loss gives some unity to our understanding of what it is to feel depressed. It does not tell us why we have lost our soul or how to get it back, but it does tell us what depressed feelings are *about.* "Not so fast," the reader may object. "One cannot lose what one never had." To which the answer is: That's right. To feel depressed one must have had experience with the soul, and almost everyone has had that experience.

Believing in the existence of souls is not quite like believing in fairies. Of course, both souls and fairies have fallen into official disrepute in secular science-bound cultures such as our own. Fairies have become the things of imagination, enchantment, medieval paintings, and children's stories. And the idea of the soul has come to be associated with theological doctrine, which means it is viewed by those of us who are secular and science bound as prescientific, fuzzy-headed, and mystical, and thus hardly worthy of serious consideration.

Fairies should probably be left where they are, in children's stories; we seem to be able to get along quite well without them, and nothing in reason, experience, or direct intuition requires that we grant them more than a tongue-in-cheek reality. It would be a shame, however, to leave the soul in the hands of the theologians.

The presence of our *own* soul is something we know by direct intuition. That intuition is so widely shared and so compelling that each of us tends to perceive the actions of others as spirited, in ways that the reactive movements of billiard balls, robots, and computers are not. And that direct intuition of our own soul is powerful enough that it has shaped many of our social institutions. Indeed, if by some strange alteration of consciousness we were to start perceiving each other as billiard balls, robots, or computers, we would have to abandon the concept of free will and personal responsibility and would probably have to strip society of its entire legal-moral fabric; for both the concept of crime and the institution of punishment are testimonies to our direct knowledge of our own souls and our faith that others have souls as well.

To acknowledge the reality of the soul it is not necessary to endorse any of the theological doctrines, specific articles of faith, or speculative ontologies that have grown up around the idea of the soul. It is not necessary to believe that a divine maker reigns over the universe, or that each individual soul is the splintered fragment of a once unshattered universal soul, or that there is a place called "heaven" where souls reside, or that souls get recycled or transmigrate, or that they move into the bodies they deserve, or that bodies can be snatched or possessed by invading spirits. It is not necessary to believe that souls materialize or that they reside in some special gland or organ.

What it is necessary to believe can be summarized in three propositions: (1) not everything that is real is material (has weight and extension in space); (2) the really real test of reality is not that something be material per se but that it have an effect on the way we understand, treat, and react to things that are; and (3) the reality of the soul is something that can be no more in doubt than the reality of ideas, values, personal identity, and all other such real things that lack weight and extension in space.

The young Leonardo da Vinci conducted several grotesque autopsies in the vain hope of finding some "thing" missing after the soul had left the body of the dead. He failed, and so has everyone since. If you try to find the soul with a scalpel, it will elude you. But, just as we can believe in the existence of memories without being able to say where they are when we are not having them, so too we can believe in souls without being able to say where they go when they wander or where they hide when they are home.

The idea of the soul is widely acknowledged even among those of us who are so secularized that we do not recognize the soul when we see it. It is what is involved when we see another person as a person and not merely as a highly intelligent robot. It is what we name when we give people a "proper" name instead of designating them with a serial number. For what is named is not merely an object, a thing in this world, but a subject as well; that subject (the so-called ghost in the machine), once properly named, continues to be honored and to have influence (for example, in legal wills) long after the body or the machine is gone. It is the soul that is involved when we hold others responsible for their actions. It is what we honor when we respect another's privacy or freedom of movement. It is what we see in others when we look beyond their visible movements and see behind those movements a dynamic center of initiative and free choice. Called the soul, the spirit, the transcendental ego, subjectivity, the free will, or the atman, it connects the person with things beyond and with others, and it is as real to each of us as it is immaterial. Lose it and you feel dead, cut off, alone, "dispirited"—depressed.

Imagine one's self entering another person's body. Imagine retaining a continuous sense of "I-ness" while replacing in succession every cell in one's body. It is not that difficult to imagine such things because one recognizes within one's self a sense of self deeper than one's possessions, one's physical appearance, one's body parts, one's tastes, one's values, or one's goals in life, and it is possible to vary every one of those things, or even give them up, and still retain a sense that something has remained the same. That is your soul, and it is not a concoction by theologians or something that disappeared with the Enlightenment or with the invention of machines or computers. It is a deeply intuitive and, apparently, a universal idea. It is an idea that makes the experience of depression something that everyone can understand.

Trying to characterize the meaning and phenomenology of depression in terms of soul loss is problematic. It begs many questions. It does not explain what causes depression or how to get rid of it. It does not answer the question whether children get depressed or whether childhood depression is related to adult depression. It does not explain the apparent worldwide predominance of depression among women, the gender difference in reported depression among adolescents and adults but not among children, or the greater number of reports of depression among European women than among Chinese women. What it does do is tell what the feeling of depression is about; and in doing so it implies that moods and emotions have meanings, that to understand a person's emotional life it is necessary to engage in conceptual analysis, and that it is possible to understand what it implies to feel depressed without knowing what "really" brought it on or how "really" to get rid of it.

Such a characterization also involves several other apparent sleights of hand, including the widespread practice of interpreting certain clusters of physical complaints (I'm tired, dizzy, and short of breath; I can't sleep; I'm losing weight; I don't care about sex) as the somatic expression of a depressed mood state. In other words, it assumes that there are alternative ways to express depression—for example, by focusing on causes, concomitants, or consequences—and that when a person tells you that he is under desertion by God he is expressing the same thing as someone who tells you he is cold, dark, and sad, who in turn is expressing the same thing as the person who tells you he can't sleep at night and has lost his appetite. Of course the three formulations are not even remotely synonymous: to lose your appetite is not quite the same thing as to feel sad or to believe that God has abandoned you. The warrant for linking these three types of formulations is that they express in three different idioms—causation, concomitance, and consequence—a concern for the same thing, the emptiness associated with soul loss. But identifying a core meaning to depression ducks the question of whether depression means the same thing to two people who feel as though they have lost their soul, one of whom believes he is a bad person under desertion by God and the other of whom believes that soul loss is a fortuitous disease for which drugs are the only sensible response. Nor does it try to link the three types of expressions of depression by referring to a common hormonal, chemical, or genetic condition; or try to establish their equivalence by referring to a common eliciting condition (for example, loss or learned helplessness); or raise doubts about whether they really are expressions of the same thing or whether they should be linked at all (yet see Chapter 8 of this volume).

Semantics and Emotions: A Developmental Puzzle

What is the role of cultural meaning systems in the growth of an emotional life?

Consider this question in terms of an emotional keyboard, with each key being a discrete emotion: disgust, interest, distress, anger, fear, contempt, shame, shyness, guilt, and so on. A key is struck when a situation or object is interpreted in a certain way—as loss, frustration, novelty, or "a little thing that squirms in the night." There is evidence to suggest that for any normal member of our species the keyboard is intact and available by the age of four years (Charlesworth and Kreutzer 1973; Campos et al. 1975; Emde, Gaensbauer, and Harman 1976; Izard 1978; Hiatt, Campos, and Emde 1979; Izard et al. 1980; Ochs 1982; Van Lieshout 1975).

The emotional keyboard of the young child is quite differentiated. Perhaps only simple tunes are played, but the young child knows the difference between the emotions listed above, and by four years of age probably experiences all of them. The image of growth as a movement from an undifferentiated system to a differentiated one seems as inappropriate for the development of emotions as it does for the development of cognition.

In recent years it has been discovered that the minds of young children are far more differentiated than was previously supposed (see Shweder 1982a; Gelman and Baillargeon 1983). Two-year-olds can distinguish the perspective of self from the perspective of others (Lempers, Flavell, and Flavell 1977; see also Shatz and Gelman 1973). Three-year-olds are able to distinguish intentional from unintentional behavior (Shultz 1980). Preschool children know the difference between conventional rules and moral rules (Nucci and Turiel 1978; Shweder, Turiel, and Much 1981). In fact, so many cognitive distinctions and competencies previously thought to be absent from the minds of young children have now been discovered that a new image has emerged. What young children lack are not complex differentiated mental structures but the knowledge and representational skills needed for talking about and making deliberate use of the complex structures available to them. Young children are able to discriminate among basic emotions (happiness, sadness, anger, surprise, fear, and so on) almost as well as adults (R. Schwartz 1981). Indeed, in some cultures the emotional experiences of four-year-olds may be more varied than those of adults. Javanese adults, for example, according to Clifford Geertz (1975), strive to smooth out their emotions to a steady affectless hum. The goal is "an inner world of stilled emotions" in which the "hills and valleys" of an emotional life are "flattened out . . . into an even level plain" (p. 49). Describing the way a young Javanese man reacted to the death of his wife, Geertz seems to imply, with his reference to meditative and mystical techniques for smoothing the emotions, that even in bereavement the Javanese succeed, at least in part, in stilling their inner life and flattening out the feeling of distress in the face of irreversible loss. Presumably if we looked at Javanese four-year-olds we would find "hills and valleys," anger and surprise, distress and disgust, and many other discrete, differentiated emotions.

While a differentiated emotional keyboard may be available to most four-year-olds around the world, the tunes that get played and the emotional scores that are available diverge considerably for adults. Some keys do not get struck at all; the emotional symphonies that do get played vary widely. Eskimos do not experience anger in situations in which Europeans would explode (Briggs 1970). What makes a Chinese feel sick makes an American feel depressed (Kleinman 1982). Wide variations are found in anxieties: men in some cultures are anxious about their masculinity; in other cultures they are anxious about their dependency (Whiting and Child 1953). Semen loss and vaginal emissions are worrisome to people on the Indian subcontinent; lack of semen loss is what worries Americans. Some peoples value formality and calm and dislike any strong expression of emotions; Samoans are nonchalant in situations in which Americans lose their cool (H. Geertz 1959). For some people, guilt has been bleached of everything but a rational concern for doing what is right; other people experience transgression with shame-terror-guilt all bound together. In Bali, where life is a stage, stage fright is the major worry (Geertz 1973). Honor and revenge still exist in the Mediterranean and the Middle East; in other parts of the world the idea of honor has not been experienced for years.

How does the distressed Javanese four-year-old become the smoothed-out Javanese adult? How does the angry Eskimo four-year-old become the angerless Eskimo adult? Little is known about the process, but some speculations are possible. One major transformation of emotional functioning is related to the emerging capacity to "decouple" elicitors from reactions and reactions from expressive signals. Young children cannot suppress the signal of an emotional state; they cannot feel but not express. Moreover, they do not easily express an emotion they do not feel, nor do they understand the social function of expressing but not feeling. They are not yet ready for the spectacle called society. They let situations get to them; they lack the concepts and detachment to redescribe events and alter their emotional reactions to them. They cry when it hurts.

There is a vivid example of decoupling in the writings of Benjamin

Lee Whorf (1956, p. 267). He points out that the sound pattern *queep* elicits a universal set of associations: *queep* is fast (versus slow), sharp (versus dull), narrow (versus wide), light (versus dark). Our associative response to *queep* is automatic, and that automatic response is probably preprogrammed and the same for the Bongo-Bongo and for us. Whorf then asks us to consider the sound pattern *deep*. *Deep* is phonetically similar to *queep* and elicits the same set of associations (fast, sharp, narrow, light) for everyone except speakers of English. For English speakers, *deep* is not simply a thing in the world, a sound pattern; it is a sound pattern with meaning, a meaning that totally overrides and alters our reaction to its sound. For English speakers, and for English speakers only, *deep* is slow, dull, wide, and dark. I suspect that the development of the emotional life of a people is not unlike the shift for English speakers from *queep* to *deep*.

Let us consider ontogenetic changes in emotional reactions to touching among Oriya Brahmans in the old temple town of Bhubaneswar, India. Touching is a universal elicitor of positive affects among newborns in our own and other species; touching is the "queep" of our emotional life (Bowlby 1969; Harlow 1973; Harlow and Mears 1979). Associated with touching is a cluster of positive feelings: comfort, security, stress reduction, attachment, nurturance. That universal early elicitor of positive affect takes on, in many contexts, exactly the opposite meaning among Oriya Brahman adults.

Ideas about touchability, untouchability, and pollution are legion in Oriya culture. Birth, death, feces, menstrual blood, "unclean" castes, "unclean" animals pollute. Oriyas protect themselves against pollution in many ways. They avoid pollutants and keep them isolated or at a distance. They wash themselves after any contact with a pollutant. They eat, drink, or apply to their skin as a purifying agent the "five products of the cow": milk, curd, ghee, urine, and dung. They wear special clothes when they defecate and remove them immediately afterward.

Each Brahman boy receives a sacred thread during a special ceremony, ideally at age seven or nine. The sacred thread is a caste insignia; for a Brahman boy it signals the end of parental permissiveness toward nudity, dietary practices, and moral responsibility. The sacred thread is worn over the left shoulder and across the right side. It is believed that the sacred thread protects its wearer against evil spirits and spirit possession. It helps keep the wearer's soul where it ought to remain for a while, in his body. The sacred thread loses protective power if it becomes polluted; thus, when Brahmans defecate the sacred thread goes over the ear. For it is believed that in the ear of every Brahman is a token of the sacred river Ganges and that draped over the ear the sacred thread will remain sacred. Indeed, if a Brahman touches a pollutant and is unable to wash immediately, he may purify himself by touching his hand to his ear.

There are many other ways in which Oriya Brahmans guard themselves against pollution. They are scrupulous about what they eat, whom they eat with, whom they accept food from, and who cooks the food they do eat. They classify cloth and utensils on the basis of their potential for pollution. Cotton is more easily polluted than silk, white cotton more easily polluted than colored cotton; earthenware plates, jars, and pots are more easily polluted than metal utensils; and so on.

One of the most dangerous sources of pollution for Oriyas is the touch of a menstruating woman, including one's mother. Adult men believe that menstrual blood is poisonous, capable of killing trees and plants, shrinking testicles, and contaminating the environment. One male informant put it this way: "If the wife touches her husband on the first day of her period, it is an offense equal to that of killing a guru. If she touches him on the second day, it is an offense equal to killing a Brahman. On the third day to touch him is like cutting off his penis. If she touches him on the fourth day it is like killing a child. So it is a sin."

Menstruating women have less exaggerated views but share with men the belief that during menstruation they are unclean and untouchable. Both men and women believe that the touch of a menstruating woman will shorten the life of the person she touches, and that anything she touches—her clothing, her bedding, her children's clothes—must be washed and purified. Consequently, a menstruating woman does not sleep in the same bed with her husband, does not cook food or leave food for returning ancestral spirits or even enter the kitchen, does not enter the family prayer room or approach the family deity, does not dress her children or wash clothing, and does not touch anyone (an exception is made for nursing infants, but all clothing is removed from the child before breast-feeding commences). For three days she does not groom herself or take a bath after dark or do anything that might tempt and attract her husband. After three days of relative isolation and seclusion she purifies herself with a special bath (preferably using turmeric paste and a bit of cow dung). On the fourth day she returns to her normal routine of bathing, cooking, feeding ancestral spirits and family members, worshiping deities, cleaning house, napping, massaging the legs of the husband's parents, and tending children. (On similar menstrual practices and pollution concepts in Madras, India, see Ferro-Luzzi 1974).

Pollution is not the same as germs, and informants clearly distinguish between them. They know about germs and do not consider them pollutants. Nor is the isolation and distancing of pollutants and agents of pollution a way of protecting people against dirt or disease. A sick woman is permitted to enter the kitchen. A menstruating woman is not.

Pollution is a less tangible thing than a microorganism, but it is just as real. Pollution has to do with sanctity, the sanctity of the temple. One must bathe before entering the temple and approaching God. Menstruating women are not allowed in the temple. Unclean castes are not allowed in the temple. No one can enter the temple for twelve days after a birth or death in the joint family. If a person dies in the temple, the temple must be purified. The temple must be cleansed if a dog, an untouchable, or a foreigner enters.

Moreover, for Oriya Brahmans in Bhubaneswar, "the temple" refers not just to the eleventh-century structure and its resident god (Lingaraj or Shiva) but also to every home and every person who lives in the shadow of Lingaraj. There is among Oriya Brahmans what might be called a "temple complex." They believe that their home is a temple to which ancestral spirits return to be fed (hence the special sanctity of the kitchen and that corner of the kitchen where food and water are daily left for returning ancestral spirits). They believe it is presided over by a family deity (hence the special sanctity of the prayer room). And they believe that the human body is a temple in which there dwells a spirit or god, the atman, the self, the observing ego.

Each of these three temples must be kept pure out of respect for God, the ancestors, and the self. The distinction between gods, ancestors, and self or between the temple as temple, the home as temple, and the body as temple is not hard and fast. Adult men think of themselves as "moving gods," and they are treated that way by their wives, who are the first to point out that the husband is to be worshiped. And although the daily ritual of washing the husband's feet and swallowing a few drops of the water is in decline in the old town, a wife does not typically eat with her husband; and if she does, it is considered shameful, comparable to eating with God. Rather, she prepares the food that is to be offered to the ancestral spirits and to the husband's spirit. Later she will offer food to herself or perhaps even eat the leftovers or remnants off her husband's plate, just as he may, on special occasions, offer food to the god in the Lingaraj temple (the so-called prasad) and then remove the leftovers to his home to be eaten.

The god in the Lingaraj temple does not eat with his wife (the goddess Parvati). Typically he eats alone, and it is not uncommon for adults in the old town to do the same. Indeed, as if deliberately to blur the distinction between self, ancestral spirits, and God, the god in the Lingaraj temple is treated as a person. The deity is awakened each morning, washed, and fed; he takes a nap; he gets sick; he visits his relatives; he goes on outings; he confesses his sins; and he chews betel (Mahapatra 1981). The distinction between the god in the Lingaraj temple, the deity and ancestral spirits in the house, and the spirit dwelling in the body is not terribly important to Oriyas. They visit the Lingaraj temple in the morning, and in the afternoon they tell you that all the gods can be found inside one's body. One is never quite sure where God ends and where you begin, but one is quite certain that life is a series of attempts to preserve or restore the sanctity of deities, in the Lingaraj temple, in the paternal home, and in one's body. Daily bathing is an ablution; daily eating is an oblation, an offering to one's self. And it is in the context of these ablutions and oblations of daily life that feelings about pollution are best understood.

"Mara heici. Chhu na! Chhu na!" is what a menstruating Oriya mother exclaims when her child approaches her lap: "I am polluted. Don't touch me! Don't touch me!" If the child continues to approach, the woman will stand up and walk away. Oriya children have no concept of menstruation or menstrual blood. There is a ceremony involving bathing and seclusion that marks the first menstruation, and the date, time, and place of the first menstruation are sometimes treated as matters of significance. Astrologers and the Oriya almanac have much to say about what it all means: if it happens on a Sunday, before 6:40 P.M., in the house of someone other than her father, she will suffer seven months of calamity and become a widow. There is even an annual festival (Raja, the festival of the Earth) during which Mother Earth bleeds and is given a menstrual bath. Despite this, the first menstruation arrives as a total shock to adolescent girls in Bhubaneswar; they are not prepared for it by anyone. Mothers explain their own monthly "pollution" to their children by telling them that they stepped in dog excrement or touched garbage, or they evade the issue. Nevertheless, Oriya children quickly learn that there is something called *mara* (the term *chhuan* is also used, and when *mara* is there their mother avoids them, stays out of her husband's bed, and out of the kitchen (indeed, "Handi bahari heichi," "I'm out of the kitchen," is the euphemism used by Oriya women to talk about menses). Most six-year-olds think it is wrong for a polluted woman to cook food or sleep in the same bed with her husband. Most nine-year-olds think that *mara* is an objective force and that all women in the world have an obligation not to touch other people or cook food while they are polluted.

In Orissa, then, touching is transformed from a universal elicitor of attachment, comfort, and security to a dreaded instrument of pollution. The transformation takes place by various means. "Don't touch me!" is heard on many occasions and in many contexts: from the menstruating mother; from the father who does not want his child to touch him in the interim between bathing (a purification ritual) and worshiping the family deity; from the grandmother who does not want the child to touch her or climb into bed with her until the child has removed all his "outside" clothes, because they have become polluted by mixing with lower castes at school. There is even a children's game on the theme, pollution "tag." Several children stand apart from a child and all together sing: "Puchu, Puchu [teasing sound]. Hadi ghare peja piichhu. Mote chhu na!" ("You drank rice water in the house of a Hadi [the lowest untouchable caste]. Don't touch me!"). The children scurry off pursued by the hand of the "polluted" child.

Touching as an instrument of pollution is only one of its transformations in Orissa. Touching the feet of a superior is also a sign of respect, deference, and apology. Young women routinely touch, indeed massage, the legs and body of their father-in-law and mother-in-law; and male friends, adults as well as children, affectionately hold hands and lounge about entwined in each other's arms. Notably, each of these touching practices has a positive valence for Oriyas yet strike many American observers as offensive, exploitative, effeminate, and slightly anxiety provoking. The point is that after early childhood the "queep" of touching is transformed through diverse cultural practices into the "deep" of touching. The emotional impact of the affective elicitors of early childhood is altered, and what ends up being touching to one people is not so touching to another.[1]

Part III

Experiments in Criticism

7.

Rethinking Culture and Personality Theory

... it is time to abandon the assumption (so prevalent till now) that everything is glued together; perhaps it is time to seriously entertain the hypothesis that nothing is glued together until proved otherwise.
—*Walter Mischel (1971, p. 23), paraphrasing Daryl Bem (1972b, p. 57)*

Most of the postulates of the culture and personality school were worked out in the 1940s and 1950s (for example, Gorer 1943; Kardiner 1945; Benedict 1946; Wallace 1952; Whiting and Child 1953). A small set of universal generalizations was advanced that seemed to make it possible to connect and interrelate so much—including the past and the present, motives and institutions, parents and gods. But those bold generalizations have not weathered empirical and conceptual scrutiny especially well. They have lost much of their predictive power and parsimony and have turned out to be restricted and context dependent in their implications. Much less is "glued together," much less is integrated, than most of us have imagined.

Four postulates are examined here: (1) the search for global traits, or the postulate that stimulus generalization has precedence over stimulus discrimination; (2) the search for childhood origins, or the postulate of the influence of the past on the present; (3) the search for comparable situations, or the postulate of an individual-difference model of cultural differences; and (4) explanation by reference to consequences, or the postulate of adaptive accommodation to an "objective" environment.

The following conclusions are drawn: (1) Individual differences in conduct are narrowly context dependent and do not widely generalize across contexts. Extant evidence for broad cultural integration is not compelling. (2) Early child care practices *per se* do not have predictable consequences for adult character. (3) Situational comparability is inversely related to cultural variation; hence an individual difference approach to cultural differences is, for the most part, inapplicable. (4) "Objective" conditions, reinforcers and other "external" stimulus events, do not guarantee the accommodation of an organism to its environment. Unless we already know a good deal about a person's goals, preferences, beliefs, ethics, and cultural meanings, most of our "universal" generalizations have little predictive power.

Four Classical Postulates of Culture and Personality Theory

Typically, investigators of culture and personality have sought linkages between social institutions and symbolic systems, on the one hand, and personality variables on the other (see, for example, Wallace 1952; Whiting and Child 1953; Whiting, Kluckhohn, and Anthony 1958; Spiro 1965, 1967; Edgerton 1971; LeVine 1973; Levy 1973; B. Whiting and J. Whiting 1975). In recent years the links have weakened, in large part because a pattern of evidence and theory has emerged that seriously challenges the relevance of the concept of personality as it has been applied in culture and personality research (see, for example, D'Andrade 1965, 1973, 1974; Mischel 1968, 1973; Shweder 1972, 1973, 1975, 1977a, 1977b, 1977c, 1977d; Fiske 1974, 1978; Ross 1977; Ross, Amabile, and Steinmetz 1977; Shweder and D'Andrade 1979). The implications of this pattern of evidence and theory are sometimes severe, especially for any approach to behavior concerned with origins in early experience and the search for global individual or cultural differences.

Postulate 1: The Search for Global Traits

POSTULATE 1A: THE SEARCH FOR GLOBAL PERSONALITY TRAITS
. . . the attitudes of the child to his father and mother, and to a lesser degree, towards his siblings will become the prototypes of his attitudes towards all subsequently met people.   (Gorer 1943, p. 108)

. . . rituals—techniques for interacting with and influencing the supernaturals—correspond to and are generalizations from modes of interaction used by children to influence their parents. (Spiro and D'Andrade 1958, p. 457)

POSTULATE 1B: THE SEARCH FOR GLOBAL CULTURAL TRAITS

... patterns of superordination and subordination, of deference and arrogance, will show a certain consistency in all spheres from the family to the religious and political organizations; and consequently the patterns of behavior demanded in all these institutions will mutually reinforce each other. (Gorer 1943, p. 108)

Religious dogmas, economic practices, and politics do not stay dammed up in neat, separate little ponds but they overflow their supposed boundaries and mingle inextricably with one another ... the most isolated bits of behavior have some systematic relationship to each other ... A human society must make for itself some design for living ... Men who have accepted a system of values by which to live cannot without courting inefficiency and chaos keep for long a fenced-off portion of their lives where they think and behave according to a contrary set of values. (Benedict 1946, pp. 11–12)

Any attempt to describe either personality or culture must address two basic questions: (1) How widely do the thoughts, emotions, and actions of a person or a people generalize across diverse stimuli, contexts, or domains? (2) To what extent can the thinking, feelings, and actions of a person or a people be sorted into a limited number of descriptive categories? The two questions are interrelated. If behavior is widely generalized it can be described with fewer categories, and vice versa.

Postulate 1 and all other typological or global-trait theories claim that individual or cultural differences in behavior are widely generalized and can be described with a relatively small number of categories (for example, extroverts versus introverts, Apollonians versus Dionysians). Although there are no absolute standards for deciding how wide is wide, or how small is small, to the extent that parsimony is a criterion of adequacy for assessing a theory, disagreements over questions of relative degree can be important.

Ruth Benedict (1934), for example, portrays a world in which a great deal hangs together. She believes that knowledge of a people's ritual conduct warrants inferences to political, economic, and military conduct. Thus she argues that people who participate in depersonalized rituals also scorn political office, avoid excess, and devalue heroism (her Apollonian type). Walter Mischel (1968), on the contrary, portrays a world that is neatly "dammed up into neat, separate little ponds." For Mischel, knowledge that a person hates his or her father does not warrant an inference to feelings about his or her boss, and knowledge that a child literally clings to its mother's apron strings implies little about other dependency measures such as seeking help or seeking attention. Along the continuum between a world in which all things are systematically interrelated and a world in which no things are, there is plenty of room for disagreement about just how widely behavior does generalize. The disagreement tends to focus on the single crucial question, How much context must be written into the definition of one's descriptive categories or hypothesized traits? It is important to recognize that the relevant question is not "Do traits exist?" but rather, "How context dependent are traits?" Individual and cultural differences clearly exist, but how generalized are they across situations?

GLOBAL PERSONALITY TRAITS: IN SEARCH OF A MISSING PHENOMENON?

For years, personality psychologists have searched for generalized consistencies in the way people differ from one another in their feelings and social behavior across diverse contexts. What they have discovered is that method variance is greater than person variance (see, for example, Burwen and Campbell 1957; Campbell and Fiske 1959; R. V. Burton 1970). Distinguishable qualities of character, such as autonomy and ascendancy, typically show higher within method associations than parallel across method associations. For example, if autonomy and ascendancy are measured by two methods, a projective test (for example, the Thematic Apperception Test) and a clinical interview, autonomy and ascendancy will correlate more positively *within* the projective test data than autonomy correlates with *itself* across the two methods. In general, features of personality-measuring instruments (the clinical interview situation, the projective test stimulus and context) have been found to be more stable than features of the people measured. Single-method research usually tells us more about social science's methodological artifacts than about anything else.

Personality psychologists have also discovered that hypothesized global-trait dispositions (for example, dependency, dominance, friendliness) typically account for no more than 9 to 15 percent of the diversity of individual differences over naturally occurring situations (see Mischel 1968, 1973; Fiske 1978; also Newcomb 1929, 1931; Raush, Dittmann, and Taylor 1959; Raush, Farbman, and Llewellyn 1960; Sears 1963; Hunt 1965; Endler and Hunt 1966, 1969; Moos 1968, 1969; Argyle and Little 1972; Shweder 1972, 1973). The most assertive child at the breakfast table is not the most assertive child in the playroom. The child who seeks help more than others is not the one who is more inclined to seek physical nearness. The man who is more likely to express his emotions to his wife is not the one who is more likely to express his emotions to his friends. The person who gets angry when contradicted is not the person who is more likely to get angry when cut in front of in line. The adult who is more hostile than others to a parent is not typically the adult who is more hostile to a boss, *nor* is he or she the one who is typically less hostile to a boss. Individual differences in the one context do not predict individual differences in the other. Different situations, stimuli, or domains seem to affect different people differentially.

Consider the relationship among the three behavioral indicators of nurturance displayed in Table 7.1. A striking feature of the results is that knowing which Rajput child is more likely to offer help to others predicts very little about which child is more likely to offer support and approval ($r = .17$) or which is more likely to make responsible suggestions ($r = -.25$). The relationships among the three items are quite weak. This result is typical of behavior observational findings.

Cross-cultural evidence from Beatrice and John Whiting's (1975) study of children's social behavior does not provide encouraging support for postulate 1. In a comparison of the behavior of 134 children from six cultures (including the Rajputs mentioned above), the highest reported level of consistency for a system of behavior (in this case "prosocial" behavior) across a set of comparable contexts (behavior to infants, to peers, and to adults) is .29 (Pearson r). For nurturant behavior the consistency coefficient is .05. Knowing that a child is more nurturant than other children to his parents predicts nothing about relative nurturance to peers. Table 7.2 summarizes evidence on the degree of consistency of individual differences for each of six systems of behavior across three types of situations (behavior to an infant versus a peer, to a peer versus a parent, and to an infant versus a parent) in the B. Whiting and J. Whiting (1975) study. The degree of generalization of individual differences is not impressive.

These failures to find support for highly generalized traits of character are not idiosyncratic. Leroy Burwen and Donald Campbell (1957), for example, initiated a study expecting to find "generalized

Table 7.1   Correlational relationship among 3 indicators of nurturance in
behavioral observations of 24 Rajput children

	2	3
1. Offers help	.17	.11
2. Offers support and approval	—	− .25
3. Makes responsible suggestions	—	—

Source: Longabaugh (1966, pp. 108–110); derived from observations by Leigh
Minturn (see Shweder 1973, p. 536).

Table 7.2   Average correlations (Pearson *r*) for the individual difference scores
of 134 children from 6 cultures across 3 types of situations
(behavior to infants vs. peers, peers vs. parents, infants vs. parents)
for 6 types of behaviors

Nurturance	.05
Aggression	.08
Dominance-dependence	.10
Intimacy-dependence	.14
Sociability	.17
Pro-social behavior	.29

Source: Adapted from B. Whiting and J. Whiting (1975, p. 163).

attitudes towards authority derived from previous encounters with
authority, especially in the early family situation" (p. 29). In the face
of "apparatus factors" (method variance) and low-consistency coef-
ficients they were forced to conclude that although "stimulus generalization is appropriate to the autistic thought processes in normal
dream states and in the waking states of extreme neurotics and psy-
chotics, it does not interfere with the waking perceptions of normal
individuals such as constituted the test population for the present
study" (p. 30). Jean Piaget (1962 [1945]) seems to have reached a
similar conclusion. He argues that broad stimulus generalizations
seem to operate only "in certain exceptional situations, such as children's play, the dreams of both children and adults, and sometimes in
states of completely relaxed thought [for example, during a psychoanalytic session]. All these are situations in which assimilation [stim-
ulus generalization] either takes precedence over accommodation [re-
sponse differentiation] or even entirely supplants it" (p. 211).

The absence of support for generalized or global traits of character
is surprising. Most of us, social scientist and layperson alike, share

certain intuitions or everyday personality theories that suggest that certain items or traits of behavior go together (for example, "smiles easily" and "introduces himself to strangers"; "gentle" and "good-natured") or are opposed (for example, "aggressive" and "friendly"; "gregarious" and "reserved") (see Brown 1965; D'Andrade 1974). Many personality psychologists and most laypeople interpret these everyday personality theories or trait and type concepts as inductive generalizations. They are held to arise out of observational experience and to summarize or encode accurately "relative frequencies of joint occurrences of various personality attributes and behavioral dispositions in other persons" (Passini and Norman 1966, p. 47; see also Brown 1965).

Recent evidence, however, challenges this view. It now appears that everyday personality theories express widely shared preexisting notions of what is like what or what is conceptually related to what (see, for example, Mulaik 1964; D'Andrade 1965, 1973, 1974; Shweder 1972, 1975, 1977a, 1977b, 1977c, 1977d; Ebbesen and Allen 1977). Moreover, these theories often have very little relation to immediately scored co-occurrence likelihoods among everyday behavioral events (see, for example, D'Andrade 1973, 1974; Shweder 1975, 1977a, 1977c). Finally, research suggests that everyday personality theories, themselves in large measure theories about conceptual relationships, systematically distort observational reports on standard personality assessment instruments (see, for example, D'Andrade 1974; Shweder 1975; Shweder and D'Andrade 1979).

It is troubling that almost all the extant evidence in support of abstract trait and type concepts (for example, dependency, ego-strength, introversion) in the personality psychology literature has been collected from interpersonal rating forms, questionnaire interviews, and personality inventories (see, for example, Cattell 1957; Sears, Maccoby, and Levin 1957; Lorr and McNair 1963; Norman 1963; Block 1965; G. M. Smith 1967). Rating forms, questionnaire interviews, and inventories turn out to be quite demanding inferential tasks in which "magical" thought processes are likely to intrude. What seems to happen is that conceptual affiliations (for example, "smiles easily" and "likes parties") and conceptual exclusions (for example, "gentle" and "managerial") dominate the judgmental process (see, for example, D'Andrade 1973, 1974; Shweder 1975, 1977a; Ebbesen and Allen 1977). Items alike in concept are judged to go together even when, as is typically the case, they do not co-occur in behavior. Thus, the data gathered from interpersonal rating forms, questionnaire interviews, and personality inventories lends illusory support to the mistaken belief that individual differences can be described in a language consisting of context-free global traits, factors, or dimensions.

Consider the pattern of intercorrelations among the five indicators of the hypothesized trait "talkativeness," displayed in Table 7.3. The data come from a study by Theodore Newcomb (1929) concerning introversion and extroversion in the behavior of boys at a summer camp. Newcomb's study is rather special in that it is possible to compare what goes with what in behavior as immediately recorded with what goes with what in behavior as summarized and judged on an interpersonal rating form by those who had kept the immediate records of behavior.

In Table 7.3 the data derived from immediate scorings of behavior suggest that there is little warrant for drawing inferences among the five indicators of talkativeness. The behavioral evidence is consistent with the notion that individual differences do not widely generalize across situations. For example, knowledge of whether or not a child talks more than others during quiet hour tells little about whether or not he will talk more than others at meals ($r = .16$).

Perhaps the most striking feature of Table 7.3, however, is the discrepancy between what goes with what in the immediate scorings of behavior and what goes with what in the ratings of those who originally kept the immediate records. For example, in the ratings, the correlation between talking during quiet hours and talking at table is .75! Raters seem to draw inferences about what goes with what that are not warranted by behavioral experience. What this suggests is that the neat package of intercorrelations among trait indicators in the personality psychology literature does not arise out of behavioral experience but rather represents a conflation of "propositions about the world with propositions about language" (D'Andrade 1965, p. 215).

PARSIMONY VERSUS CONSISTENCY: WHEN IS TOO MUCH CONTEXT NOT A GOOD THING?

As a result of repeated failures to find impressive support for generalized or global traits of character (see Burwen and Campbell 1957; Endler and Hunt 1966, 1969; Mischel 1968, 1973), the emphasis in personality psychology has shifted from processes of generalization to processes of discrimination and differentiation. This "divide and conquer" strategy of splitting up trait concepts to accommodate

Table 7.3 Intercorrelations among behavioral indices of "talkativeness" for 30 boys at camp, derived from immediate scorings of behavior (italicized) and from subsequent observer ratings (not italicized)

	1	2	3	4	5
1. Tells of his own past and of exploits.	—	*.52*	*.05*	*.29*	*.20*
2. Gives loud and spontaneous expressions of delight or disapproval.	.67	—	*.03*	*−.14*	*.08*
3. Goes beyond only asking and answering necessary questions in conversations with counselors.	.61	.68	—	*−.11*	*.48*
4. How is the quite hour spent?	.97	.88	.66	—	*.16*
5. Spends a lot of time talking at the table.	.66	.92	.77	.75	—

Source: Adapted from Newcomb (1929, pp. 42, 48).

person-situation interaction effects creates its own special difficulty, the unparsimonious proliferation of theoretical categories.

A trait-splitting strategy is possible for personality theorists because the relevant question in research on individual differences is not whether individual differences generalize, but across how many and across which particular contexts the generalizations that exist are to be found. Suppose we discover (as we have: Sears 1963) that the global-trait concept of dependency cannot be used to consistently describe children's social behavior; that is, children who seek attention a lot are not the ones who cling to their mother's apron strings. Using a consistency criterion, we simply rewrite the original trait concept, dividing it into two independent concepts. We no longer speak of "children who are dependent." Instead we speak of "children who seek attention" and "children who seek physical nearness." If we subsequently find that children who seek attention from their mothers in the playground are not the ones who seek attention from their mothers at home, we again rewrite our trait concepts to include more context. We speak of "children who seek attention from their mothers in the playground" and "children who seek attention from their mothers at home."

Consistency is not a hypothesis. It is an incorrigible presupposition or criterion by reference to which trait theorists either admit or exclude a particular trait concept. Consistency dictates how much context we must write into our definition of a hypothesized trait. Since, logically, trait consistency can *always* be preserved by writing more and more context into trait concepts, it follows that it is not consistency we are in a position to assess, but rather the degree of generalization of a trait. We strive to find a level of description at which our behavioral indicators are internally consistent or homogeneous. With this in mind, the implication of Mischel's (1968) evidence becomes clear. With consistency as the criterion, trait concepts have to get very complex and context dependent—for example, children who ask their mothers to watch them build things when other children of the same sex are watching, or perhaps cultures in which people generalize at the expense of detail but only when talking about interpersonal situations during a clinical interview (Inkeles, Hanfmann, and Beier 1958, p. 11). And we have to employ a great many such complex concepts to account for behavioral diversity (though it is to be hoped not as many such complex concepts as there are behaviors to describe). If we are permitted to introduce enough context into the specification of our trait concepts we can always discover consistencies; children who ask their mothers to watch them build things when other children of the same sex are watching may do it regardless of the time of day, regardless of the number of same-sex peers watching, regardless of the object being built, and so on. We can always discover (some kind of) consistencies, but at a cost, the sacrifice of parsimony.

How much context should we be allowed to write into our definition of trait categories? How many trait categories should we be permitted to contrive? There seems to be no logical way to decide between two possible answers to these questions: (1) the nomothetic scientist's response: Write in only as much context and use only as many categories as *parsimony* permits; (2) the idiographic clinician's response: Write in as much context and use as many categories as are needed to discover the *consistencies* in behavior.

There is nothing inherently wrong with the clinician's response. Clinical insight has always involved the appreciation of context-person interactions, and clinical methodology often produces long and complex lists of the ways in which specific situations affect a specific person in a special way. In fact there is considerable evidence that "idiosyncratic" or "interactive" effects, "the particular 'meaning' that a particular situation" has for a particular person, are the major determinants of behavior (Raush, Farbman, and Llewellyn 1960; also Endler and Hunt 1966; Moos 1968, 1969; Argyle and Little 1972). As mentioned above, the man who is more likely than others to express his emotions to his wife is not typically the man who is more likely than others to express his emotions to his friends. The rub is that such listmaking does not bring us any closer to the construction of a general explanatory scheme. When complexity is applauded instead of simplified, the pursuit of universal explanatory theory has been abandoned. Postulate 1 will not lead us to parsimony. At the personality level, it does not enable us sufficiently to reduce the diversity of ways in which individuals differ from one another.

OTHER REACTIONS TO THE ABSENCE OF GLOBAL TRAITS

There are a number of other ways to react to the pattern of evidence discussed above. One is to suggest that better methods will one day produce evidence more consistent with a global-trait approach to personality.

Robert LeVine (1973), for example, in a discussion of the problems of studying personality cross-culturally, notes that evidence in the personality literature is not encouraging: "different methods of measuring the 'same' disposition correlate poorly or not at all, yielding differing distributions of results for the same group of individuals" (p. 173). He remarks that "behavior measured in psychological experiments and testing situations is strongly, sometimes overwhelmingly, influenced by the interactive settings in which observation and measurement take place" (p. 175). He states that "the behavior that personality psychologists regard as symptoms of person-specific dispositions have not shown the expected transituational generality," and that dispositional theories of personality have not produced "accurate predictions as a purely inductive approach to individual behavior" (pp. 176, 177).

It is LeVine's view that dispositional theories of personality "have made little headway towards confirmation" (1973, p. 178), in large part because evidence collected in laboratories, classrooms, and clinics is restricted and artificial. LeVine raises the hope that a return to the clinical methods of psychoanalysis (which he characterizes in terms of the logic of physiological, ecological, and embryological research) will make it possible to identify unities and mechanisms underlying the diversity of situation-specific responses (pp. 178, 182–184). He concludes that it would be "premature" to reject a "dispositional view" of the person (p. 177).

LeVine's perspective is challenging, and I agree that nothing in the evidence on the absence of trans-situational generality of individual differences (that is, across tests, situations, or common trait indicators) requires us to reject a dispositional view of the person. Such a rejection would not only be premature; it would leave us with no way to make sense of those individual differences in comparable contexts that do occur. What is required is a rejection of the view that dispositions are widely generalized. The main problem is that dispositions may have to be defined too narrowly with reference to contexts, test situations, and so on (for example, the disposition to get angry when a big car cuts into line at a gas station; the disposition to give whole-card responses, W, on the Rorschach test), so narrowly defined that we might well ask: Of what theoretical worth are such dispositions? The evidence that dispositions are narrowly context dependent does not come only from tests and contrived laboratory observations. Some of the most convincing and damaging evidence is "ecological" in LeVine's sense (see, for example, Newcomb 1929; Shweder 1973; B. Whiting and J. Whiting 1975; and Tables 7.1, 7.2 and 7.3, above). Finally, it would be encouraging if some small set of underlying transformational principles (for example, inversion, displacement, projection), when consistently applied, actually permitted us theoretically to equate apparently diverse individual differences. The rub, as I see it, is that the adult who hates his or her parent does not typically have a predictable affectual relationship with a boss (by inversion or extension).[1]

Another type of reaction to the context specificity of individual differences is to explicitly adopt an idiographic approach to personality assessment. Thus, Daryl Bem (1974) has persuasively argued that it is possible to "predict certain behaviors across certain situations for certain people but not beyond that" (p. 513; see also Bem 1972a).

It is tempting to assume that trait breadth itself is a normally distributed variable (see, for example, Newcomb 1929). Given any trait (for example, extroverted, dependent, egotistical), most people will mix together behavior items that should not go together from the point of view of the trait category; at the tails of the distribution a few people will display noticeable generality. It may also be the case that for any person there is some feature of his behavior that will tend to be consistent, although there will be no way of knowing what feature this will be for any person without having already observed the consistency itself. The main difficulty with Bem's approach is the one discussed above in connection with the "clinician's response": One can predict too few of the people too much of the time.

CULTURAL INTEGRATION

At the cultural level of analysis, postulate 1 is more difficult to assess. There is very little systematic evidence on the extent of thematic generalization across domains such as the domestic, the economic, the political, and the religious. It is the impression of some ethnographers (for example, Geertz 1973, pp. 406–407) that within any culture every theme has a "subdued opposite." And it is certainly the impression of this writer that the portrait one gets of a culture is intimately related to the methods used to study it (see Benedict 1946 and Triandis et al. 1968 for two very different views of the extent to which Japanese and American cultures are alike). Once in a while there are even intimations in the literature on national character that the way cultures differ from one another cannot be generalized from one domain to another (for example, Inkeles, Hanfmann, and Beier 1958, p. 11). Nonetheless, impressions and intimations do not a science make. At the moment the degree of thematic generalization at the cultural level cannot be judged with confidence, and one can only look forward to more systematic research on cultural integration. There are, however, two studies worth mentioning.

Francesca Cancian (1975) sets out to discover the "norms" of Zinacantecos in Chiapas, Mexico. She introduces the notion of a norm hierarchy, that is, the relative importance of rules concerning religious versus economic versus political versus kinship behavior. Cancian tries to infer a Zinacanteco's norm hierarchy by two different methods. Zinacantecos have well-developed ideas about the extent to which actions such as sending one's children to school, renting farmland in the distant yet fertile lowlands, or using a Western doctor are consistent with their religious, economic, political, or kinship norms. For example, the use of a Western doctor (in addition to a shaman) is thought to be inconsistent with Zinacanteco religious norms. Cancian discovers that the norm hierarchy implied in the way people make decisions about whether to use a Western doctor, send children to school, and so on is entirely different from the norm hierarchy that one would discover by asking people which norms are important to them. How one studies a people's norms seems to be decisive for what one finds. Method variance may well be decisive for an ethnographer's construction of cultural reality.

A second relevant study is Rex Costanzo's (1974) reanalysis of some of the data in Whiting and Child's classic volume *Child Training and Personality* (1953). *Child Training and Personality* presents evidence on thematic generalization across two cultural domains: socialization customs, and beliefs about illness. Cultural differences in socialization customs are shown to relate consistently to cultural differences in beliefs about the causes of illness. Whiting and Child's most dramatic finding is the significant cross-cultural correlation between customs promoting oral socialization anxiety in childhood (for example, early and severe weaning from the breast) and beliefs that the causes of illness are oral (for example, "It must have been something I ate"). Whiting and Child also discover a statistically significant relationship between anxiety-producing socialization customs and beliefs about the causes of illness in the area of aggression (for example, severe punishment for physical aggression and the belief that aggressive wishes make you sick). Three other socialization and illness explanation systems (the anal, the sexual, and the dependent) tend to converge but fall short of statistical significance.

The interpretation of these findings is made complicated in interesting ways by Costanzo's multitrait/multimethod reanalysis (see Campbell and Fiske 1959) of the Whiting and Child data, reproduced in Table 7.4. The table shows the degree of correlation both within and between all possible pairs of the five socialization systems and the five parallel illness-explanation systems. For example, whereas oral socialization anxiety is significantly related to oral explanations of illness (.49), it is more highly associated (too highly associated) with anal and sexual explanations of illness (.60 and .67, respectively). Moreover, oral socialization anxiety predicts anal and sexual illness explanations (.60 and .67, respectively) better than these illness explanation systems are predicted by anal and sexual socialization customs (.45 and .33, respectively).

The notion of cultural integration receives only equivocal support from the evidence in Table 7.4. While every socialization system is positively related to its parallel illness explanation system (.49, .45, .33, .25, .47), there are just too many instances in which nonparallel systems are more highly correlated. For example, dependent socialization anxiety is positively correlated to dependent illness explanations (.25), but it is more highly associated with every one of the four other illness explanation systems (.37, .37, .31, .30, respectively). Also, on the average, the intercorrelations among the five different socialization systems are as highly correlated with each other as any of them is correlated with its equivalent illness explanation system. For example, the oral socialization anxiety/dependent socialization anxiety coefficient (.75) is greater than either the oral socialization anxiety/oral illness explanation coefficient (.49) or the dependent socialization anxiety/dependent illness explanation coefficient (.25). The case for cultural integration in Whiting and Child's data is probably debatable. E. Terry Prothro (1960), for example, in a factor analytic study of Whiting and Child's variables, concludes that cross-

Table 7.4 Multitrait/multimethod analysis of 5 socialization anxiety systems and 5 illness explanation systems

	Socialization Anxiety					Illness Explanation				
	Oral	Anal	Sex	Dep	Agg	Oral	Anal	Sex	Dep	Agg
Socialization anxiety										
Oral	—									
Anal	.43 (49)	—								
Sexual	.43 (54)	.47[a] (48)	—							
Dependent	.75[a] (55)	.47[a] (48)	.25 (53)	—						
Aggressive	.27 (58)	.03 (47)	.62[a] (55)	.11 (53)	—					
Illness explanation										
Oral	.49[a] (65)	-.12 (49)	-.40 (61)	.37 (57)	-.47[a] (64)	—				
Anal	.60[a] (65)	.45 (49)	.45[a] (61)	.37 (57)	.13 (64)	.58[a] (75)	—			
Sexual	.67[a] (65)	-.10 (49)	.33 (61)	.31 (57)	.40 (64)	.52[a] (75)	.67[a] (75)	—		
Dependent	.09 (65)	-.04 (49)	-.51[a] (61)	.25 (57)	-.06 (64)	.03 (75)	-.08 (75)	-.08 (75)	—	—
Aggressive	.27 (65)	-.02 (49)	.01 (61)	.30 (57)	.47[a] (64)	.08 (75)	.16 (75)	.27 (75)	.13 (75)	—

Source: Costanzo's (1974) reanalysis of Whiting and Child's (1953) intermediate and high-confidence data.

a. Significant at the .05 level (two-tailed).

Note: Coefficient of correlation = Yule's Q (for dichotomous ordinal data).

Note: Numbers in parentheses are cell base frequencies.

cultural childrearing norms "cannot be described as permissive or nonpermissive. Rather they must be described as more or less permissive on orality-sexuality, on anality-independence, and on aggression. It is not even accurate to refer to the 'permissiveness for dependency' in a given culture, for dependence is not unifactorial" (p. 152). Nonetheless, Prothro does discover some clustering of variables around an orality-sexuality factor and anality-independence factor. One possible inference from Costanzo's results in Table 7.4 is that when the people of a culture think a lot about the human body they tend to be scrupulously concerned with it when they raise their children (see Chapters 6 and 9 of this volume). This interpretation has plausibility but should probably be viewed with some caution. As Prothro (1960) remarked with regard to a possible "hypochondria" factor in his study, it "might represent [the] ethnographer's generalized concern and lack of concern with illness rather than the culture's concern or lack of it" (p. 153).

Postulate 2: The Search for Childhood Origins

... habits established early in the life of the individual influence all subsequent learning, and therefore the experiences of early childhood are of predominant importance.   (Gorer 1943)

In 1971 Herbert Barry and Leonora Paxson published information on what it is like to be an infant or young child in each of 186 societies (see also Barry et al. 1977). Barry and Paxson's numerical codes concerned thirty-four parameters of childhood experience, including the nighttime sleeping proximity of mother, father, and infant; the identity of principal caretakers; the amount of body contact between infants and their caretakers; the type of infant-carrying device and carrying position; the age of weaning and "elimination control"; and the age at which motor skills develop. Barry and Paxson introduce their codes with the following justification: "Infancy may be of special interest to some analysts of culture and personality because of the widely accepted belief that experiences early in life have important influences on the development of adult character" (1971, p. 466).

Barry and Paxson are, of course, correct. Most studies in culture and personality ultimately try to explain adult personality characteristics by reference to the causal influence of specific child care practices. Many of these studies (for example, Erikson 1950; Whiting and Child 1953; J. Whiting 1949, 1964, 1971; Shirley and Romney 1962;

Ayres 1967) focus on exactly the kinds of childhood variables that Barry and Paxson code.

To what extent does the past influence the present? Postulate 2 is widely endorsed, but how well does it stand up in the face of evidence on the longitudinal stability of individual differences in conduct? The question is difficult to answer, primarily because of the lack of good observational evidence on behavior in the developmental literature. What little evidence there is, however, is not terribly strong.

For example, William Caudill and Carmi Schooler (1973) report dramatic differences between Japanese and American caretakers and their children for behavioral events involving activity level, affect display, and dependency. Like most culture and personality theorists, Caudill and Schooler believe that early and significant childhood experiences (in this case the behavior of caretakers) produce distinctive underlying qualities of character. These qualities of character are supposed to account for the anticipated longitudinal stability of individual behavioral differences.

Caudill and Schooler perform a very sensible test of postulate 2. They first try to predict, within each culture, a six-year-old's behavior from information about the caretaker's behavior during the child's infancy. They find fewer significant correlations than would be expected by chance. Then they relax their test and try to predict the child's behavior at age two and one-half years from the caretaker's behavior in infancy. The test fails dreadfully. Finally, they try to predict the six-year-old's behavior from the child's own behavior at age two and a half. Again, nothing.

Dismayed by their results, Caudill and Schooler note that "although even with the most valid measures one would not necessarily expect complete consistency in the individual's behavior over time, the level of individual inconsistency in the present data is unbelievable" (1973, p. 337). Caudill and Schooler do not reexamine postulate 2, but they are puzzled by their failure to validate their intracultural predictions. They offer two speculations: (1) perhaps the data are unreliable; (2) perhaps there are threshold effects that render measures of monotonicity inappropriate. Caudill and Schooler may be right, but this failure to find confirmation for postulate 2 should probably not be dismissed, especially since it is not unique to studies that use systematic and detailed behavior observational techniques.

Sibylle Escalona and Grace Heider (1959), for example, try to predict the behavioral characteristics of thirty-one preschool children (ages thirty-two months to sixty-six months) from observations of their "reaction tendencies" in infancy. First the authors assess the longitudinal stability of individual differences by applying the same set of 134 rating scales (for example, "impulse control," "speed or tempo") to summary descriptions of each child's behavior at the two ages. Then they intercorrelate the two sets of ratings separately for each child. Across the thirty-one children, the average correlation between the two time-lagged descriptions of behavior is .24 (uncorrected for attenuation). The range extends from −.17 to .51. Perhaps even more startling is the finding that random comparisons of children across the two sets of behavioral ratings (for example, child 1 in infancy compared with child 2 at preschool age) are correlated on the average at .18. The standard deviation is .30. As Escalona and Heider point out, "this means that the five percent level of the distribution is .65. None of the predictions can be said to be better than chance by this criterion" (p. 138). They reject the criterion.

Stella Chess, Alexander Thomas, and Herbert Birch (1959) further discuss the problematical status of postulate 2. They examine the consequences of early child care practices in the areas of feeding, discipline, toilet training, sleeping, and instruction. In general they discover that children show "differing responses with parents whose approaches have been similar" and "similar responses with parents whose approaches have differed" (p. 798). They conclude that "the available published data do not confirm the hypothesis that the pattern of child care practiced by the parent in the child's early life has a clear-cut, consistent effect on the personality of the older child or adult" (p. 793; see also Kagan and Klein 1973; and Kagan 1976). Parents sometimes come to recognize the truth of this conclusion by the time they have finished raising their second child, who typically turns out to be disposed differently from the first child.

Postulate 3: The Individual-Difference Model of Cultural Differences

> Personality refers to more or less stable internal factors that make one person's behavior consistent from one time to another, and different from the behavior other people would manifest in *comparable situations*. (Child 1968, p. 83; emphasis added)

The individual-difference concept of personality has influenced culture and personality research. The literature is rich in such formulations as, the Tuscarora modal personality type displays a fear of rejection and punishment by the environment and a strong urge to be allowed to become passive and dependent (Wallace 1952, p. 75), or the Burmese monk lacks self-confidence and has a greater-than-average fear of female and mother figures (Spiro 1965). Nevertheless, despite its popularity, the individual-difference conceptualization of personality may be inappropriate for cross-cultural research. Its application to cross-cultural materials seems to lead to bafflement and paradox.

WHAT IS PERSONALITY THEORY ABOUT?

What is it that psychologists have tried to explain by means of the individual-difference concept of personality, and are the conditions for applying the concept likely to be met in cross-cultural research? Irvin Child's (1968) definition, as given above, is a useful starting point. Let us examine the implications of the element of situational comparability in Child's definition.

To understand the concept of personality, one must recognize that not everything a person does is personality relevant. There are many true statements about behavior that are simply irrelevant to personality theory. Personality theorists are not interested in explaining why people talk more in debating clubs than in libraries, or touch more in bedrooms than in kitchens. They are not interested in explaining why the pupil of a person's eye contracts more in sunlight than in a dark room.

Among the things that are not grist for the personality theorist's mill are behaviors demanded by the situation and behaviors that any rational person would do under the circumstances. The point is fundamental but often overlooked. Differences between the anxiety level of one Trukese man who is having a familiar sexual experience with his brother's wife and that of another who is sailing a canoe on high seas in a gale may tell us only about differences between sailing and sex (or sex with a brother's wife, or familiar sex with a brother's wife). Similarly, we would not want to make personality claims about differences in the altruism or helping behavior of two cultures if those cultures also differed in the number of bystanders who typically witness "altruistic occasions." Helping behavior is to a large extent "demanded by the situation." The greater the number of bystanders, the less likely it becomes that anyone will help (Latané and Darley 1970).

A characteristic difference in behavior is not necessarily paralleled by a characteristic difference in character. A people's behavior can be altruistic without their having corresponding altruistic personalities.

The same can be said for authoritarianism or any other type of behavior. For example, Roger Barker (1971) explains the social behavioral differences between an American and English town without reference to personality at all. He presents evidence that levels of participation and responsible social behavior are higher in cultures in which behavior settings are relatively deficient in personnel. He then goes on to claim that "people in the Midwest *have* to participate to a greater degree than in Yorkdale," and that if the English were imported to the Midwest they would "have to participate also, and this would occur immediately with no learning period involved" (p. 30). As Mischel (1969) notes, "dispositional theories try to categorize behaviors in terms of hypothesized historical psychic forces that diverse behaviors serve; but it is also possible to categorize behaviors in terms of the unifying evoking and maintaining conditions that they jointly share" (p. 1016). The two types of categorizations should not be confused.

Personality theory has a subject matter. But even to begin a personality analysis we must show that the behavioral differences we are trying to explain are not "demanded by the situation" or "what any rational person would do under the circumstances." In effect this means that we must be able to demonstrate that the relevant behavioral differences have been observed in the same or equivalent situations. It is with reference to the equivalence or comparability of the situations in which individuals from different cultures are observed that doubts arise about the relevance of the individual-difference concept of personality to cross-cultural studies.

HOW COMPARABLE ARE SITUATIONS ACROSS CULTURES?

Anthropologists can rarely treat a difference in the conduct of two peoples as if it were an indication of a difference in personality. Spiro was fully aware of this as early as 1955. He commented upon the role of Rorschach testing in psychological anthropology by noting that the Rorschach test

> provides us with a yardstick against which genuine personality variables, in contrast to patterned-response variables, can be measured. This proposition requires some explanation. A culture, psychologically viewed, consists of a configuration of stimulus situations and the customary responses to those situations which have been learned by the members of a given society. Hence, in demonstrating that

emotional and behavioral differences are to be found within different socio-cultural contexts we have not demonstrated the existence of personality difference at all. We have merely shown that different stimuli evoke different responses. What we must demonstrate, if we are to show personality differences, is that peoples reared in different socio-cultural contexts respond differently to the *same* stimuli. We must, in short, be able to observe the responses of different peoples to a stimulus that is identical for all of them and to which they have not already learned a culturally patterned response.   (1955, p. 257)

Child and Spiro seem to agree. To talk of differences one must first demonstrate likeness or equivalences. To talk of personality differences one must observe behavioral differences in equivalent situations. (I hasten to add that to talk of personality *factors* one must observe consistent differences over a *set* of equivalent situations. See postulate 1). The crucial question then becomes, How are we to decide that the differential responses we observe are in fact differential responses to an equivalent set of stimuli? How are we to establish the equivalence or comparability or alikeness of the situations or contexts in which our observations of differences are made?

There is another way to ask this question. With respect to which particular descriptive components must stimuli (situations, contexts, environments) be shown to be equivalent? How many descriptive components are to be written into our specification or definition of a behavioral situation before we test for situational equivalence? From a logical point of view there are a number of conceivable answers.

At one extreme we have Spiro's 1955 proposal that stimulus or situational equivalence is established whenever the (for lack of a better term) "objective" properties of the stimulus situation are identical *from the point of view of the outside observer.* For example, Spiro suggests that the verbal responses of people around the world can be treated as comparable because they have been asked to interpret the same ten inkblots. Occasionally, although not characteristically, Le-Vine (1973) argues in the same way. He suggests that one of the reasons "bureaucratic institutional structures" such as schools and hospitals can be used as a universal framework for the detection of personality differences is that schools and hospitals are organized around similar physical settings, in particular, classrooms, clinics, and wards (p. 247).

I believe we should feel uneasy with Spiro's proposal. Allen Newell and Herbert Simon's (1972) discussion of the difficulty of defining a task environment in human problem-solving research suggests why. Newell and Simon ask us to imagine an experiment in concept attainment

> A sequence of stimuli is presented to a subject, who is asked to classify each as an instance, or noninstance, of a concept (as yet unknown to him). He is informed whether each reply is right or wrong . . . if the subject refuses to try the task, is obviously inattentive, or undertakes to spoof the experimenter—we would not regard it as an experiment in concept attainment. We would also reclassify the experiment if it turned out that the subject could not discriminate among the stimuli because the light was too dim or because his eyes could not resolve the differences among them. In these cases, we would call it an experiment in visual sensation, or possibly, in perception.   (1972, p. 54)

This very simple example reminds us that a situation (environment, context, setting) is more than its physical properties as defined by an outside observer (also see Labov 1970; Cole and Bruner 1971). It is a situated activity defined in part by its goal *from the point of view of the actor.* "What any rational person would do under the circumstances" depends upon what the person is trying to accomplish. Two individuals moving about in a boxing ring are not in comparable situations if one of them is Jack Johnson and the other is Muhammad Ali, or if one is a boxer and the other a referee; and differences in their behavior may tell us only about the difference between trying to win a fight in the early twentieth century and doing so in the late twentieth century, or the difference between trying to enforce the rules of boxing and trying to exploit the rules to one's advantage. Boxing and refereeing are two distinct forms of activity, and only behavioral differences within each activity can be used to make inferences about distinctive features of the boxer or referee (in contrast to inferences about boxing versus refereeing).

This is probably the reason many culture and personality theorists (for example, LeVine 1973, p. 247) have postulated certain universal goals (for example, controlling sexual and aggressive impulses, defending the ego against anxiety) as a framework within which to study cross-cultural variations in personality. One difficulty with a "universal goals" strategy is that it restricts investigation to a very small subset of the goals actually pursued by any people, most of which are not universal. A more important difficulty is that once we concede that our definition of a behavioral situation must include the actor's goals and that two situations are equivalent only if the actors in the respective situations share the goals, we are on a very slippery slope. If our answer to the question, What kind of situation is this person in? must make reference to the actor's goals, then certainly it must also make reference to the means that the actor views as potentially admissible (and thinkable?) to accomplish these purposes.

Imagine a test of boxing skill in which a contestant is placed in a boxing ring for a fifteen-round match against Muhammad Ali. The goal is the usual one in contemporary boxing: score more points than your opponent or by your own agency (slips don't count) cause him to remain ten seconds off his feet. Our contestant is knocked down in the first round, but his friends, relatives, and supporters rush into the ring and help him to his feet. In the second round our contestant comes out of his corner with a sledge hammer, and Ali is left unconscious on the mat for the rest of the day. How do we assess the contestant's behavior? Clearly we do not view it as an instance of his boxing skill. Boxing is a form of activity defined not only by its goals, but also by a detailed (even if implicit) list of ways in which the goal can be legitimately accomplished. *Thus, we must write what we usually call traditions and norms into our very definition of a behavioral situation.* Since forms of activity, goals, traditions, and norms constitute a large part of what we mean by culture, it would seem to follow that two actors are in comparable or equivalent situations only to the extent that they are members of the same culture! Who is the more skillful boxer, Muhammad Ali or Jack Johnson? The question seems unanswerable; there is no yardstick that permits comparison, since the two men fought under dissimilar conditions. Ali had the option to score more points than his opponent; Johnson could win only by knockout. Furthermore, in Johnson's day there was no limit on rounds, audience interference was not tabooed, and defensive dancing was unthinkable. The very things that make the two actors members of different activity subcultures (their goals, traditions, techniques, and so on) make it impossible to place them in comparable contexts.

It would seem to follow that the difference in the anxiety level of two Kikuyu boys both about to be circumcised after having been masked, marked, secluded, and hazed in an initiation ceremony might warrant a personality analysis. But what of the difference in the anxiety level of the Kikuyu adolescent about to "go under the knife" and the Jewish thirteen-year-old about to read from the Torah?

The individual-difference concept of personality creates an irresolvable dilemma for cross-cultural researchers. If we force situational comparability by simply writing very little into our definition of a behavior situation—for example, we claim comparability by pointing at those ten inkblots, or by noting that all people go through rituals of status transition, or by pointing out that "every human being lives in a world in which there are others who are also seeking food and water" (Sears 1961, p. 449)—it becomes nearly impossible to discriminate between personality-relevant behaviors and "what any rational person would do under the circumstances" (given that culture's definition of the situation). The concept of culture and the concept of personality become hopelessly blurred, and we, as theorists, do little more than personify cultural differences. We must recognize that descriptions such as "the Dobu are more competitive and less cooperative than the Zuni" (based on Benedict 1934, pp. 91, 112, 154) or "the extremest of Russian atheists is on better speaking terms with God than are the devout of other lands, to whom God is always something of a mystery" (based on Sapir 1924, p. 408) are merely reports of differences between two or more populations. They are mute concerning the causes of such differences, such as the history, or character of a people. The personification of cultural differences is not what culture and personality are about. Moreover, it is a hazardous business. As has been demonstrated (Shweder 1973) there is no reason to expect that the ways individuals differ from one another within any or all cultures have anything to do with the ways cultures differ from one another.

On the other hand, if we write a great deal into our definition of a behavioral situation (for example, the actor's goals, the actor's understanding of the possible means, the actor's evaluations of the likelihood that each available means will accomplish the desired goal), then whatever the actor does will seem to be demanded by the situation. It is what any rational person would do, given *that* perception of the circumstances. The actor's personality will seem irrelevant and will disappear from our analysis.

Personality psychologists resolve this dilemma, the choice between vacuous commonalities and incomparable differences, quite pragmatically. They participate in the same culture as the people they study. Thus, they can sometimes reasonably assume that their notion of the actor's situation approximates the actor's notion. Unfortunately for cross-cultural researchers the individual-difference model of personality (postulate 3) presupposes the common cultural background of those whose behavior is being compared. It does not lend itself to cross-cultural comparisons.

A final remark concerning postulate 3: cross-cultural situational comparability is a "problem" because it is a prerequisite for carrying out a personality or character analysis of two or more peoples. It should not be confused, however, with another problem, that of identifying transcultural variables. Robert Sears (1961), for example, asks what the criteria are for "defining both a street fight and the telling of malicious gossip as indices of aggression" (p. 453). There are many possible answers to this type of question—for example, that the two indices have face validity, go together in behavior, and have similar empirical relationships to relevent external variables. Sears lists four criteria of his own (for example, that the same antecedent-consequent relations be demonstrable in all cultures). It is somewhat depressing that Sears's criteria have rarely (if ever) been met in cross-cultural research. But the main point here is that it is possible for a variable (for example, aggression) to have transcultural universality without its being a *personality* variable (see Shweder 1973). The incidence of street fights and gossip may rise and fall together across neighborhoods, cities, states, or whole nations. We may even want to talk about some situations eliciting more aggression (fights, gossip) than other situations. We can do this without ever being tempted to use the variable to describe individual differences across comparable situations.

Postulate 4: Explanation by Reference to Consequences

> Animals and men do, in the long run, exhibit those responses which lead to satisfying after-effects... (Tolman 1934)

There are two kinds of events that culture and personality theorists typically explain by reference to consequences: (1) the development of modal personality types and (2) the motivational integration of culture. Consequences are introduced into their explanations by invocations of (1) the concept of rational choice, (2) Darwin's notion of natural selection, or (3) the law of effect (see Gorer 1943; Barry, Child, and Bacon 1959; LeVine 1966, 1973, pp. 115–135). Although one or the other of these schemata plays a part in most explanations in the social sciences, the concept of rational choice and the law of effect must be contextualized and subjectivized to such an extent that they lose their parsimony and predictive power, while the notion of natural selection begs many of the questions that concern social scientists the most.

One of the ways culture and personality theorists explain the formation of modal personality types is by applying established learning theory generalizations about the functional relationships between instrumental acts (operants) and their consequences (positive and negative reinforcements). The assumption is that human behavior is predominantly learned and that learning takes place "by differential reward and punishment chiefly meted out by other members of the society" (Gorer 1943, p. 107). For example, Herbert Barry, Irvin Child, and Margaret Bacon (1959; see also Barry, Bacon, and Child 1967), in a discussion of hunting and gathering societies, argue that the frequency, degree, consistency, and immediacy of reward for self-reliance and achievement "shape children into venturesome, independent adults who can take initiative in wresting food daily from nature" (p. 63). In other words, we can predict an act's likelihood of occurrence from information about its attendant positive and negative consequences. Personality formation is referenced to the "objective" constraints of the social environment.

After culture and personality theorists have explained the formation of individual character by reference to so-called objective conditions, they analyze the sociocultural domain as though it were fashioned to correspond either directly or inversely to features of the modal personality of societal members. Thus, Geoffrey Gorer (1943) assumes that "when childhood wishes and frustrations are shared by a majority of a population, social and cultural institutions will be evolved to gratify them, and existing social and cultural institutions and those borrowed from other societies will be modified to congruence with these wishes" (p. 108). Similarly, Melford Spiro and Roy D'Andrade (1958) assume that "unless the personalities of the members of the group are consonant with the various traditions of the group, they will not in the long run be motivated to learn and/or transmit the traditions" (p. 456).

Culture and personality theorists frequently introduce person variables (for example, wishes, frustrations, conflicts, motives) as prior objective constraints that select for or against sociocultural institutions and thereby influence their evolution. Thus the persistence of a cloistered monastic tradition in Burmese Buddhism is interpreted as an accommodation to the passive dependency, homosexuality, and excessive fear of female figures latent in the Burmese male character

(Spiro 1965). Thus the belief in benevolent gods responsive to prayer is interpreted as an adaptation to motivational tendencies established in childhood with respect to nurturant parents who were responsive to verbal and nonverbal solicitations such as crying, whining, and begging (Spiro and D'Andrade 1958). Thus adolescent initiation rituals emphasizing aggressiveness, martial skills, and other "hypermasculine" virtues are interpreted as a defensive adjustment to the gnawing persistence throughout childhood of anxious concerns over whether one's sexual identity is male or female. The ritual ends all doubt (J. Whiting 1964).

The historical or ontogenetic process producing an adaptive accommodation between personality variables and sociocultural institutions is not always made explicit in culture and personality studies. Nevertheless, there are only three possible ways to explain behavior by reference to consequences: (1) the concept of rational choice, (2) Darwin's notion of natural selection, and (3) the law of effect.

RATIONAL CHOICE

The concept of rationality refers to any choice "whose probability of success is not exceeded by that of any available alternative"; it refers to any behavior that on the basis of available information "offers optimal prospects of achieving its objectives" (Hempel 1962, p. 7).

A rational orientation is one of calculation. It involves assessing alternative means to determine which will most efficiently accomplish one's ends—that is, maximize one's benefits and minimize one's losses with reference to some goal. John Harsanyi argues that the concept of rationality is important to social scientists because "if a person acts rationally, his behavior can be *fully explained* in terms of the goals he is trying to achieve. When we say that Napoleon's strategy in a particular battle was rational, this means that his strategy choice can be explained essentially by pointing out that this was the best strategy for him to choose in terms of his military objectives at the time" (quoted in Allison 1971, p. 31).

Mischel (1973) seems to have turned to rational-choice analysis as an alternative to a global-trait approach to personality. In various studies on self-control behavior (for example, Mischel and Staub 1965) he argues that choice is a function of the expectation that it will lead to an outcome and the actor's evaluation of that outcome. Mischel demonstrates that delays in gratification are related to the actor's expectation of success under various experimentally controlled contingency conditions. Delay times are highly manipulable under experimental conditions that alter either the actor's expectations about chances for success or the actor's evaluations of the outcomes. When children are provided with differential information about such success likelihoods, it is not difficult to alter their self-control behavior.

One of the limitations of the concept of rational choice is that its application depends upon numerous qualifications that substantially erode its predictive power. For example, Simon (1957) has noted that, from the point of view of an omniscient observer, human rationality is a "bounded rationality" severely limited by cognitive and symbolic constraints:

> The intended rationality of an actor requires him to construct a simplified model of the real situation in order to deal with it. He behaves rationally *with respect to this model,* and such behavior is not even approximately optimal *with respect to the real world.* To predict his behavior we must understand the way in which this simplified model is constructed, and its construction will certainly be related to his psychological properties as a perceiving, thinking and learning animal.   (P. 199; emphasis added)

Thus, upon examination it turns out that we cannot fully explain or predict the behavior of a rational actor by reference to goals alone. We must also know, for example, the order in which admissible alternatives will be searched out and considered. This is because actors do not consider all the alternatives and then pick the one with the optimal prospects for goal attainment. Rather they select the first alternative that is "good enough," or "satisfices" (Simon 1957; Allison 1971). Some would argue that there is a cost to searching among alternatives.

Rationality is not a hypothesis. It is presupposition or criterion. (In this respect the concept of rational choice is like the concept of consistency in postulate 1.) The relevant consistency question is not, Is behavior consistent? but rather, Where are the consistencies that exist to be found? Similarly, the relevant rationality question is not, Is behavior rational? but rather, With respect to what can the behavior be seen as rational by an outside observer? We assume that behavior is rational and then use the concept of rationality as a criterion to decide how much we need to know in advance of our explanations. For example, it seems that Simon's (1957) account of "satisficing" is not really an abandonment of the notion that an actor selects an alternative that "offers optimal prospects of achieving its objectives." Rather,

Simon seems to ask, With respect to what is the actor optimizing? It is the criterion of rationality that leads him to introduce notions such as the actor's "simplified model of the real situation." Similarly, Freud was led to introduce the notion of unconscious goals by his commitment to the concept of rationality, as well as concern for the question, With respect to what can phobic, compulsive, and hysterical behavior be seen as rational? This presuppositional status of the concept of rational choice is most apparent in the following remark by Walter and Harriet Mischel (1976): "Even the noblest altruism [that is, *apparently* acting against one's interests for the benefit of others] supported by the "highest" levels of moral reasoning [for example, it is "right" to help others regardless of the personal consequences] still depends on expected consequences, although the consequences are often temporally distant, are not in the immediate external environment, are not easily identified, and reside in the actor himself rather than in social agents" (pp. 97–98).

The relevant question, then, is not whether behavior is rational. The relevant question is: How bounded is that rationality and what specifically are the boundaries? The boundedness of the concept of rationality will be inversely related to its parsimony and directly related to its emptiness as a predictive principle (although even if it is ineffectual as a predictive principle it will still have utility as a criterion for discovering the limits of rational choice such as the sacred, the traditional, the unconscious). The more we have to know about an actor before we can predict his or her behavior, the less helpful is the concept of rationality.

How bounded is the concept of rationality? How many "givens" must be introduced before it can be applied? How much must we already know about an actor and his or her behavioral context before we can go about predicting behavior? We can answer these questions by explicating the way rational choice operates as an explanatory scheme. (The scheme is often referred to as "practical inference" or "practical reason"; see von Wright 1971; Sahlins 1976a).

Rational choice is, perhaps, the concept most frequently employed in explaining the behavior of everyday life (see Lewis 1978). Question: During his trip to Europe in 1977, why was Jimmy Carter received so warmly in Poland? Answer: Poland had a sluggish economy, and its leaders wanted to expand trade with the United States (CBS Evening News, December 29, 1977). Why does a particular individual take a particular course of action? In answering this question, we usually assume that the individual in question had some goal toward which the action was an optimal means (see Allison 1969). More explicitly, a rational choice explanation takes the following form (as described by Hempel 1962; also see Von Wright 1971).

Step 1. *People are rational agents;* that is, their actions are under voluntary control (which, as we shall see later, is not equivalent to being under conscious control; we must admit the possibility of unconscious decisions). If we had reason to believe that a particular individual was in the throes of an epileptic seizure, or in a hypnotic trance, or under the influence of drugs, or in any other way coerced into acting, we would not try to explain that person's behavior in terms of the rational choice concept. When it comes to knee jerks, the concept of rationality is out of place (Fitzgerald 1973).

Step 2. *A particular person, a rational agent, is in a situation of type S.* A description of the situation must include the following: (1) the person's goals (the concept of rational choice does not help to explain behaviors that are not goal directed, are done for their own sake, or are ends in themselves or merely matters of habit, such as doodling and *perhaps* certain forms of ethical conduct; see Weber 1958; Black 1975); (2) the person's perceived means, that is, a list of the behaviors thought to be sufficient to bring about the desired goal, one of which the person believes must be selected if the goal is to be attained (if there is no such list there can be no rational choice); and (3) the person's calculations concerning the efficiency and relative cost of each possible method for attaining the desired goal.

Step 3. *In a situation of type S anyone who is a rational agent will do such-and-such,* that is, select the behavioral alternative that on the basis of available information and beliefs seems to offer the optimal prospect of success (see Hempel 1962).

Step 4. *Therefore, the person in question did such-and-such.*

There are two noteworthy features to this explanatory pattern. The first is that step 3 (the claim that in a given situation all rational agents would select the alternative that offers optimal prospects of success) is not a generalization based on experience. It is an assumption that we must make because if we were to deny it we would have no way to make sense of the behavior of rational agents. In fact we often use the assumption implicit in step 3 to ascertain an individual's goals, perceived means, and so on (step 2); and we typically do this in the light of what that person has already done (step 4).

Imagine we observe a man proceeding out into a cold winter's night to catch something to eat. He tells us he is in search of a rabbit, that he will certainly be gone for several hours, and that he may in fact come back empty-handed, cold, and hungry. On his way out the door he discovers a dead rat in a trap; he promptly tosses it into his garbage heap. As observers, what interpretative use do we make of such behavior? Do we reject step 3? Do we argue that the man has failed to select an alternative that he believes offers optional prospects of achieving his goal? I think not. What we do is revise our understanding of his goals. "Something to eat" does not include rats. In fact, we would be willing to do more than simply revise our notion of his goal; we would postulate unconscious goals before we would doubt the assumption expressed in step 3.

The second noteworthy feature of the rational choice form of explanation is that to use it to predict an individual's behavior we must already know an enormous amount about that individual. We must know which alternatives are actually going to be considered. All people typically fail to consider potentially optimal alternatives. They may fail to do so because the order of search among admissible alternatives has already produced a satisficing solution (after we have found a "decent" candidate for a job, how long should we go on searching for the "perfect" candidate?); because they are unaware of a potentially optimal alternative or hold erroneous beliefs about its efficiency; because they classify it as "sacred" and hence not as something to be considered as a means to an end (for example, some Christians would not regard a wooden cross as potential firewood); or because the alternative violates traditional rules about how goals are to be attained (one does not use a sledgehammer to fell one's opponent in boxing, or eat rats to satisfy one's hunger).

To predict behavior by means of the concept of rational choice we must already know the actor's state of mind, goals, sources of information, beliefs, ethics, and cultural traditions. Given that the actor is not under duress, has a goal in mind, has this particular goal in mind, defines these particular alternatives as alternatives, considers these alternatives in this particular order—given all that, the actor's behavior can be "fully explained." The parsimony and predictive power of the concept of rational choice are severely limited by all these historical, clinical, and ethnographic "givens" that it presupposes.

This seems to be what Marshall Sahlins (1976a) has in mind when he argues:

The "opportunity costs" of our economic rationality are a secondary formation, an expression of relationships already given by another kind of thought, figured a posteriori within the constraints of a logic of meaningful order. The food taboo on horses and dogs thus renders unthinkable the consumption of a set of animals whose production is practically feasible and which are nutritionally not to be despised. Surely it must be practicable to raise *some* horses and dogs for food in combination with pigs and cattle. There is even an enormous industry for raising horses as food for dogs. But then, America is the land of the sacred dog.   (P. 171)

NATURAL SELECTION

Rational choice is a prerogative of actors; natural selection is a prerogative of environments. Both processes have been championed as ways of explaining behavior by reference to consequences. The concept of rational choice inevitably leads to a detailed historical, clinical, and ethnographic subjectivization of decision making. A "rational choice" analysis ultimately must examine the unparsimonious intricacies of the actor's point of view if it is to explain behavior.

The concept of natural selection, on the other hand, explains solely by reference to the "objective" conditions of an environment. Subjective categories such as "goal," "awareness of alternatives," " 'evaluation of outcome likelihoods," and "preference orderings" have no proper place in a Darwinian account (although Popper and Eccles 1977, pp. 11–14, maintain that evolutionary processes become more understandable if one makes reference to an animal's "subjective aims and purposes"—animals, it is argued, choose, alter, even construct their own selective environments). The causative influence of consequences is direct. The only consequences that are theoretically relevant are those that threaten the survival of the organism and its ability to reproduce or duplicate its kind. Viability or persistence is the only criterion for assessing the adequacy of an alternative; by definition, only "fit" alternatives survive. For a Darwinian, the expression "this species is 'fit' but has a very limited reproductive potential" is a contradiction in terms.

Darwinians restrict their concerns to those consequences that reduce an organism's ability to reproduce. By doing this they avoid the need for subjective categories. This is certainly one of the appeals of Darwinism, but it comes at a price. That price is silence on a central issue for most social scientists, namely, Of all the conceivable viable alternatives, why this one and not some other (see Sahlins 1976a, 1976b)?

An explanation by reference to the process of natural selection tells us about the limits of what is possible. It tells us which of a large class of occurrences could not persist. Gregory Bateson (1967) has aptly termed it "negative explanation."

Explanation by elimination can go only so far. Natural selection is a theory of persistence; it is concerned with *regeneration*, not with generation. It tells us nothing about why certain events occur; its only answer to the question, Why this viable alternative and not some other viable alternative? is an appeal to chance or randomness. At its limits Darwinism is indeterminate.

Natural selection is a variety of functional explanation, and its indeterminate nature is typical of such. Functional explanations have the following form (see Hempel 1959):

1. There is some entity (for example, a population of honeybees) that functions adequately (that is, perpetuates its kind) in some environment.
2. This entity (those bees) functions adequately (perpetuates its kind) in that environment only if it is able to satisfy some necessary condition (for example, locate food resources).
3. If such-and-such a trait (for example, a language for communicating the location of pollen) was present in this entity, then the necessary condition would be satisfied.
4. Hence, the trait is present in the entity.

There are two difficulties with functional explanations of this type, both discussed by Carl Hempel (1959). The first is the tacit assumption that systems are self-regulating, that is, develop appropriate traits for meeting their needs. "That adaptation has occurred seems obvious. That it does so most of the time or even very often is completely unclear" (Lewontin 1976, p. 21). The second difficulty is the fallacy of affirming the consequent. If such-and-such a trait (for example, the dance language of honeybees) satisfies some necessary condition (for example, locating food resources), it does not follow that satisfaction of some necessary condition (food resources are routinely located) must occur as a result of that trait ("if $p \rightarrow q$" does not imply "if $q \rightarrow p$"). (In fact honeybees typically rely on smell, not on dance languages, to locate food resources; see Gould 1975.) It is rare indeed when there is only one trait that nature can "design" to satisfy a necessary condition for survival.

Bateson (1967), however, believes that, by a process of elimination, Darwinism can provide a uniquely determinate account of what persists (that is, "*only* if $p \rightarrow q$"). Bateson likens natural selection "to the form of logical proof by *reductio ad absurdum*. In this species [*sic*] of proof, a sufficient set of mutually exclusive alternative propositions is enumerated, e.g., "P" and "not P," and the process of proof proceeds by demonstrating that all but one of this set are untenable or "absurd." It follows that the surviving member of the set must be tenable within the terms of the logical system" (p. 29).

Bateson's analogy is not entirely compelling. Unlike the "events" that occur within logical or mathematical systems, the events that concern empirical scientists cannot typically be partitioned into exhaustive, mutually exclusive alternatives (for example, we cannot always tell whether a particular organism is a vertebrate or an invertebrate, a plant or an animal; see Rudd 1954); alternatives overlap with one another. Moreover, there are no rules or algorithms for specifying or interdefining all the possible events that can occur within the terms of the system (see Cavell 1969, chapter 1; Ziff 1972, chapter 4; also Toulmin 1971; Shweder and LeVine 1975). Natural systems, unlike logical and mathematical ones, are not tautological.

Finally, Bateson's analogy disguises the indeterminate nature of Darwinian explanations and seems to encourage "the fallacy of an a priori fitness course" (Sahlins 1976b, pp. 82–83). Sahlins identifies the fallacy by reference to various Darwinian explanations of the spawning behavior of the Pacific salmon. In the process of a "long and dehabilitating swim upstream" the female salmon "undergoes certain organic changes that optimize her egg-bearing capacity, such as atrophy of the digestive system" (p. 82). These changes also guarantee the salmon's death. According to Sahlins, quoting sociobiologist E. O. Wilson, a typical Darwinian account of the salmon's spawning behavior argues that "if a female salmon laid only one or two eggs, the reproductive effort, consisting primarily of the long swim upstream, would be very high. To lay hundreds more eggs entails only a small amount of additional effort" (ibid.). In rebuttal Sahlins points out the hidden indeterminancy of the natural selection process: "if selection will go so far as to atrophy the digestive tract in favor of a single reproductive explosion that also kills the organism, why should it not as easily effect structural changes that will allow the salmon to spawn twice or more to the same fitness effect, as for instance sturgeons do?" (p. 83). Facetiously, Sahlins remarks:

> The problem is this course or some other was precluded not by a natural selection but by an analytic one. The salmon was taken as an a priori limited being with only one possible solution to the evolutionary problem of resource allocation to fitness, by a premise not

motivated in the nature of evolution itself. The salmon is going to have only one chance to lay eggs, and that at very considerable cost. Once this set of conditions is taken as given, all other evolutionary possibilities to the same net fitness effect may be conveniently ignored. (P. 83)

Hence we have "the fallacy of the a priori fitness course."

Neo-Darwinian theorists (for example, Campbell 1965; Toulmin 1972; LeVine 1973) have argued that Darwinism is more than just a theory of organic evolution. These theorists advance it as an explanatory scheme of such generality that it can account for organic evolution, trial-and-error learning, the evolution of science, and the development of personality.

In an important paper, Donald Campbell (1965, pp. 26–27) argues that "the most exciting contribution of Darwin is in his model for the achievement of purposive or ends-guided processes through a mechanism involving blind, stupid, unforesightful elements." The specifications of the model are as follows. Given three kinds of hypothetical events, an accommodation of a system to the objective constraints of its surrounding environment becomes inevitable:

1. The occurrence of haphazard variations. Campbell points to the mutation process in organic evolution and the exploratory process in trial-and-error learning.
2. The differential elimination of variants as a result of the selective pressures of the environment. Campbell points to the differential survival of certain mutants in organic evolution and the differential reinforcement of certain responses in trial-and-error learning.
3. The reproduction of those variants that are retained. Campbell points to the duplication process of the chromosome-gene system in plants and animals and the memory system in learning.

Campbell thus gives an abstract formulation of the law of effect while arguing that it is the psychologist's analogue to Darwin's notion of natural selection. Behavioral outcomes or consequences (for example, rewards and punishments) are viewed as selective criteria that either differentially propagate or differentially eliminate certain behavioral variants, thereby "shaping" behavior to environmental constraints. Campbell's attempt to equate natural selection with the law of effect is provocative, but even at this high level of generality it does not succeed. The law of effect, unlike the concept of natural selection but very much like the concept of rational choice, can "explain" only by reference to subjective categories; it does not guarantee the adaptation or accommodation of an organism to the constraints of its environment.

THE LAW OF EFFECT

The law of effect states that the effect of an act, including its rewards and punishments, is included among the future causes of the act (see Thorndike 1933). The general claim is that behaviors are controlled by the events or stimuli that follow them. More specific claims concern the degree and manner of control of subsequent stimuli over preceding behaviors. For example, one principle states that the greater the delay between behavior and consequences, the less the consequence influences future behavior. Another principle (the principle of variable-ratio intermittent reinforcement) states that the more random the occurrence of a consequence around a designated average number of consequences of that particular kind per some fixed number of behaviors of a particular kind, the more likely the behavior will persist even when the consequences fail to occur.

The law of effect is not as easy to understand as it first appears. Interpretative difficulties emerge as soon as one asks, Is the law of effect a lawlike statement? Is it an empirical generalization capable of disproof? There is reason to believe it is not. One reason is that if the law of effect is an empirical proposition, as Edward Thorndike (1933) seems to have believed, then the case against it is overwhelming; it would have to be rejected.

The consequences of an act often do not alter the future likelihood of occurrence of the behaviors that preceed them. For example, John Garcia and Robert Koelling (1966; see also Seligman and Hager 1972) tried to train laboratory rats (ninety-day-old Sprague-Dawley males) to avoid drinking water. Two kinds of drinking water, "tasty water" and "bright and noisy water," were paired with two kinds of aversive consequences of water drinking, X-ray-induced nausea and electrical shock. The rats were unable to associate the occurrence of electrical shock with the "tasty water" or to associate the occurrence of nausea with the "bright and noisy water." They failed to link the occurrence of shock with their efforts to drink "tasty water" even when act and outcome were nearly simultaneous. The rats suffered shock and came back for more. Similarly, there is evidence that the pecking behavior of pigeons persists even if it costs the pigeon grain (Williams and Williams 1969), and that the locational preference of rats for black over white areas is not reversed by the experience of shock in the black area (Allison, Larson, and Jensen 1967).

In addition, there is evidence that the particular way in which the effect of a behavior influences that behavior, when there is an influence, is unpredictable *from the effect alone.* For example, in rats and pigeons, the larger a food reward, the more rapid the extinction of the behavior. In turtles and goldfish the relationship between amount of reward and rate of extinction is just the opposite (Bitterman 1975, p. 701). Similarly, partial or intermittent reward produces greater resistance to extinction in rats than does consistent reward, but not so for African mouth breeders (Bitterman 1975, p. 703). The extent and type of influence that a consequence will have on the preceding behavior cannot be predicted from *only* knowledge of the consequence itself.

There is a great deal more evidence that the actual consequences of an act are independent of its future occurrence (see Seligman and Hager 1972). But it would be a misguided effort to recount it. The evidence has no bearing on the law of effect because the law of effect is not an empirical generalization; it is a definition of what is to count as a consequence (or reinforcer) of a behavior. Consequences (or reinforcers) are by definition those subsequent events that alter the future probability of the occurrence of preceding behaviors.

The law of effect simply specifies what class of subsequent events (those that change the future probability of occurrence of preceding behaviors) we should be interested in studying. Like any other definition, the relationship between its terms is circular and tautological (see Chomsky 1964). The reward or nonrewards (that is, reinforcers) following an act alter its future probability of occurrence. How are we to know whether some subsequent event is a reinforcer? It is a reinforcer only if it changes the future probability of the occurrence of the preceding act. Thus evidence that the drinking behavior of rats is unaffected by subsequent shock or that food decrements do not alter pecking behavior in pigeons merely indicates that shock and food are not reinforcers in those instances.

At first glance it seems perplexing that the law of effect is either wrong or circular. One way out of this interpretative conundrum is to recognize that not all circularities are vicious ones. Once we recognize that the law of effect is merely a definition of a reinforcer, we can turn away from the misguided question, Is the law of effect true or false? (definitions are neither true nor false) to the more relevant question, Is the law of effect useful?

To assess the usefulness of the law of effect, we must see if we are able to predict which subsequent events will serve as reinforcers without having to carry out a detailed contextual analysis of a particular organism's behavior in a particular environment. Are we in fact able to predict reinforcers in this way? Unfortunately the answer seems to be no. Knowledge of which events will reinforce is knowledge of a great deal more than simply which event will follow an act.

David Premack (1965), for example, has mounted an impressive case that there are no intrinsic reinforcers. The subsequent occurrence of, say, shock, food, or intracranial stimulation may or may not influence the future likelihood of the occurrence of preceding behaviors. Sometimes shock suffering, food ingesting, and intracranial stimulation are reinforcers; sometimes they themselves can be reinforced. It all depends. What it depends upon, though very simple, is highly contextual and profoundly subjective.

To identify what can be reinforced and what will serve as a reinforcer we must first discover the organism's *preferences* or goals (as measured by duration of activity selection under free-choice conditions). These preferences vary from organism to organism, situation to situation, and time to time. Premack (1965) presents considerable evidence in support of the following claims:

1. For any pair of responses the more probable response will reinforce the less probable response.
2. Reinforcement is a relative property. The most probable response of a set of responses will reinforce all members of the set; the least probable will reinforce no member of the set.
3. The reinforcement relationship is reversible. If the probability of the occurrence of two responses can be reversed in order, so can the reinforcement relationship between the two responses. (Pp. 132–133)

For example, if a rat would rather explore its cage than drink water (as measured by the duration of time it freely spends in each activity), then the subsequent opportunity to explore can be used to increase the future probability of occurrence of water-drinking behavior but not the reverse. But if the rat would rather drink than explore its cage, it is now water drinking that can be used to reinforce exploration. It seems that even hard-nosed behaviorists must allow for the actor's point of view before behavior can be explained; the concept of the reinforcer is ultimately a subjective category. Reinforcers are not independent objective features of an external environment.

The selective criteria with respect to which an organism (or person) adapts its behavior turn out to be the organism's (or person's) own goals. Behaviors that enable the organism to attain its goals are repeated. Gain leads to repetition. All this sounds like rational choice cloaked in a different idiom.

It seems that the law of effect is either wrong or tautological. To the extent that it is a tautology, it is not the kind of tautology that permits powerful context-free predictions about behavior. One cannot specify what will be a reinforcer until one already knows all about the actor's preferences. These can only be learned from a detailed contextual analysis of the actor's behavior.

Nothing that I have said denies the existence of a reinforcing relationship between particular events in everyday life. Taking off from Lewontin's observation, "That [reinforcement] occurs seems obvious. That it does so most of the time or even very often is completely unclear" (1976, p. 21). Of course, all members of a society (and most learning theorists) acquire a good deal of context-dependent knowledge about what subsequent events will have what effects on what behaviors under what circumstances for which class of persons (or species of organisms). But the knowledge *is* context dependent. Whatever predictive validity we achieve presupposes that one already knows all about the subject's preferences and the special conditions that affect them. There are no context-free reinforcers. The reinforcement relationship is a "secondary formation."

DUTY AND DESIRE RECONSIDERED: THE CONGRUENCE OF THE INDIVIDUAL AND SOCIAL

We are now in a position to reconsider the claim that culture and personality are consonant (congruent, integrated, isomorphic) and the related formulation that sociocultural institutions are constrained by, and ultimately adapt to, previous motivational variables. The epistemological status of the claim is not unlike that of the law of effect. For example, if we treat the claim that there is motivational integration of culture as an empirical generalization, it is probably wrong. On the one hand, Rorschach test evidence suggests that with respect to personality variables "individuals within cultures vary much more among themselves than they do from individuals in other cultures" (Kaplan 1954, p. 16). On the other hand, there is evidence that affective variables (including "anxiety") are not global traits and display a specificity like the personality traits discussed under postulate 1 (see Endler and Hunt 1966, 1968). The person who gets angry when contradicted is not the person who gets angry when pushed aside in a ticket line. There seems to be too much specificity and overlap of personality variables across populations to permit a systematic account of the striking differences that exist between populations in their social and cultural institutions.

Finally, the postulate of shared motivations is not always required to account for those instances of cultural integration that do occur. Given the complex pattern of results that emerges from Costanzo's (1974) reanalysis of Whiting and Child's (1953) data on socialization anxiety and explanations of illness (see Table 7.4), one is tempted to reconsider a position entertained and then dismissed by Whiting and Child (1953): "[cultural] integration might be directly between 'projective systems' (which would then not merit the name) and child training practices, personality characteristics being quite irrelevant" (p. 310). As mentioned earlier, a people that thinks a lot about the human body may be more scrupulously concerned with it than some other people when raising children. As far as I can tell, this null hypothesis has yet to be rejected (see also Benedict 1928 for an alternative "cognitive set" theory of cultural integration). (See chapters 6 and 9 of this volume.)

However, claims concerning the motivational integration of culture need not be interpreted as empirical generalizations. Rather, they can be interpreted as definitions of individual-social congruence. What do we mean when we say that a belief (for example, monotheism) or an institution (for example, adolescent initiation ceremonies) is congruent (consonant, isomorphic) with a group's personality? The best definition I can offer runs as follows: One's personality is congruent with the beliefs of one's culture and the institutions of one's society to the extent that one's ends and motives can be satisfied by means of those beliefs and institutions.

This definition of individual-social congruence (or integration) directs attention to the class of ends and motives that is satisfied by any particular belief or institution. The relevant theoretical question for culture and personality theory becomes, To what extent can we predict the end or motive that is satisfied, exclusively from knowledge of the belief or institution? Unfortunately, here as elsewhere, our predictive successes are rather limited.

The relationship of ends and motives to beliefs and institutions is many-to-many. Any particular motive can be satisfied by a wide (though not infinite) range of beliefs or institutions. Any particular belief or institution is compatible with diverse motives. It is because of this many-to-many relationship that Reinhard Bendix (1952) argues that normative behavior is psychologically unrevealing. He notes that it is, of course, possible for a theorist to construct "an analogous psychological syndrome" for any cultural belief or social institution;

for example, the compulsive character type of psychoanalytic lore has been advanced as a personification of German Nazi values emphasizing hard work, discipline, sacrifice, devotion, and will power. But, Bendix points out, the psychological syndrome and the cultural institution do not require one another and empirically go together only as an exception, not as a rule.

In a similar vein, Spiro (1961) argues that "a knowledge of a person's social roles would not even lead to an accurate prediction of those aspects of his personality that are caught up in their performance . . . (1) different drives may be canalized by the same goal, which is attained by the performance of the same role; (2) the same drive may be canalized by different goals, which are attained by the performance of different roles; and (3) different drives may be canalized by the same goal which is attained by the performance of different roles" (p. 115). Sahlins (1976b) formulates the many-to-many relationship thus:

> There is no necessary relation between the phenomenal form of a human social institution and the individual motivations that may be realized or satisfied therein . . . Men may be moved to fight out of love (as of country) or humaneness (in light of the brutality attributed to the enemy), for honor or some sort of self-esteem, from feelings of guilt, or to save the world for democracy . . . compassion, hate, generosity, shame, prestige, emulation, fear, contempt, envy, greed—ethnographically the energies that move men to fight are practically coterminous with the range of human motivations. (pp. 7–8)

Sahlins and Spiro seem to concur: there is no reason to expect that we can predict an actor's particular motive from what she or he does (or believes).

Rethinking Culture and Personality Theory: A Breakdown of the Action Schema

> Men may violently disagree about the purposes behind a given act, or about the character of the person who did it, or how he did it, or in what kind of situation he acted; or they may even insist upon totally different words to name the act itself. But be that as it may, any complete statement about motives will offer some kind of answers to these five questions: what was done (act), when or where it was done (scene), who did it (agent), how he did it (agency), and why (purpose). (Burke 1969, p. xv)

In a unit act there are identifiable as minimum characteristics the following: (1) an end, (2) a situation, analyzable in turn into (a) means and (b) conditions, and (3) at least one selective standard in terms of which the end is related to the situation. It is evident that these categories have meaning only in terms which include the subjective point of view, i.e., that of the actor.   (Parsons 1968, p. 77)

I believe most culture and personality theorists would agree with both Robin Horton (1967) and H. L. A. Hart (1961): (1) To construct a scientific theory is to elaborate "a schema of forces or entities (*of a limited number of kinds and governed by a limited number of general principles*) operating 'behind' or 'within' the world of common sense observation" (Horton 1967, p. 51; emphasis added); and (2) In the last resort, a scientific theory's claim to forward our understanding of nature is dependent on its power to predict what will occur, which is based on generalizations of what regularly occurs (Hart 1961, p. 184, paraphrased). That is, a good theory is both parsimonious (it explains a lot and does so with relatively few categories and principles) and valid (it has predictive utility). In the social sciences, however, the predictive success of culture and personality theory seems to be inversely related to its parsimony, and vice versa. Parsimony and validity cannot be simultaneously achieved.

With predictive success as a criterion, none of the parameters of Kenneth Burke's (1968, 1969) or Talcott Parsons' (1968) action schemata seem to lead to a parsimonious theory of human conduct. As we have seen, an "agent-act" emphasis (an emphasis on "personality" or "the correspondence between a man's character and the character of his behavior"; Burke 1968, p. 446) leads us to complexity, highly specific act-context-person interaction effects, and the recognition that "it all seems to depend" (see postulates 1 and 2). An "agency-purpose" emphasis (an emphasis on rational choice or the principles governing the selection of means to accomplish ends) leads us to the limits of rationality and to the details of the historical, cultural, and clinical idiosyncrasies of the actor (see postulate 4). An "act-act" emphasis (an emphasis on the law of effect or the principles governing the way certain events have subsequent control over preceding events) suffers the same fate (see postulate 4). Finally, a "scene-act" emphasis (an emphasis on "circumstances," the "situation," or the way "objective conditions" regulate conduct via natural selection) leads us into noncomparability on the one hand (see postulate 3) and indeterminacy on the other (see postulate 4). In summary, human conduct does not readily lend itself to description in terms of a universal scheme of forces or entities "of a limited number of kinds and governed by a limited number of general principles."

There is a striking similarity and convergence between this conclusion and the one drawn by certain ethologists, ethnologists, and psychologists concerned with social behavior. Blurton Jones and Mel Konner (1976), for example, doubt the very possibility of a general theory of animal behavior. They suggest that the best we can do is "simply to know a lot about each animal" (p. 347). Clifford Geertz (1973) adopts somewhat the same position. He argues that theory building in cultural anthropology should be aimed at making "thick description" possible instead of either generalizing across cases or trying to "subsume them under a governing law" (Perhaps Geertz should have said "universal law"; a generalization within cases is still a governing law.) Explicitly endorsing the logic of clinical inference he believes that generalizations are possible only within cases, that is, that generalizations in cultural anthropology are restricted in their scope and limited in their power. What this means is that to understand human conduct adequately one must engage in the unparsimonious proliferation of context-dependent insights; that is the conclusion demanded by all the evidence on interaction effects. Harold Raush, Allen Dittmann, and Thaddeus Taylor (1959, p. 371) provide an illustration from children's social behavior:

> On the whole, 34 percent of all responses produced by children towards adults were coded as hostile. One of the children, Frank, exhibited 60 hostile out of a total of 161 interactions with adults, an average of 37 percent hostile responses. However, in the arts and crafts setting, a teaching situation, only 9 percent of his behavior towards adults was hostile in orientation; this was in contrast with an average of 28 percent hostile responses by all children toward adults in arts and crafts. At meal time, the case was reversed. There, 48 percent of Frank's behavior towards adults was hostile in orientation in contrast to the lower group average of 29 percent.

Raush, Dittmann, and Taylor conclude that the effects of individual differences on social behavior are "considerably enhanced" when they are examined separately within each setting. Different settings affect different children in different ways. This clinical recognition of interaction effects anticipates the retreat from universal explanatory theory reflected in the work of Jones and Konner (1976) and Geertz (1973). That sense of withdrawal is found in Cronbach (1975), who argues that "generalizations decay," and in Campbell (1972), who claims that "for the social and psychological issues that concern the students of culture, higher-order interactions are the rule, and main effects, *ceteris paribus* generalizations, the rare exception. Complex interdependencies, highly contingent relationships and context dependencies characterize the relationships among the aspects of culture and personality" (p. xi). Nonetheless there are retreats and there are retreats.

Those seeking a universal explanatory theory that is both parsimonious and valid may soon arrive at an unexpected and disquieting fork in the road. One signpost reads: "Anything can be explained; little can be predicted." The other signpost reads: "Anything can be predicted; little can be explained." Neither choice is acceptable.

The first road has been well traveled by the proverbial peasant described by Geertz (1973) who shoots holes in fences and then paints bull's-eyes around them. Much that passes for social science is little more than the promiscuous generation of interpretations within the grammar of some unassailable world view (for example, Darwinian, Marxian, Freudian, behaviorist, structuralist) for events that have already happened. There is a certain satisfaction that comes from being able to explain *any* possible outcome, but it should be severely tempered by Hart's (1961) reminder. Our respect for a theory is related to its predictive success, not to its ability to translate any occurrence into its flexible idioms.

Down the second road, successful prediction becomes a nonexplanatory activity. One can predict anything, and *with enough prior information* about event likelihoods one can often do it reasonably well. All one needs to assume is that "behavior at [time] $t + 1$ will be [only] marginally different from behavior at the present time" (Allison 1969, p. 702). Not infrequently, the best prediction of behavior at $t + 1$ is simply t. For example, D'Andrade (1974, pp. 181–185) has shown that the best prediction one can make about what a group or individual is going to do is to guess that it will do what it has done most frequently in the past (see also Mischel 1968, p. 106). Of course to do this, one must already know all about how the group or individual about whom predictions are being made has previously behaved. $T + 1$ predictions are very costly; moreover, they typically fail to explain the phenomenon or render it theoretically intelligible. At the fork in the road, I would turn back. (For example, turn back to Chapter 2 of this volume.)

8.

Suffering in Style: On Arthur Kleinman

Arthur Kleinman's *Social Origins of Distress and Disease* (1986a) is the most important book to be written in medical anthropology in a long time. The work is stimulating, passionate, sophisticated, balanced, and theoretically up-to-date. It sets out an inspiring agenda for the anthropological study of suffering. It raises profound questions about psychic and physical pain, spiritual embodiment, and somatization and about the possibilities of cross-cultural understanding and translation of the subjective states of the "other." It entertains the view that forms of suffering vary across cultures and historical epochs. It advocates a holistic, dialectical, interactionist view of the interrelationships between mind, body, society, culture, and nature. It advances a sociopolitical causal ontology of loss, defeat, and social injustice for the explanation of suffering (angst and amines make room for oppression; ego isolation and neurotransmitters make room for adverse social conditions), inevitably leading the thoughtful reader to consider the range of causal ontologies or theodicies (biomedical, moral, sociopolitical, interpersonal, psychological) that might get invoked, and are invoked in different regions of the world, to define the circumstances of suffering. Elsewhere, Kleinman (1986b)

313

has called on anthropologists to develop a "forceful cultural critique and a more complex anthropological alternative to the current paradigm of social epidemiology (p. 508)." *Social Origins* presents just such a cultural critique and complex alternative.

One central theme in *Social Origins* is the evaluation of claims that neurasthenia and depression should be designated illness experiences, disease entities, or both. The exegesis is brilliant and complex, a stimulating fluctuating evaluation by a master of dialectics and interactionism, trying in the name of the virtues of holism to do the best that can be done with that now famous, ambiguous, polysemous, and shaggy distinction between illness and disease. In the following pages I hope to open a critical dialogue about the usefulness of the polysemous illness/disease distinction as an analytic tool in the cross-cultural study of suffering. I have some doubts.

First, however, I shall summarize the key research problem and findings of *Social Origins,* relying as little as possible on the global distinction between illness and disease, though along the way unpacking a few of its many parameters of meaning. This summary formulation should be read as an exercise in interpretation; it is my way of telling the story about the relationship of neurasthenia and depression as I see it revealed by Kleinman's agenda-setting research in China.

In Kleinman's version of the story, told in the language of illness and disease, neurasthenia, when viewed as an illness experience, is interpreted as somatized depression, and depression, viewed as a disease entity, is identified as its underlying disease. Depression, viewed as an illness experience, is interpreted as a less disguised or less transformed or perhaps more psychologized version of the same underlying disease, depression, again viewed as a disease entity (1986a, pp. 1, 66, 165). What precisely depression is *as a disease entity* (that is, as distinct from an illness experience) is intimated but not fully told, although it is linked, in the reconstruction of life histories and in theory, to demoralizing and psychically painful social conditions—job dissatisfaction, school failure, financial difficulties, and other defeats and losses on various micro sociopolitical fronts, associated, in this instance, with macro sociopolitical upheavals in China (for example, the Cultural Revolution).

Kleinman forthrightly invites a healthy skepticism from his readers and designs his book with sensitivity to the hazards of cross-cultural "translation," so as to stimulate and encourage debate about his theoretical models. Thus stimulated and encouraged, I am going to try to tell the story of *Social Origins* with a slightly different punch line.

In my telling of the story I am going to distinguish forms of suffering (for example, the experience of neurasthenia or depression) from the causal ontologies or theodicies that are invoked to explain them (for example, a biomedical ontology of organ pathology/physiological impairment/hormone imbalance, or a moral ontology of transgression/sin/karma, or a sociopolitical ontology of oppression/injustice/loss, or an interpersonal ontology of envy/hatred/sorcery, or a psychological ontology of anger/desire/intrapsychic conflict and defense).

Suffering, as I will use the term, signifies the experience of disvalued and unwanted subjective states (feelings, sensations, emotions, ideas); its meaning overlaps with aspects of the concept of illness as defined by Leon Eisenberg (1977) and Kleinman (1986a), namely, the experience "of disvalued changes in states of being and in social function" (Eisenberg 1977, p. 11), "the way individuals . . . perceive symptoms, categorize and label those symptoms, experience them, and articulate that illness experience through idioms of distress and pathways of help seeking" (Kleinman 1986a, p. 225). Suffering takes on *form* when it becomes organized and meaningful and is experienced and expressed as suffering of a certain kind, for example, as depression or as neurasthenia.

In contrast, a *causal ontology or theodicy,* as I will use the expression, signifies the events and processes going on in some other order of reality (biomedical, moral, sociopolitical, interpersonal, psychological) that are thought to generate or cause the experience of suffering. The notion of a causal ontology or theodicy converges in meaning with one *special* sense of the concept of disease as used by Kleinman (1986a, pp. 146–147), namely, the interpretation of a sufferer's problem as a specific abnormality in some nosological system, without prejudice as to the type of nosological system (biomedical, astrological, moral) used in the interpretation.

For reasons I shall enumerate later I prefer the distinction between "forms of suffering" and "the causal ontologies or theodicies invoked to explain them" to the distinction between "illness" and "disease" (which presupposes, and hence privileges, a biomedical view of the world and its biomedical discourse, in the very act of seeking a supplement to biomedicine and revaluing its residues). But first I want to summarize the key research problem and findings in *Social Origins,* using only the first set of terms.

The research problem can be stated as follows: There is a form of suffering called "depression," and there is a form of suffering called "neurasthenia." It appears that neurasthenia, but not depression, is a popular form of suffering in China, and that neurasthenia, but not depression, is a popular diagnosis of suffering by Chinese psychiatrists. It also appears that depression, but not neurasthenia, is a popular form of suffering in the United States and Europe, and that depression, but not neurasthenia, is a popular diagnosis of suffering by Western psychiatrists. Finally, it seems that a century ago neurasthenia was a popular form of suffering in the United States and Europe, but that recently it has gone out of style and is no longer even listed as a form of suffering in the American Psychiatric Association's standardized manual for diagnosis of psychopathology (DSM-III).

Kleinman goes to China in 1980. His field site is the psychiatric outpatient clinic at the Second Affiliated Hospital of the Hunan Medical College (formerly known as the Yale-in-China Medical College). He selects 100 patients diagnosed by Chinese psychiatrists as suffering from neurasthenia. After a clinical interview and assessment using the DSM-III manual (which, remember, has no diagnostic category for neurasthenia), he diagnoses most of them (87) as suffering from depression. Follow-up interviews are conducted with 76 of the patients and second follow-ups with 23. Three years later Joan and Arthur Kleinman collect detailed case histories from 21 of the original patients; 13 of those case studies are presented in the book. Although emotional and psychological disturbances are either not salient in the minds of these Chinese patients or are not discussed readily in their reporting of complaints (1986a, pp. 75, 81), careful scrutiny and sensitive questioning uncover the following kinds of subjective states in a prototypical case (for example, pp. 107, 109): headache, low self-esteem, fatigue, sadness, dizziness, feelings of hopelessness, insomnia, anxiety. The Chinese call that neurasthenia; the DSM-III and Kleinman call it depression.

The finding is suggestive. It raises the question, Could it be that, whatever the label and whoever the diagnostician, neurasthenia and depression are really the same form of suffering, in China and in the West, a century ago and today?

Social Origins establishes that the answer to that question ought to be no. Neurasthenia and depression are distinct forms of suffering whose popularity waxes and wanes across cultures and across history (even though, as Kleinman hypothesizes, they may have a common sociopolitical causal ontology—engendered by defeats and losses of one kind or another—and may be responsive to the ingestion of similar substances). The original finding, that patients in a Chinese psy-

chiatric clinic who are diagnosed by the Chinese as suffering neurasthenia would be diagnosed by Westerners using the DSM-III as
suffering depression, turns out to be a red herring, as we shall see.

Are neurasthenia and depression different labels for the same form
of suffering, or are they different forms of suffering? And how does
one go about answering such a question? There are a variety of parameters in terms of which one can assess the sameness or difference
of two forms of suffering. *Social Origins* is an outstanding book, in
part, because it explores or speculates about almost every one of
them.

One can ask, Are they the same or different with respect to their
significance, their denotation, their connotation, their practical consequences, their causal ontologies and their responsiveness to therapeutic interventions of various kinds? As I read and interpret *Social
Origins*, Kleinman's research establishes that neurasthenia and
depression are quite distinguishable and separate forms of suffering.

For one thing, neurasthenia and depression signify different things.
By *signification* I mean the ideas, notions, concepts, or properties implied by a term or expression. Neurasthenia signifies a form of suffering experienced as brain fatigue or frayed nerves or worn-out fibers
or depleted juices, the run-down feeling of overloaded and straining
central nervous system (CNS) circuitry or of sluggish blood, a form
of suffering experienced and expressed by the sufferer as an affliction
of the central biological operating systems of the body. Depression, in
contrast, signifies a form of suffering experienced as demoralization
and hopelessness, the resignation and loss of animus of a dispirited
ego, a form of suffering experienced and expressed by the sufferer as
an affliction of the central goal-striving systems of the soul or ego.

Second, neurasthenia and depression denote different things. By *denotation* I mean the events, states and objects selected out and
pointed to by virtue of what is signified by a term or expression. Neurasthenia denotes a set of subjective states, primarily headaches, dizziness, insomnia, tiredness, weakness, and muscle tension, interpreted
as intrinsic or inherent aspects of the experience of CNS fatigue, or
precious bodily fluid (blood or semen) depletion. Depression denotes
a set of subjective states, primarily sadness, hopelessness, self-depre-
cation, and anxiety, interpreted as direct expressions of the anguish
of a demoralized soul or ego.

Third, neurasthenia and depression have different connotations. By
connotation I mean the noncriterial attributes, extrinsic aspects, and
secondary associations that sometimes accompany a form of suffer-

ing, but are connected to it only as a derivative concomitant. For example, the concept "surgeon" does not signify "male," nor does it denote a set of objects that are male; the set of objects it denotes are picked out and selected for membership in the set without regard to their maleness. "Surgeon," however, does connote maleness at least to Americans, because in America most objects picked out for membership in the set of objects denoted by "surgeon" happen to be male. Yet from the point of view of the significance and denotation of the concept "surgeon," its association with maleness is incidental and extrinsic, a happenstance.

Neurasthenia and depression have different connotations. The connotation of neurasthenia is a set of extrinsic or incidental subjective states that may or may not accompany it, as secondary psychological derivatives. That connotative set includes feelings of sadness, hopelessness, anxiety, and resignation. They are the kind of feelings—psyche responding to soma—that some people experience after they become convinced that their central nervous system has become depleted of energy or that their blood is drying up. Depression also has its connotation, a set of subjective states that may or may not accompany it, yet are understandable as secondary "vegetative" derivatives: the loss of appetite that may accompany sadness, the fatigue that may accompany the loss of hope, the headaches that express a lowering in self-esteem—soma responding to psyche. In the former case we have a psychological derivative of neurasthenic suffering, in the latter case a somatized derivative of depressive suffering. Indeed, from the limited perspective of an elicited list of symptoms, the two forms of suffering (neurasthenia plus its psychological derivatives, depression plus its somatic derivatives) may be diagnostically difficult to tell apart.

As should now be apparent, neurasthenia and depression, as forms of suffering, bear the following fascinating relationship to each other: the denotation of the one is a connotation for the other. The denotation of neurasthenia (headaches, fatigue) is the connotation for depression; the denotation of depression (sadness, resignation) is the connotation for neurasthenia. Yet the two sets of denotata (or, alternatively put, the two sets of connotata) need not, and often do not, occur together in patients.

The finding from the psychiatric clinic at the Hunan Medical College was a red herring. It just so happened that in that patient population the two sets of denotata happened to co-occur. When that occurs a mere list of symptoms is ambiguous, and diagnosis with the DSM-III can be hazardous; for we may be led to misclassify neurasthenia as depression or, worse yet, to conclude that neurasthenia is depression.

Fortunately, as Kleinman discovered, the two sets of denotata do not always co-occur. There are large numbers of people around the world who suffer neurasthenia unambiguously and without the optional connotations that might be (mis)construed as the denotations of depression. In the Taiwanese primary care unit also investigated by Kleinman, 57 percent of patients suffering neurasthenia did not meet the DSM-III criteria for depression (1986a, pp. 102, 204). Kleinman's data here converge with evidence from an Indian psychiatric outpatient clinic (Jindal, Rastogi, and Rana 1978), where only twenty out of sixty-one patients suffering from neurasthenia displayed symptoms that might be (mis)construed as the denotata of depression.

Similarly, the dysphoric subjective states denotative of depression (sadness, hopelessness, low self-esteem, loss of interest in the world, anxiety) need not be associated with the subjective states denotative of CNS fatigue (headaches, dizziness, weakness). There are people who experience depression without those somatic derivatives that might be (mis)construed as the denotata of neurasthenia, although it does appear that many people who experience depression without somatic derivatives experience it in association with secondary psychological derivatives instead (for example, indecision, guilt, fantasies of death).

The rub is that in those cases in which both the denotative and the connotative features are present, a mere listing of symptoms will not help us to distinguish neurasthenic suffering from depressive suffering; and if we make a diagnosis using an inappropriate or wrong "theory" about what is denotative and what is connotative (that is, our prior notion of the significance of the suffering, or an institutionalized canon of significances such as the DSM-III) we may be led to misclassify neurasthenia as depression, or vice versa.

Fourth, neurasthenia and depression also have different pragmatic consequences. Because of the different things neurasthenia and depression signify and denote as forms of suffering, they are appraised differently in the context of Chinese and American social institutions and cultural values. In China depressed, demoralized, and hopeless souls are stigmatized with the label of political disengagement (1986a, p. 94). Depression is the wrong form of suffering for China, a genre too embarrassingly personal for public display (p. 154). It is more suitable for the values and tastes of the American white middle class, where, as Kleinman puts it so eloquently, it expresses "the heroic romance of the lonely individual testing his existential condition by being obdurately solitary, the equity of each independent person naked before his just god ... the narcissistic conception of man's ultimate, ego-centric rights, the bitter disillusionment with sentimentality at not 'making it' in the marketplace" (pp. 178–179). CNS fatigue, however, was the right form of suffering for China in 1980 and perhaps also in nineteenth-century Europe and the United States. Suggestive of having become physically run down or depleted by the pressures and hard works of life, it was an acceptable rationalization for failure and a locally rational and legitimate excuse for time off from work and for requesting a change in jobs.

Although neurasthenia and depression are distinct and separable as forms of suffering, Kleinman argues in *Social Origins* that they share a common sociopolitical causal ontology, engendered by defeat, loss, vexation, and oppression within local power hierarchies (pp. 79, 167–168, 174, 181).

Social Origins describes in sociopolitical terms the humiliations and frustrations (job loss, school failure, financial difficulties, family problems, marital struggles, and so on) of the neurasthenic, many of them victims of the Cultural Revolution and antiright campaigns in China. Deeply pathetic life experiences are narrated without pathos, yet with great sympathy and power.

> Some experienced such overwhelmingly destructive personal tragedies that they developed major personality changes: a few became so deeply embittered that every aspect of their lives radiated anger and hatred and alienation; others withdrew with fear and hurt into the inner privacy of the isolated self, diminishing performance to match greatly reduced expectations, to protect against further losses. Yet others organized their lives around their repeated and multiple losses as prolonged or even continuous grief reactions.   (1986a, pp. 170–171)

Kleinman hypothesizes a universal sociopolitical causal ontology as a worldwide explanation of neurasthenic and depressive suffering (1986a, pp. 79, 167–168). This is a bit surprising, for Kleinman is very sensitive to the dangers of overgeneralization from one or two culture areas and from a limited data base, and he is well aware that, when it comes to forms of suffering such as neurasthenia and depression, people's representations or descriptions of the nature of their suffering and its causes can be part of the suffering it describes. He quotes Nelson Goodman approvingly to the effect that reality is not independent of our version of it, and "there are many worlds if any" (pp. 143, 165).

So the postulation of a universal causal process is slightly bewildering and raises several questions. Why should sociopolitical forces and events cause neurasthenia and depression independently of our representation of those forces and events? Is it not our *representation* of sociopolitical forces and events that defines the terms of our involvement with and reactions to those forces and events? Perhaps what is meant by the claim of universal causation is that on a worldwide scale sociopolitical forces and adverse social conditions are represented in a similar way, that there is a universal pattern of construal leading to the experience of either CNS fatigue or demoralization. Yet why should representations of the *causal ontologies* for neurasthenia and depression be any more universal than are representations of the *experience* of neurasthenia and depression and of their significance, denotation, connotation, or practical consequences?

A cross-cultural survey of explanations for illness by George Peter Murdock (1980) suggests that preferred causal ontologies for suffering are unequally distributed around the world and cluster in geographic regions. A reasonable even if skeptical response to *Social Origins* is that the sociopolitical causal ontology (defeat, injustice, loss, and oppression) preferred by the Chinese (and by some other cultures) as an explanation for their suffering may play an important part in making them sick and in their meaningful reconstruction and representation of their life history, yet it remains to be seen whether it is a universal or even privileged cause of neurasthenia and depression.

After reading *Social Origins* and the sociopolitical causal discourse of Chinese patients I turned to my files of interviews, texts, and field records (including discourse during healing sessions) from research with traditional Hindus in Orissa, India. Using a computerized indexing system, I retrieved all materials in which mention was made of illness, sickness, or suffering. In that South Asian corpus sociopolitical causal explanations for suffering (references to oppression, injustice, adverse social circumstances or even references to stress, pressure, and strain) were rare, although loss (for example, the death of a child) was certainly mentioned as a proximate cause of suffering.

Several alternative causal ontologies were prevalent in the South Asian corpus. The most common was a moral causal ontology, notable for its references to transgression, sin, divine retribution, sacrifice, austerity, sanctity, and karma, associated with the notion that a loss of moral fiber is a prelude to disaster and physical suffering, which is its natural outcome and just desert. "What sinful work have I done that now I am suffering [without a child, with leprosy, as a widow]?" "What mistake have I made that the goddess is bothering me?" Life histories are sometimes narrated in those terms.

There was also an interpersonal causal ontology, notable for its references to sorcery, black magic, the evil eye, bewitchment, and spirit attack, and associated with the notion that we can be made sick by the envy and hatred and ill will of people who want us to die, suffer, or fail (on spirit attack as a cause of suffering see Nuckolls 1986).

There was a biomedical causal ontology, notable for its references to hot and cold foods, and associated with the notion of humors and substances that affect the brain and the notion of precious bodily fluids (blood and semen) that enhance physical well-being. Indeed, in the South Asian context one can imagine excessive masturbation as a plausible cause of neurasthenia and/or depression. The masturbator, conscious of his uncontrolled and "sinful" depletion of what he thinks of as an essential life force, feels weakened and guilty, and demoralized by his inability to exercise authority over his body (see Kelly 1987; also Kleinman 1986a, pp. 76–77).

There was also a psychological causal ontology, associated with the notion that unfulfilled desires (for example, never getting married and missing the experience of a family life) can make us sick. And an astrophysical causal ontology, notable for its references to horoscopes and malevolent planets and inauspicious periods. One case of suffering most relevant to neurasthenia and depression (the healer described the client's condition as sluggishness, biliousness, feelings of sorrow, fickle-mindedness, indecisiveness, forgetfulness, accompanied by chills and sleeplessness) was explained by reference to arrangements of the stars, which come and go.

One looks forward to much future research in medical anthropology addressed to the question of whether across the various cultures or cultural regions of the world, a sociopolitical causal ontology gives a better account of neurasthenia and/or depression, or provides a more powerful means for the meaningful reconstruction and representation of a life of suffering, than does any of those other causal ontologies. It seems not unreasonable to postulate that a people's causal ontology for suffering plays a part in causing the suffering it explains, just as a people's representation of a form of suffering may be part of the suffering it represents.

Those last remarks speak to an unresolved and perhaps unresolvable tension in *Social Origins*. Kleinman seeks a golden mean between a constructivist (or interpretivist) view of reali*ties*, understood in terms of what some philosophers would call "intentional" categories, and a transcendent conception of a "broader reality" that everyone ought to accept in the name of a universal science of so-called natural kinds (1986a, pp. 67, 143–144, 165). According to some philosophers, science seeks to discover natural kinds, which are classes of events that exhibit a causation independent of what they mean to us, independent of our involvement with them, independent of our experience of them or evaluation of them, independent of our aesthetic or emotional response to them. Constructivists (or interpretivists) in contrast, seek to discover intentional categories, which are classes of events that exhibit whatever causation they may have by virtue of what they mean to us, by virtue of our conceptions and representations of them and reactions to them. Black holes and hydrogen are natural kinds. Windsor chairs and punk hairdos are intentional categories.

There is a complex tension in *Social Origins* between constructivism and science, between intentional categories and natural kinds. At times Kleinman speaks approvingly of the constructivist position of Nelson Goodman that "there are many right world-versions, some of them irreconcilable with others," world-versions, whose multiplicity cannot be reduced by empirical evidence (1986a, pp. 143, 165). At other times he speaks of those same purportedly irreconcilable world-versions as the "iron cage of incomparable localism," suggesting that they are really merely alternative idiomatic versions of some broader reality that a universal science should be able ultimately to describe (pp. 67, 144, 165).

Kleinman's holistic, dialectical interactionism leads him to look in both directions and to try to have it both ways. He proposes to reduce the tension between the idea of irreconcilable culture-specific world-versions and the idea of a broader or universal natural world by interpreting forms of suffering such as neurasthenia and depression in a constructivist discourse of intentional kinds (what he calls "illness experiences," which are responsive to social evaluation, and hence may be culture specific) while interpreting their causation in a scientific discourse of natural kinds (what he calls universal "diseases"). It remains to be seen whether this is a golden mean (a creative tension) between constructivism and science or whether, as some critics will be bound to suggest, it is the famous middle path between right and wrong.

As I interpret it, it is the resounding, and utterly persuasive, constructivist message of *Social Origins* that somewhere in between a literal lesion and a literary trope there is a lot of room for a broken heart. What that means is that frayed nerves, tired blood, splitting heads, and broken hearts can be thought of as the metonymies of suffering; they give poetic expression by means of body-part metaphors to forms of embodied suffering experienced through the body parts used to express them (see Haviland n.d.). (That poetic suffering is sometimes redescribed in the discourse of biomedicine as "somatization".)

Of course, splitting heads do not split, broken hearts do not break, tired blood continues to circulate at the same rate, and frayed nerves show no structural pathology. Yet metonymies using body parts to express suffering are a good example of the kind of "symbolic reticulum" (a favored expression in the book) that Kleinman investigates and promotes. That symbolic reticulum provides a bridge across the gap between the unseen and unseeable subjective world of our feelings, sensations, emotions, and thoughts (our states of mind) and the seeable, directly manipulable world of concrete objects, in this case the inanimate juices, fibers, and organs of our body made soulful through suffering as well as mindful of a fall from grace. (See Chapter 9 of this volume.) That symbolic reticulum stretches across a vast sea of suffering, sometimes described by biomedical healers, for lack of an adequate comprehension, as a "functional" disorder of the relevant body part, with no apparent organic pathology, no apparent structural deficits and no apparent physiological impairment outside the normal range.

We might describe that sea of suffering as "illness without disease" (Eisenberg 1977), an oxymoron if formulated within the reductionist monistic discourse of biomedicine. The head is splitting, but the CAT scan is normal and there is no brain tumor. The chest is caving in, but the treadmill test looks fine. Must something be biomedically wrong? Or do we just throw up our hands and say "Tension headache; next patient please"?

The suffering of the (apparently) biomedically fit is our contemporary version of the classic problem of Job—the suffering of the (apparently) righteous. Such suffering—of the righteous or the biomedically fit—is an insult to our ontological sensibilities and raises deep questions about the types of causal forces that might be out there causing it.

The classical problem of Job can be resolved by postulating that

Job must have sinned (if not in this life then in a previous one) and that the suffering of the righteous is merely apparent. Similarly, the contemporary problem of Job can be resolved by sticking to a single causal ontology, postulating that all suffering is biochemical and that if we suffer we must not be biomedically fit; we must simply have not yet discovered the problem.

Social Origins demurs from any such single-minded reductionist monism and from those types of dualism that permit no interaction between mind and body. The book elaborates an interactionist position, arguing that there is a great deal more to the causation of physical and psychic suffering than biomedicine can comprehend, and much "transduction" from adverse social conditions into psychic pain and from psychic pain into the experience of physical suffering.

Kleinman actually denounces dualism in general (1986a, pp. 39, 162–163) and calls it "scientifically untenable" (p. 39). As I read his objections, however, they are really aimed at a much narrower and extreme view, a view certainly not held by Descartes, who is sometimes parodied in these terms, that mind and body are separate, unconnected, autonomous domains, each acting totally independently from the other. Dualism is not reducible to that view, and Kleinman's interactionism, as far as I can judge, is a type of dualism. Karl Popper, a dualist and an interactionist, thinks interactionism is the philosophy of mind and nature promoted by common sense; it distinguishes the mental from the physical yet acknowledges that, for example, intending or willing to do something can cause a physical movement, and that a physical cut can cause the subjective experience of pain.

As I understand it the issue at stake in the mind/body controversy is not whether commonsensical folk report that such things happen. The issue is whether such things happen in the way they are represented by common sense or by some scientific observers—thoughts and things represented as distinguishable ontological realms influencing one another. The problem is to make theoretically credible such a possibility (how precisely, and by what means, does "transduction" take place between thoughts and things?) or, alternatively, to explain the possibility away—by representing thoughts as things (monistic materialism) or things as thoughts (monistic idealism), without replacing one perplexing problem with another. It is not at all clear to me how science can resolve the differences between monists and dualists, since the differences in all cases are metaphysical differences over how to represent the facts. In another context Kleinman (1986a) formulates a brilliant statement to the effect that the "conceptual framework" within which research is organized is beyond assessment by scientific findings (p. 165). I do not see why conceptual frameworks for talking about mind and body should be exceptions to that formulation.

Finally, it is noted in *Social Origins* that neurasthenia and depression are responsive to the same class of ingested substances (1986a, pp. 91–92, 164–165). Kleinman mentions some of the difficulties involved in interpreting that point of similarity between neurasthenia and depression. American psychiatrists interpret the ingested substances as antidepressant drugs. A few Chinese psychiatrists interpret the ingested substances as antineurasthenic drugs. Yet both interpretations are gratuitous, for the causal ontology is poorly understood that links the ingested substances to symptom relief.[1]

I suppose we could go further, arguing that symptom relief via ingested substances per se does not even establish the type of causal ontology (biomedical, moral, interpersonal) relevant for explaining the suffering. Certainly in many parts of the world where spirit attack is a preferred explanation for suffering there is an expectation that possessing spirits do not like substances of certain kinds (for example, mustard seeds), which are therefore ingested therapeutically to drive the spirit out. It is also conceivable that today's efficacious ingested substance might turn out to be a kind of broad-spectrum anesthesia (or "opium of the people") for psychic, spiritual, and physical pain, and thus neutral as to causal ontology.

So far in this interpretative summary I have relied as little as possible on the notions of illness and disease. Without those notions the story told in *Social Origins* is stimulating, powerful, and easy to comprehend, and it goes like this: neurasthenia and depression are distinct forms of suffering (the first popular in China, the second in contemporary Europe and the United States), both precipitated by the same cause—adverse social conditions, oppression, defeat, loss, and humiliation. The differential popularity in China and the contemporary West of the two forms of suffering is understandable in the light of various cultural and institutional differences between the two societies, and here they are . . .

Yet Kleinman wants to say more (1986a, pp. 1, 66, 165). He wants to say that depression is not only a form of suffering (an illness experience) but also a universal disease. And he wants to say that neurasthenia (as an illness experience) is really a somatized variety of depression, the underlying disease. It is right there in the argument, with the designation of depression as a disease (apart from an illness experience) and neurasthenia as somatized depression, that I get confused and a bit nervous. And what I think makes me confused and nervous is that shaggy distinction between illness and disease.

Eisenberg (1977) describes the distinction between illness and disease in an essay that is marvelous and uplifting in every respect except its specifications for the distinction between illness and disease. Let us consider and worry a bit about some of its multifarious and shifting meanings.

An initial specification is that "patients suffer 'illnesses'; physicians diagnose and treat 'diseases'" (p. 11). This implies one or the other or both of two things: (1) the difference between illness and disease is a difference in perspective (patient versus physician; also described as lay versus professional); (2) the difference between illness and disease is a difference in mode of activity (suffering versus diagnosis and treatment). It is unclear from the specification, however, what to say of a sufferer who diagnoses and treats himself. Has he diagnosed and treated an illness or a disease? Does the answer depend on whether the sufferer diagnosing and treating himself is lay or professional?

To complicate things further there is much uncertainty about what the difference in perspective (patient versus physician, or lay versus professional) is supposed to amount to. Is it the difference between a novice perspective versus expert perspective? a local folk perspective (perhaps by an expert) versus a universal scientific perspective (perhaps by a novice)? a nonbiomedical perspective versus a biomedical perspective? an incorrect biomedical perspective versus a correct biomedical perspective? a perspective that views any system in its interactions with other systems versus a perspective that analyzes each separated system in its own terms? a perspective inclusive of the generalized concerns of a sufferer versus a perspective narrowly focused on the causal and treatment concerns of the diagnostician? Does it matter whether the diagnostician adopts the causal ontology of contemporary biomedicine? What if the diagnosis is "semen loss" or "spirit possession" or "divine retribution" or "demoralizing social conditions"? Are those diseases, according to the definition?

Eisenberg (1977) elaborates the definition as follows: "*illnesses* are experiences of disvalued changes in states of being and in social function; *diseases,* in the scientific paradigm of modern medicine, are abnormalities in the structure and function of body organs and systems" (p. 9). What is left pregnantly ambiguous here is whether the disease concept is to be defined by the biomedical causal ontology of modern medicine, or whether the biomedical causal ontology of modern medicine is merely being used as an optional illustration of the disease concept. Could the definition just as well have read: Diseases, in the scientific paradigm of modern Ayurvedic medicine, are somatic imbalances of the ratios of wind, water, fire, earth, and ether? or perhaps, Diseases, in the scientific paradigm of modern astrology, are malevolent configurations of planets, stars and moons? Or are those not disease categories because they do not correspond to the causal categories of modern Western medicine? Or are they to be treated as disease categories, but as false or fictive ones?

The illness/disease distinction, because it is pregnant with meaning, has undoubtedly served an important purpose in alerting biomedical professionals that there is a great deal more to suffering than biomedicine can comprehend and in defining a broad and promising research agenda for medical anthropology and for a social and holistic medicine (for spectacular statements in that regard see Eisenberg 1977; Kleinman 1986c). Yet it is precisely because the illness/disease distinction is so pregnant with meaning that I have some doubts about its analytic usefulness. Its interacting meanings are too volatile to control and just fickle enough to be exasperating.

This is how Kleinman's subtle and stimulating analysis of the cultural construction of suffering gets told in the ambiguous and polysemous (and exasperating) language of illness and disease. In some contexts (1986a, pp. 66, 165), neurasthenia is judged to be an illness experience but not a disease (depression is judged to be the underlying disease process), and depression is judged to be both an illness experience and a disease process. In such contexts, when neurasthenia is judged to be an illness experience but not a real disease we are encouraged to view it (from the perspective of universal science) as somatized depression.

Here I get a little confused. If a disease process is different from an illness experience *and* if depression is a disease process (as well as an illness experience), then what precisely is that depressive disease process that is other than an illness experience, and how do we know that neurasthenia is a somatized version of it? Is the depressive disease process that is said to underlie the illness experience of both neurasthenia and depression a sociopolitical disease process; that is, is the "disease" the demoralizing social circumstances that are a major focus of the book? That is, is the concept of disease being used here in a nonbiomedical sense? Or is the underlying depressive disease a biomedical disease process (1986a, pp. 1, 58, 66)?

Depressive disease is described at least twice in *Social Origins* as a "psychobiological template" for a "universal core depressive disorder" (1986a, p. 66) and as "characterized by psychobiological dysfunctions which appear to be universal" (p. 1); and, at least once, that psychobiological template is described as "the outcome of the interaction between personal vulnerability (psychological-physiological state), major stressful life events, coping processes and the social support . . . [within local contexts of power] that influence how risk, stress, and resources are configured and systematically interrelate" (p. 168). Yet those expressions and formulations are not really helpful in comprehending depression as a disease (versus illness experience); for the idea of a psychobiological dysfunction seems designed to be ambiguous with respect to the concept of illness and the concept of disease, and we are left wondering just what it is that is disordered and is psychobiological and is other than neurasthenia or depression as illness experiences, which, as illness experiences, are two culture-specific forms of suffering.

One possible interpretation of the argument, staying within the language of illness and disease, is that adverse sociopolitical circumstances cause "psychic pain," which is experienced and expressed either in the (disguised) idiom of physical pain (neurasthenic illness) or in the (direct?) idiom of psychic pain (depressive illness).

By that interpretation depressive disease denotes a hypothesized moderator variable called "psychic pain." That hypothesized moderator variable makes it possible for an outside comparative analyst to think of neurasthenia and depression (the illness experiences) as alternative and distinct ways of experiencing the same thing, the hypothesized psychic pain.

Yet if we follow that line of reasoning we end up with a rather Platonic moderator variable, and it is a rather psychological Platonic variable at that: an abstract pain that exists prior to or independently of its qualitative experience as either neurasthenia or depression, yet is the common cause of both. Still, whatever one thinks of Platonic moderator variables, why should we call psychic pain a disease rather than an illness? Is any type of imagined or constructed cause to be referred to as a disease? Shouldn't the discourse of biomedicine be kept where it belongs and works so well—with infections, organ pathologies, physiological impairments, and so on?

Yet still another difficulty remains, if we keep talking in the language of illness and disease. If both the neurasthenia and depressive illness experiences are to be explained by means of the same underlying disease process, why should the depressive illness experience be treated as the more fundamental or privileged? Why should the neurasthenic illness experience be interpreted as somatized depression, treating depression as the disease underlying both illnesses? Why not interpret the experience of depressive illness as emotionalized neurasthenia, treating neurasthenia as the disease underlying both illnesses?

Even more deeply, why should the language for *any* illness experience (a form of suffering) be used to describe an "underlying" disease process or entity? Whether one defines *disease* narrowly, from the perspective of contemporary Western biomedicine, or broadly, as the nosological categories of any kind of healer, diseases are by definition (or is it by mythopoeic conception?) postulated events taking place in a separate order of reality (biomedical, moral, sociopolitical, psychological) of a different logical type from the illness experience they are meant to explain. If there are diseases (whether biomedical, moral, sociopolitical, or what have you) that explain the experience of neurasthenic or depressive suffering, why shouldn't they be described in the "natural kind" language of disease instead of in the "intentional" language of illness?

In other contexts (for example, 1986a, pp. 94–95, 165–166) Kleinman judges neurasthenia to be an illness experience *and* a disease process, though not for the same reasons that he judges depression to be an illness experience and a disease process. In most of those contexts, neurasthenia is judged a disease because the Chinese (and the World Health Organization) have a biomedical causal ontology for explaining the neurasthenic illness experience (1986a, pp. 152, 160, 166). Whether their biomedical explanation is correct or not is treated as beside the point; it is argued that neurasthenia should be retained as a disease category even if Chinese professionals are wrong and it has no biomedical foundation.

Depression, in contrast, is judged a disease not only because American psychiatry has postulated a biomedical causal ontology for explaining the depressive illness experience or because Kleinman believes there is a sociopolitical causal ontology (mediated by abstract psychic pain) for explaining it. In judging depression (but not neurasthenia) a disease, Kleinman speaks from the perspective of the detached scientist, and it becomes relevant in evaluating the disease designation to decide whether depression really is a disease truly accountable by means of the proposed causal ontologies.

Kleinman, who is a veritable master of the illness/disease distinction, is well aware of all these difficulties. He makes explicit mention of many of them, generating many questions, promising few definitive answers, inviting a healthy skepticism from his readers; and none of my stated concerns about the analytic cumbersomeness of the distinction and its elusive shifts in aspect and perspective detracts from the stimulation and sheer intellectual pleasure that results from trying to stay with him through his virtuoso exercise. It is hardly his fault that the biomedical discourse of our culture (for example, the disease concept) is so ill suited for representing and comprehending some major forms of suffering.

Kleinman, on the other hand, comprehends those forms of suffering very well, and his arguments seem most convincing when they are disencumbered of the biomedical rhetoric of illness and disease. Neurasthenia and depression are distinct forms of suffering, which, as intentional categories, can be compared with each other because the denotation of the one is the connotation of the other, and vice versa. They go in and out of style in different cultures and at different times for reasons that cultural anthropology is well suited to illuminate. Perhaps they have a common cause in adverse sociopolitical circumstances, a hypothesis that social medicine is well suited to investigate on a worldwide scale. As far as I can judge, except for requirements internal to the biomedical language of illness and disease, there is no necessity for Kleinman to construct neurasthenia as somatized depression or for *Social Origins* to speak about social causation in the rhetoric of disease.

The publication of *Social Origins* is a major event. If we keep faith with the spirit of the book it will alert us to the way psychiatric disease concepts are used to constitute the reality they describe, and it will occasion a deep reconsideration of the telos in our contemporary culture of a medical anthropology and social psychiatry. In this review essay I have tried, in my own way, to honor *Social Origins* (and its esteemed author) with a critical interpretative reading of some of the book's central arguments. It is precisely because those arguments are so profound and important that they deserve close and critical engagement. *Crescat scientia, vita excolatur:* Let knowledge grow, so life may be enriched.

9.

How to Look at Medusa without Turning to Stone: On Gananath Obeyesekere

And they are three, the Gorgons, each with wings
And snaky hair, most horrible to mortals.
Whom no man shall behold and draw again
The breath of life . . .
—*A narration concerning Perseus and Medusa in*
Edith Hamilton's Mythology *(1942, p. 143)*

According to modern legend, heroes and other men and women of vision do not turn away from what there is to see, and they take their risks. Unlike Perseus, Gananath Obeyesekere dared to look upon the snakelike hair and hideous face of his Medusa, a female fire walker and ecstatic at Kataragama on the island of Sri Lanka, and, as he reports in *Medusa's Hair* (1981, p. 7), he became very anxious. If feeling anxious is one way of feeling petrified, we might say that Medusa turned Obeyesekere into stone.

At Kataragama Obeyesekere experienced petrification through looking. His goal in *Medusa's Hair* is to examine the meaning of the matted hair that embellishes the head of female ecstatics at that pilgrimage site, so that we might look without turning to stone. Honoring Obeyesekere, this meditation and commentary upon *Medusa's Hair* is intended as a fragment of a version of a continuing modern legend about unpetrified viewing.

The Meditation

Obeyesekere's book carries on a tradition in which anthropologists have perplexed one another about the meaning of head hair. What

332

anthropologists mean when they talk about the meaning of head hair is not merely a list of features distinctive or characteristic of head hair (slender threadlike outgrowth located on top of the head, composed of elongated epidermal cells, cuttable without pain, and so on), but the use of head hair to express a state of mind, a belief or desire, an idea or emotion, a subjective state; and what they like to perplex each other about are the answers to three interrelated questions:

1. What are the various kinds of things that are done to head hair (cut short, grown long, tied up, let down, and so on) by various kinds of people (relevant statuses to be defined) on various kinds of occasions (relevant occasions to be defined)?
2. What state of mind (belief, desire, idea, emotion, subjective state) is expressed or made manifest by this or that manipulation of head hair by this or that person on this or that occasion?
3. Are there theories about how the world works, how society works, how the mind works, or what hair is like that help us understand what state of mind is being expressed by what people do to their hair on particular occasions, and why they bother to do it?

The last question has several subparts, which, for sake of clarity, should be examined separately:

a. Why is head hair per se (and the particular thing done to it—shaving it off; tearing it out) used to express some particular state of mind (for example, grief)?
b. How are we to understand why some particular state of mind (for example, grief) is the state of mind expressed on some particular occasion (for example, funerals)?
c. What is the relationship between the state of mind expressed (for example, grief) and the actual state of mind (that is, the subjective experience) of the person doing the expressing?
d. What are the interpersonal consequences of using one's hair to express some particular state of mind on some particular occasion?
e. What are the intrapsychic consequences of using your hair to express some particular state of mind on some particular occasion?

A doctrine called conventionalism can serve as a useful straw person in discussions about the meaning of hair. The doctrine of conventionalism holds that the link between an expressive symbol and the state of mind it expresses on a particular occasion is sufficiently explained by reference to the existence of a social agreement to express that particular state of mind, in that particular way, on that particular occasion. The doctrine expounds a "principle of arbitrariness," which asserts that, from the point of view of designing an expressive code, any expressive symbol could, in principle, serve just as well as any other expressive symbol to express any state of mind, on any occasion. The principle implies that, for any society, the use of certain expressive symbols, and not others, to express certain states of mind, and not others, is solely the product of a historically formed consensus to use symbols that way, a consensus now conventionalized into customary usage. The doctrine of conventionalism denies that there is any theory about how people work or what hair is like that can help us understand what state of mind (for example, grief) is being expressed by what people do to their hair (for example, shave it off, tear it out) on particular occasions (for example, a funeral).

An advocate of a full-blown doctrine of conventionalism would answer the five subquestions as follows:

1. Only social consensus can explain why it is hair rather than any other vehicle of meaning that plays a part in expressing grief.
2. Only social consensus can explain why it is grief rather than any other state of mind that is expressed at funerals.
3. No relation can be assumed to exist between the state of mind expressed with one's hair and the actual state of mind of the person doing the expressing, for social consensus requires of its actors only the occasion-appropriate expression of an agreed-upon state of mind (for example, show grief at funerals), and not the subjective experience of it.
4. The expression (or nonexpression) of a state of mind has significant interpersonal consequences, which is the only reason for expressing a state of mind.
5. The expression of a state of mind has negligible intrapsychic consequences, for actors cannot be assumed actually to experience the state of mind they express, and their actual state of mind may well be different from the state of mind that is expressed.

No one, as far as I know, is an advocate of a full-blown doctrine of conventionalism for the analysis of the meaning of head hair; not even Sir Edmund Leach (1958), who flirted with the doctrine yet sharply pulled back from it. Leach flirted with conventionalism by insisting that the state of mind expressed through hair on a ritual occasion neither reflects nor creates a parallel state of mind in the subjective experience of the person doing the expressing. In his view, the expression of a state of mind at funerals was sufficiently explained by reference to its interpersonal consequences. For example, he recounted that at Trobriand mourning ceremonies "all those suspected of hostile intentions against the deceased are required to make a symbolic gesture [shaving the head hair] which says 'I loved the deceased'" (p. 152, quoting Malinowski).

Yet Leach also developed a theory about how the mind works, and what hair is like, that might explain the shaving off or removal of head hair on certain ritual occasions. Commenting on a book by Charles Berg (1951), Leach (1958, p. 154) posited a panhuman folk psychobiology in which, consciously or unconsciously, the human head is likened to a penis, head hair is likened to semen, long hair is expressive of sexuality unharnessed, short or tightly bound hair is expressive of sexual restraint, and the shaving or removal of head hair on ritual occasions (prototypically, during death rituals) makes manifest the idea of celibacy or castration.

It was a tidy theory, but then along came C. R. Hallpike (1969), who spoiled all the fun. He pointed out that the castration hypothesis had difficulty with certain embarrassing facts: in some cultures not just men but also women shave their head during funeral rites; other body mutilations besides haircutting occur in the context of mourning; beards and other facial hair are more suggestive of genitals than is head hair, yet they are not as likely to be shaved during funeral rites; and, in some parts of the world, it is celibate ascetics who adorn themselves with long hair. Hallpike posited an alternative panhuman folk psychobiology in which the self or the soul is thought to be located in the head, and head hair, closely associated with the head and lending itself to painless manipulation, stands in as a representation of the whole person and can be used to express a state of mind. He went on to argue that hairiness is a prominent feature of animals. Animals lived in a wild state outside society, which explains why long hair is found on intellectuals, hippies, and others who live in a state of mind outside, or in rebellion against, a controlling social regime; and which explains why short hair and a shaved head (for example, a military cut) can be used to express the idea of living within society in subordination to a disciplinary regime.

Before long Paul Hershman (1974) came up with a challenging case for both Leach and Hallpike: in Punjabi mourning rituals, the men shave their heads yet the women let their hair down and leave it disheveled for several days. To Hershman it seemed implausible to argue that the women were in a heightened state of sexuality while the men were sexually impotent. It seemed equally implausible to argue that the women entered a position outside society while the men did not.

The story about the meaning of hair is further enriched by evidence on death practices from other parts of India and by local native interpretations of those practices. During Oriya Brahman death rituals, for example, the script for events is ideally played out as follows: on the tenth day after a death, the family barber shaves or trims the head hair and beard of male family members; the barber's wife cuts the nails of female relatives. While cutting the hair, the barber wears a special cloth or napkin to avoid pollution, and when the haircutting and nail-cutting are over, everyone, including the barber, takes a ceremonial bath. The barber also washes his instruments, and women wash their hair. All this occurs at the end of a period of mandated fasting, dietary restrictions, sexual abstinence, and withdrawal from routine business affairs.

Now it is certainly possible to liken fingers and toes to a phallic head, to liken nails to head hair, and to view nail-cutting as the female's equivalent of castration. It may even be possible to view the hair shaving and nail-cutting (and the fasting and the abstinence) as subordination to the authority or regime of the deceased, or to view symbolic castration as merely a body-part metaphor for expressing the idea of powerlessness under someone else's rule. Nevertheless, some of my Oriya Brahman friends have their own doctrinal account of what it all means.

They think there is a lot of pollution caused when someone dies, which potentially jeopardizes the successful transmigration of the soul of the deceased. To protect that transmigrating soul from pollution they undertake a project to turn their own bodies into what might be referred to as toxic-waste sites. First cleansing their bodies through fasting and sexual abstinence, they absorb into themselves the pollution of the corpse, thereby facilitating the purification, distillation, and migration of the soul of the dead. During that process of turning oneself into a toxic-waste site, pollution absorbed into the body is thought to concentrate in the extremities: fingers, toes, and head; and head hair is viewed as an especially effective net for catching the pollution of the corpse. Shaving the hair and cutting the nails on the tenth day are like emptying out the vacuum cleaner. That, along with a bath and a new set of clothes, restores people to the workaday world, after completing their moral obligation to assist the soul of their relative as it separates from its corpse.

That nails and head hair should receive special attention in the process of pollution management is not difficult to understand. The area under the nails is a site where dirt concentrates and collects, a concrete analogue to pollution. And many things, from dirt to aromas to lice, get in one's hair, and stay there, until they are washed out. If smoke and smells in a room are going to get into hair, then certainly the pollution will too.

The doctrine of head hair as a toxic-waste site has broad application. Menstruating women are not allowed to brush their hair, for they will stroke their pollution into the environment; and if hair is combed on the day of ancestor worship (*sraddha*), the ancestral spirits will not enter the house to be fed.

Yet native testimony supports other meanings as well, meanings suggestive of potency and power, subordination and castration, respect and rebellion; and all the meanings have a tendency to spill over into one another.

> When the Baba came to Bhubaneswar, he stayed, at first, at the Dharmasala. He warned everyone not to open the door to his room. There was a man named Malia, who attended to the Baba and carried his stick. Not heeding the warning, Malia looked into the Baba's room. The power of God was standing there in the room. The Baba was doing meditation, while standing and chanting. His matted hair was spreading on the floor like snakes. Malia screamed, closed the door and ran up the stairs. Immediately he started vomiting and defecating. He became sick. His eyelids closed. It seemed as if he was on the brink of death. (A narration concerning Malia and the Baba, told in 1984 by a male Brahman resident of Bhubaneswar, India)

Energized during meditation and spreading like snakes to the floor, his hair, a magnet for the collection and concentration of divine power, was an awesome sight, causing mortification to those who dared to look. Apparently head hair is an all-purpose containment site, which can be used to store up either pollution or divinity, or perhaps even personal vitality.

In the Oriya mind snakes and matted hair are associated with the power and vitality of Maheswar (Siva), who not only is depicted and pictured as having long matted hair but who also stores up semen in his body and wears a snake around his neck, all the while as the snake raises its hood above Siva's head. (See the depiction of Siva on page 21.)

Yet witches also have hair extending to the ground, and it is told that when a witch is caught, instead of killing her one cuts off her hair.

I once witnessed in Orissa a "paranoid" episode and the articulation of a "delusion of grandeur," in which a man I knew who worked as a driver verbalised in great agitation to me and others his terror of the police, and claimed to have once been the powerful and prominent inspector general of police of Cuttack. "That was before they cut off my hair," he said.

One informant described the cutting of head hair during death rites as a form of penance, a self-mortification designed to pay homage to the deceased and to express grief: "You cut off your hair because you can't afford to cut off your head."

Shaving one's hair is sometimes associated with lowering one's head, as a sign of respect to parents, elders, and gods. F. M. Senapati, the brilliant Oriya writer, has a delightful story to tell about hair and obeisance. Reminiscing about his childhood, he remembers that elders never accepted water from any children unless they tied their long hair up in a knot. Under the influence of foreigners and an English education, Oriya schoolchildren cut off their long hair as a gesture of rebellion against their orthodox parents, and perhaps in anticipation of the "punk" hair styles of the 1980s.

When it comes to the meaning of head hair and other expressions by the body, everyone rejects the full-blown doctrine of conventionalism, although perhaps no one rejects fully all parts of the doctrine. The most vulnerable parts of the doctrine are the answers to questions a and b above. Social agreement and a historically contingent consensus are insufficient to explain the use of certain parts and exuviae of the human body, and not others, to express certain states of mind, and not others.

An obvious example of that insufficiency is the case of crying at funerals and at other mourning ceremonies. Putting aside the question (c above) of whether this or that individual, or any individual, is actually in a grief-stricken state of mind, it is a fact that in almost every society "shedding tears" is a featured mode of emotional display and expression at funerals (Rosenblatt, Walsh, and Jackson 1976); and that fact beckons to be explained. Whatever it is that links the expressive symbol (shedding tears), the expressed state of mind (sorrow), and the occasion (funerals) goes far beyond historical coincidence or social agreement.

Understood as expressive symbols, the body and its parts and exuviae are not like the phonetics of a language. Unlike the characteristically arbitrary relationship between a sound pattern and the meaning it conveys (let's put poetry to the side), it is more than mere convention that links a body part to the state of mind it expresses. John Haviland (n.d.), for example, has surveyed the way body-part metaphors (hard-nosed, weak-kneed, foot-loose) are used to refer to states of mind in thirty languages, from diverse language families. He discovers many referential regularities across languages: for example, the skin is used to refer to irritability, the knees to servility, the hands to control. Head hair is widely used to express fear. "It was a hair-raising experience," "His hair stood on end," and so on. Fingernails and toenails do not appear in his data.

The existence of a core of referential universals for body-part metaphors seems to require some qualifications of the principle of arbitrariness as a general doctrine. An expression such as "hard-hearted" or "tight-fisted" or "weak-kneed" is not an opaque idiom. Haviland discovers, for example, that the chest and upper interior organs (for example, the heart) are appropriated universally as symbols of emotionality and feeling. A friend of mind once described his ulcer as caused by flakes from his granite heart. Body metaphors such as "granite heart" have, as Haviland notes, a "clear and obvious" reference to a particular state of mind; and those expressions that are not entirely clear (for example, in the Australian aboriginal language of Guugu Yimidhirr a greedy person is referred to as a "hand penis") seem to light up some aspect of experience (a greedy person does with his hand what some people would like to do with their penis), once they are explained.

Instead of being arbitrary, there seems to be a moderate degree of motivation to the way body parts and words for body parts get used to give expression to states of mind. One interpretation of Haviland's findings is that certain aspects of physiological, motoric, and interpersonal functioning—grasping, buckling at the knees, body hair standing on edge—provide a minimal universal ground for a folk psychology of body meanings.

The Commentary

When it comes to understanding the meaning of the matted hair of his female ecstatics Obeyesekere rejects most parts of the doctrine of conventionalism, including those retained by Leach; although, as we shall see, what he retains (the idea of local rationality) has the potential to renovate the doctrine in significant ways.

For one thing, he believes that the linkage between matted hair and the state of mind it expresses is not arbitrary; each lock is snakelike, and each snakelike lock, a displaced representation of a penis emerging from the head, is, according to Obeyesekere, a vehicle of meaning well suited to the message it conveys (1981, p. 34). Second he believes that the matted hair adorning the head of his female ecstatics makes manifest a state of mind (I am connected to God's power, possessed by his *śakti,* female energy source) that is actually experienced by those doing the expressing (pp. 34, 44–46).

Obeyesekere not only looks at Medusa; he talks to her, about her family life and her life history. From that interview material he makes his case for the special suitability of matted hair as a symbol of god's power, and he traces the interconnections between the state of mind expressed by Medusa's hair and the state of mind experienced by Medusa. He shows, for example, that for Medusa to make manifest through her hair a connection to god's power is personally to assert a denial of castration (that is, a denial of powerlessness) (1981, pp. 33, 36, 38), and that the snakelike matted hair on the head of a female ecstatic communicates to its wearer, can be used by its wearer to communicate to others, a conviction not to yield to the demands (for example, sexual demands) of local authorities (for example, a husband) (p. 64).

Finally, Obeyesekere suggests that to express through body symbolism a state of mind has significant intrapsychic consequences (for example, eliminating unconscious feelings of guilt), as well as interpersonal ones (1981, pp. 45, 77, 91). The body not only expresses a state of mind, the expression of which has public effects; the body doing the expressing is also experienced personally as a state of mind by the person whose body it is.

It is not Obeyesekere's substantive interpretation of the meaning of matted hair that makes *Medusa's Hair* an important book. What makes it an important book is that Obeyesekere defies conventional wisdom, which is the wisdom of conventionalism (1981, pp. 14–15, 102). He tries to integrate an understanding of how states of mind are expressed by means of the body, with an understanding of how expressions by the body are actually experienced (by the body) as a state of mind. He defines a class of expressive performances for which to express a state of mind while in no way experiencing that state of mind is, by definition, an impossible thing to do; then he documents the existence of that class of expressive performances. In so doing he contributes three fragments to our modern legend of unpetrified viewing: (1) the personal symbol, (2) the universal unconscious, and (3) the cultural construction of what counts as fantasy and what counts as reality. To those fragments I think we need, in good faith, to add (4) the idea of an unpetrified text.

Obeyesekere's notion of a personal symbol, properly understood, refers not to a type of symbol, but rather to the conditions definitive of a special class of expressive performances. That class of expressive performances has the following defining conditions: (1) *optionality;* nothing in the culture mandates that the person must get involved in the expressive behavior (1981, p. 140); (2) *local rationality;* the culture defines the state of mind made manifest by the symbols as real, objective, or normal and does not define the state of mind expressed as unreal, subjective, or fantastic (pp. 34–35, 101–102); (3) *psychological relevance;* personal involvement with the expressive behavior can be shown to be psychologically useful, giving expression to, and thereby lending a sense of reality and objectivity (local rationality) to, actual states of mind that, if left unexpressed, would be psychologically dysfunctional for the person (pp. 45, 91, 102, 104, 165).

Obeyesekere's focus on so-called personal symbols is a strategic methodological move against full-blown conventionalism. Much of the anthropological discussion of the meaning of hair has fixed on a somewhat different and special class of expressive performances, those that are mandated on ritual occasions. A distinctive condition of ritualized or stylized or mandated expressions of a state of mind (for example, tearing at one's hair to express grief at a funeral or on a stage) is that very little can be deduced about the actual state of mind (subjective experience) of a person from the fact that the person expressed herself or himself in that way at that time. On ritual occasions, the subjective experience of a person might be consonant with his or her expressed state of mind, yet it need not be.

Obeyesekere introduces the notion of a personal symbol, and searches for examples of it. He does that precisely because he recognizes that on ritual occasions (or on any other occasion when there are substantial interpersonal consequences to expressing a certain state of mind) one cannot assume any close fit between the expression of a state of mind and the subjective experience of it. Indeed, he flatly rejects the postulate, characteristic of some classic formulations in culture and personality theory, that ritualized expressions of a state of mind will become part of a cultural tradition only if they are concordant with, or express, a parallel state of mind in the psychological makeup of a people (1981, pp. 119–120, 136). (See Chapter 7 of this volume.) Thereby granting that the relationship between public expression and private experience is indeterminate for the case of ritualized expressions of a state of mind, Obeyesekere pins his critique of the generalized doctrine of conventionalism on the existence of a class of expressive performances known as personal symbols.

By definition, expressive behavior with a personal symbol resolves psychological difficulties for the individual (the psychological relevance condition) while validating the collective sense of reality of the group (the local rationality condition). According to Obeyesekere the display of matted hair by his female ecstatics fits the definition. The snaky hair makes manifest a locally rational state of mind (possession by a god or spirit, and connectedness to his power), yet the expression of that state of mind is functionally related to an actual state of mind (anxiety over powerlessness or castration; guilt over a desire to rebel against subordination to the rule of local authority figures?) in the private world of the Medusa. The punch line of *Medusa's Hair* is something like this: since *(a)* the idea of a personal symbol is, by definition, inconsistent with the assumptions of conventionalism, and *(b)* personal symbols exist, therefore, *(c)* not all expressive behavior can be assimilated to a doctrine of conventionalism.

We should expect that there will be some controversy about the definition and existence of personal symbols. All three conditions definitive of a personal symbol are in some measure problematical. The optionality condition is, perhaps, the least important of the three.

I think I know what the optionality condition means. It means that growing matted locks is not a mandatory form of expressive behavior for someone of Medusa's status, and that in choosing to grow matted locks there are no "external" payoffs that might motivate her to express a state of mind that is not her own.

I also think I know when the optionality condition does not apply. It does not apply if one grows snakelike matted hair solely to avoid social stigmatization or solely to avoid displeasing one's parents or solely for the sake of any other interpersonal consequences (for example, growing matted locks solely in order to discourage one's husband from making sexual demands).

I find it much harder to know when the optionality condition does apply; for expressive behavior is never devoid of interpersonal consequences, and it is always conceivable that the interpersonal consequence might be the sole motivation for the behavior. Perhaps the optionality condition applies only when it is possible to show that the expressive behavior has an intrapsychic payoff as well as an interpersonal one. If that is so, it would appear that expressive behavior is optional to exactly the extent that it is psychologically relevant; and, thus, we really need only two conditions to define a personal symbol, psychological relevance and local rationality.

Freud is the inspiration for Obeyesekere's theory of psychological relevance (1981, pp. 114, 132, 194). He takes from Freud several things: (1) the idea that there are "deep motivations," that is, universal unconscious states of mind (the desire to rebel against, or do harm to, authority figures; self-reproach over the desire to rebel against, or do harm to, authority figures; the desire to be taken care of; fears about being powerless or "castrated") that, if left unexpressed, would be psychologically dysfunctional; (2) the idea that it can be therapeutic to make manifest a deep motivation, especially if the expression of that unconscious state of mind lends to that state of mind, now expressed, a sense of objectivity, reality, or normalcy; (3) the idea that there exist universal unconscious mental processes, such as identification, projection, free association, and various mental procedures for the defense of the psyche against anxiety; (4) the idea that early childhood experiences (for example, "infantile fixations on significant others") are especially decisive for the formation of unconscious states of mind.

Using those ideas Obeyesekere tries to bridge the gap between the public expression and subjective experience of a state of mind. He links, for example (1981, pp. 26–27, 132–133), the matted locks of one Medusa to her castration fears or feelings of powerlessness, and the fire walking and hook swinging of another Medusa to her masochistic desires, all the while tracing the origins of deep motivations to childhood events—lengthy breast feeding, ambivalence to mother, severe inhibitions of sexual and aggressive desires, and so on.

I think it is a bit unfortunate that Obeyesekere accepts uncritically Freud's mythic vision that deep motivations are pervasive and enduring and that they have their origins in early childhood experience and family life practices. Far more important, however, than Obeyesekere's particular appropriation of Freud to establish the psychological relevance of expressive performances is his more general thesis, that there may be a universal folk psychobiology lending personal and public significance to the human body as a vehicle for expressing and experiencing states of mind. This thesis must be taken seriously even as we disagree about how much of folk psychobiology is universal or about how the universals are to be described.

In my view Freud's theory has appeal and fascination because it is a special instance of a more abstract psychobiological theory, widely distributed among the cultures of the world. Doctrinal variations on that abstract theory can be found, not only in the writings of Freud, but also in the folk psychobiologies of ancient Greece and among Zoroastrians, Hindus, Orthodox Jews, and New Guinea highlanders (see Boyce 1977; Grunfeld 1982; Parker 1983; Meigs 1984). The theory, in basic form, posits the human body as an abode for the self or as a temple for an indwelling spirit or soul. So fundamental is the belief that the self, spirit, or soul is normally connected to the body, that the dignity and sanctity of the self are managed, experienced, and made manifest through the body, its parts, its erogenous zones, and its exuviae. And although, in folk theory, it is recognized that souls may wander and selves may become detached or depersonalized, so intimate is the link of self and body that bodily boundaries are used to give expression to the very idea of the subject (for example, through metaphors for subjectivity such as "internal," "inside the head," "interior"), and physical manifestations, such as illness, are thought to be related to the moral career of the person. Indeed, on a worldwide scale, one of the more popular ideas about illness is that it is caused by mismanaging one's body (mouth and genitals) with regard to food and sex and failing to show the proper attitude of identification or respect (Oedipus comes to mind) to things that are superior and good (for example, parents, elders, and gods). Violating food taboos causes illness. So does adultery. So does blasphemy or defamation. Or so it is widely believed in folk psychobiology (Murdock 1980).

The folk theory, in abstract, posits two complementary processes for managing the dignity of the self. One process involves casting out of the body what is bad or below the self; the other process involves incorporating into the body what is good or above the self. Each process has numerous analogues and extensions.

For casting the bad and lowly out of the body there are, according to folk theory, various rituals of extrusion: washing off dirt, defecating waste, vomiting or spitting out what is toxic, starving or bleeding or sweating out impurities, beating or driving out evil spirits, scapegoating your sins, projecting or repressing malevolent impulses. Successful extrusions are associated with feelings of dignity, purity, wellbeing, and relief. Feelings of dignity are also sustained by various avoidance practices, which deny entrance to the body to things that are dirty, disgusting, undignified, polluting, or evil (unthinkable deeds, unspeakable thoughts, untouchable objects, unviewable events, tabooed foods). There are, of course, complementary rituals of incorporation of the good and of the elevated: swallowing, touching, looking, inhaling, embracing, identifying, internalizing; and they are also associated with feelings of dignity, purity, well-being, and relief.

That is about all the theory one needs to see psychological relevance in the hair growing, spirit possession, fire walking and hook swinging of the female ascetic-ecstatics at Kataragama. Each Medusa uses her body to express a state of mind (for example, the feeling of being connected to god's power); and the state of mind expressed through the body is part of a project of self- or soul maintenance, sustaining a sense of personal dignity or purity by extruding, for example, evil spirits (*pretas*) and incorporating the *śakti* of god.

That sense of personal dignity could not be sustained, however, unless the state of mind expressed also satisfied Obeyesekere's third condition for a personal symbol, the condition of local rationality. For while it is definitive of a personal symbol (for example, matted hair) that, by means of its very expression, the state of mind expressed becomes psychologically functional (for example, in maintaining personal dignity), that effect will not occur unless the state of mind expressed is interpreted by members of one's community as proportionate to, or commensurate with, reality.

Obeyesekere powerfully documents cross-cultural variations in local rationality. In Sri Lanka, for example, given local understandings of penance and the expiation of sin, it is credible to express a desire to nearly starve oneself to death; and, given local conceptions of what is real and what is unreal, there is some plausibility in the belief that one's body has been invaded by an ancestral spirit or possessed by a god.

It seems beyond doubt that there are significant cross-cultural variations in the extent to which expressed states of mind are viewed as normal. There are also significant cross-cultural variations in which states of mind remain unexpressed and get pushed to some mental fringe, because, if expressed, they would be diagnosed as abnormal or strange. Feelings of superiority are not easy to express in some subcultures in the United States; whereas, in many parts of South Asia one can look someone in the eye and say "I am better than you are." Feelings of selfishness are not easy to express in many parts of South Asia, whereas in some subcultures in the United States one can look someone in the eye and extol self-interest as a virtue. In some subcultures today in the United States it is even possible to enhance one's sense of dignity by expressing the belief that god, sin, and the devil do not exist. Someone who did that in England in the sixteenth century risked being branded an enemy of reason, perhaps even diagnosed as suffering from delusions. Neither reality nor fantasy is independent of our version of it; and although every culture draws a distinction between what is objective versus subjective, real versus unreal, perceived versus made up, there is not always cross-cultural consensus in cultural doctrine about whether such things as devils, evil ancestral spirits, or deep malevolent unconscious motivations are objective and real or subjective and imagined.

Obeyesekere displays brilliance, insight, and sensitivity in using the psychological relevance and local rationality criteria to illuminate the expressive performances of his Medusas. Nevertheless, I do not think he presses the local rationality criterion quite far enough. Pressing the local rationality criterion far enough means never absolutely privileging one's own local conception of rationality when giving an account of the expressive performances of others. Obeyesekere does not completely avoid that pitfall, although it remains an open question whether the pitfall is avoidable.

The arguable difficulty with *Medusa's Hair* is that Obeyesekere himself does not believe that (for example) malevolent ancestral spirits and possessing gods in fact exist as external agents in nature. He believes they are anthropomorphized entities "created anew by individuals" (1981, p. 117). And, on the basis of that secular view of what is objective and what is subjective, he invites us to view Medusa's expressed state of mind (I am possessed by a god; I am being harmed by a malevolent ancestral spirit) as a psychologically useful fantasy, and to view public cultural discourse about ancestral spirits and possessing gods as part of a mythic or magical world view (pp. 86, 100–101).

Obeyesekere eloquently describes what is lost as a result of demythologizing and disenchanting the world, in a secular society devoid of ghosts, gods, spirits, and other functional fantasies. Nevertheless, throughout *Medusa's Hair* we are theoretically primed to view her through the lens of our own secular conception of what is real and what is fantasy; and we are never encouraged to escape from the perception that female ascetic-ecstatics in Sri Lanka, with their matted locks, spirit possession, fire walking, and hook swinging derive their psychological benefits by confusing fantasy with reality, while remaining innocent of their innocence.

Obeyesekere assumes that ancestral spirits are illusory, and that culture has imposed a meaning that lends an air of local rationality to a fantasy whose public expression thereby has psychological benefit. Yet, strangely, Obeyesekere's Medusa herself encourages the reader to imagine another possible perspective from which to view her. That alternative perspective is to start with the assumption that malevolent ancestral spirits do exist and can get into one's body, that they are experienced, and that the cultural representation of their existence and a person's experience of their existence lights up an aspect of reality that has import for the management of the self.

Culture, from this latter viewpoint, is not so much "a set of meanings that human beings impose on the world" (Obeyesekere 1981, p. 110), in which the emphasis is on the imposition of meaning, and the world on which meanings get imposed is either left undefined or is predefined (for example, ancestral spirits do not exist; p. 117). Rather, by this view, culture is a version of the natural world as presented and illuminated by an interpretative scheme, in which the emphasis is on the illumination of reality and the most pressing question is, How is it possible for an interpretative scheme to present us with a world that is more or less livable and meaningful? (See the Introduction and Chapter 1 of this volume.)

Given the assumption, Medusa's assumption, that (for example) spirits exist, there are two ways for interpretation by an outside observer to proceed; and the way one goes depends on one's answer to the question, Is the natural world in which I live already a world in which spirits exist? If the answer is yes, then, in that instance, local rationality is not so local, and what looked like a real difference in conception of the natural world can be dismissed as merely a difference in the idiom used to express a shared idea. If the answer is no, then it may be time to cast some new light on the natural world and to engage in some unpetrified viewing, in a process of realities hopping.

Is the natural world presented to us by our own interpretative schemes of a world in which there exist malevolent ancestral spirits who can enter the body and wreak havoc on one's life? The answer to that question is not as obvious as it may seem, and in this instance I find it surprisingly difficult to make up my mind. I find it difficult to make up my mind because I find it so easy to think of what we call the "unconscious" as an alien force in the body that can drive behavior to self-destructive ends; and it is commonplace in some circles to imagine that the alien force is the shadowy trace of the persona of one's relatives. In which case, reference to spirit possession and reference to a destructive impulse from the unconscious mind may simply be different ways of speaking about the same real, nonmythic, non-fantastic thing.

The alternative is to interpret spirits as real things that have not yet been fully represented in the natural world given to us by our own interpretative schemes; and to try to reconceive our interpretative assumptions so that we can light up reality in a somewhat different way. As Nelson Goodman (1984) notes: "One might say there is only one world but this holds for each of the many worlds" (p. 284; see also Shweder 1986).

What does that alternative mean in terms of the expressive behavior of female ascetic-ecstatics in Sri Lanka? I think it means we try to see things in the terms of an interpretative scheme that presents us with a natural, nonmythic, nonfantastic world in which the unwelcome spirit of an ancestor can hover about causing illness and misfortune, and in which the welcome power of a god can, under special circumstances, be put to use in the service of personal dignity and self-management. If we succeed in illuminating the natural world as it is for the interpretative community at Kataragama, then their local rationality is the only rationality we need, and the states of mind experienced and expressed in that natural world (being in connection with God's power; being possessed by an ancestral spirit) will be no less psychologically functional or dysfunctional for also being real.

Thus, in the end, the power in *Medusa's Hair* does not derive solely from Obeyesekere's announced perspective on expressive performances: the perception of a Medusa in the grip of a psychologically pleasing fantasy, which we, as outside observers, can distinguish from reality. Rather, the great appeal of the book is that during the act of looking at Medusa, Obeyesekere's perspective on Medusa leads us beyond itself to other ways of seeing her. In other words, the *śakti* in *Medusa's Hair* is the power of an "unpetrified text" read by an "unpetrified viewer," who keeps shifting perspective so that neither the reader nor Medusa is frozen into stone. And while it is certainly true that Medusa's ideas about reality can momentarily be viewed as mythic, it is only for a moment that we can view them that way; for Medusa's so-called mythic ideas invite us to reconsider our very distinction between myth-fantasy and reality, and thus she leads the unpetrified viewer to see the natural world in a somewhat different light.

Here I need to say more about unpetrified texts and unpetrified viewing. If the reading of *Medusa's Hair* can put us in an unpetrified state of mind, perhaps we should try to understand better that rather special, and legendary, state of mind.

The Legend

Modern legend, the legend of an existential ego capable of detaching itself from or transcending any fixed point of view, tells that there exists a special class of texts, "unpetrified texts." Here by a *text* I mean any object or event that is a vehicle of meaning, and by *meaning* I mean all the implications and suggestions to which one ought to be led in comprehending a text. There are two features definitive of unpetrified texts: (1) meaning many things is what the text means; and (2) it is through every attempt to make the text mean only one thing that an unpetrified viewer is led more and more deeply into the text's multiplicity of meanings. When an unpetrified text is viewed by an unpetrified viewer every attempt to bind in a self-contained meaning drives the interpretation of the text into another semantic territory. There is also a moral to this fragment of my version of the legend: unpetrified texts deserve unpetrified viewers.

Technically speaking, the attempt to bind in a self-contained meaning, to make a text mean only one thing, can be referred to as a homonymic test. The attempted application of the homonymic test is not only an inevitable feature of interpretation, it is an indispensable procedure for distinguishing petrified from unpetrified texts. Petrified texts pass the homonymic test; unpetrified texts do not.

It is definitive of the homonymic test that one treats the text, rather than the meaning of the text, as multiple. Homonymic entries in dictionaries are exemplary of the procedure. The basic idea is to treat as merely apparent the unity of a text with multiple meanings, by dividing up the text, not into versions of the same text, but rather into independent texts, one text for each meaning.

Thus, for example, the sound pattern *gross,* a text in English, easily passes a homonymic test. Instead of one unpetrified text, whose meaning is its multiplicity of reactivating implications, *gross* is a petrified text, reasonably interpreted as three separate texts (gross 1: revolting, vulgar, crude; gross 2: an aggregate of twelve dozen things; gross 3: total earnings exclusive of deductions), each text with a single self-contained meaning that does not activate the others. Petrified texts are readily assimilated to a homonymic procedure. Unpetrified texts resist such homonymic separation, because each of a multiplicity of meanings leads on to the next.

There is probably no general standard for judging the relative worth of petrified versus unpetrified texts; both types of texts exist and play their different parts in our way of life. It was once commonplace to argue that for a text to be properly scientific its meaning must be petrified (fixed and unitary), although that view is no longer so common or well placed. In the Judeo-Christian cultural tradition the book of Job is a worthy exemplar of an unpetrified text, and so is the story of Medusa and her hair. Each interpretation of the text activates yet another, and the process of shifting perspectives is not meant to ever come to an end.

Yet resist as they may, unpetrified texts can, by brute force, be terrorized, and turned into stone. Petrified viewers invariably petrify unpetrified texts, either by ignoring significant details of the text or by failing to ask precisely those questions that might flood the text with other meanings. Remember the moral: unpetrified texts deserve unpetrified viewers. Petrified viewing is fine for petrified texts.

One of the joys of an unpetrified text is that getting all the facts aligned with any one perspective or theory is impossible, and every attempt to do so leads on to another perspective or theory, which is the point of the exercise; to keep talking without ever putting things to an end. Indeed, arguments among unpetrified viewers who study the meaning of things sometimes go something like this.

> I think people who are afraid of snakes are afraid because a snake reminds them of a penis.
>
> I think not: people who are afraid of snakes are not afraid of penises.
>
> I still think so: people who are afraid of snakes are afraid because a snake reminds them of a penis, but not just any penis; it reminds them of a penis that has been severed from the body. It reminds them of a castrated penis, and it is the idea of castration that makes them anxious and is made manifest by the presence of a snake.
>
> I still think not: people who are most afraid of snakes are nearly always women, and it is men, not women, who ought to be most anxious about potential castration, for it is men who have the most to lose.
>
> I still think so: potential castration is not as anxiety provoking as actual castration, and from an anatomical point of view women are castrated men. A snake reminds a woman of what she has lost, for to look at a penis without a body is to think of a body without a penis. And what is a body without a penis? It is body with a vagina, a degraded form, which women loathe and think of as dirty or polluted.
>
> I still think not: it would be strange to say that monkeys experience castration anxiety, yet monkeys are afraid of snakes; and those women who are terrified by snakes are also terrified by other animals, such as birds, frogs, or spiders.

Here the argument carries on, with retorts such as "What do monkeys have to do with people? for they may both be afraid of snakes, but not for the same reason" and "What do frogs have to do with snakes? for they may both be objects of fear, but not for the same reason."

Disagreements of that sort are not meant to be settled; and the fact that they do not get settled does not bring, and should not bring, discussion to an end. Unpetrified texts are the textual analogues of a Necker cube. The more you stare at it the less stable it becomes, and each time you think you have a fixed view of the face of the cube that is forward, the cube switches face. Yet you keep looking, precisely because through looking you are led out of one perspective on things and into another. Or so it is told by the modern legend of unpetrified viewing; which is, it turns out, the legend of cultural anthropology.

The story of Medusa and her hair is an unpetrified text, and it deserves an unpetrified viewing. Historically, many frozen glances and fixed interpretations have fallen on Medusa and her sisters; yet, taken together, and placed side by side, the various interpretations activate one another without destroying the integrity of the text. In one viewing, by Apollodorus (Hamilton 1942), the focus is upon the anomalous figure of the Gorgons, with fishlike scales, birdlike wings, reptile-like hair, and the face of a human; and the terror comes from looking at their mutant form, "each with wings and snakey hair" (p. 143); for Apollodorus, *stony* means dead.

In another viewing, by Freud (1955 [1940]), the focus shifts to the decapitated head of Medusa; and the horror comes from looking, not at the mutant form of an intact Gorgon, but rather at a partial form, Medusa's head, severed from its body, and so reminiscent of a penis after it has been castrated. In Freud's viewing the meaning of Medusa is the castration anxiety (fear of powerlessness?) suggested by the severed head. The snaky hair, because it is still attached to the head, mitigates the horror, by representing an uncastrated penis. *Stony* means becoming erect or stiffening; it is the consolation of knowing that you still have a penis.

In Ovid's viewing the meaning of Medusa turns to shame, and the idea of averting the eyes. Alone of all the Gorgon sisters it was Medusa who had snakelike hair. And why? "She was very lovely once, the hope of many an envious suitor, and of all her beauties her hair most beautiful—at least I heard so from one who claimed he had seen her. One day Neptune found her and raped her, in Minerva's temple, and the goddess turned away and hid her eyes behind her shield, and punishing the outrage as it deserved, she changed her hair to serpents" (Ovid 1955, p. 106). For Ovid it is the snakes that are horrifying, and they are meant to frighten away from Medusa's body those who would do evil. A Gorgon head, we are told in one viewing (*Encyclopaedia Britannica* 1984, 4:637), protects against the evil eye or—what amounts to the same thing—evil intentions. A free association comes to mind: those who looked on Medusa did not hide their own evil intentions toward her, and perhaps, because of their cruelty and lack of compassion, they turned hardhearted into stone.

Thomas Bulfinch (1942) adds a touch of envy, the envy of the goddess Minerva or Athena, that perhaps all-too-helpful goddess who guided the hand of Perseus as he cut off the head of the unsuspecting Medusa, asleep in her home. Medusa "was once a beautiful maiden whose hair was her chief glory, but as she dared to vie in beauty with Minerva, the goddess deprived her of her charms and changed her beautiful ringlets into hissing serpents" (p. 116). From placing those interpretations side by side it becomes apparent that there is more to an unpetrified text than meets the eye from any one perspective, and that it is by shifting perspectives that we learn how to see.

Unlike Obeyesekere, Perseus never looked at the face of Medusa, nor did he try to comprehend her inner life. Instead, eyes averted, he simply killed her. It was a borderline cowardly act. The plot is well known. First, through intimidation, Perseus extorted from the Gray Women information leading him to Medusa's faraway island abode. The Gray Women looked upon the world with a single eye, which they passed from forehead to forehead; Perseus stole the eye and used it as a bribe. Then, heavily armed with expert methodology, the shield of Athena (which functioned as a mirror), the sword of Hermes, a magic bag, winged sandals and a hat of invisibility, our "hero" stole up on a sleeping Medusa, cut off her head, and gave it to Athena, who used it to petrify others.

Modern heroes may seem more cerebral than Perseus and, perhaps, less methodical, but certainly not less noble. Obeyesekere did not kill or decapitate his Medusa. Instead, gazing in anxiety at her ugly face and snakelike matted hair, he tried to see through the less visible world of her subjective life, so that later we might look at things horrible (Medusa) and awesome (the Baba) without turning into stone.

Conclusion

Artful Realism

Naive realism is the experience of reality as an immediacy contained within appearances, as experienced, for example, in the extraordinary achievements of "ordinary" visual perception. It is the experience of a relationship between inside and outside, so proportionate, coincidental, and graceful that no difference is noticed between the real and the apparent, and no disharmony felt between the nature of an object or stimulus and the nature of our response to it or representation of it.

Naive realism is a highly addictive experience for reality-seeking human beings; once they have had it they cannot keep off it. "Ordinary" perception is to the eye as Nirvana is to the mind, and what they have in common is the experience of reality as transparent, inherently compelling, and indistinguishable from experience.

It is probably a good thing that, in reality, the real and the apparent are not conflated, and that, when it comes to appearances, reality is not *that* immediate or close at hand. Because if it were, we could never make use of reality to explain appearances; we could not talk of sunlight as "the shadow of God" or of dreams as communications received over a noisy channel from a distant realm; and no one would ever write about artful realism.

Naive realism, the experience of subject-object indissolubility, is an experience you can have whether you are extraordinary (in the case of Nirvana) or ordinary (in the case of visual perception). But it is not something you can subscribe to, or think about, like a philosophy or a theory. To "think about" anything is to separate subject and object, and to think about the unity of subjectivity and objectivity is to acknowledge them as *two* things conflated, which requires that you draw precisely the subject-object distinction that is the denial of naive realism.

Just as it takes sophistication to write a simple sentence, it takes artfulness to achieve naive realism. Naive realism is the direct, transparent, close-at-hand experience of reality. Artful realism is the theoretical account of how that experience of immediacy is achieved, when, if you think about it, reality must always be beyond experience, transcending appearance, distant, hidden, buried within, or at the very least separate and somewhere else.

Artful Realism: Premodern, Modern, and Postmodern

That beyondness or separateness of the real has been represented by artful realists across the ages in many ways: as a signal obscured by noise; as a hidden force operating behind the visible world; as a transcendent realm of gods and heroes elevated in comparison with mortal folk; as a distant realm, perhaps a lost age of truth, when the world was free from error, distortion, and sin, of which the present world of experience is but the decadent trace; or as an observing ego or spirit exiled in the interiority of a human body and unable to reach out beyond the skin or the retinal image to a mindless world exterior to the senses.

Across the ages artful realists have proposed many theories about the nature of the gap between appearance-sensation-experience and reality, the reasons for it, and how the gap might be bridged, if at all.

The most popular premodern theories are quite heroic (and thus antiegalitarian and antidemocratic), placing a good deal of confidence in the testimonials of the possessed and the visions of "seers" and in the extraordinary sightedness of virtuosos and experts credited with a special ability to make "contact" and to peer into reality as it really is.

The remaining artful realists, a diverse collection of modern and postmodern scholars, scientists, and artists, seem to have difficulty with the premodern idea that knowledge of the really real should be established on the basis of "revealed" truths or from the miraculous experiences of a self-privileging elite claiming special powers for sensing. The modern and postmodern periods are more egalitarian and bureaucratic, and their intellectual middlemen and mediums (those who bridge the gap) do not have X-ray vision or keener ears able to listen carefully to voices that no one else can hear. Modern middlemen have tricks of the trade and rules and procedures and "formal" methods and mirrors and manuals and titles; postmodern mediums have their imagination, and they rely a lot on their wits.

A very modern-sounding theory about the nature of the gap between appearance-sensation-experience and reality, dating from at least the twelfth century, goes something like this. By the time the truths about reality (including so-called revelations) reach our minds they have been viewed through the eyes of a very mortal seer who may have been in need of glasses, and who did not speak our dialect, written down by a scribe who made transcription errors, translated by someone who was not perfectly bilingual, and narrated by a storyteller who got the emphasis all wrong.

In that artful modern conception of realism is born a hermeneutic methodism whose goal is to preserve or restore the fidelity of the original signal or message or "text" through the control of bias and the methodical estimation and elimination of distortion. Shattered images and grotesque forms become objects of experimentation and fascination.

Postmodern realists demur, suspecting there is madness in the method of the modern. Postmodern realists see no way across the gap between appearance-sensation-experience and reality, except through an irrepressible act of imaginative projection. Reality, according to postmodern theories, is not only just obscured from sight; it is intrinsically invisible, like a black hole.

A black hole (the analogy is to confinement in the "black hole of Calcutta") is a densely compacted star possessing gravitational forces so intense that it keeps imprisoned within itself, and will not release, its own light particles. If reality is a black hole it is fundamentally cut off from sensation and appearances; staring very hard in its direction does not help, for it can be known only speculatively and by conjecture.

So a postmodern artful realism has emerged, with the argument that the postulation of our own internal mental constructs as unseen external forces and entities is an indispensable feature of reality-seeking thought, including the best of science. An implication of the argument: what Derrida calls the "metaphysics of presence," consisting of all those asymmetrical relationships of the subject to the object, the apparent to the real, the immediate to the distant, the visible to the hidden, the inside to the outside, and the superficial to the deep, is not something we can choose to do without. For, as Derrida notes, all too briefly, "nothing is conceivable" without it. Reality-testing is, unavoidably, a metaphysical act, implicating the knower as well as the known.

A Parable for Artful Realists

Speaking of metaphysics and epistemology, there is a story told in anthropological circles about three baseball umpires conversing about how they call balls and strikes.[1] The first umpire says, "I calls 'em as I sees 'em." The second says, "I calls 'em as they are." The third says, "They ain't nothing' 'til I calls 'em."

The story is usually told by a narrator in a Nietzschean frame of mind, eager to aphorize and to liberate his audience from the burdensome and phantasmagoric idea of objective constraint or of a reality hidden behind appearances. I shall try to transform the story into a parable for artful realists.

In a story with three voices it is a distinct disadvantage not to have the final word. In the Nietzschean telling of the story it is a subject inventing his own objects ("They ain't nothin' 'till I calls 'em") who has the authoritative voice, and speaks last. Yet a different effect can be produced by reordering the sequence of voices.

As the story is usually told, an empiricist enters as the first voice. He speaks in the lowbrow idiom of a baseball umpire ("I calls 'em as I sees 'em"), suggestive of an unsophisticated and guileless sensibility. That impression is reinforced by his message, a straight, simpleminded, earnest avowal of his honesty in reporting what he sees.

The second voice is that of a naive realist. Since you can't think naive realism but can only experience it, when the second umpire tries to express himself, directly telling his direct experience ("I calls 'em as they are"), he sounds strident and overconfident.

The story has started with the voice of a pious empiricist. With the naive realist it continues with the lowbrow voice of an innocent, who discredits himself by talking in incorrigible tones as though he were Superman, or a seer, equipped with transparent eyes and X-ray vision. Apparently unreflective in matters concerning "the metaphysics of presence," the second umpire experiences no gap between the subjective "internal" representation of a thing and the objective "external" thing represented. Prearranged among the voices to give artless expression to feelings of immediacy, the voice of the second umpire blusters in its oblivious certitude.

The story concludes with a voice of authority. Appearing foremost because he comes last, the third umpire speaks for a reality-constituting subject, reminding us indirectly but truthfully ("They ain't nothing' 'till I calls 'em") of all those questionable calls ("Strike three, you're out!") that we had to accept as binding because there was no higher court of appeal. His lowbrow idiom reinforces his devilish authority (or is it his power?) as the conversation takes a light-hearted turn away from simplicities toward guile and sophistication.

Yet the authority and sophistication of the reality-constituting umpire are undermined and diminished by generating a variation on the story in which the voices are arranged in a different order. In that version it is the first umpire, describing how he calls balls and strikes, who says "They ain't nothin' 'till I calls 'em." The second umpire says, "I calls 'em as they are." The third says, "I calls 'em as I sees 'em."

Here the voice that speaks first sounds nihilistic, arrogant, and jejune. Perhaps it is because the first umpire is so haughty in his solipsism ("They ain't nothin' 'till I calls 'em") that the voice of the second ("I calls 'em as they are") no longer sounds naive. Instead it seems to index and make salient its presupposition, which is that familiar and useful truism for baseball umpires: every pitch is either a strike or not a strike, and no pitch is both. The voice of the third umpire ("I calls 'em as I sees 'em") rounds out the message, seemingly instructing paternalistically our peurile nihilist in a most important fact of life for baseball umpires: if you do not even *try* to "call 'em as they are" you're not going to last very long in this league.

A highbrow translation and transcription of the conversation might read like this:

"How do you call balls and strikes?" Translation: What do you have to say about the gap between appearance-sensation-experience and reality?

"I calls 'em as I sees 'em." Translation, to quote Ernest Gellner (1985): "What piece of *evidence* could ever turn up which would show that the external world is something *more* than just experience? Whatever piece of evidence turned up would be, precisely, just one *further experience*" (p. 15).

"I calls 'em as they are." Translation: Appearances, sensations, and experiences are not all of the same kind. Without the idea of reality we could not explain sensations, nor could we distinguish between perception and hallucination, truth and error, or a reminiscence and a fantastic daydream. When it comes to the metaphysics of presence—the here and now brought to us from up above or from far away or from deep inside or from right before the eyes or from "through a glass darkly"—"nothing is conceivable" without it.

"They ain't nothin 'till I calls 'em." Translation: The metaphysics that is present is put there by the human mind. The most fanciful idea of all is the notion that the world can be described, inscribed, or specified independently of our involvement with it and experience of it. Without us there is no game in town. There certainly is no game of baseball. And, without the game of baseball there are no "balls" or "strikes." Naked reality, alas, is in eternal purdah; she can never let herself be seen. It is dressed up, in style, that she appears in public, clothed in those preconceptions we left for her outside the bedroom door.

Should we choose, once and for all time, among the three umpires, or among the three sensibilities (premodern, modern, and postmodern)? Not if all that is mental is a never-ending process of overcoming partial views. Not if reality is incapable of being represented completely, when represented from any one point of view, and incapable of being represented intelligibly, when represented from all points of view at once.

In the realm of artful realism every court needs a jester, just as it needs a king, and a loyal opposition. The king, thinking he has dominion over all of external reality, will eventually go out of his mind; and there will be madness in the methods of even the most loyal opposition. Which makes it ever so much more important that the jester not lose his head.

Notes

1. Post-Nietzschean Anthropology

1. For a frontal assault on fallacies in relativistic thinking in anthropology see Spiro 1986. Recent expositions, defenses, and critiques of relativism can be found in Wilson 1970; Hollis and Lukes 1982; Shweder and LeVine 1984; Clifford and Marcus 1986; Fiske and Shweder 1986. Also see Geertz 1984.
2. For a detailed ethnographic account of Islamic theories of satanic beings and jinns and of various contemporary South Asian conceptions of illness and therapeutic practice, see Kakar 1982.

2. Cultural Psychology: What Is It?

1. I am uncertain of the origin of the expression *cultural psychology*. It appears and reappears with varying meanings in the writings of nineteenth- and twentieth-century social and psychological theorists, including those of Michael Cole (1989), Alan Howard (1985), and James Peacock (1984).

   In defining cultural psychology I shall assume, as did the ancients, that a proper appreciation of a thing integrates its taxonomic and narrative contexts (its being with its becoming). That assumption is characteristic of teleological approaches to definition and understanding, and it is associated with the following conception of reality or nature: what is real or in the nature of things is what a thing of a certain kind strives to become so as to realize its identity and become excellent, developed, and exemplary of its kind.

   The teleological approach to definition may sound old-fashioned or premodern, which is not surprising, since teleology, and all that it implied about nature, society, and persons, was one of the casualties of modern thinking in the West. It was replaced in the Enlightenment by a positive science conception: the natural order as unanimated, deterministic, and indifferent to human affairs and to all other mental events. Thus, in modern consciousness, the idea of what was proper or excellent or elevated or cultivated became detached from the idea of what was natural (see Chapter 1). One consequence of that separation was that all the traditional and central normative ideals for human functioning and development—ideas of the good, the right, the beautiful, etc.—were deprived of natural or objective force, while the idea of a natural norm was reduced to a nonevaluative statistical notion, the so-called value-neutral positive science idea of regularly occurring or repetitive events. Natural science and normative ethics, is and ought, got in the habit of moving through modern times in entirely divorced ways, and social science suffered for it.

Yet teleology still has some things to recommend it, not the least of which is the opportunity it affords to move seamlessly back and forth between descriptions of what something is and descriptions of what something ought to be; to see an as-yet-unrealized regulative ideal immanent and active in the development of instances of its kind; and to promote what is natural in the light of what is.

Hence this essay, which is itself part of a teleological process, lending assistance, quite purposefully, to the discipline of cultural psychology in an attempt to help it discover, and hence realize, its nature.

2. At any historical moment, of course, what has been constituted as true, beautiful, or good within some one, then existing, intentional world might also happen, as a matter of contingency, to have been constituted that way within each of all the then-existing intentional worlds. In other words, there may well be some intentional truths that are true universally.

However, since an intentional truth becomes true only by virtue of its embeddedness in some particular intentional world, it follows that there is no sense of necessity associated with a universal intentional truth.

A universal intentional truth is universally true because it has been constituted as true within each of the then-existing particular intentional worlds, which is no guarantee that it must of necessity be true within every existing intentional world, past or future, or within every imaginable one.

3. For those general psychologists who are, by metaphysical choice or second nature, materialists, reductionists, and incorrigible utopians, there is also an additional aim, someday to locate Plato's transcendent realm of fixed ideas in some physical realization in the brain or the nervous system, or on chromosome 11.

It may well have been René Descartes, a latter-day Platonist, who interiorized the ancient search for the transcendent, and first tried to postulate a physical realization—localized in the pineal gland—for an abstracted central processor of the mind, the "I".

4. Descartes, of course, tried an alternative Platonist route to the central processor, the route of rationalism (deductive reasoning from undeniable premises, for example, "I think, therefore I am") rather than the route of empiricism (inductive reasoning from sense data or observations). Adhering to his

principle of radical doubt, Descartes treated as deceptive or illusory or exterior all sensations and stimulus materials and tried to reconstruct the logically necessary features of the central processing mechanism through deductive reasoning alone.

Both rationalism and empiricism are the offspring of the Platonic imagination, which fancies routes of direct access to a fixed and uniform reality. General psychology is the empiricist child of Platonism, while its rationalist sibling lives on in the philosophy of mind and language, in normative ethics, and in the field of artificial intelligence.

If there is to be a cultural psychology it will have to synthesize rationalism and empiricism into something else or provide an alternative to both. C. S. Peirce's (1940) notion of abductive reasoning as the indispensable assistant to the "unaided rationality" of logic and sense data is a promising starting point. One version of Peirce's notion, if I understand it, is this: transcendent realities can be imagined but never seen or deduced, for they are constructions of our own making, which sometimes succeed in binding us to the underlying reality they imagine by giving us an intellectual tool—a metaphor, a premise, an analogy, a category—with which to live, to arrange our experience, and to interpret our experiences so arranged. In other words, the abductive faculty is the faculty of imagination, which comes to the rescue of sensation and logic by providing them with the intellectual means to see through experience and leap beyond empty syllogisms and tautologies to some creative representation of an underlying reality that might be grasped and reacted to, even if that imagined reality cannot be found, proved, or disproved by inductive or deductive rule-following.

The fact that you cannot get beyond appearances to reality with the methods of science or the rules of logic (or, for that matter, through meditative mysticism) does not mean that you should stop trying to imagine the really real, or that the imagination *must* be disrespectful of sense data or deductive logic, or that "anything goes."

Of course there are times and places when it makes good sense to be disrespectful of sense data and of logical deductions, especially when they lead you places where there is good reason not to go.

5. For a discussion of how the field of geophysics had to get free of the standards of Newtonian mechanics in order to gain some self-respect and make progress see Richter (1986) on the topic of plate tectonics. For a discussion of the importance in the social sciences of not waiting around for our Newton see Converse (1986).

6. From the interpretative framework of cultural psychology researchers in general psychology might be construed as participant observers in the special sociocultural and procedural world of laboratory life, where they talk to and observe the reactions of informants—most often college-age students—from some specific cultural and historical tradition, typically their own.

7. Of course I am being very selective and contemporary here. Cultural psychology has many ancestral spirits, including Abelard, Herder, Hegel, Heidegger, and Brentano. A short list of important contemporary texts critiquing one aspect or more of the Platonist conception of a central processing mechanism includes Lévy-Bruhl (1910), Wittgenstein (1968 [1953]), Kuhn

(1962), Garfinkle (1967), Toulmin (1972), Geertz (1973), Goodman (1968), MacIntyre (1981), Fish (1980), Lakoff (1987), and Putnam (1987).

8. One of the great ancestral spirits of cultural psychology, whose work deserves to be honored and revived, is Edward Sapir, who tried to define an interdisciplinary agenda for anthropology, psychology, and linguistics.

Hardly anyone in the social sciences (historians are an exception) reads things more than ten years old these days, let alone a poetic, Aristotelian essay from 1924 written by an anthropological linguist and published in a sociology journal. The anthropological linguist in question is Edward Sapir, the less honored, though more formidable, intellectual figure behind the so-called Sapir-Whorf "linguistic relativity" hypothesis. Yet in 1924, just before joining the University of Chicago, Edward Sapir published an article in the *American Journal of Sociology* entitled "Culture: Genuine and Spurious," in which he conceived of the way traditions and individuals, cultures and psyches, might conspire to make each other up and excellent. Sections of the essay could well have been subtitled "A Manifesto for a Cultural Psychology." A genuine culture, Sapir argued, is not an externally imposed set of rules or forms or a "passively accepted heritage from the past," but rather a "way of life" (p. 321), gracefully proportioned to the beliefs, desires, and interests of its bearers, with which it is indissociably linked. A genuine culture consists of institutions, resources, and ideals that assist individuals in cultivating precisely those reactions, skills, and mental states that have "the sanction of a class and of a tradition of long standing" (p. 309). In a genuine culture there are processes at work aimed at the achievement of a harmonious, interdependent balance between psyche and culture. Traditional ideals for a good and proper life are made salient through diverse forms of representation—art, artifacts, ritual, language, folklore, mundane practice—and individuals deliberately and creatively come to terms with and use those ideals to refashion their selves, thereby revivifying and confirming the tradition. In a genuine culture, processes of cultural maintenance and personal maintenance serve each other. The tradition gives to the self "the wherewithal to develop its powers" and "a sense of inner satisfaction, a feeling of spiritual mastery" (p. 323).

Sapir was concerned that the alienation of culture from psyche had, in modern times, become real and pervasive. He held out as a mission for anthropology the examination of the processes by which genuine or unalienated cultures integrate cultural and personal symbols. Cultural psychology promises to carry on where Sapir left off.

9. Relevant here is the work of the so-called Edinburgh school (Woolgar, Pinch, Collins, Barnes, and others) in the sociology of science, as well as the work of Donald McCloskey and Allan Megill on the rhetorics of science. See, for example, Barnes and Shapin (1979), Latour and Woolgar (1981), McCloskey (1985), and Collins (1981).

10. It has become increasingly recognized among anthropologists that speculative ontologies and other cultural "texts" can be misleading guides to operative beliefs, which is one reason that the idea of "metaphors we live by" (Lakoff and Johnson 1980b) in our personal and interpersonal functioning has taken hold.

11. My use of the Scarr and McCartney framework to talk about person-environment interactions should not imply that those authors are engaged in an exercise in cultural psychology, or that my appropriation and extension of their logical scheme is a comment, one way or the other, upon behavioral genetics. The framework of positive (active, reactive, passive) versus negative (active, reactive, passive) relationships is totally detachable from any concern with the genetic determination of behavior.

    I might add that the behavioral geneticists seem all too fascinated with, indeed overjoyed by, the idea of positive person-environment relationships and far too little concerned with the ubiquity of negative ones. At its core the field of behavioral genetics displays strong Platonist tendencies and is relatively innocent of the idea of intentional persons and intentional worlds. Robert Plomin (1986) and Daniel G. Freedman (1974) are exceptions.

12. Of course, in some other intentional worlds parents react to the onset of maidenhood by encouraging their teenage daughters to date, go to parties, and get out of the house.

    If I had to divide all the cultures of the world into two types, putting aside everything else, I would partition them into those in which boys and girls are pushed together at puberty and those in which they are kept apart—kissing-game cultures versus purdah cultures. I suspect that many other aspects of value and practice are associated with that division.

13. Such a review would include philosophical work on intentionality and partial translatability (Brentano, Derrida, Gadamer, Goodman, Heidegger, MacIntyre, Manicus, Rorty); linguistic work on discourse processes, performative utterances, and the pragmatics of language use (Austin, Dunn, Grice, Haviland, Heath, Labov, Peggy Miller, Much, Fred Myers, Ochs, Schieffelin, Searle, Silverstein, Slobin); cognitive work on framing effects, construal, and the representation of knowledge (D'Andrade, Holland, Ed Hutchins, Kahneman, Kempton, Nisbett, Charles Nuckolls, Quinn, Ross, Schank, Siegler, Trabasso, Tversky); literary work on rhetoric inside and outside of science (Booth, Clifford, de Man, Fish, Geertz, McCloskey, Barbara H. Smith); sociological work on situated meanings and the construction of realities, including scientific realities (Cicourel, Latour, Mehan, Pinch, Woolgar); critical interpretative work on social and psychological theory (Bernstein, Bloor, Bourdieu, Mike Cole, Gergen, Goodnow, Lave, Haskel Levi, Tambiah); medical work on "placebo," psychosomatic effects, and the body as an intentional system (Csordas, Gendlin, Good, Kleinman); developmental work on social referencing and the socialization of emotions (Campos, Camras, Dunn, Emde); clinical work on the role of cultural myths and stories in the self-regulation of emotional states (Doi, Herdt, Kakar, Spiro, Zonis); anthropological work on person-centered ethnography (Gregor, LeVine, Robert Levy, Obeyesekere, Scheper-Hughes, Whiting and Whiting); ethnographic work on the socialization of motivations, attitudes, and subjective states in institutional settings—families, schools, military units (Bletso, Csikszentmihaly, Edgerton, Alan Fiske, Phil Jackson, Ogbu, Lois Peak, G. W. Skinner, Stodolsky, Weisner); psychological and anthropological work on narrative and dialogue (Bruner, Cohler, Crapanzano, Nancy Stein); and ethno-psychological work on the representation of self and subjective states

(Michael Bond, Fogelson, Paul Harris, Heelas, Karl Heider, Lutz, Joan Miller, Triandis, Geoffrey White).

6. Menstrual Pollution, Soul Loss, and the Comparative Study of Emotions

1. One objection raised to my semantic approach to the development of emotional functioning, in a personal communication from Daniel G. Freedman, is that "there is no universal infancy any more than there is a universal adulthood." What Freedman has in mind is a line of research, much of it conducted by himself and his associates (Freedman 1974; also see Super 1981), indicating that there are racial and population differences in neonatal temperament and responsiveness to certain stimulus events. For example, under conditions of partial air blockage (a cloth is placed over a newborn's mouth or nose), Oriental babies are, on average, more passive and less agitated than Caucasian babies. The implication of Freedman's objection is that emotional differences between populations of adults will be matched by parallel or analogous innate differences in the emotional functioning of babies in those populations.

   It would be a forceful challenge to the semantic approach if different cultural practices were "reflections" or "crystallizations" of innate differences in responsiveness—for example, if Oriya Caucasian newborns displayed significantly greater aversive responses than American Caucasian newborns to dirt or excreta or being touched, or if Tahitian or Eskimo six-month-olds did not display the face of anger when their wrists were confined to their sides or when a desired object was held just out of reach. Although a lot more evidence is needed before the issue can be settled with confidence, it is my bet that Tahitian and Eskimo six-month-olds will display situation-appropriate anger, that Javanese four-year-olds will clearly discriminate between a variety of basic emotions (e.g., surprise, anger, sadness, disgust, fear), and that Oriya babies are not born with feelings of untouchability.

7. Rethinking Culture and Personality Theory

1. This critique of the personality trait approach reads to me today, more than a decade after the critique was written, as a parody cum reductio ad absurdum of the tired old opposition between the nomothetic and the idiographic. In my struggle to get free of the opposition I tried to show how personality disposition concepts become trivialized as they become encumbered, as they must, by the albatross of contextual qualifiers, yet I didn't quite liberate myself entirely from the language of dispositions. These days it seems to me less fruitful to worry about the relative breadth of proposed dispositional concepts and more fruitful to raise doubts about the entire conceptual apparatus that treats persons as vessels for *autonomous* mental states of any kind, whether broad and abstract or narrow and context-specific. What a person is predictably disposed to do as viewed from the outside (for example, seek attention from mother) is neither a causal explanation nor an interpretative understanding of why he or she does it. See Shweder and Sullivan (1990) for an alternative conception of the person as a "semiotic subject."

8. Suffering in Style

1. As I understand it, one of the persisting anomalies from biochemical research on the experience of depression is that the postulated biochemical disturbances—of enzymes involved in catecholamine synthesis or norepinephrine in CNS pathways—typically turn out to be of low magnitude, and, more important, unlike classic metabolic pathologies the biochemical levels of the sufferer are typically within the statistical range of the biochemical levels for normals in the population.

10. Conclusion

1. I first heard the story from David M. Schneider. Perhaps everyone else did, as well.

References

Allison, G. T. 1969. Conceptual models and the Cuban missile crisis. *American Political Science Review* 63:689–718.

———. 1971. *Essence of Decision: Explaining the Cuban Missile Crisis*. Boston: Little, Brown.

Allison, J., D. Larson, and D. Jensen. 1967. Acquired fear, brightness preference, and one-way shuttlebox performance. *Psychonomic Science* 8:269–270.

American Psychiatric Association. 1980. *Diagnostic and Statistical Manual of Mental Disorders*. 3d ed. Washington, D.C.

Argyle, M., and B. R. Little. 1972. Do personality traits apply to social behavior? *Journal for the Theory of Social Behavior* 2:1–35.

Austin, J. L. 1962. *How to Do Things with Words*. Oxford: Clarendon Press.

Ayres, B. 1967. Pregnancy magic: A study of food taboos and sex avoidances. In C. S. Ford, ed., *Cross-Cultural Approaches*. New Haven, Conn.: HRAF Press.

Barker, R. G. 1971. Individual motivation and the behavior setting claim. In W. W. Lambert and R. Weisbrod, eds., *Comparative Perspectives on Social Psychology*. Boston: Little, Brown.

Barnes, B., and S. Shapin. 1979. *The Natural Order: Historical Studies of Scientific Culture*. Beverly Hills: Sage.

Barry, H., M. K. Bacon, and I. L. Child. 1967. Definitions, ratings, and bibliographic sources for child training practices of 110 cultures. In C. S. Ford, ed., *Cross-Cultural Approaches*. New Haven, Conn.: HRAF Press.

Barry H., I. L. Child, and M. K. Bacon. 1959. Relation of child training to subsistence economy. *American Anthropologist* 61:51–63.

367

Barry, H., L. Josephson, E. Lauer, and C. Marshall. 1977. Agents and techniques of child training: Cross-cultural codes. *Ethnology* 16:191–230.

Barry, H., and L. M. Paxson. 1971. Infancy and early childhood: Cross-cultural codes. *Ethnology* 10:466–508.

Bateson, G. 1967. Cybernetic explanation. *American Behavioral Scientist* 10:29–32.

Beck, A. T. 1976. *Cognitive Therapy and Emotional Disorders.* New York: New American Library.

Bem, D. 1972a. Constructing cross-situational consistencies in behavior: Some thoughts on Alker's critique of Mischel. *Journal of Personality* 40:17–26.

———— 1972b. Self-perception theory. In L. Berkowitz, ed., *Advances in Experimental Social Psychology.* Vol. 6. New York: Academic Press.

———— 1974. On predicting some of the people some of the time. *Psychological Review* 81:506–520.

Bendix, R. 1952. Complaint behavior and individual personality. *American Journal of Sociology* 58:292–302.

Benedict, R. 1928. Psychological types in the cultures of the Southwest. *International Congress of Americanists* 23:572–581.

———— 1934. *Patterns of Culture.* New York: Houghton Mifflin.

———— 1946. *The Chrysanthemum and the Sword.* New York: New American Library.

Berg, C. 1951. *The Unconscious Significance of Hair.* London: Allen and Unwin.

Berlin, B., and P. Kay. 1969. *Basic Color Terms: Their Universality and Evolution.* Berkeley: University of California Press.

Bitterman, M. E. 1975. The comparative analysis of learning. *Science* 188:699–709.

Black, M. 1975. Reasonableness. In M. Black, ed., *Caveats and Critiques.* Ithaca: Cornell University Press.

Block, J. 1965. *The Challenge of Response Sets.* New York: Appleton-Century-Crofts.

Bloom, A. 1987. *The Closing of the American Mind.* New York: Simon and Schuster.

Booth, W. 1988. *The Company We Keep: An Ethics of Fiction.* Berkeley: University of California Press.

Bostwick, G. L. 1976. A taxonomy of privacy: Repose, sanctuary, and intimate decision. *California Law Review* 64:1447–83.

Bowlby, J. 1969. *Attachment and Loss.* Vol. 1: *Attachment.* New York: Basic Books.

Boyce, M. 1977. *A Persian Stronghold of Zoroastrianism.* Oxford: Clarendon Press.

Briggs, J. L. 1970. *Never in Anger.* Cambridge, Mass.: Harvard University Press.

Brown, R. 1965. *Social Psychology.* New York: Free Press.

Bruner, J. S. 1966. On cognitive growth II. In J. S. Bruner, R. R. Olver, and P. M. Greenfield, eds., *Studies in Cognitive Growth.* New York: Wiley.

Bruner, J. S., R. R. Olver, and P. M. Greenfield, eds. 1966. *Studies in Cognitive Growth.* New York: Wiley.

Bulfinch, T. 1942. *The Age of the Fable.* New York: Heritage Press.

Burke, K. 1968. Dramatism. In David L. Sills, ed., *International Encyclopedia of the Social Sciences*. Vol. 7. New York: Macmillan and The Free Press.

────── 1969. *A Grammar of Motives*. Berkeley: University of California Press.

Burton, M. L. 1968. Multidimensional scaling of role terms. Ph.D. diss.. Stanford University.

Burton, R. V. 1970. Validity of retrospective reports assessed by the multitrait-multimethod analysis. *Developmental Psychology* 3:1–15.

Burwen, L. S., and D. T. Campbell. 1957. The generality of attitudes towards authority and nonauthority figures. *Journal of Abnormal and Social Psychology* 54:24–31.

Campbell, D. T. 1965. Variation and selective retention in socio-cultural evolution. In H. R. Barringer, G. Blanksten, and R. Mack, eds., *Social Change in Developing Areas*. Cambridge, Mass.: Schenkman.

────── 1972. Herskovits, cultural relativism, and metascience. In F. Herskovits, ed., *Cultural Relativism*. New York: Random House.

────── 1986. Science's social system of validity-enhancing belief change and the problems of the social sciences. In D. W. Fiske and R. A. Shweder, eds., *Metatheory in Social Science*. Chicago: University of Chicago Press.

Campbell, D. T., and D. W. Fiske. 1959. Convergent and discriminant validation by the multitrait-multimethod matrix. *Psychological Bulletin* 56:81–105.

Campos, J. J., R. N. Emde, T. Gaensbauer, and C. Henderson. 1975. Cardiac and behavioral interrelationships in the reactions of infants to strangers. *Developmental Psychology* 5:589–601.

Campos, J. J., and C. R. Stenberg. 1981. Perception, appraisal, and emotion: The onset of social referencing. In M. E. Lamb and L. R. Sherrod, eds., *Infant Social Cognition*. Hillsdale, N.J.: Lawrence Erlbaum Associates.

Cancian, F. 1975. *What Are Norms?* New York: Cambridge University Press.

Cattell, R. B. 1957. *Personality and Motivation Structure and Measurement*. New York: World.

Caudill, W. A., and C. Schooler. 1973. Child behavior and child rearing in Japan and the United States: An interim report. *Journal of Nervous and Mental Disease* 157:323–338.

Cavell, S. 1969. *Must We Mean What We Say?* New York: Charles Scribner and Sons.

Charlesworth, W. R., and M. A. Kreutzer. 1973. Facial expressions of infants and children. In P. Ekman, ed., *Darwin and Facial Expression*. New York: Academic Press.

Chess, S., A. Thomas, and H. Birch. 1959. Characteristics of the individual child's behavioral responses to the environment. *American Journal of Orthopsychiatry* 29:791–802.

Child, I. L. 1968. Personality in culture. In E. F. Borgatta and W. W. Lambert, eds., *Handbook of Personality Theory and Research*. Chicago: Rand McNally.

Chomsky, N. 1964. A review of B. F. Skinner's *Verbal Behavior*. In J. A. Foder and J. J. Katz, eds., *The Structure of Language*. Englewood Cliffs, N.J.: Prentice-Hall.

Cicourel, A. V. 1974. *Cognitive Sociology.* New York: Free Press.

Clifford, J. 1988. *The Predicament of Culture.* Cambridge, Mass.: Harvard University Press.

Clifford, J., and G. E. Marcus, eds. 1986. *Writing Culture.* Berkeley: University of California Press.

Climent, C. E., B. S. M. Diop, T. W. Harding, H. H. A. Ibrahim, L. Ladrido-Ignacio, and N. N. Wig. 1980. Mental health in primary health care. *WHO Chronicle* 34:231–236.

Cohn, J. F., and E. Z. Tronick. 1983. Three-month-old infants' reaction to simulated maternal depression. *Child Development* 54:185–193.

Colby, A., L. Kohlberg, J. Gibbs, D. Candee, A. Hewer, C. Power, and B. Speicher-Dubin. 1987. *Measurement of Moral Judgment: Standard Issue Scoring Manual.* New York: Cambridge University Press.

Cole, M. 1989. Cultural psychology: A once and future discipline? Manuscript. [Available from Michael Cole, Department of Communication, University of California at San Diego.]

Cole, M., and J. S. Bruner. 1971. Cultural differences and inferences about psychological processes. *American Psychologist* 26:867–876.

Cole, M., and J. Gay. 1972. Culture and memory. *American Anthropologist* 74:1066–84.

Cole, M., and S. Scribner. 1974. *Culture and Thought: A Psychological Introduction.* New York: Wiley.

Collingwood, R. 1972. *An Essay on Metaphysics.* Chicago: Henry Regnery.

Collins, H. M. 1981. Stages in the empirical programme of relativism. *Social Studies of Science* 11:3–10.

Conklin, H. 1955. Hanunoo color categories. *Southwestern Journal of Anthropology* 11:339–344.

Converse, P. E. 1986. Generalization and the social psychology of "other worlds." In D. W. Fiske and R. A. Shweder, eds., *Metatheory in Social Science: Pluralisms and Subjectivities.* Chicago: University of Chicago Press.

Cook, M., S. Mineka, B. Wolkenstein, and K. Laitsch. 1985. Observational conditioning of snake fear in unrelated Rhesus monkeys. *Journal of Abnormal Psychology* 94:591–610.

Costanzo, R. 1974. A reanalysis of the Whiting and child data using the multitrait-multimethod matrix. Manuscript, Committee on Human Development, University of Chicago.

Courtright, P. 1988. Public lecture at University of Chicago.

Cronbach, L. J. 1975. Beyond the two disciplines of scientific psychology. *American Psychologist* 30:116–127.

D'Andrade, R. G. 1965. Trait psychology and componential analysis. *American Anthropologist* 67:215–228.

——— 1973. Cultural constructions of reality. In L. Nader and T. W. Maretzki, eds., *Cultural Illness and Health.* Washington, D.C.: American Anthropological Association.

——— 1974. Memory and the assessment of behavior. In T. Blalock, ed., *Measurement and the Social Sciences.* Chicago: Aldine-Atherton.

——— 1981. The cultural part of cognition. *Cognitive Science* 5:179–196.

——— 1984. Cultural meaning systems. In R. A. Shweder and R. A. LeVine, eds., *Culture Theory: Essays on Mind, Self, and Emotion*. New York: Cambridge University Press.

——— 1986. Three scientific world views and the covering law model. In D. W. Fiske and R. A. Shweder, eds., *Metatheory in Social Science: Pluralisms and Subjectivities*. Chicago: University of Chicago Press.

——— 1987. A folk model of the mind. In D. Holland and N. Quinn, eds., *Cultural Models in Language and Thought*. New York: Cambridge University Press.

D'Andrade, R. G., and M. Egan. 1974. The colors of emotion. *American Ethnologist* 1:49–64.

Derrida, J. 1977. *Of Grammatology*, trans. Gayatri C. Spivak. Baltimore: Johns Hopkins University Press.

Douglas, M. 1973. *Rules and Meanings*. Harmondsworth: Penguin.

Driver, H. E. 1966. Geographical-historical versus psycho-functional explanations of kin avoidances. *Current Anthropology* 7:131–145.

Dumont, L. 1960. World renunciation in Indian religions. *Contributions to Indian Sociology* 4:3–62.

——— 1970. *Homo Hierarchicus*. Chicago: University of Chicago Press.

Durkheim, E., and M. Mauss. 1963. *Primitive Classification*. Chicago: University of Chicago Press.

Dworkin, R. 1977. *Taking Rights Seriously*. Cambridge, Mass.: Harvard University Press.

Ebbesen, E. B., and R. B. Allen. 1977. Further evidence concerning Fiske's question: "Can personality constructs ever be validated?" Manuscript, Department of Psychology, University of California, San Diego.

Edgerton, R. B. 1971. *The Individual in Cultural Adaptation*. Berkeley: University of California Press.

Eisenberg, L. 1977. Disease and illness. *Culture, Medicine, and Psychiatry* 1:9–23.

Ekman, P. 1989. The argument and evidence about universals in facial expressions of emotion. In H. Wagner, ed., *Handbook of Social Psychophysiology: Emotion and Social Behavior*. London: Wiley.

Emde, R. N., T. Gaensbauer, and R. J. Harman. 1976. *Emotional Expression in Infancy*. New York: International Universities Press.

Endler, N. S., and J. McV. Hunt. 1966. Sources of behavioral variance as measured by the S-R inventory of anxiousness. *Psychological Bulletin* 65:336–346.

——— 1968. S-R inventories of hostility and anxiousness. *Journal of Personality and Social Psychology* 9:309–315.

——— 1969. Generalizability of contributions from sources of variance in the S-R inventories of anxiousness. *Journal of Personality* 37:1–24.

Erikson, E. 1950. *Childhood and Society*. New York: W. W. Norton.

Ervin-Tripp. S. 1976. Speech acts and social learning. In K. Basso and H. Selby, eds., *Meaning in Anthropology*. Albuquerque: University of New Mexico Press.

Escalona, S., and G. M. Heider. 1959. *Prediction and Outcome*. New York: Basic Books.

Evans-Pritchard, E. E. 1937. *Witchcraft, Oracles, and Magic among the Azande*. Oxford: Clarendon Press.

Ferro-Luzzi, G. E. 1974. Women's pollution periods in Tamiland. *Anthropos* 69:113–161.

Feyerabend, P. 1975. *Against Method*. Atlantic Highlands, N.J.: Humanities Press.

Findley, J. D. 1979. Comparisons of frogs, humans, and chimpanzees. *Science* 204:434–435.

Fish, S. 1980. *Is There a Text in This Class?* Cambridge, Mass.: Harvard University Press.

Fiske, D. W. 1974. The limits for the conventional science of personality. *Journal of Personality* 42:1–11.

—— 1978. *Strategies for Personality Research*. San Francisco: Jossey-Bass.

—— 1986. Specificity of method and knowledge in social science. In D. W. Fiske and R. A. Shweder, eds., *Metatheory in Social Science: Pluralisms and Subjectivities*. Chicago: University of Chicago Press.

Fiske, D. W., and R. A. Shweder, eds. 1986. *Metatheory in Social Science: Pluralisms and Subjectivities*. Chicago: University of Chicago Press.

Fiske, S. T., and M. G. Cox. 1979. Person concepts: The effects of target familiarity and descriptive purpose on the process of describing others. *Journal of Personality* 47:136–161.

Fitzgerald, P. J. 1973. Voluntary and involuntary acts. In A. R. White, ed., *The Philosophy of Action*. London: Oxford University Press.

Fortes, M. 1959. *Oedipus and Job in West African Religion*. Cambridge: Cambridge University Press.

Foucault, M. 1965. *Madness and Civilization*. New York: Random House.

Frake, C. O. 1962. The ethnographic study of cognitive systems. In T. Gladwin and W. C. Sturtevant, eds., *Anthropology and Human Behavior*. Washington, D.C.: Anthropological Society of Washington.

Frazer, J. G. 1890. *The Golden Bough: A Study in Magic and Religion*. London: Macmillan.

Freedman, D. G. 1974. *Human Infancy*. Hillsdale, N.J.: Lawrence Erlbaum Associates.

Freud, S. 1955 [1940]. Medusa's head. In James Strachey, ed., *The Standard Edition of the Complete Psychological Works of Freud*. Vol. 18. London: Hogarth Press.

—— 1959 [1907]. Obsessive actions and religious practices. In James Strachey, ed., *The Standard Edition of the Complete Psychological Works of Sigmund Freud*. Vol. 9. London: Hogarth Press.

—— 1962 [1929]. The question of lay analysis. In James Strachey, ed., *The Standard Edition of the Complete Psychological Works of Sigmund Freud*. Vol. 20. London: Hogarth Press.

Friedman, M. n.d. Scientific objectivity in historical perspective. Manuscript, Department of Philosophy, Northwestern University.

Friedman, M., and R. Friedman. 1980. *Free to Choose*. New York: Harcourt Brace Jovanovich.

Gada, M. T. 1982. A cross-cultural study of symptomatology of depression. *International Journal of Social Psychology* 28:195–202.

Garcia, J., and R. Koelling. 1966. Relation of cue to consequence in avoidance learning. *Psychonomic Science* 4:123–124.

Garfinkle, H. 1967. *Studies in Ethnomethodology.* Englewood Cliffs, N.J.: Prentice-Hall.

Geertz, C. 1973. *Interpretation of Cultures.* New York: Basic Books.

—— 1975. On the nature of anthropological understanding. *American Scientist* 63:47–53.

—— 1984. Anti anti-relativism. *American Anthropologist* 86:263–278.

—— 1988. *Works and Lives.* Stanford: Stanford University Press.

Geertz, H. 1959. The vocabulary of emotion. *Psychiatry* 22:225–237.

Gellner, E. 1985. *Relativism and the Social Sciences.* Cambridge: Cambridge University Press.

—— 1988. The stakes in anthropology. *American Scholar* 57:17–30.

Gelman, R., and R. Baillargeon. 1983. A review of some Piagetian concepts. In P. Mussen, ed., *Handbook of Child Psychology.* Vol. 3: *Cognitive Development.* New York: Wiley.

Gerety, T. 1977. Redefining privacy. *Harvard Civil Rights–Civil Liberties Law Review* 12:233–296.

Gergen, K. J. 1973. Social psychology as history. *Journal of Personality and Social Psychology* 26:309–320.

—— 1986. Correspondence versus autonomy in the language of understanding human action. In D. W. Fiske and R. A. Shweder, eds., *Metatheory in Social Science: Pluralisms and Subjectivities.* Chicago: University of Chicago Press.

Gilmour, J. S. L. 1937. A taxonomic problem. *Nature* 139:1040–42.

—— 1951. The development of taxonomic theory since 1851. *Nature* 168:400–402.

Glick, J. 1968. Cognitive style among the Kpelle. Paper presented at the annual meeting of the American Educational Research Association, Chicago.

Goffman, E. 1971. *Relations in Public.* New York: Harper and Row.

Goodman, N. 1968. *Languages of Art.* New York: Bobbs-Merrill.

—— 1972. Seven strictures on similarity. In N. Goodman, ed., *Problems and Projects.* New York: Bobbs-Merrill.

—— 1978. *Ways of Worldmaking.* New York: Hackett.

—— 1984. Notes on the well-made world. *Partisan Review* 51:276–288.

Goody, J. 1977. *The Domestication of the Savage Mind.* New York: Cambridge University Press.

Goody, J., and J. Buckley. 1974. Cross-sex patterns of kin behavior: A comment. *Behavior Science Research* 9:185–202.

Gorer, G. 1943. Themes in Japanese culture. *Transactions of the New York Academy of Science* 5:106–124. Reprinted in M. Mead and M. Wolfenstein, eds., *Childhood in Contemporary Cultures.* Chicago: University of Chicago Press, 1955.

Gould, J. L. 1975. Honey bee recruitment: The dance-language controversy. *Science* 189:685–693.

Gould, S. J., et al. 1977. The shape of evolution: A comparison of real and random clades. *Paleobiology* 3:23–40.

Greenfield, P. M. 1972. Oral or written language: The consequences for cognitive development in Africa, the United States, and England. *Language and Speech* 5:169–178.

Gregor, T. 1981. "Far, far away my shadow wandered . . ." Dream symbolism and dream theories of the Mehinaku Indians of Brazil. *American Ethnologist* 8:702–720.

Grunfeld, I. 1982. *The Jewish Dietary Laws.* Vol. 1. London: Soncino Press.

Hallpike, C. R. 1969. Social hair. *Man,* n.s., 4:254–264.

—— 1979. *The Foundations of Primitive Thought.* Oxford: Clarendon Press.

Hamilton, E. 1942. *Mythology.* New York: New American Library.

Harlow, H. F. 1973. *Learning to Love.* New York: Ballantine Books.

Harlow, H. F., and C. Mears. 1979. *The Human Model.* Washington, D.C.: U. H. Winston.

Hart, H. L. A. 1961. *The Concept of Law.* London: Oxford University Press.

Hartshorne, H., and M. A. May. 1928. *Studies in the Nature of Character.* Vol. 1: *Studies in Deceit.* New York: Macmillan.

Haviland, J. B. n.d. Inner states and body metaphor. Manuscript, Department of Linguistics, Reed College.

Hempel, C. G. 1959. The logic of functional analysis. In L. Gross, ed., *Symposium on Sociological Theory.* New York: Harper and Row.

—— 1962. Rational action. *Proceedings and Addresses of the American Philosophical Association* 35:5–23.

—— 1965. Science and human values. In C. G. Hempel, ed., *Aspects of Scientific Explanation.* New York: Free Press.

Hershman, P. 1974. Hair, sex, and dirt. *Man,* n.s., 9:274–298.

Hesse, M. 1972. In defense of objectivity. *Proceedings of the British Academy* 58:275–292.

Hiatt, S., J. J. Campos, and R. N. Emde. 1979. Facial patterning and infant emotional expression: Happiness, surprise, and fear. *Child Development* 50:1020–35.

Hirsch, E. D. 1967. *Validity in Interpretation.* New Haven: Yale University Press.

—— 1976. *The Aims of Interpretation.* Chicago: University of Chicago Press.

Hochschild, A. R. 1979. Emotion work, feeling rules, and social structure. *American Journal of Sociology* 85:551–575.

Holland, D., and N. Quinn. 1986. *Cultural Models in Language and Thought.* New York: Cambridge University Press.

Hollis, M., and S. Lukes. 1982. *Rationality and Relativism.* Cambridge, Mass: MIT Press.

Horton, R. 1967. African traditional thought and Western science. Parts 1 and 2. *Africa* 37:50–71 and 159–187.

—— 1968. Neo-Tylorianism: Sound sense or sinister prejudice? *Man,* n.s., 3:625–634.

Howard, A. 1985. Ethnopsychology and the prospects for a cultural psychology. In G. M. White and J. Kirkpatrick, eds., *Person, Self, and Experience.* Los Angeles: University of California Press.

Hunt, J. McV. 1965. Traditional personality theory in the light of recent evidence. *American Scientist* 53:80–96.

Inkeles, A., E. Hanfmann, and H. Beier. 1958. Modal personality and adjustment to the Soviet socio-political system. *Human Relations* 11:3–22.

Izard, C. E. 1978. Emotions as motivations: An evolutionary-developmental perspective. In R. Dienstbier, ed., *Nebraska Symposium on Motivation*. Lincoln: University of Nebraska Press.

Izard, C. E., R. R. Huebner, D. Risser, G. C. McGinnes, and L. M. Dougherty. 1980. The young infant's ability to produce discrete emotion expressions. *Developmental Psychology* 16:132–140.

Jackson, S. W. 1980. Two sufferers' perspectives on melancholia: 1690s to 1790. In E. T. Wallace and L. C. Pressley, eds., *Essays in the History of Psychiatry*. Columbia, S.C.: William S. Hall Psychiatric Institute.

Jespersen, O. 1934. *Language: its Nature, Development, and Origin*. London: Allen and Unwin.

Jevons, W. S. 1920. *The Principles of Science*. London: Macmillan.

Jindal, R. C., V. S. Rastogi, and S. S. Rana. 1978. A study of general weakness in psychoneurosis. *Indian Journal of Psychiatry* 20:277–280.

Jones, N. B., and M. J. Konner. 1976. !Kung knowledge of animal behavior. In R. B. Lee and I. DeVore, eds., *Kalahari Hunter Gatherers*. Cambridge, Mass.: Harvard University Press.

Kagan, J. 1976. Resilience in cognitive development. In T. Schwartz, ed., *Socialization as Cultural Communication*. Berkeley: University of California Press.

Kagan, J., and R. E. Klein. 1973. Cross-cultural perspectives on early development. *American Psychologist* 28:947–961.

Kakar, S. 1978. *The Inner World: A Psychoanalytic Study of Childhood and Society in India*. Oxford: Oxford University Press.

———— 1982. *Shamans, Mystics, and Doctors*. Boston: Beacon Press.

Kaplan, B. 1954. A study of Rorschach responses in four cultures. *Papers of the Peabody Museum of American Archaeology and Ethnology, Harvard University* 42:2.

Kardiner, A. 1945. *Psychological Frontiers of Society*. New York: Columbia University Press.

Kelly, W. R. 1987. The reasons for *Dhat* syndrome, or fear of semen loss in India. Manuscript, Department of Anthropology, University of Chicago.

Kleinman, A. 1982. Neurasthenia and depression: A study of socialization and culture in China. *Culture, Medicine, and Psychiatry* 6:117–190.

———— 1986a. *Social Origins of Distress and Disease*. New Haven: Yale University Press.

———— 1986b. Summary of *Social Origins of Distress and Disease*. *Current Anthropology* 27:499–509.

———— 1986c. Some uses and misuses of the social sciences in medicine. In D. W. Fiske and R. A. Shweder, eds., *Metatheory in Social Science: Pluralisms and Subjectivities*. Chicago: University of Chicago Press.

Kohlberg, L. 1966. Cognitive stages and pre-school education. *Human Development* 9:5–17.

———— 1969. Stage and sequence: The cognitive-developmental approach to socialization. In D. A. Goslin, ed., *Handbook of Socialization Theory and Research*. New York: Rand McNally.

———— 1971. From is to ought: How to commit the naturalistic fallacy and get away with it in the study of moral development. In T. Mischel, ed., *Cognitive Development and Epistemology*. New York: Academic Press.

———— 1981. *The Philosophy of Moral Development*. Vol. 1. New York: Harper and Row.

Kohlberg, L., C. Levine, and A. Hewer. 1983. Moral stages: A current formulation and a response to critics. In J. A. Meacham, ed., *Contributions to Human Development*. Vol. 10. New York: Karger.

Kroeber, A. L. 1909. Classificatory systems of relationship. *Journal of the Royal Anthropological Institute* 39:77–84.

Kruskal, J. B., and R. Ling. 1967. How to use the Yale version of MDSCALE, a multidimensional scaling program. Manuscript, Department of Social Relations, Harvard University.

Kuhn, T. 1962. *The Structure of Scientific Revolutions*. Chicago: University of Chicago Press.

LaBarbera, J. D., C. E. Izard, P. Vietze, and S. Parisi. 1976. Four- and six-month-old infants' visual responses to joy, anger, and neutral expression. *Child Development* 47:535–538.

Labov, W. 1970. The logic of non-standard English. In F. Williams, ed., *Language and Poverty*. Chicago: Markham Press.

Labov, W., and D. Fanshel. 1977. *Therapeutic Discourse: Psychotherapy as Conversation*. New York: Academic Press.

Lakoff, G. 1987. *Women, Fire, and Dangerous Things*. Chicago: University of Chicago Press.

Lakoff, G., and M. Johnson. 1980a. The metaphorical structure of the human conceptual system. *Cognitive Science* 4:195–208.

———— 1980b. *Metaphors We Live By*. Chicago: University of Chicago Press.

Latane, B., and J. M. Darley. 1970. *The Unresponsive Bystander: Why Doesn't He Help?* New York: Appleton-Century-Croft.

Latour, B., and S. Woolgar. 1981. *Laboratory Life: The Social Construction of Scientific Facts*. Beverly Hills: Sage.

Laurendeau, M., and A. Pinard. 1972. *Causal Thinking in Children*. New York: International Universities Press.

Leach, E. R. 1958. Magical hair. *Journal of the Royal Anthropological Institute* 88:147–164.

———— 1972. Anthropological aspects of language: Animal categories and verbal abuse. In W. A. Lessa and E. Z. Vogt, eds., *Reader in Comparative Religion*. New York: Harper and Row.

Leary, T., and H. S. Coffey. 1955. Interpersonal diagnosis: Some problems of methodology and validation. *Journal of Abnormal and Social Psychology* 50:110–124.

Leff, J. 1980. *Psychiatry around the Globe: A Transcultural View*. New York: Marcel Dekker.

Lempers, J. D., E. R. Flavell, and J. H. Flavell. 1977. The development in very young children of tacit knowledge concerning visual perception. *Genetic Psychology Monographs* 95:3–54.

LeVine, R. A. 1966. Toward a psychology of populations: The cross-cultural study of personality. *Human Development* 9:30–46.

—— 1973. *Culture, Behavior, and Personality.* Chicago: Aldine.

—— 1976. Patterns of personality in Africa. In G. A. DeVos, ed., *Responses to Change.* New York: Van Nostrand–Reinhold.

—— 1984. Properties of culture: An ethnographic account. In R. A. Shweder and R. A. LeVine, eds., *Culture Theory: Essays on Mind, Self, and Emotion.* New York: Cambridge University Press.

—— n.d. Environments in child development: An anthropological perspective. Manuscript, School of Education, Harvard University.

Levinson, D., and M. J. Malone. 1980. *Towards Explaining Human Culture: A Critical review of the Findings of Worldwide Cross-Cultural Research.* New Haven, Conn.: HRAF Press.

Lévi-Strauss, C. 1963. *Structural Anthropology.* New York: Basic Books.

—— 1966. *The Savage Mind.* Chicago: University of Chicago Press.

—— 1969a. *The Elementary Structures of Kinship.* Boston: Beacon Press.

—— 1969b. *The Raw and the Cooked.* New York: Harper and Row.

Levy, R. I. 1973. *Tahitians: Mind and Experience in the Society Islands.* Chicago: University of Chicago Press.

—— 1984. Emotion, knowing, and culture. In R. A. Shweder and R. A. LeVine, eds., *Culture Theory: Essays in Mind, Self, and Emotion.* New York: Cambridge University Press.

Lévy-Bruhl, L. 1910. *Les fonctions mentales dans les sociétés inférieures.* Paris: Alcan.

Lewis, M., and J. Brooks. 1978. Self-knowledge and emotional development. In M. Lewis and L. A. Rosenblum, eds., *The Development of Affect.* New York: Plenum Press.

Lewis, M., and L. Michalson. 1982. The socialization of emotions. In T. Field and A. Fogel, eds., *Emotion and Interaction: Normal and High-Risk Infants.* Hillsdale, N.J.: Lawrence Erlbaum Associates.

Lewis, P. 1978. Levels of explanations in everyday life. Manuscript, Committee on Human Development, University of Chicago.

Lewontin, R. 1976. Adaptation. Manuscript, Department of Biology, Harvard University.

Longacre, R. 1983. *The Grammar of Discourse.* New York: Plenum Press.

Longabaugh, R. 1966. An analysis of the cross-cultural study of children's social behavior. In The Structure of Interpersonal Behavior: A Cross-Cultural Analysis. Final report, Research Project No. s 106. Ithaca, N.Y.: Cornell University. Manuscript.

Lorr, M., and D. M. McNair. 1963. An interpersonal behavior circle. *Journal of Abnormal and Social Psychology* 2:823–830.

—— 1965. Expansion of the interpersonal behavior circle. *Journal of Personality and Social Psychology* 2:823–880.

Luria, A. 1976. *Cognitive Development: Its Cultural and Social Foundations.* Cambridge, Mass.: Harvard University Press.

Lutz, C. 1982. The domain of emotion words on Ifaluk. *American Ethnologist* 9:113–28.

McClosky, D. 1985. *The Rhetoric of Economics*. Madison: University of Wisconsin Press.

MacIntyre, A. 1981. *After Virtue: A Study in Moral Theory*. Notre Dame: University of Notre Dame Press.

——— 1985. Relativism, power, and philosophy. *Proceedings and Addresses of the American Philosophical Association*. Reprinted in M. Krausz, ed., *Relativism: Interpretation and Confrontation*. Notre Dame: University of Notre Dame Press, 1989.

Mahapatra, M. 1981. *Traditional Structure and Change in an Orissa Temple*. Calcutta: Punthi Pustak.

Malleus Maleficarum. 1928 (1489). London: John Rodker.

Marriott, M. 1976. Hindu transactions: Diversity without dualism. In B. Kapferer, ed., *Transactions and Meaning*. Philadelphia: Institute for the Study of Human Issues.

Marsella, A. J. 1980. Depressive experience and disorder across cultures. In H. C. Triandis and J. G. Draguns, eds., *Handbook of Cross-Cultural Psychology*. Boston: Allyn and Bacon.

Mathew, R. J., M. L. Weinman, and M. Mirabi. 1981. Physical symptoms of depression. *British Journal of Psychiatry* 139:293–296.

Meigs, A. S. 1984. *Food, Sex, and Pollution*. New Brunswick, N.J.: Rutgers University Press.

Mezzich, J. E., and E. S. Raab. 1980. Depressive symptomatology across the Americas. *Archives of General Psychiatry* 37:818–823.

Milgram, S. 1974. *Obedience to Authority*. New York: Harper and Row.

Miller, G. 1956. The magical number seven, plus or minus two: Some limits on our capacity for processing information. *Psychological Review* 63:81–97.

Miller, J. G. 1982. Culture and the development of social explanation. Ph.D. diss. University of Chicago.

——— 1984. Culture and the development of everyday social explanation. *Journal of Personality and Social Psychology* 46:961–978.

Miller, P. 1982. Teasing: A case study in language socialization and verbal play. *Quarterly Newsletter of the Laboratory of Comparative Human Cognition* 4:29–32.

Miller, P., and L. L. Sperry. 1987. The socialization of anger and aggression. *Merrill-Palmer Quarterly* 33:1–31.

Mineka, S., and R. Keir. 1983. The effects of flooding on reducing snake fear in Rhesus monkeys. *Behavior Therapy Research* 21:527–535.

Mineka, S., R. Keir, and V. Price. 1980. Fear of snakes in wild- and laboratory-reared Rhesus monkeys (*Macaca Mulatta*). *Animal Learning and Behavior* 8:653–663.

Mischel, W. 1968. *Personality and Assessment*. Stanford: Stanford University Press.

——— 1969. Continuity and change in personality. *American Psychologist* 24:1012–18.

——— 1971. The construction of personality: Some facts and fantasies about cognition and social behavior. Address of the chairman, Section II, Division 12, American Psychological Association, Washington, D.C.

———— 1973. Towards a cognitive social learning reconceptualization of personality. *Psychological Review* 80:252–283.

Mischel, W., and H. N. Mischel. 1976. A cognitive social-learning approach to morality and self-regulation. In T. Lickona, ed., *Moral Development and Behavior*. New York: Holt, Reinhart and Winston.

Mischel, W., and E. Staub. 1965. Effects of expectancy on working and waiting for larger rewards. *Journal of Personality and Social Psychology* 2:625–633.

Moos, R. H. 1968. Situational analysis of a therapeutic community milieu. *Journal of Abnormal Psychology* 73:48–61.

———— 1969. Sources of variance in responses to questionnaires and in behavior. *Journal of Abnormal Psychology* 74:405–412.

Morgan, L. H. 1871. *Systems of consanguinity and affinity of the human family*. Washington, D.C.: Smithsonian Institution.

Much, N. C. 1983. The microanalysis of cognitive socialization. Ph.D. diss., University of Chicago.

Much, N. C., and R. A. Shweder. 1978. Speaking of rules: The analysis of culture in breach. In W. Damon, ed., *New Directions for Child Development: Moral Development*. San Francisco: Jossey-Bass.

Mulaik, S. A. 1964. Are personality factors raters' conceptual factors? *Journal of Consulting Psychology* 28:506–511.

Murdock, G. P. 1971. Cross-sex patterns of kin behavior. *Ethnology* 10:359–368.

———— 1980. *Theories of Illness: A World Survey*. Pittsburgh: University of Pittsburgh Press.

Nagel, T. 1979. Subjective and objective. In T. Nagel, ed., *Mortal Questions*. New York: Cambridge University Press.

Nerlove, S., and A. K. Romney. 1967. Sibling terminology and cross-sex behavior. *American Anthropologist* 69:179–187.

Newcombe, T. M. 1929. *The Consistency of Certain Extrovert-Introvert Behavior Patterns in 51 Problem Boys*. New York: Teacher's College, Columbia University.

———— 1931. An experiment designed to test the validity of a rating technique. *Journal of Educational Psychology* 22:279–289.

Newell, A., and H. A. Simon. 1972. *Human Problem Solving*. Englewood Cliffs, N.J.: Prentice-Hall.

Nietzsche, F. 1982. *The Portable Nietzsche*, ed. and trans. Walter Kaufmann. New York: Viking Penguin.

Nisbett, R. E. 1980. The trait construct in lay and professional psychology. In L. Festinger, ed., *Retrospections on Social Psychology*. New York: Oxford University Press.

Norman, W. T. 1963. Toward an adequate taxonomy of personality attributes: Replicated factor structure in peer nomination personality ratings. *Journal of Abnormal and Social Psychology* 67:574–583.

Nucci, L., and E. Turiel. 1978. Social interaction and the development of social concepts in pre-school children. *Child Development* 49:400–407.

Nuckolls, C. 1986. Culture and causal thinking. Ph.D. diss., University of Chicago.

Obeyesekere, G. 1981. *Medusa's Hair: An Essay on Personal Symbols and Religious Experience.* London and Chicago: University of Chicago Press.
———— 1985. Depression, Buddhism, and the work of culture in Sri Lanka. In A. Kleinman and B. Good, eds., *Culture and Depression.* Berkeley: University of California Press.
Ochs, E. 1982. Affect in Samoan child language. Paper presented at the Stanford Child Language Research Forum, Stanford, 1982. (Available from Elinor Ochs, Department of Linguistics, University of Southern California.)
Ochs, E., and Schieffelin, B. B. 1984. Language acquisition and socialization: Three developmental stories and their implications. In R. A. Shweder and R. A. LeVine, eds., *Culture Theory: Essays on Mind, Self, and Emotion.* New York: Cambridge University Press.
O'Flaherty, W. D. 1984. *Dreams, Illusions, and Other Realities.* Chicago: University of Chicago Press.
O'Flaherty, W., and J. D. M. Derrett. 1978. *The Concept of Duty in South Asia.* New Dehli: Vikas.
Orley, J., and J. K. Wing. 1979. Psychiatric disorders in two African villages. *Archives of General Psychiatry* 36:513–520.
Osgood, C. E. 1964. Semantic differential technique in the comparative study of cultures. *American Anthropologist* 66:171–200.
Osgood, C. E., W. H. May, and M. S. Miron. 1975. *Cross-Cultural Universals of Affective Meaning.* Urbana: University of Illinois Press.
Ovid. 1955. *Metamorphoses,* trans. Rolfe Humphries. Bloomington: Indiana University Press.

Paradise, E. B., and F. Curcio. 1974. Relationship of cognitive and affective behaviors to fear of strangers in male infants. *Developmental Psychology* 10:476–483.
Pareto, V. 1935. *The Mind and Society.* New York: Harcourt, Brace.
Parker, R. 1983. *Miasma: Pollution and Purification in Early Greek Religion.* Oxford: Clarendon Press.
Parsons, T. 1968. *The Structure of Social Action.* Vol. 1. New York: Free Press.
Passini, F. T., and W. T. Norman. 1966. A universal conception of personality structure: *Journal of Personality and Social Psychology* 4:44–49.
Peacock, J. L. 1984. Religion and life history: an exploration in cultural psychology. In E. M. Bruner, ed. *Text, Play and Story: The Construction and Reconstruction of Self and Society.* Washington, D.C.: American Ethnological Society.
Peirce, C. S. 1940. *The Philosophy of Peirce: Selected Writings.* London: Routledge and Kegan Paul.
Pepper, S. C. 1972. *World Hypotheses: A Study in Evidence.* Berkeley: University of California Press.
Perelman, C. 1963. *The Idea of Justice and the Problem of Argument.* New York: Humanities Press.
Phillips, D. C. 1976. *Holistic Thought in Social Science.* Stanford: Stanford University Press.

Piaget, J. 1962 [1945]. *Plays, Dreams, and Imitation in Childhood*, trans. C. Gattegno and F. M. Hodgson. New York: W. W. Norton.

―――― 1965 [1932]. *The Moral Judgment of the Child*, trans. Marjorie Gabain. New York: Free Press.

―――― 1966. Need and significance of cross-cultural studies in genetic psychology. *International Journal of Psychology* 1:3–13.

Pinch. T. J. 1977. What does a proof do if it does not prove? A study of the social conditions and metaphysical divisions leading to David Bohm and John von Neumann failing to communicate in quantum physics. In E. Mendelsohn, P. Weingart, and R. Whitley, eds., *The Social Production of Scientific Knowledge*. Boston: D. Reidel.

Plomin, R. 1986. *Development, Genetics, and Psychology*. Hillsdale, N.J.: Lawrence Erlbaum Associates.

Popper, K. R., and J. C. Eccles. 1977. *The Self and Its Brain*. New York: Springer International.

Praharaj, G. C. 1931–1940. *Purnachandra Ordia Bhashokosha: A lexicon of the Orya language*. Vols. 1–7. Cuttack: Utkal Sahitya Press.

Premack, D. 1965. Reinforcement theory. In D. Levine, ed., *Nebraska Symposium on Motivation*. Lincoln: University of Nebraska Press.

Price-Williams, D. R. 1975. *Explorations in Cross-Cultural Psychology*. San Francisco: Chandler and Sharp.

Prothro, E. T. 1960. Patterns of permissiveness among preliterate peoples. *Journal of Abnormal and Social Psychology* 61:151–154.

Putnam, H. 1981. *Reason, Truth and History*. Cambridge: Cambridge University Press.

―――― 1987. *The Many Faces of Realism*. La Salle, Ill.: Open Court Publishing.

Quine, W. V. O. 1969. Natural kinds. In W. V. O. Quine, ed., *Ontological Relativity and Other Essays*. New York: Columbia University Press.

Radcliffe-Brown, A. R. 1940. On joking relationships. *Africa* 13:195–210.

Ramanujan, A. K. 1983. The Indian Oedipus. In L. Edmunds and A. Dundes, eds., *Oedipus: A Folklore Casebook*. New York: Garland.

Rapoport, J. 1989. *The Boy Who Couldn't Stop Washing*. New York: E. P. Dutton.

Raush, H. L., A. T. Dittman, and T. J. Taylor. 1959. Person, setting, and change in social interaction. *Human Relations* 12:361–377.

Raush, H. L., I. Farbmann, and L. G. Llewellyn. 1960. Person, setting, and change in social interaction II: A normal control study. *Human Relations* 13:305–332.

Read, K. E. 1955. Morality and the concept of the person among the Gahuku-Gama. *Oceania* 25:233–282.

Rescher, N. 1988. *Rationality*. London: Oxford University Press.

Richter, F. 1986. Non-linear behavior. In D. W. Fiske and R. A. Shweder, eds., *Metatheory in Social Science: Pluralisms and Subjectivities*. Chicago: University of Chicago Press.

Roberts, J. M., and B. Sutton-Smith. 1962. Child training and game involvement. *Ethnology* 1:66–185.

Rorty, R. 1979. *Philosophy and the Mirror of Nature*. Princeton: Princeton University Press.

Rosaldo, M. 1980. *Knowledge and Passion*. Cambridge: Cambridge University Press.

—— 1984. Towards an anthropology of self and feeling. In R. A. Shweder and R. A. LeVine, eds., *Culture Theory: Essays on Mind, Self, and Emotion*. New York: Cambridge University Press.

Rosch, E. 1975. Universals and cultural specifics in human categorization. In R. W. Brislin, S. Bochner, and W. J. Lonner, eds., *Cross-Cultural Perspectives on Learning*. New York: Wiley.

—— 1978. Principles of categorization. In E. Rosch and B. B. Lloyd, eds., *Cognition and Categorization*. Hillsdale, N.J.: Lawrence Erlbaum Associates.

Rosch, E., and C. B. Mervis. 1975. Family resemblances: Studies in the internal structure of categories. *Cognitive Psychology* 7:573–604.

Rosch, E., C. B. Mervis, W. D. Gray, D. M. Johnson, and P. Boyes-Braem. 1976. Basic objects in cultural categories. *Cognitive Psychology* 8:382–439.

Rosenblatt, P. C., R. P. Walsh, and D. R. Jackson. 1976. *Grief and Mourning in Cross-Cultural Perspective*. New Haven, Conn.: HRAF Press.

Ross, L. 1977. The intuitive psychologist and his shortcomings: Distortions in the attribution process. In L. Berkowitz, ed., *Advances in Experimental Social Psychology*. Vol. 10. New York: Academic Press.

Ross, L., T. M. Amabile, and J. L. Steinmetz. 1977. Social rules, social control, and biases in social perception processes. *Journal of Personality and Social Psychology* 35:485–494.

Rudd, J. T. 1954. Vertebrates, without erythrocytes and blood pigments. *Nature* 173:848–850.

Sahlins, M. 1976a. *Culture and Practical Reason*. Chicago: University of Chicago Press.

—— 1976b. *The Uses and Abuses of Biology*. Ann Arbor: University of Michigan Press.

Sapir, E. 1924. Culture: Genuine and spurious. *American Journal of Sociology* 29:401–429. Reprinted in D. Mandelbaum, ed., *Selected Writings of Edward Sapir in Language, Culture and Personality*. Berkeley: University of California Press, 1963.

—— 1929. The status of linguistics as a science. *Language* 5:207–214.

Scarr, S., and K. McCartney. 1983. How people make their own environments: A theory of genotype → environment effects. *Child Development* 54:424–435.

Schank, R., and R. Abelson. 1977. *Scripts, Plans, Goals, and Understanding*. Hillsdale, N.J.: Lawrence Erlbaum Associates.

Schelling, T. C. 1984. *Choice and Consequence*. Cambridge, Mass.: Harvard University Press.

Schneider, D. M. 1965. Kinship and biology. In A. G. Coate et al., eds., *Aspects of Analysis of Family Structure*. Princeton: Princeton University Press.

—— 1968. *American Kinship: A Cultural Account*. Englewood Cliffs, N.J.: Prentice-Hall.

———— 1984. *A Critique of the Study of Kinship*. Ann Arbor: University of Michigan Press.

Schwartz, B. 1981. *Vertical Classification*. Chicago: University of Chicago Press.

Schwartz, R. 1981. A developmental study of children's understanding of the language of emotion. Ph.D. diss., University of Chicago.

Searle, J. R. 1979. A taxonomy of illocutionary acts. In J. R. Searle, ed., *Expression and Meaning*. Cambridge: Cambridge University Press.

Sears, R. R. 1961. Transcultural variables and conceptual equivalence. In B. Kaplan, ed., *Studying Personality Cross-Culturally*. New York: Harper and Row.

———— 1963. Dependency motivation. In M. R. Jones, ed., *Nebraska Symposium on Motivation*. Lincoln: University of Nebraska Press.

Sears, R. R., E. E. Maccoby, and H. Levin. 1957. *Patterns of Child Rearing*. New York: Harper and Row.

Selby, H. A. 1974. *Zapotec Deviance*. Austin: University of Texas Press.

———— 1975. Semantics and causality in the study of deviance. In M. Sanches and B. G. Blount, eds., *Sociocultural Dimensions of Language*. New York: Academic Press.

Seligman, M. E. P., and J. Hager. 1972. *The Biological Boundaries of Learning*. New York: Appleton-Century-Crofts.

Shatz, M., and R. Gelman. 1973. *The Development of Communication Skills: Modification in the Speech of Young Children as a Function of Listener*. SRCD Monograph 38, no. 5. Chicago: University of Chicago Press.

Shepard, R. 1962a. The analysis of proximities: Multidimensional scaling with an unknown distance function I. *Psychometrica* 27:125–140.

———— 1962b. The analysis of proximities: multidimensional scaling with an unknown distance function II. *Psychometrica* 27:219–246.

———— 1963. Analysis of proximities as a technique for the study of information processing in man. *Human Factors* 5:33–48.

———— 1987. Toward a universal law of generalization for psychological science. *Science* 237:1317–23.

Shirley, R. W., and A. K. Romney. 1962. Love magic and socialization anxiety: A cross-cultural study. *American Anthropologist* 64:1028–31.

Shultz, T. R. 1980. The development of the concept of intention. In W. A. Collins, ed., *The Minnesota Symposia on Child Psychology*. Vol. 13. Hillsdale, N.J.: Lawrence Erlbaum Associates.

Shweder, R. A. 1972. Semantic structures and personality assessment. *Dissertation Abstracts International 33*, 2452B (University Microfilms no. 72–79, 584).

———— 1973. The between and within of cross-cultural research. *Ethos* 1:531–543.

———— 1975. How relevant is an individual difference theory of personality? *Journal of Personality* 43:455–484.

———— 1977a. Illusory correlation and the M.M.P.I. controversy. *Journal of Consulting and Clinical Psychology* 45:917–924.

———— 1977b. Illusory correlation and the M.M.P.I. controversy: Author's reply to some of the allusions and elusions in Block's and Edward's commentaries. *Journal of Consulting and Clinical Psychology* 45:936–940.

—— 1977c. Likeness and likelihood in everyday thought: Magical thinking in judgments about personality. *Current Anthropology* 18:637–638. Reprinted in P. N. Johnson-Laird and P. C. Wason, eds., *Thinking: Readings in Cognitive Science*. Cambridge: Cambridge University Press.

—— 1977d. *Reply* [to commentary on Likeness and likelihood in everyday thought: Magical thinking in judgments about personality]. *Current Anthropology* 18:652–658.

—— 1980a. Rethinking culture and personality theory part III: From genesis and typology to hermeneutics and dynamics. *Ethos* 8:60–94.

—— 1980b. Factors and fictions in person perception. A reply to Lamiell, Foss, and Cavenee. *Journal of Personality* 48:74–81.

—— 1982a. Beyond self-constructed knowledge: The study of culture and morality. *Merrill-Palmer Quarterly* 28:41–69.

—— 1982b. Fact and artifact in trait perception: The systematic distortion hypothesis. In B. A. Maher and W. Maher, eds., *Progress in Experimental Personality Research*. Vol. 11. New York: Academic Press.

—— 1982c. Liberalism as destiny. *Contemporary Psychology* 27:421–424.

—— 1982d. On savages and other children. *American Anthropologist* 84:354–366.

—— 1984a. Anthropology's romantic rebellion against the enlightenment: Or there's more to thinking than reason and evidence. In R. A. Shweder and R. A. LeVine, eds., *Culture Theory: Essays on Mind, Self, and Emotion*. New York: Cambridge University Press.

—— 1984b. Preview: A colloquy of cultural theorists. In R. A. Shweder and R. A. LeVine, eds., *Culture Theory: Essays on Mind, Self, and Emotion*. New York: Cambridge University Press.

—— 1986. Divergent rationalities. In D. W. Fiske and R. A. Shweder, eds., *Metatheory in Social Science: Pluralisms and Subjectivities*. Chicago: University of Chicago Press.

Shweder, R. A., and R. G. D'Andrade. 1979. Accurate reflection or systematic distortion? A reply to Block, Weiss and Thorne. *Journal of Personality and Social Psychology* 37:1075–84.

—— 1980. The systematic distortion hypothesis. In R. A. Shweder, ed., *Fallible Judgment in Behavioral Research*. San Francisco: Jossey-Bass.

Shweder, R. A., and R. A. LeVine. 1975. Dream concepts of Hausa children: A critique of the "Doctrine of invariant sequence" in cognitive development. *Ethos* 3:209–230. Reprinted in T. Schwartz, ed., *Socialization as Cultural Communication*. Berkeley: University of California Press, 1976.

Shweder, R. A. and R. A. LeVine, eds., 1984. *Culture Theory: Essays on Mind, Self, and Emotion*. New York: Cambridge University Press.

Shweder, R. A., M. Mahapatra, and J. G. Miller. 1987. Culture and moral development. In J. Kagan and S. Lamb, eds., *The Emergence of Moral Concepts in Early Childhood*. Chicago: University of Chicago Press. Reprinted in J. W. Stigler, R. A. Shweder, and G. Herdt, *Cultural Psychology: Essays on Comparative Human Development*. New York: Cambridge University Press, 1990.

Shweder, R. A., and M. A. Sullivan. 1990. The semiotic subject of cultural psychology. In L. Pervin, ed., *Handbook of Personality.* New York: Guilford.

Shweder, R. A., E. Turiel, and N. C. Much. 1981. The moral intuitions of the child. In J. H. Flavell and L. Ross, eds., *Social Cognitive Development.* Cambridge: Cambridge University Press.

Silverman, M. 1976. Psychoanalytic theory: The reports of my death have been greatly exaggerated. *American Psychologist* 31:621–637.

Simmel, A. 1968. Privacy. *International Encyclopedia of the Social Sciences* 12:480–487.

Simon, H. A. 1957. *Models of Man: Social and Rational.* New York: Wiley.

Sivananda, Swami. 1979. *What Becomes of the Soul after Death?* Shivanandanagar, India: Divine Life Society.

Smith, G. M. 1967. Usefulness of peer ratings of personality in educational research. *Educational and Psychological Measurement* 27:967–984.

Smith, H. 1961. *Accents of the world's philosophies.* Publications in the Humanities, no. 50. Cambridge, Mass.: Department of the Humanities, Massachusetts Institute of Technology.

Smith, M. W. 1952. Different cultural concepts of the past, present, and future. *Psychiatry* 15:395–400.

Sneath, P. H. A. 1961. Recent developments in theoretical and quantitative taxonomy. *Systematic Zoology* 10:118–139.

Sokal, R. R. 1974. Classification: Purposes, principles, progress, prospects. *Science* 185:1115–23.

Sokal, R. R., and P. H. A. Sneath. 1963. *Principles of Numerical Taxonomy.* San Francisco: W. H. Freeman.

Soloman, R. 1976. *The Passions.* Austin: University of Texas Press.

——— 1984. Getting angry: A critique of the Jamesian theory of emotions in anthropology. In R. A. Shweder and R. A. LeVine, eds., *Culture Theory: Essays on Mind, Self, and Emotion.* New York: Cambridge University Press.

Spiro, M. E. 1955. Symposium: Projective testing in ethnography. *American Anthropologist* 57:245–270.

——— 1961. Social systems, personality, and functional analysis. In Bert Kaplan, ed., *Studying Personality Cross-Culturally.* New York: Harper and Row.

——— 1965. Religious systems as culturally constituted defense mechanisms. In M. E. Spiro, ed., *Context and Meaning in Cultural Anthropology.* New York: Free Press.

——— 1967. *Burmese Supernaturalism: A Study in the Explanation and Reduction of Suffering.* Englewood Cliffs, N.J.: Prentice-Hall.

——— 1982. Collective representations and mental representations in religious symbol systems. In J. Maquet, ed., *On Symbols in Anthropology.* Vol. 3. Los Angeles: University of California Press.

——— 1983. *Oedipus in the Trobriands.* Chicago: University of Chicago Press.

——— 1984. Some reflections on cultural determinism and relativism with special reference to emotion and reason. In R. A. Shweder and R. A. LeVine, eds., *Culture Theory: Essays on Mind, Self, and Emotion.* New York: Cambridge University Press.

—— 1986. Cultural relativism and the future of anthropology. *Cultural Anthropology* 1:259–286.

—— 1990. On the strange and familiar in recent anthropological thought. In J. Stigler, R. Shweder, and G. Herdt, eds., *Cultural Psychology: Essays on Comparative Human Development*. New York: Cambridge University Press.

Spiro, M. E., and R. D'Andrade. 1958. A cross-cultural study of some supernatural beliefs. *American Anthropologist* 60:456–466.

Sroufe, L. A. 1979. Socioemotional development. In J. Osofsky, ed., *Handbook of Infant Development*. New York: Wiley.

Stenberg, C. R., J. J. Campos, and R. N. Emde. 1983. The facial expression of anger in seven-month-old infants. *Child Development* 54:178–184.

Stephens, W. N., ed., 1962. *The Oedipus Complex: Cross-Cultural Evidence.* New York: Free Press.

Stephens, W. N., and R. D'Andrade. 1962. Kin-avoidance. In W. N. Stephens, ed., *The Oedipus Complex: Cross-Cultural Evidence*. New York: Free Press.

Stevenson, I. 1960. The evidence for survival from claimed memories of former incarnations. *Journal of the American Society for Psychical Research* 54:51–117.

—— 1977. The explanatory value of the idea of reincarnation. *Journal of Nervous and Mental Diseases* 164:305–326.

Stigler, J. W. 1984. "Mental Abacus": the effect of abacus training on Chinese children's mental calculation. *Cognitive Psychology* 16:145–176.

Stigler, J. W., and R. Baranes. 1988. Culture and mathematics learning. In E. Rothkopf, ed., *Review of Research in Education*. New York: AERA.

Stigler, J. W., L. Chalip, and K. F. Miller. 1986. Consequences of skill: The case of abacus training in Taiwan. *American Journal of Education* 94:447–479.

Stiles, N., and D. Wilcox. 1974. *Grover and Everything in the Whole Wide World Museum*. New York: Random House.

Super, C. M. 1981. Behavioral development in infancy. In Ruth Monroe, Robert Monroe, and B. Whiting, eds., *Handbook of Cross-Cultural Human Development*. New York: Garland Press.

Super, C. M., S. Harkness, and L. M. Baldwin. 1977. Category behavior in natural ecologies and in cognitive tests. *Quarterly Newsletter of the Institute for Comparative Human Development* 1:4–7.

Sweetser, D. A. 1966. Avoidance, social affiliation, and the incest taboo. *Ethnology* 5:304–316.

Thorndike, E. L. 1933. A proof of the law of effect. *Science* 77:173–175.

Tolman, E. C. 1934. Theories of learning. In E. L. Thorndike et al., *Comparative Psychology*. New York: Prentice-Hall.

Toulmin, S. 1971. From logical systems to conceptual populations. In R. C. Buck and R. S. Cohen, eds., *Boston Studies in Philosophy of Science*. Hingham, Mass.: Reidel.

—— 1972. *Human Understanding*. Vol. 1. Princeton: Princeton University Press.

Trevor-Roper, H. R. 1967. The European witch-craze of the sixteenth and seventeenth centuries. In H. R. Trevor-Roper, ed., *Religion, the Reformation, and Social Change*. London: Macmillan.

Triandis, H. C., et. al. 1968. Cultural influences upon the perception of implicative relationship among concepts and the analysis of values. Group Effectiveness Research Laboratory, Department of Psychology, University of Illinois Technical Report No. 56 (68-1). Manuscript.

Trilling, L. 1972. *Sincerity and Authenticity.* Cambridge, Mass.: Harvard University Press.

Tversky, A., and D. Kahneman. 1973. Availability: A heuristic for judging frequency and probability. *Cognitive Psychology* 5:207–232.

————— 1974. Judgment under uncertainty: Heuristics and biases. *Science* 185:1124–31.

Two murder trials in Kordefan. 1920. *Sudan Notes and Records,* 245–259. Transcripts.

Tylor, E. B. 1889. On a method of investigating the development of institutions: Applied to laws of marriage and descent. *Journal of the Royal Anthropological Institute of Great Britain and Ireland* 18:245–272.

————— 1958 [1871]. *Primitive Culture.* New York: Harper Torchbooks.

Van Lieshout, C. F. M. 1975. Young children's reactions to barriers placed by their mothers. *Child Development* 46:879–886.

von Gebsattel, V. E. 1958 (1938). The world of the compulsive. In R. May, E. Angel, and F. Ellenberger, eds., *Existence.* New York: Basic Books.

Vonnegut, K. 1988. *Slaughterhouse-Five.* New York: Dell.

von Wright, G. H. 1971. *Explanation and Understanding.* Ithaca: Cornell University Press.

Wallace, A. F. C. 1952. The modal personality of the Tuscarora Indians as revealed by the Rorschach test. *Bureau of American Ethnology Bulletin* 150.

————— 1972. *The Death and Rebirth of the Seneca.* New York: Random House.

Wason, P. C., and P. N. Johnson-Laird. 1972. *The Psychology of Reasoning.* London: Batsford.

Watanabe, S. 1969. *Knowing and Guessing.* New York: Wiley.

Weber, M. 1958. *The Protestant Ethic and the Spirit of Capitalism.* New York: Charles Scribner and Sons.

Werker, J. 1989. Becoming a native listener. *American Scientist* 77:54–59.

Werner, H., and B. Kaplan. 1956. The developmental approach to cognition: Its relevance to the psychological interpretation of anthropological and ethnolinguistic data. *American Anthropologist* 58:866–880.

White, G. M. 1980. Conceptual universals in interpersonal language. *American Anthropologist* 82:759–781.

Whiting, B. B., and J. W. M. Whiting. 1975. *Children of Six Cultures.* Cambridge, Mass.: Harvard University Press.

Whiting, B. B., and C. P. Edwards. 1988. *Children of Different Worlds: The Formation of Social Behavior.* Cambridge, Mass.: Harvard University Press.

Whiting, J. 1959. Sorcery, sin, and the superego. In *Nebraska Symposium on Motivation.* Lincoln: University of Nebraska Press. Reprinted in C. S. Ford, ed., *Cross-Cultural Approaches.* New Haven, Conn.: HRAF Press, 1967.

————— 1964. The effects of climate on certain cultural practices. In W. Goodenough, ed., *Explorations in Cultural Anthropology.* New York: McGraw-Hill.

—— 1971. Causes and consequences of the amount of body contact between mother and infant. Paper presented at the American Anthropological Association meetings, November 18, New York City.

—— 1977. A model for psychocultural research. In P. H. Leiderman, S. R. Tulkin, and A. Rosenfield, eds., *Culture and Infancy: Variations in Human Experience.* New York: Academic Press.

Whiting, J., and I. Child. 1953. *Child Training and Personality.* New Haven: Yale University Press.

Whiting, J., R. Kluckhohn, and A. Anthony. 1958. The function of male initiation ceremonies at puberty. In E. Maccoby, T. Newcomb, and E. Hartley, eds., *Readings in Social Psychology.* New York: Holt.

Whiting, J., and B. B. Whiting. 1975. Aloofness and intimacy of husbands and wives: A cross-cultural study. *Ethos* 3:183–207.

Whorf, B. L. 1956. *Language, Thought, and Reality: Selected Writings of Benjamin Lee Whorf.* Cambridge, Mass: MIT Press.

Williams, D., and H. Williams. 1969. Auto-maintenance in the pigeon: Sustained pecking despite contingent non-reinforcement. *Journal of the Experimental Analysis of Behavior* 12:511–520.

Wilson, B. R. 1970. *Rationality.* Oxford: Basil Blackwell.

Witkowski, S. R. 1972. A cross-cultural test of the proximity hypothesis. *Behavior Science Notes* 7:243–263.

Wittgenstein, L. 1968 [1953]. *Philosophical Investigations,* trans. G. E. M. Anscombe. New York: Macmillan.

Ziff, P. 1972. *Understanding Understanding.* Ithaca: Cornell University Press.

Acknowledgments

I view these essays as a pale, distant, and insufficient recollection of the spirit of Peter Abelard. There is a postmodern irony in the fact that the "Socrates of the Gauls" is best remembered for his romantic connections with Heloise. Yet in the early years of the twelfth century it was Abelard who wrote that controversial book entitled *Sic et Non* (Yes and No), a compilation of equally authoritative yet divergent views on the nature of nature and the law. Persecuted for much of his life because his reasoning was so corrosive of dogma, Abelard projected himself forward in time by dedicating his autobiography to unknown future friends. One suspects he would have been fond of the West in the late twentieth century, where, it is to be hoped, his deconstructive spirit will continue to live on.

Hindu ascetics have known for a long time that free thinking—the deconstructive questioning of established things—is best pursued in a cave, the premodern analogue of an armchair. In postmodern times the cave and the armchair have been replaced by the jumbo jet. Parochial truths rarely survive unexamined through the irreality of the international transit lounge (the "duty-free" zone, as they say) and the astonishment of border crossings.

While some of the thoughts for these essays come from out of the cave, the armchair, and the jumbo jet, many of them were written in the ivory tower of the University of Chicago, where I am a co-conspirator in a surprisingly successful plot against disciplinary parochialism: the Committee on Human Development.

Although I am not at all sure just what it is that is tested by the test of time (the Committee on Human Development celebrated its fiftieth anniversary in 1990), it may well be the longest surviving interdisciplinary graduate program in the United States. It is my good luck that psychological anthropology, more properly "cultural psychology," has, from the beginning been fundamental to the intellectual agenda of the Committee on Human Development. For this I have my predecessors Lloyd Warner, Robert Havighurst, William Henry, Bernice Neugarten, Melford E. Spiro, and Robert A. LeVine to thank, and my current colleagues as well, especially Bert Cohler, Mihaly Csikszentmihalyi, Raymond Fogelson, Daniel G. Freedman, Eugene Gendlin, Gilbert Herdt, Peggy Miller, James Stigler, and Marvin Zonis.

Well represented these days within the Gothic quadrangles of the University of Chicago are the three intellectual traditions and frameworks that go under the labels Platonism, positivism (or positive science), and historicism (or cultural relativism). A reconsideration of the possibilities for a cultural psychology is a form of engagement and struggle with the judgments of all three frameworks. My understanding of those traditions has been enriched through ongoing participation in the Practical Reason Workshop of the University of Chicago Divinity School, organized by Donald Browning, Philip Jackson, and Jerome Wakefield; the Rational Choice Workshop, organized by Gary Becker and James Coleman; and the Cross-Cultural Workshop and Person, Body, Culture ("P.C.B.") Workshop of the Committee on Human Development.

For well over a decade Haskel Levi and Marvin Zonis have kept alive at the University of Chicago a remarkable informal faculty seminar known as "Grounds" where Platonism, positivism, and historicism have been encouraged to argue with each other in the context of a family affair. We all keep coming back, eagerly.

I have Lindsay Waters, my thoughtful and sympathetic editor at Harvard University Press, to thank for the very idea of *Thinking Through Cultures.* The book is a selection of essays spanning the years 1979–1989. During that time I spent a year (1982–83) in Orissa, India, renewing old friendships and initiating a longer-term research project on the cultural psychology of moral evaluations. I was also privileged to spend a year (1985–86) as a John Simon Guggenheim Fellow and as a Fellow at the Center for Advanced Study in the

Behavioral Sciences, on that magic mountain above the campus of Stanford University.

Overheard one day at lunch at the Center was a Woody Allen type remark from another fellow: "How could they invite me here. They have ruined my life. I'll never be happy again!" That the prophesy has not come true for me is largely thanks to my mentors, colleagues, students, and friends, those who have kept me alert and on my toes and have contributed so much to the life of the mind and to my mind. A short list includes: Ashoy Biswal, Rita Biswal, Wayne Booth, Anatole Broyard, Jerome Bruner, Roy G. D'Andrade, M. K. Das, Gagan Dash, Alan Fiske, Donald Fiske, Daniel G. Freedman, Clifford Geertz, Eugene Gendlin, Alan Gewirth, Kenneth Gergen, David Greenstone, John Haviland, Janellen Huttenlocher, Jerome Kagan, Arthur Kleinman, Mark Lepper, Haskel Levi, Robert Levy, John Lucy, Robert A. LeVine, Manamohan Mahapatra, P. K. Makadam, Hazel Markus, Joan Miller, S. K. Misra, John Miyamoto, Nancy C. Much, Richard Nisbett, Charles Nuckolls, Babaji Patnaik, Deborah Pool, K. S. Ramachandran, Frank Richter, David Rosenhan, Lee Ross, Paul Rozin, Jan Smedslund, Nilamani Senapati, Candy Shweder, Melford E. Spiro, Nancy Stein, Maria Sullivan, Thomas Trabasso, Elliot Turiel, Evon Vogt, Thomas Weisner, Beatrice Whiting, John W. M. Whiting, William Wimsatt and Stanton Wortham. I hope this collection will keep the conversation going.

Support over the years from the John Simon Guggenheim Foundation and from the Spencer Foundation, the National Institute of Child Health and Human Development, and National Institute of Mental Health, and the Social Sciences Division of the University of Chicago is most gratefully acknowledged. Whitney Seymour and Nancy L. Dray assisted me in innumerable ways in the preparation of the book. Ann Hawthorne of Harvard University Press taught me what copy editing, philology, and linguistic politics are all about.

The original titles and publication sources of the essays in this volume are listed below. They are reprinted, with minor changes, with the permission of the publishers and coauthors.

Chapter 1. "Post-Nietzschian Anthropology: The Idea of Multiple Objective Worlds." *Relativism: Interpretation and Confrontation,* edited by Michael Krausz (Notre Dame: University of Notre Dame Press, 1989). Chapter 1 incorporates a few paragraphs from "Divergent Rationalities," *Metatheory in Social Science: Pluralisms and Subjectivities,* edited by Donald W. Fiske and Richard A. Shweder. © 1986 by the University of Chicago Press.

Chapter 2. "Cultural Psychology: What Is It?" In *Cultural Psychology: Essays on Comparative Human Development,* edited by James W. Stigler, Richard A. Shweder and Gilbert Herdt. © 1990 by Cambridge University Press.

Chapter 3. "Does the Concept of the Person Vary Cross-Culturally?" In *Cultural Conceptions of Mental Health and Therapy,* edited by Anthony J. Marsella and Geoffrey M. White. © 1982 by Kluwer Academic Publishers. Recipient of the 1982 American Association for the Advancement of Science (AAAS) Socio-Psychological Prize.

Chapter 4. "The Social Construction of the Person: How Is It Possible?" In *The Social Construction of the Person,* edited by Kenneth J. Gergen and Keith E. Davis. © 1985 by Springer-Verlag.

Chapter 5. "Determinations of Meaning: Discourse and Moral Socialization." In *Moral Development Through Social Interaction,* edited by William M. Kurtines and Jacob L. Gewirtz. © 1987 by Wiley and Sons, Publishers.

Chapter 6. "Menstrual Pollution, Soul Loss and the Comparative Study of Emotions." In *Culture and Depression,* edited by Arthur Kleinman and Byron J. Good. © 1985 by the University of California Press.

Chapter 7. "Rethinking Culture and Personality Theory." *Ethos: Journal of the Society for Psychological Anthropology* 7:255–278 (part 1), 7:279–311 (part 2). © 1979 by American Anthropological Association. (Part 3 is available in *Ethos* 8:60–94.)

Chapter 8. "Suffering in Style." *Culture, Medicine and Psychiatry* 12:479–497. © 1988 by Kluwer Academic Publishers.

Chapter 9. "How to Look at Medusa without Turning to Stone." *Contributions to Indian Sociology,* 21, no. 1. © 1987 by Institute of Economic Growth, Delhi, with permission of the copyright holder and the publisher, Sage Publications India Private Limited, New Delhi.

Conclusion. "Artful Realism." *Via: Journal of the Graduate School of Fine Arts, University of Pennsylvania,* no. 9. © 1988 by the University of Pennsylvania's Graduate School of Fine Arts.

Index

Abductive reasoning, 97, 361n4
Abelard, Peter, 70–72, 361n7
Abortion, 235
Accusations, as speech acts, 199
Adanson, Michael, 175
Adansonian taxonomy, 175–183
Adaptive accommodation, 269–270
Adler, Mortimer, 12
Age of truth, 163, 234
Anthropology: aims of, 68, 72; cognitive, 88; cultural, 12, 13, 38–40, 46, 47, 54–55; fragmented, 93; general, 91; legend of, 351; medical, 96, 313, 322, 328, 331; post-Nietzschean, 27–72; psychological, 87–90; symbolic, 48; theory in, 49
Anthropology, concepts and stances in: arbitrariness, 119–121, 334, 338–339; astonishment, 1, 8, 10, 11–12, 13, 23; avoidance relationships, 162, 236, 248–250; comparisons, 269, 288–293, 310; conformity, 121, 218–219; consensus (social), 121, 334, 338; constituted worlds, 74–76; constructivism, 323, 324; development (differentiation metaphor), 259; developmentalism, 4, 31, 33, 114, 117–119, 136–146, 155, 161; discourse analysis, 186, 192–202, 363n13; discourse and socialization, 196–202; diversity, 7, 29–34, 39, 76; dramaturgy and society, 248–249; duty-based societies, 170, 174; egocentrism, 149, 153–155; ethnocentrism, 4, 27; ethnomethodology, 96; ethnopsychology, 90–91; ethnoscience, 91, 95; ethnosemantics, 91, 95; etics vs. emics, 85; evolutionism, 113, 117–119, 136–146; expression and experience, 333, 342–343; expressive symbolism, 333–339, 340–343; extrusion, 344; folk psychobiology, 335, 343–345; global mind, 18; incorporation, 344–345; individualism, 47, 49, 53–55, 68, 113, 123–124, 149–151, 153–155, 157, 169; intentional worlds, 74–76, 79, 97, 99, 360n2; intersubjectivity, 197, 202; irrationalist theories, 58–59; joking relationships, 163, 248–250; linguistic relativity hypothesis, 362n8; multiple objective worlds, 29; multiplicity, 5–6, 67, 187, 229; narrative, 158, 170, 188, 216, 219, 220, 223, 321–322, 363; null-reference arguments (Nietzschean), 39–40, 42, 46, 48–50, 57; ordinary language use, 225–226,

393